Masculinity in the Modern West

For my father, Edward Forth

It is a durable, ubiquitous, specious metaphor, that one about veneer (or paint, or pliofilm, or whatever) hiding the noble reality beneath. It can conceal a dozen fallacies at once. One of the most dangerous is the implication that civilization, being artificial, is unnatural: that it is the opposite of primitiveness ... Of course there is no veneer, the process is one of growth, and primitiveness and civilization are degrees of the same thing.

– Ursula Le Guin, *The Left Hand of Darkness* (1969)

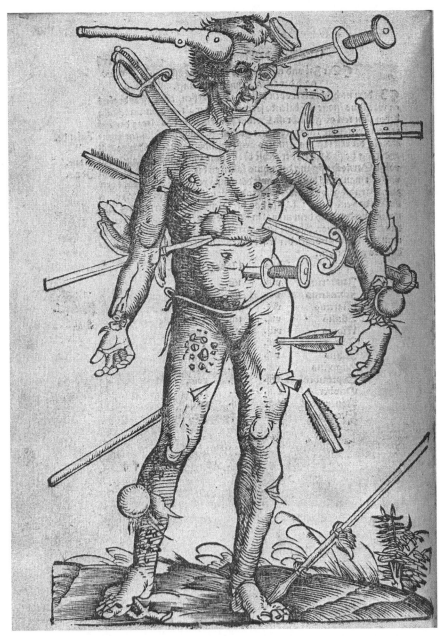

Frontispiece: Hans von Gersdorff, *Feldtbüch der Wundartzney: newlich getruckt und gebessert* (Strasburg: Hans Schotten züm Thyergarten, 1528). Courtesy of the National Library of Medicine.

Masculinity in the Modern West

Gender, Civilization and the Body

Christopher E. Forth

First published 2008 by
PALGRAVE MACMILLAN
Houndmills, Basingstoke, Hampshire RG21 6XS and
175 Fifth Avenue, New York, N.Y. 10010
Companies and representatives throughout the world

PALGRAVE MACMILLAN is the global academic imprint of the Palgrave Macmillan division of St. Martin's Press, LLC and of Palgrave Macmillan Ltd. Macmillan® is a registered trademark in the United States, United Kingdom and other countries. Palgrave is a registered trademark in the European Union and other countries.

ISBN-13: 978–1–4039–1240–4   hardback
ISBN-10: 1–4039–1240–8   hardback
ISBN-13: 978–1–4039–1241–1   paperback
ISBN-10: 1–4039–1241–6   paperback

This book is printed on paper suitable for recycling and made from fully managed and sustained forest sources. Logging, pulping and manufacturing processes are expected to conform to the environmental regulations of the country of origin.

A catalogue record for this book is available from the British Library.

Library of Congress Cataloging-in-Publication Data

Forth, Christopher E.
   Masculinity in the modern west : gender, civilization and the body /
   Christopher E. Forth.
      p. cm.
   Includes index.
   ISBN 1–4039–1240–8 (alk. paper) – ISBN 1–4039–1241–6 (alk. paper)
      1. Body, Human–Social aspects. 2. Masculinity. 3. Men–Identity.
   I. Title.
   HM636.F67 2008
   306.4–dc22
                                                              2008015904

10   9   8   7   6   5   4   3   2   1
17 16 15 14 13 12 11 10 09 08

Printed and bound in Great Britain by
CPI Antony Rowe, Chippenham and Eastbourne

Contents

List of Illustrations

Acknowledgments

If, as Flaubert once claimed, writing history is like drinking an ocean in order to piss a teacup, then this warm and frothy cup would not have been remotely possible without a considerable amount of assistance. My greatest thanks goes to the many scholars in the history of culture, gender and masculinity whose work has been so important to the ideas developed in this book. Whether they knew it or not, the following individuals all offered helpful suggestions, recommended useful readings, and/or served as able guides to the many issues raised in this book: Beth Abraham, Robert Aldrich, Sam Birbeck, Rachel Bloul, David Buchbinder, Ana Carden-Coyne, Ivan Crozier, Karen Downing, Alastair Greig, Susan Kassouf, Helen Keane, Katrina Lee Koo, Will Kuby, Jill Matthews, Gino Moliterno, Robert Nye, Nick Quass, Jennifer Ridden, Mark Seymour, Peter Stanley, Carolyn Strange, Judith Surkis, Lorenzo Veracini, Ben Wellings, Kevin White, Christine Winter and Robert Wood. I am especially grateful to those generous people who read and commented on all or part of the manuscript: David Buchbinder, Karen Downing, Christina Jarvis, David Kuchta, Jill Matthews, Robert Nye, John Powers, Lorenzo Veracini, Michael Wilson, Robert Wood, and the anonymous reader for Palgrave.

I must also thank Jenny Kay for sharing with me her honors research on metrosexuality; Sven Mönter for his masters thesis on the Sonnenorden; David Tjeder for his doctoral dissertation on middle-class manhood in Sweden; Ofer Nur for his dissertation on Jewish youth movements; and Robert Wood for his honors thesis on dietetics and sexuality. My many conversations with Lorenzo Veracini have sharpened my awareness of the relationship between settler colonialism, civilizational critiques, and dreams of regenerated manhood. I regret not having had the time, space or expertise to develop these ideas more fully in the present work. On the many occasions when I wasn't talking to anyone, the following helped keep the juices flowing, notably Albert Ayler, Frank Black, Peter Brotzmann, John Coltrane, The Lowest of the Low, Maeror Tri, Daniel Menche, Merzbow, Neutral Milk Hotel, The Pixies, Éliane Radigue, System of a Down, Tool, The Tragically Hip and John Zorn.

I would also like to acknowledge the support of Luciana O'Flaherty, who commissioned this book while working at Palgrave, Michael Strang, who inherited it after her departure, and Barbara Slater, whose copyediting helped smooth out the wrinkles and clarify murky areas. I am also indebted to the excellent research assistance provided in Canberra by Susan Pennings and Art O'Brien, as well as that of Julia McLaren and the Centre Parisien d'Études et de Documentation pour l'Enseignement et le Rayonnement du Français (CPED-

ERF). As always, the efficient staff of the ANU's Inter-Library Loan division kept me well-supplied with what probably seemed like an endless series of requests. Some of this book's broader arguments were developed in my undergraduate course, "Real Men: Manhood and Identity in the Western World," and I am grateful to the critical feedback and recommendations supplied by ANU students over the years. However it was much-needed release from teaching that allowed me to bring this book to completion. Many thanks to Frank Lewins, who, as Head of the School of Social Sciences, was able to arrange for teaching relief that allowed me to make some early headway on this project. Further teaching relief and financial assistance were provided by a Discovery Grant from the Australian Research Council.

As always, my greatest thanks goes to my wife Jennifer and to our boys, Declan and Logan, for supporting me when I needed time to write and for enriching my life the rest of the time.

Introduction
Civilization and its Malcontents

"I hate sweating." These, the first words spoken by the detective Elijah Baley in Isaac Asimov's novel, *The Robots of Dawn* (1985), provide an interesting way of approaching some of the problems that haunt Western conceptions of masculinity. What moves Baley to utter these words is his physical discomfort at being separated from the City of the future, a fully enclosed megalopolis within which one usually has a more controlled and predictable experience of the body. Asimov offers some clues as to why Baley might respond in this manner:

> One *never* perspired (unless one wished to, of course) in the City, where temperature and humidity were absolutely controlled and where it was never absolutely necessary for the body to perform in ways that made heat production greater than heat removal.
> Now *that* was civilized.

In Asimov's novel, as in much of modern history, the experience of being "civilized" is a peculiarly bodily, and often gendered fact. With its protection from the elements and mechanized labor force, the City is implicitly described as feminine, a "womb," as Baley puts it, and, given his own desire to travel off-world, the source of considerable personal ambivalence. Like most Earth people of the future, Baley has become completely dependent upon civilized comforts, even to the point of viewing space travel as a threatening prospect. This fact places Earthlings like Baley in a position of weakness vis-à-vis those humans who had colonized other worlds centuries before. "Again and again he accepted the City as the womb and moved back into it with glad relief. He knew that such a womb was something from which humanity must emerge and be born. Why did he always sink back this way?"[1] As a detective Baley is not exactly heroic or tough; more logical than intuitive, he is no hard-boiled shamus. Yet, as Asimov's imagery suggests, every agoraphobic and sweaty step

1

that Baley takes from his urban womb is one step closer to freedom, adult-hood and, implicitly, manhood, both for humanity and for himself. All city dwellers are thus childlike (if not fetal) in this scenario, not least because their womb-like world satisfies their creature comforts and makes arduous or risky physical activity unnecessary. With the city at its heart, "civilization" is at cross-purposes both with the "mature" autonomy that seems assured through muscular exertion and a willingness to dispense with material comforts. Ironically, the only way Earthlings can move forward is by taking a few steps back, mainly by unlearning their habits of comfort and idleness to become reacquainted with the harsher experiences of exertion, discomfort, and, yes, even a little sweat.

The misgivings about being overly "civilized" that Asimov dramatizes in this futuristic scenario tap into the longstanding problems of the body that have resonated in the Western world for centuries. Historically speaking, the act of thrusting oneself away from comfort and security in order to face trials, endure pains, defend one's nation or conquer new worlds has been regarded as an essentially male set of practices, things that (despite evidence to the contrary) women have long been thought incapable of doing by virtue of their different corporeal "natures." Yet however much masculinity is approached as the straightforward expression of male anatomy, the accomplishment of mas-culinity is usually likened to the result of a *process*, typically one that involves some degree of physical or symbolic violence.

This is hardly a novel idea. In 1944, five years before Simone de Beauvoir famously claimed that "One is not born, but rather becomes a woman," the critical theorists Max Horkheimer and Theodor Adorno asserted that "Men had to do fearful things to themselves before the self, the identical, purposive, and virile nature of man, was formed, and something of that recurs in every childhood." Just as de Beauvoir observed that "it is civilization as a whole that produces this creature ... which is described as feminine," Horkheimer and Adorno admitted that these "fearful things" that constitute manhood are not things that, once administered, can be easily put aside; rather they require endless reinforcement and repetition that underscore the constructed nature of the masculine self. "The strain of holding the I together," they explain, "adheres to the I in all stages; and the temptation to lose it has always been there with the blind determination to maintain it."[2]

Exploring the recurring tensions between the creation of this male "I" and the tendencies and temptations of modern civilization sheds light on how masculinity, like any form of personal identity, is a dynamic and ultimately unachievable process.[3] A relatively durable set of dispositions and habits acquired during one's childhood and adolescence (and clung to with "blind determination"), the performance of gender is also prone to failures, lapses and refusals. No gender identity can ever be said to be "stable." Rather it is founded and thrives upon this constant tension. Attempts to ground gender differences in the bedrock of "nature" must conceal this secret history of becoming. Thus any history of masculinity must also be the story of weakness denied.

Yet a "history of masculinity" is itself an exercise in pluralism. As many scholars agree, in practice masculinities are always multiple, complex and often contradictory. They are not easily reduced to a single stereotype, set of qualities or horizon of aspirations. Being a man can surely imply aggressive or violent forms of behavior, but it can also entail "softer" forms of expression, sometimes moral or cultural, at other times conciliatory and connective. Arguably there is no single "hegemonic masculinity" that dominates gender representations in society at large; rather masculinities are defined according to the specific expectations of different sectors of the social world, the relationships among different male groups and, of course, between men and women. What counts as acceptable masculinity in one domain would not necessarily hold true in others, and certainly not for men at every stage of the life course.[4]

Moreover, the heterogeneity of masculinities cannot simply be reduced to the structural dominance of men in society, politics and the economy that is often termed "patriarchy," even if most men indirectly benefit from that dominance.[5] This is one reason why men have at various time been able to enjoy considerable power and yet still feel inadequate and defensive about their masculinity.

Judging from the widespread academic and media claims today about a "crisis of masculinity" in the Western world, one might guess that inadequacy and defensiveness are common feelings among many men, though the pervasiveness of and rationale for this anxiety are the subject of considerable disagreement. Most scholars concur that the very term "crisis" is simply inadequate. If there is no stable or non-critical period to be found prior to the disturbance in question (and historians have not found one), then the very idea of a crisis makes little sense.[6]

Others draw upon the work of Judith Butler and other contemporary theorists to argue that, given the constructed nature of the self described above, some sense of crisis is endemic to any attempt to form a coherent and unified identity. Still others have seen in the rhetoric of crisis a performative strategy seeking to bring about the very disruption being described, whether as a reactionary attempt to shore up male privileges during periods when such authority is challenged,[7] or as an exercise in misandry by those who "want such a crisis to exist because they wish to redefine the male role and masculinity itself out of existence."[8] To be sure, claims that manhood is in trouble have been mounting in recent decades, no doubt as a partial reaction to the modest gains made by women, homosexuals and people of color since the 1960s. But if allegations of crisis are only reactions against the social and economic challenges of marginalized groups, how do we account for earlier manifestations of gender disturbance, especially during periods when white, middle-class men seemed to enjoy unprecedented socio-economic power? Without seeking to establish the ontological basis for perceived crises of masculinity, we still need to sketch the conditions of possibility that have made the discourse of gender crisis (whether or not this precise term is used) such a recurring component of modern life. Focusing on the male body may provide some clues. Beginning with the time-honored assumption that bodily difference is what undergirds and authorizes male supremacy, this book proposes that one reason the language of crisis recurs in the West is because the material and experiential circumstances that provide the framework through which certain men assert their dominance over women, children and other men are themselves fraught with contradictions that gnaw at the corporeal basis upon which androcentrism stands. In other words, the very male body that has been viewed as the bedrock of normative masculinity is itself subject to environmental conditions that diminish its capacity to generate properly "masculine" practices and habits. In historical terms these conditions have largely developed in the Western world since the sixteenth century, and are often included under the umbrella term "modernity": the rise of secular forms of political authority, large-scale monetary economies, the decline of religious world-views and the emergence of a secular, materialist and individualist ethos. With the end of the feudal order, traditional societies with fixed hierarchies gave way to more dynamic social relationships organized around class- and sex-based divisions of labor, particularly in countries where capitalism dominated.

Those who equate masculinity with patriarchy seem to assume the relative stability of these features of modernity, at least insofar as they have persistently reflected the interests of white male elites. Yet the changes generated by modernity and modernization processes have always been attended by resistance and ambiguity, not least because they threaten traditional institutions and habits while displacing people who are unable or unwilling to adapt. Like other vectors of difference such as class and race, gender is enmeshed in a complex web of social relationships, institutional frameworks and representational schemes that have undergone a series of dislocations connected to the general experience of modernity. Marshal Berman provides a succinct description of this paradoxical situation: "To be modern is to find ourselves in an environment that promises us adventure, power, joy, growth, transformation of ourselves and the world – and, at the same time, that threatens to destroy everything we have, everything we know, everything we are."[9] Many of the things that Berman's definition includes are conventionally "masculine" activities and experiences that suggest a divide between male and female encounters with modernity, and in his account the perspective of women is largely ignored.[10] Yet I would like to linger over the *simultaneity* upon which Berman's definition of modernity clearly insists. Not only do these processes of progress and decline occur contemporaneously in space as well as time, but, insofar as modernity is also described as "a mode of vital experience," they occur in the very bodies in which these two vectors intersect. In a world where everything is "pregnant with its opposite," as Karl Marx claimed, one might expect to see the same transformative potential unfolding within bodies as well.

Put differently, the recurrence of "crisis" as a means of describing masculinity at various historical moments is to some extent made possible by the paradoxes that lurk at the heart of modernity's relationship with masculinity and the male body. After all, modernity is continually troubled by what Ulrich Beck describes as "counter-modernity," a discourse that "absorbs, demonizes and dismisses the questions raised and repeated by modernity" by positing "constructed certitudes" in the face of the liquefying tendencies of modernization. Arising with and in reaction to modernity, counter-modern impulses seek to renaturalize many of the things that modernity sends into motion, often by imagining a new modernity purged of its unhealthy or "feminizing" components. As Beck suggests, a more complex view of modernity would discover "the simultaneity of contradictions and dependencies of reflexively modern and counter-modern elements and structures in the image of 'modern' society."[11] Insistence upon an essential, embodied and recuperable masculinity lurking beneath the veneer of civilization is one of the most durable examples of a counter-modernity that asserts itself within and against modernity.

As a cultural history of the male body since 1700, this book argues that developments central to modernity at once reinforce and destabilize the representation of masculinity as an unproblematic quality of male anatomy. These conditions reflect what we might call the *double logic of modern civilization*, a process that promotes and supports the interests of males while threatening to undermine those interests by eroding the corporeal foundations of male privilege. Civilization, in short, both supports and dismantles the "natural" rationale for male dominance. This double movement reflects and is influenced by a number of other paradoxes commonly associated with modernity. In its promotion of hard work, for instance, the Protestant ethic encourages the creation of commodities that generate wealth and thus forms the conditions that encourage their consumption as well as either a disinclination or lack of necessity for further work. This contributes in part to the gendered dialectic between "feminine" self-gratification and "masculine" self-control that inflects many Western discourses about consumption. A similar paradox pertains to the history of technology, where the great machines that extend male powers also threaten to constrain or diminish them at the same time. More paradoxes await as we move into the realm of culture and knowledge, for the premium placed on the alleged intellectual superiority of Westerners has been closely tied to the high rates of mental illness, nervous disorders and suicide in "advanced" societies. Finally there is the temporal dimension to attend to, for the forward-looking tendencies of modernity have invariably compelled nostalgic longings for "primitive" worlds and experiences deemed "lost" through the creative destruction of development or the softening tendencies of modern conveniences and habits.[12] It is hardly surprising that the masculinity so closely associated with these developments would emerge as the most triumphant yet imperiled consequence of modernity.

Rather than presenting a history of men and masculinities in all their manifestations, this book seeks to understand the instabilities of Western masculinity by focusing on the male body itself. As the point of intersection between physically robust ideals of masculinity and the more polite, sedate and comfortable realities of modern existence, the body offers a useful perspective on the paradoxes that perennially haunt representations of Western manhood. If, as R.W. Connell suggests, the "materiality of male bodies matters ... as a referent for the configuration of social practices defined as masculinity,"[13] then we need to pay special attention to the relationship between the enduring fantasies of a less restrained, physically vibrant and even aggressive definition of manhood and the more sedentary conditions of modern life that have emerged since the sixteenth century. Despite the plurality of masculinities that can coexist at any given time, it remains true that whenever critics engage with the gendered paradoxes of modernity, a quite specific form of essentialized and embodied (and usually absent or submerged) masculinity becomes the object of loss and grief. This book explores the history of this version of masculinity and provides some explanations for its seemingly eternal recurrence in the modern West.

THE USUAL SUSPECTS

Before beginning, it is worth spending some time defining the terms to be employed in this book. Concepts as slippery as "modern" and "modernity" are notoriously difficult to pin down, and any interrogation of their implications for gender, sexuality and the body risks becoming a virtually endless task.[14] The same difficulty renders the concept of "civilization" equally problematic. Frequently connected to conceptions of the modern, almost as a synonym for intellectual, industrial and material development, it too has been defined and employed in a variety of ways and to various ends.[15] However, when viewed specifically in terms of the experiential conditions of the lifeworld, we find that civilization is a remarkably clear notion that provides ways of engaging with the long-term relationship between the male body and the "masculine" behaviors traditionally assigned to it. A distinction between "civilized" and "primitive" or "savage" peoples has been around for millennia, but these recurring verbs and adjectives referring to civility and cultivation did not become solidified into the noun "civilization" until the 1750s. As Jean Starobinski points out, this term

> drew together the diverse expressions of a preexisting concept. That concept included such notions as improvements in comfort, advances in education, politer manners, cultivation of the arts and sciences, growth of commerce and industry, and acquisition of material goods and luxuries. The word referred first to the process that made individuals *civilized* (a preexisting term) and later to the cumulative result of that process. It served as a unifying concept.

Starobinski adds that civilization also functioned as a durable concept that "could take on a pluralist, ethnological, relativistic meaning yet retain certain implications of the most general sort."[16] This broad definition of modern civilization has been a common feature of "developed" countries throughout the modern era.[17]

As a moral ideal, civilization was implicitly patriarchal, for by insisting upon the domestication of women it transformed mothers and wives into the moralizing agents of society while refusing them access to the world of politics, the professions and ideas.[18] Yet to the extent that civilization's implications for the body have been characterized by both progress and decline, for women as well as men, its effects upon gender relations and representations defy easy categorization. Just as new medical knowledge and initiatives have helped to ameliorate health problems, cure diseases, improve nutrition and extend longevity, the poor ventilation, inadequate sunshine and fresh air, sanitary problems, adulterated food and pollution that have accompanied urbanization and industrialization offer negative indices of modernity's impact upon health and well-being. For our purposes three developments implicit to the original concept of civilization have had profound implications for the male body and the vexed notions of masculinity that are attached to it. Refined manners and self-control, education and culture, and material comfort and luxuries: these three developments have continued to characterize the cultural trends of those developed urban societies commonly associated with the "West." Sedentary lifestyles constitute a fourth development pertaining to the body that has shadowed the concept of civilization, less as a value to be celebrated than as an unsavory fellow traveler of the other three.

Emerging as lived realities for increasing numbers of Westerners from the early modern era onward, these four overlapping aspects of civilization are repeatedly cited as the main corporeal disadvantages of modern life. Despite their origins in elite circles, they have become relevant for larger segments of the population as Western societies and economies shifted toward intellectual and largely sedentary "service" industries during the nineteenth century and especially since the Second World War. The refined manners that grease the wheels of sociability are frequently contrasted to the putatively more direct and authentic expressions of simpler times; the cerebral regimens that consti- tute the training ground for most modern professions are counterposed morally and medically to more physically active and risky male occupations; the consumer luxuries that inevitably accompany material abundance and which are a spur to industry are frequently denigrated as fostering an "effem- inate" submission to appetite, appearances and vice supposedly absent in earlier, simpler times; finally, the sedentary existence that seems implicit in this polite, cerebral, and consumer-oriented society is almost always con- demned as the exact opposite of manly action and health, the root cause of obesity and muscular atrophy that were meant to be "cured" through sports and military training. Although capable of being articulated in a variety of ways and inflected by the specific experiences of different national con- texts, distinctions between refinement and coarseness, mental and manual labor, self-indulgence and self-denial, and idleness and activity consti- tute some of the basic structuring principles of modern culture. When men in Western societies have sought the main sources of their physical devia- tions from masculine ideals, these, the "usual suspects," are most often identified and rounded up for questioning in an investigation that has no foreseeable end.

These modern developments affect the body both as representation and lived experience; yet "the body" that has become the topic of so much scholarly attention in recent years is often considered as a figure of discourse or just another synonym for sexuality. It is thus treated in ways that are some- what abstract (the body stands for the opposite of mind and reason) and surprisingly reductive (the body is just another word for desire).[19] The "male body" analyzed in this book revolves primarily around the physical attributes and capacities that, according to traditions whose roots extend into the pre- modern era, have been closely associated with the qualities that men ought to possess. Bravery, strength, endurance and sexual potency figure prominently in most lists of ideal male bodily attributes, as do grace, beauty and harmony of form. Yet this body is also expected to perform more subtle functions. Saddled with the expectation of being capable of enduring discomfort, whether due to manual labor, physical ailments, inclement weather, enemy armies or just irritating people, the male body is conceptualized as an ideally bounded entity, equipped with psychological and physical resources that maintain a sharp distinction between self and other while containing (or at least channeling) aspects of emotional life, which in the case of men often include the feelings of fear, sorrow, love and aggression. Historically speaking, the bodily and emotional boundaries of men and women have often been considered to be qualitatively different, with the male imagined as being more capable of resisting external influences, whether physical or moral. Under the best circumstances, the body functions as both the material foundation of moral qualities and as a kind of armor for males in their dealings with the world. If the bounded male ego can be likened to a fortified "castle" or "tower of self," then the body constitutes its psychosomatic stones and mortar.[20]

Given the way in which the body has been shaped since the sixteenth century, these four faces of civilization have had consequences for how masculinity has been viewed in the modern world, both spatially and temporally. Likening civilization to a "veneer" has the effect of relocating the signs of "true" masculinity from the surface level of manners and sociability to the depths of biological manhood, especially in drives toward sexuality and aggression that are often said to be "repressed" by social constraints. At various moments throughout modern history, masculinity is typically represented as an inner "essence" that is submerged, but never fully concealed, by the surface play of civilization. Yet this displacement from surface to depth is overwritten by a temporal discourse consisting of extended and updated versions of classical warnings about the dangers of becoming soft in an increasingly commercial society. Operative in Britain and America as well as in France, Germany and the Netherlands, in the eighteenth century a discourse of ancient civic republicanism provided a potent means of criticizing many of the "softening" aspects of commercial society as instances of "effeminacy." Critiques of this softness were often posited by using neoclassical artistic styles depicting muscular and heroically bounded male bodies.

Yet if many critics urged men to adopt a more austere "republican" stance in relation to such factors as luxury, manners, education and physical activity, this prescription for health and morality was undermined through the cyclical nature of political time that classical republicanism entailed. Ever since antiquity, republics had been considered inherently unstable political forms that would inevitably degenerate through luxury and vice into more abject associations. Appeals to the superior virility of classical manhood were thus always rather tentative propositions. As Stefan Dudink suggests, the idea of effeminacy implied that

> masculinity – and the political liberty it supported – could never be assumed but always had to be guarded or regained, and therefore it called for permanent vigilance and constant action. ... Effeminacy ... was an "intimate other", a danger residing in the history of the political community and the individual citizens themselves, a danger that could always

return and the blame for which could not be securely projected onto other communities.

Informed by a neoclassical concern with the life cycles of civilizations, the specter of effeminacy has continued to structure male subjectivity to the present, even though explicit references to masculinity are often euphemized in the seemingly more inclusive and gender-neutral categories of "the people" and "the nation."[21]

The temporality of masculinity is thus often structured around a tension between a corrupt "now," and an "after" that – depending on one's point of view – is cast either as refreshingly improved or (more likely) depressingly worse. When viewed in terms of male bodily concerns, modern masculinity is conceptualized through a narrative of absence that is almost inevitably identified with lack and loss, resulting in nostalgia for an imagined corporeal plenitude that has become less practical (yet fantasmatically celebrated nevertheless) as modernization has proceeded.[22] This nostalgic longing is played out in complex ways. With the corrupting city standing at the center of modern civilization, it is not surprising to see many insist that rugged manhood only exists elsewhere, notably in villages, forests and mountains, or at sea. However, to the extent that the city is also represented as a space partly inhabited by the "savage" masses and their dangerous pleasures, the so-called urban jungle has always functioned as zone of wildness within civilization itself. More often, though, for the malcontents of civilization "true" masculinity is located else*when*, imaginatively projected either into the halcyon days of yore or a post-apocalyptic future where it crawls from the wreckage of a moribund society. And if some idealized masculinity does appear in the here and now, it must bear the residual traces of these other times and places. The future tends only to be viewed positively when male bodies are tempered by the values of old.

This is not to say that every critique of civilization amounts to a wholesale rejection of everything that civilization entails; rather such critiques more often demand infusions of more "natural" ways of thinking and living to offset civilization's excesses. In such debates civilization is haunted less by "barbarism" than by a lack of "authenticity" in relation to the capacities and needs of the body. Without intervention, in other words, civilization and feminization tend to march hand-in-hand. Yet intervention is the key. If polemical writings often cast the relationship between civilization and masculinity in the oppositional pairs of surface and depth or present and past, reform discourses that target gender usually defend civilization so long as it is purified of its negative elements, often through the infusions of the "primitive." To borrow the terms of Ulrich Beck once more, we might view this "true" masculinity as a form of counter-modernity that enables the "conscious allowing of questions to disappear in constructed, sometimes even scientifically fortified certitude [that] makes the anti-civilizing impulse the possible victor over the self-restraint of civilization."[23] More succinctly put, modern masculinity is never free of reactionary impulses.[24]

Examining the history of male bodies in light of the problem of civilization provides an illuminating means of approaching distinctions based on sexual difference, sexual orientation, race and class. That women are integral to representations of male identity has been amply demonstrated, with much important scholarship demonstrating how localized "crises" of masculinity often coincide with changes in the social, political and economic location of women. Indeed, women have been cited as a perennial cause of male sexual impotence, whether through witchcraft, demands for sexual satisfaction or campaigns for equal rights.[25] Whereas women have been identified as problematic in their own right, as the most tangible examples of "the feminine" women have also been considered central to "civilization" as described above. Some nineteenth-century evolutionary thinkers argued that the unfolding of civilization was conducive to sexual differentiation (and that, phylo-genetically speaking, women were closer to primitives and animals than to white men). Yet this claim was rivaled by an older one that pointed out how civilized lifestyles produced men who were, at least in terms of behavior, uncomfortably similar to women. One reason for this was the privileged place women have had in the inculcation of manners, culture and propriety, modes of sociability periodically resented by men as a form of "feminization" that has allegedly allowed women to dominate at certain times.

Credited with helping to raise men from savagery to civility, women have been at once celebrated and resented for their efforts, and in some cases have even been blamed as the central *cause* of whatever men find repugnant about civilization.[26] "Indeed," asked the young Leo Tolstoy, "from whom do we get sensuality, effeminacy, frivolity in everything, and many other vices, if not from women? Who is to blame that we lose our innate qualities of boldness, resolution, reasonableness, justice, and others, if not women?"[27] The relationship of these qualities to women is not as obvious as Tolstoy would have us believe. As Sarah Watts reminds us, "Fear of women is not fear of *women* as such, but a metaphorical reduction of many other fears that signal the loss of singularity and independence."[28] Arguably, what Tolstoy really despised was a whole way of life that allowed women to emerge in this light, a situation he condemned in *The Kreutzer Sonata* (1889) while nevertheless continuing to cite women as the cause of it all. Women thus stand at the heart of many anxieties about the male body, but often as symbols and agents of the very civilizing/feminizing process that elite males have both encouraged and resented since the early modern era. From this perspective the Manichean distinctions that have often been made between male and female bodies (and the mental and moral qualities attributed to each) seem like reaction formations against a counter-discourse that views civilization as a process of feminization that threatens to collapse the strict sexual dimorphism that has been so highly prized in the modern West. Male ambivalence about women is thus a complex phenomenon that is interconnected with ambivalence about civilization.

If the conditions of modern civilization have made categorical distinctions between two sexes hard to sustain, maintaining the existence of *three* "sexes" has posed even more difficulties. After all, same-sex relationships have been widely considered to be closely associated with urban modernity. Many historians have highlighted the centrality of the city to the formation of gay subcultures, sometimes arguing that one is simply not possible without the other. Whereas some claim that homosexual communities have a precondition in urban settings, the sociologist Henning Bech goes so far as to claim that "homosexual existence is a phenomenon *of* the city and not just something occurring *in* the city."[29] To the extent that "civilization" is a term that cannot be separated from the development of urban centers and the distinctive styles of life made possible there, since the eighteenth century many have argued that the conditions of city life have fostered same-sex relationships as *forms of desire* as well as distinct communities. Just as moralists and doctors warned of the connection between the city and a spectrum of sexual and physical dangers (masturbation, prostitution, nervousness and constipation figure high on the list), they also contended that the origins of "deviant" sexuality could be readily traced to the "feminizing" conditions of urban life, with special attention paid to sedentary lifestyles devoted to appearances, study or imagination, and luxurious self-indulgence.

This focus on the environment in the development of same-sex desire was never completely eclipsed by the more biologistic turn of the nineteenth century. Despite sexual science's periodic recasting of the homosexual as a "third sex" since the 1850s, the "invert" was often viewed less as a new sexual "species" than as the result of hereditary degeneration, which was itself conceptualized as the cumulative result of unhealthy urban conditions over generations. Hence, whether over the long or short term, in many quarters the fact of men loving men was often viewed as a symptom rather than a cause of effeminacy, or at least of feminizing habits that are often connected to the "softer" lifestyles made possible by modern civilization.[30] While contemporary essentializing references to the "gay gene" threaten to affirm homosexuals as a third sex yet again, if we consider some of the recent books and even religious camps currently devoted to gay "reparation therapy," it is evident that environmental and developmental arguments have hardly lost their allure. If the distinctive lifestyles of modern civilization supposedly make men gay, a solid dose of the "primitive" has often been prescribed as an antidote, as something that might "make men" of them.

When we consider the interplay between civilization and masculinity, race and class are far more problematic categories than sexual difference and orientation. It is by now widely recognized that white Westerners have employed the concept of civilization as a yardstick of socio-economic advancement, technological innovation and cultural refinement, both in relation to non-Western peoples and the lower orders of their own countries. Starobinski makes the point that the circulation of the concept of civilization encouraged Europeans to think more clearly about its opposite, for "the use of the same term, *civilization*, to describe both the fundamental process of history and the end result of that process established an antithesis between civilization and a hypothetical primordial state (whether it be called nature, savagery, or barbarism)."[31] Yet this hypothetical "natural" state was never an entirely abject category, but was often employed as a springboard for critiques of the "effeminate" luxury and refinement that were viewed as the almost inevitable consequences of civilized society. Every pompous celebration of the white man's modernity may be viewed as another "constructed certitude" that circumvents the shadow side of this privileged concept (that is, a narrative that posits civilization as a process of physical and moral decline or instinctual repression that threatens to constrain or destroy masculinity). Like many yardsticks, then, "civilization" features two units of measure, in this case assessing either the degree of a people's progress or the extent of their deviation from "nature."

As the boon and bane of "advanced" societies, the Janus-faced nature of modernity highlights the complex ways in which Western elites engaged with other peoples in the world. We know that the imperialist imagination selectively cast various indigenous peoples as "primitive" and "effeminate" when compared to their Western conquerors. Whether this effeminacy was explained with reference to environmental, cultural or biological differences, if we look closer at the *content* of that effeminacy we see many of the same corporeal shortcomings that Westerners bemoaned in their own societies, notably self-indulgence, sedentariness and physical weakness. Ann Laura Stoler rightly notes that "external colonialism provided a template for conceptualizing social inequities in Europe and not solely the other way around,"[32] and the constant problematization of the white bourgeois male body reveals an ongoing anxiety about the West's ability to preserve boundaries even within and around the bodies of its most privileged representatives, and not merely those internal populations of proletarians, criminals, women and the insane. Despite ethnocentric rhetoric presenting Western civilization as a shining beacon to the rest of the world, what the French called their "mission to civilize" thinly concealed European ambivalence about the potentially feminizing consequences of their own culture, especially when travelers' reports and guidebooks condemned in colonial peoples the same character flaws widely observed in the metropole. Yet by the same token, Western men have also been increasingly ready to appropriate those aspects of subjugated groups, both at home and abroad, which seem to be "primitive" in salutary and even therapeutic ways. To borrow Alastair Bonnett's provocative phrase, when couched in global terms the perceived tensions between masculinity and civilization contributed to a "crisis of whiteness" that has unfolded since the eighteenth century.[33]

Many of these tensions developed over time and became more prominent as societies modernized themselves; yet the way in which these tensions have been played out reflects an important geographical dimension. Indeed, historically the discourse of civilization has implied a cultural topography where the relative "center" of civilization (in the early modern period, this was Western Europe, particularly France and northern Italy) related in complex ways to a range of cultural and geographic "peripheries," be they national cultures (Russia, the Germanic states), settler societies (North America, Australia, New Zealand, South Africa) or overseas colonies (India, Indochina and so on). As the concept of civilization expanded and engaged with traditional customs across the West, countries that aspired to possess polished manners, consumer goods or industrial power necessarily looked beyond their borders to assess the extent or excess of modernization among their own populations. Just as conduct books, fashion guides and dueling manuals were disseminated, translated, debated and emulated wherever elevated manners were considered worth cultivating, so too were the medical, social and political discourses that tirelessly warned of the dangers of modern lifestyles. Needless to say, similar ideas were expressed in the novels, plays, artworks and films that also migrated across national boundaries throughout the modern era. Here too the endless games of emulation and distinction played themselves out against a backdrop of the interarticulated categories of gender, race and class. However much we must attend to the specificities of national differences, notions of masculinity, like the very concept of civilization, were and remain part of a largely transnational conversation.[34]

Although a close examination of settler and colonial societies does not take place in this book, I would suggest that these locations extended and renegotiated metropolitan anxieties about manhood and city life. In Australia, New Zealand and North America, settlers often represented the potential for moral and physical regeneration through the encounter with harsh and physically taxing new conditions. This subjection of the body to rigorous ordeals and conflict with indigenous peoples is an example of what Richard Slotkin calls a "regeneration through violence"[35] of older, decadent and "effeminate" societies. As much as colonists might have been later denigrated by metropolitan elites as "the white trash of their time,"[36] this coarseness could be readily transformed into a virtue by laborers, convicts, frontiersmen and others for whom hard work, a harsh landscape and a difficult climate rendered refined manners, comforts and sensibilities as irrelevant as they were potentially dangerous. Many overseas colonies could thus represent themselves as more virile and authentic than their "mother" countries by turning the gendered logic of civilization against an effete and decadent Old World. This almost never meant a wholesale rejection of that world, but rather an obsessive tendency to move back and forth between these somewhat contradictory ways of representing manhood. Hence the oases of European luxury and refinement that were constructed in the higher elevations of colonies like India and Indochina, the famous hill stations and resorts that tried to emulate the comforts and temperatures of "Home" while providing a space in which fragile white bodies might overcome some of their vulnerabilities. As emissaries of civilization women naturally played an important role in reinforcing the white European's connection to metropolitan culture, and thus reconciling the implicit contradiction Penny Edwards observes between the "native itineracy and colonial settledness" that was "embodied in the figure of the itinerate, colonizing, European male."[37] One of the enduring paradoxes of modernity and manhood is that even those seeking to escape civilization have found it difficult to go for long without it.

Finally, it is hardly surprising to see that, as settlement unfolded in countries like Australia, New Zealand and the United States, each of these societies reproduced metropolitan tensions between the refined and unhealthy city and robust country lifestyles, thus embarking upon the path toward an urban modernity that sought to emulate the culture and conveniences of European cities while displacing its most distinctive national myths into rural contexts.[38] The "bush myth" in Australian history is a case in point, for in many respects this valorization of a tough, rugged and coarse manhood over the more refined, educated and consumer-oriented urban (or "English") existence merely recapitulates and extends the structural tension between a "hard" masculinity and a "soft" civilization that recurs in most Western countries. What is widely called the "cultural cringe" is a sign of Australians' compensatory need to measure up to the cultural standards set overseas, even as their national mythology often locates "Australianness" elsewhere.[39] In other words, while the tense relationship between civilization and its malcontents is always shaped by local differences, the double logic of modern civilization has tended to reproduce itself throughout these variations. Founded upon the central paradoxes of modernity, a "crisis of masculinity" is a recurring, even structural feature of life in our world.

MASCULINITY IN THE MODERN WEST

A broad canvas and a synthetic imagination are needed in order to sketch these developments. Many histories of masculinity rarely move beyond the boundaries of particular nation-states or closely-linked countries, and to date there have been no attempts to conceptualize manhood using a wider geographic and temporal scope. To remedy this situation, this book offers a synoptic reconceptualization of modernity, masculinity and the body in the West since 1700. Proceeding in the expansive spirit of George Mosse's classic study, *The Image of Man: the Creation of Modern Masculinity* (1996), it provides a more complex elaboration of Mosse's important claim that the reigning "stereotype of masculinity was conceived as a totality based upon the nature of man's body."[40] It argues that our modern nostalgia for an imagined corporeal plenitude defined by simpler, more rough and bellicose qualities may be usefully traced to the late medieval and early modern periods, and that this nostalgia has functioned as a rhetorical strategy in struggles among men and between nations for several hundred years. Behind all of these permutations and strategic deployments has lurked the specter of civilization's continuing capacity to soften and corrupt bodies and minds. By showing how gender, class and race intersect in historical perceptions of the body, this book necessarily proceeds in an eclectic manner, bringing into dialogue the histories of war, sport and physical education with those of culture, consumption and medicine. These disparate themes become coherent when approached through the core components of civilization to which they frequently refer. If this book mainly emphasizes developments and discourses pertaining to elite circles, it is to show that the lifestyles associated with these groups have, in their general tendencies toward sedentary, non-manual occupations and consumer-oriented sensuality, by the twenty-first century become standard for large segments of the Western population. It is also within those circles that the greatest anxieties about masculinity seem to have manifested themselves, spreading throughout the culture along with the inculcation of middle-class values and practices. What had once been the corporeal privilege and burden of elites has now come within the reach of many more people.

With such a wide scope, this book does not pretend to offer complete and exhaustive coverage. For practical reasons, it is structured in a thematic as well as a loosely chronological manner, with each chapter examining the place of masculinity and the male body in relation to a particular set of issues associated with the lifestyles of modern society. It focuses on select developments in Britain, France, Germany, Russia and the United States, with occasional references to Australia, Italy, the Netherlands and Scandinavia. This emphasis on transatlantic and northern European regions is useful for the light it sheds on the relationship between the historical "center" of civilization and its peripheries, thus revealing how countries removed from one another geographically and culturally could engage with a relatively similar set of concerns about manhood in the modern world, even if the "solutions" proposed reflected local requirements. Finally, it seeks to expand our understanding of the multiple levels on which masculinity can be said to be "embodied," and thus considers a range of corporeal experiences and representations that move beyond the usual preoccupation with penises, pecs and biceps.

Part One examines the changes in corporeal prescriptions and experiences that have attended the creation of the modern gentleman since the sixteenth century. The first chapter provides a deep thematic background to the four major aspects of modern civilization that have been so frequently cited as endangering the male body by seeking their origins in the early modern era and charting their development through the early eighteenth century. The second chapter examines the paradox of the gentleman in the eighteenth and nineteenth centuries, a figure poised between a socially-required concern with manners, self-control and proper deportment, and the persistent anxiety that excessive attention to such matters risked rendering a man effeminate. The instability of gentlemanly behavior reflects tensions between the imperatives toward respectability and manners and the enduring belief that a more authentic masculinity lurks beneath these conventions and may at times be expressed through coarse and indecorous behavior.

Part Two examines several key and overlapping areas of corporeal experience with particular attention to the relationship between personal and collective bodies during the eighteenth and nineteenth centuries. Chapter 3 unpacks the gendered implications of good health during this period, revealing tensions between the sedentary and cerebral occupations that most clearly characterize modern civilization and the debilities that such professions inevitably seemed to produce. If manners and reason were often touted as the most desirable attributes for middle-class men around 1800, most doctors agreed that genteel masculinity was constantly threatened by excessive devotion to study and sedentary lifestyles. Robust masculinity seemed much more evident among peasants, proletarians and some indigenous peoples, thus contributing to a crisis of whiteness from the eighteenth century onward. Chapter 4 further mines this medical vein by examining the problematic relationship between bodily "appetites" and the lifestyles of male elites through the late nineteenth century. It reveals the many interconnections among the appetites for food, drink and sex during the eighteenth and nineteenth centuries, and demonstrates how the conditions of modern life were often cited as the source of physical and moral problems in all of these areas. Chapter 5 extends the foregoing analysis of civilization's deleterious impact upon the body by inquiring into the role played by effort, pain and violence in relation to the proposed rehabilitation of "soft" men and the formation of the nation as an embodied entity, mainly through military training, gymnastics and sports as practices that promised to harden the male body by removing it from the "softening" routines of modern life. If men were to survive modern life, it was suggested, they had to incorporate aspects of both the savage and the civilized in a balance that would prove virtually impossible to sustain.

Part Three proceeds both thematically and chronologically to show how these bodily concerns have been interwoven with anxieties about masculinity and modernity since the 1880s. Chapter 6 considers the complex and sometimes contradictory fantasies of metamorphosis that fired the masculine imagination around the turn of the twentieth century. Special attention is given to the tensions between evolutionary progress and corporeal degeneration that were crystallized in the figure of the white-collar worker. According to many critics, these tensions might be resolved through practices and ideologies that emphasized the virtues of the "primitive" as an essential counter-force to the corrupting tendencies of the modern city. Chapter 7 extends this discussion of metamorphosis to the level of technology by revealing the double logic of machines in their relationship with male bodies from around 1900 to the 1940s. From the interplay between industrial machines and muscular manhood to fantasies of man-machine fusions through aviation and the automobile, this chapter shows how the rhetoric of machine-like "men of steel" allowed certain societies to negotiate the gap between a mechanized modern world and the "natural" hardness of the body, a virtue that played a significant role in European fascisms. In its survey of developments since World War II, Chapter 8 considers the commercialization of primitiveness as a way of negotiating the continuing tensions between modern lifestyles and the attractions of traditional male images.

By adopting such a broad scope, this book seeks to chart continuities amidst the ever-changing landscape of modern life. To be sure, masculinity is an inherently unstable and even elastic cultural construction, one capable of being disrupted as well as validated depending upon where and when it is being articulated. Yet as a set of ideals, attributes and potentialities that are closely associated with the body, certain continuities may be discerned when viewed over *la longue durée*. It is its very elasticity that allows masculinity to "snap back" by withdrawing its implicit possibilities while delivering the sting that such sudden contractions often entail. This book provides a history of that sting.

Part One

Making and Unmaking the Gentleman

1
Four Faces of Civilization,
c. 1500–1750

In his recent synthetic analysis of masculinity and warfare, Leo Braudy notes that the history of masculinity,

> like the history of many cultural attitudes as well as physiological responses, is a history of changes by which previously successful ways of engaging with the world became increasingly irrelevant to new conditions. Nevertheless they often persist, even when their usefulness is gone and masculine styles that had been beneficial to the larger community turn out to be destructive.[1]

Benefiting from a view of masculinity over a broad sweep of time, Braudy's description of how traditional habits can persist in contexts that no longer require them is close to what Raymond Williams means when he says that "residual" cultural elements are quite often bound up with novel cultural forms, where utopian projections of the future often contain idealized elements of the past fused with new relationships and technologies. No matter how oppositional a residual element may be in relation to the dominant culture, Williams continues, "some part of it, some version of it – and especially if the residue is from some major area of the past – will in most cases have had to be incorporated if the effective dominant culture is to make sense in these areas."[2]

Modern masculinities have frequent recourse to residual practices and representations, such as when middle-class men resort to euphemisms of combat or manual work in order to describe their considerably more cerebral and less physically demanding conditions of life and labor. That the stereotypically muscular and coarse masculinity of the warrior, proletarian or peasant is often presented as more "authentic" than that of the bourgeois does not necessarily upset the social system that allows the latter to exercise power in a more general and effective sense. Rather, in this scenario socially-dominated masculinities can easily be articulated through the gendered prism of the discourse of "civilization," not as styles of manhood that actually *do* dominate, but as a prescriptive collection of qualities which *should* predominate (and thus dominate) if modern society were to overcome its current decadence and corruption (that is, its "effeminacy"). Just as contemporary life may provide several possible paths to the future, so too has the spectrum of masculinities offered different ways of imagining that future.

This chapter shows how traditional ideals of masculinity centered around corporeal robustness and martial values survived the transformation of elite male lifestyles during the early modern period, and continued to haunt the gender identities of upper-class males, even as their everyday circumstances were being gradually oriented towards a very different reality. It examines four significant and overlapping tensions that have shaped the ideals and anxieties surrounding the male body: directness and manners; arms and letters; virtue and luxury; and action and sedentariness. These tensions have not been (and, arguably, cannot be) resolved by civilization, mainly because it is often "civilization" itself that is called into question by most normative prescriptions regarding masculinity and the male body. The belief that there is something physically and morally debilitating in a life of ease, leisure and contemplation is an enduring one in the West, and whereas the negative effects of civilization have been observed in women and men alike, many have claimed that a slide into "effeminacy" is the lot of men whose lives are not marked by action, struggle, hardship and pain. Of course such misgivings halted neither the civilizing process nor slowed modern tendencies toward professions and lifestyles marked by leisure, ease and cerebral pursuits. Finally, one should view these tensions as rhetorical strategies that, in addition to occurring in conjunction with each other, were also capable of being mobilized by different types of men at different times.

MANNERS AND DISCIPLINE

The word "manners" often calls to mind the systems of formal niceties that allow an individual to move smoothly through social networks, and is sometimes seen as almost synonymous with etiquette or politeness. My use of the term is looser than this, referring instead to an array of codes and practices instilled in individuals so that their bodily actions, emissions and emotional expression are curbed in the interests of maintaining decorum and politeness, however variably the latter may be defined at different times and in different places. Understood as durable and acquired dispositions and modes of comportment, manners constitute a central element of what Pierre Bourdieu calls the "habitus," wherein through years of training and mimesis certain gestures and movements become second nature, an intrinsic part of one's social being. Above all, these bodily performances develop in social contexts that encourage, validate and evaluate them, thus making them seem even more natural.[3] Discipline, self-control and the enclosure of the body are at the heart of this understanding of manners. Of course all societies, past and present, impose certain behavioral constraints upon their members, so in many respects self-control is virtually a universal requirement of human culture. What differs across cultures is the definition of the person who is meant to impose these restrictions and his or her relationship to society as a whole. In the early modern West, manners were part of a repertoire of rules and practices that aimed at crafting more or less self-contained, disciplined and self-regulating bodies, constituting what Norbert Elias has termed *homo clausus*, or a conception of the individual as a closed entity separated from others and from the world at large.[4] Of course this is not to suggest that such self-contained individuality was (or could ever be) fully achieved, but that bodily containment was becoming more of an ideal for elites during this period.

The historical context for this broad transformation can be sketched briefly. The consolidation and expansion of European states during the sixteenth century were based to a significant degree upon the military might of monarchs who no longer needed to rely heavily upon the loyalty of aristocrats in order to exercise their power. In this sense bellicosity and civilization certainly went hand-in-hand, with more powerful monarchs increasingly claiming a monopoly on the legitimate use of physical force from this period onward.[5] This could only be achieved by minimizing tensions within the ruling class that might threaten the sovereignty of the monarch. Significantly, this was sometimes referred to as the "domestication" of the nobility. What is sometimes described as an "identity crisis" on the part of the sixteenth-century aristocracy must also be viewed as a crisis of noble manhood, which found itself poised between a vanishing world where combat and military training were paramount and one in which civil and administrative obligations were increasingly understood as an aristocrat's proper vocation.[6] In such a world, expressions of interpersonal aggression were socially destabilizing in that they undermined the monarch's capacity to rule directly. As Martin J. Weiner reminds us, "it is not too much to say that the 'civilizing process' was fundamentally and deeply gendered ... The nature of new restrictions on impulsiveness varied: while the 'civilizing' of women proceeded particularly around their sexuality (a well-known story), that of men, by contrast, focused primarily around their aggression."[7] For instance, the evolution of table manners during the sixteenth century was inextricably bound up with a growing insistence that men curb the very aggressive impulses that, in an earlier time, would have helped to affirm their manhood.

If there is a "zero degree" to the civilizing process – that is, a state of absolute wildness – it is surely an imagined one; yet even fantasies about wildness play a part in this process. As Robert Bartra suggests, "The very idea of a contrast between a wild natural state and a civilized cultural configuration forms part of an ensemble of myths serving to sustain the identity of the civilized West."[8] The projection of wildness is thus an essential ingredient of civilization itself, and a recurring motif in the history of masculinity. In medieval mythology the valor of knights was a code-bound affair that was often contrasted to the sheer brutality of the legendary wild men, whose violence sprang from bestial drives with no concern for laws or codes.[9] Thus the "civility" engendered by the court society may be viewed as a further refinement of Germanic warriors whose manners were no doubt coarser still than those of the knights of chivalric romance. Nevertheless, the martial lifestyle was not easily set aside when the warrior was at court, nor did many think that it should be. Courtly romances of the twelfth century revealed what Peter Burke rightly identifies as "the unstable mixture of chivalry with courtesy, the values of the battlefield with those of the court." Drawing upon Christian ethics, the earliest courtesy books endeavored to soften the rowdy and coarse behavior of knights so as to minimize potentially divisive altercations, especially when at the court of the king. Yet by around the twelfth century behavior at court was taken as a standard for all people to emulate, so that in time these prescriptions about self-control were extended to commoners as well (Figure 1.1).[10]

What distinguished late medieval courtesy books from the conduct manuals of the sixteenth and seventeenth centuries was the former's strong emphasis on ceremonial deference for specific occasions rather than on the *courtois* body as an ideal in itself.[11] With Baldassare Castiglione's influential *Il libro del Cortegiano* (1527), the elegance and grace of the nobleman were explicitly meant to temper the violent potential of the warrior. Hence the importance that Castiglione placed on the ideal courtier being at once elegant and virile, graceful and strong, courteous and physically fit. Echoing Ovid's claim that "the point of art is to conceal art," *Il Cortegiano* proposed the ideal of *sprezzatura*, a calm self-confidence capable of being manifested at any time, what has been aptly dubbed a form of "contrived spontaneity."[12] For the soldier and diplomat Castiglione, some degree of bellicosity was a critical ingredient in the perfect courtier, whose "true profession ... ought to be in feates of armes [which he should] practise lively and to bee known among other of his hardines." The aesthetic dimension of these bravura displays is also worth noting, for as a result of these exercises and feats his body should be comely in shape and countenance, well-proportioned, and demonstrating "strength, lightnesse and quicknesse." Although ideally muscular, the courtier should not be overly so, lest he be dull-witted and "unapt for all exercise of nimblenesse, which I much desire to have in the Courtier." Castiglione's martial ideal was obviously meant as a corrective to the kind of man who, in his view, often appeared at court. Hence his courtier should have an attractive countenance,

Figure 1.1   A gallant courtier in elaborate costume walking the street with smoking pipe and horn in hand, with descriptive verse. Reproduction of a woodcut (London, *c.* 1620). Wellcome Library, London.

but "not so soft and womanish as many procure to have [who] pampre them selves in everie point like the most wanton and dishonest women in the world." Pampering oneself represented an excess of softness and thus an unmanning of oneself, in terms both of self-display and self-indulgence, as we will see below. Such men who wished to appear as women must be counted among "common Harlots" and thus "banished, not onely out of princes courtes, but also out of the company of gentlemen."[13]

With over 153 editions in several languages by 1850, *Il Cortegiano* was an immensely popular book, but one whose influence really peaked during the sixteenth century. After its initial publication, Castiglione's book was quickly followed by other manuals that modified its basic precepts in important ways, thus reflecting how, as the nobility became relatively more pacified, demonstrations of martial valor were no longer considered practical or advisable peacetime forms of behavior. As a partial consequence, the emphasis on martial physicality all but disappeared from many later conduct books, especially those directed toward a more "bourgeois" readership.[14] For instance, Desiderius Erasmus's popular manual *De Civilitate morum puerilium* (1530) owed much to Castiglione's example, but said nothing about martial skills or even physical health when instilling manners in boys, an omission probably due to the author's humanistic contempt for warfare and chivalric values.[15] Yet bellicosity was also of little concern in Giovanni della Casa's equally celebrated *Galateo, or The Book of Manners* (1558). For della Casa this omission was less a matter of disdain than practicality: of course there were many heroic and noble virtues that a man might embody, but in everyday life courtesy and charm were required far more frequently. Whereas Castiglione had insisted that the courtier would need to demonstrate his prowess on a more or less regular basis, according to della Casa, "those who are endowed with courage and strength are seldom called upon to show their valour by deeds."[16] Although this displacement of martial valor from the courtly scene – or the transformation of physical aggression into more symbolic forms of violence – may suggest a transformation of values from a mere softening of muscular force to its virtual replacement, the continuing emphasis that other writers placed on battlefield prowess indicates the clash during this period of competing discourses of how the male body should be deployed.[17]

We must remember that the self-regulation recommended by conduct manuals was never a merely personal affair, but was a widely-accepted tool of social stability that was even valued at the level of political theory. Through widely translated books like *De Constantia Libri Duo* (1584) and *Politicorum sive Civilis Doctrinae Libri Sex* (1589), Justus Lipsius had a profound impact on early modern rulers, army leaders and bureaucrats, mainly because he revealed a connection between the construction of powerful states and the inculcation of self-discipline among political and social elites. In his writings the classical values of introspection, self-control, toleration and moderation comprised the virtues of the model citizen in a way that echoed the style of comportment recommended in conduct manuals. Control of one's gestures, emotions and bodily functions were public performances that strengthened the body politic. Most importantly, Lipsius updated classical Stoicism by making room for action and involvement in public affairs, thus grafting the manly ideal of action onto that of disciplined self-control. This ethic of self-mastery served as a template for the conduct of noblemen and bourgeois alike, who subscribed to what Charles Taylor sees as

> the growing ideal of a human agent who is able to remake himself by methodical and disciplined action. What this calls for is the ability to take an instrumental stance to one's given properties, desires, inclinations, tendencies, habits of thought and feeling, so that they can be *worked on*, doing away with some while strengthening others.[18]

What applied to subjects pertained to the king as well. If medieval representations of power had usually insisted upon physical vigor and heroic deeds, by the seventeenth century portraits of sovereigns placed more emphasis on refinement and elegance, though, like most nobles, they retained the symbolic trappings of their military heritage.[19]

Following Elias, one can discern in this new emphasis on self-control three interrelated effects on perceptions of bodily boundaries and social relationships. On one level, the inculcation of manners encouraged one to recoil from the bodies of others, thus sharpening a person's impressions of his or her own self-containment while ideally coming to regard another's personal boundaries as inviolable. Indeed, many a duel was fought when physical inviolability was thought to be threatened. Yet what one recoiled from in the bodies of others was a coarseness, even animality, that was also present within oneself. Thus the wedge that divided individuals from one another was mirrored in a person's relationship with him or herself. Finally, lest we assume that all of this boundary-building did little more than create neatly atomized individuals, it was precisely the watchful eyes and judgments of others that kept this process on track. The civilizing process thus accelerated the lived experience of being a self-contained bodily unit while binding individuals together ever more tightly in what Elias calls ever-lengthening "chains of interdependence." Central to this development was a displacement of warrior manhood from the outer world of physical enemies and obstacles to the inner world of aggressive passions. Assuming that aggressive and erotic passions are "drives" that demand expression,

Elias sees this as the reinstallation of the battlefield in the world of male fantasy.

> Life becomes in a sense less dangerous, but also less emotional or pleasur-able, at least as far as the direct release of pleasure is concerned. And for what is lacking in everyday life a substitute is created in dreams, in books and pictures. So, on their way to becoming courtiers, the nobility reads novels of chivalry; the bourgeoisie contemplate violence and erotic passion in film ... But at the same time the battlefield is, in a sense, moved within. Part of the tensions and passions that were earlier directly released in the struggle of man and man, must now be worked out within the human being.[20]

By requiring the internalization of the battlefield and the stylization of interpersonal tension, among men "civilization" was clearly war waged by other means and on other fronts. Yet, as Elias suggests, the image of direct physical confrontation has remained a lingering component of masculine ideals in the West. Whereas scholars today are often inclined to underscore the *cultural* currency of these nostalgic ideals, throughout the centuries critics of the supposed decline of masculine force have couched their complaints in the most visceral of terms, as if the "essence" of manhood resides in a lost or repressed warrior or hunter heritage now covered over by a sociable veneer. The tension between the courtier and the knight was often expressed as a dis-tinction between appearance and reality, dissimulation and directness, and even repression and expression. These gendered oppositional pairs have func-tioned as rhetorical strategies wherein the effeteness of established elites could be denigrated as "effeminate" in comparison with the purportedly more direct, plain-spoken, if not more "authentic" behavior of social competitors. These distinctions also worked across national borders, and could be cited in the name of nationalist campaigns to shrug off "foreign" customs in order to rekindle more authentic local traditions and habits. By threatening to render men overly concerned with appearances or prompting them to "repress" their aggressive or sexual urges in excessive ways, self-control has remained a problematic, albeit indispensable, foundation for the creation of modern masculinities.

Equating masculinity with rationality or self-control thus fails to account for the ways in which men have also relied upon *irrationality* and a *loss of control* as signs of male "freedom." As the inculcation of discipline installed one style of masculinity while seeking to supplant a rougher, more traditional and putatively more "free" or "natural" ideal, so the codes of conduct that aimed at producing new bodies also ignited interest in the very behaviors they condemned and (at least hypothetically) sought to eradicate. After all, the court societies that were supposedly centers of civilized conduct were also rampant with drunkenness, gambling, gluttony and sexual excesses.[21] As we will see frequently in the pages that follow, appeals for a reformation of male manners were often accompanied by fantasies about the very activities being proscribed. Therefore, however much the psychosocial make-ups of individuals have clearly changed since the medieval period, one must not exaggerate the *success* of these prescriptive texts and pedagogic practices: there were always counter-pressures to their insistence on discipline and modesty, such as the case of young Restoration courtiers with a penchant for "streaking" naked through the streets of London. "This kind of joke," Anne Bryson perceptively observes, "and the more usual forms of 'gentlemanly' extravagance in conduct, effectively inverted the 'civil' values of hierarchy, locating social superiority in freedom from rules and restraints, and locating inferiority in an obligation to self-control."[22] Prescribed codes of masculine comportment thus varied according to mitigating factors like age, rank and context. Depending upon who and where one was, embodied masculinity could be expressed as much through self-indulgence as through self-control. This negotiation between "rough" and "refined" forms of masculinity is a recurring feature of manhood in the modern world, as is the idea that certain forms of explosive personal expression (and even loss of control) are distinctly male privileges.[23]

ARMS AND LETTERS

The inculcation of manners may have softened the rowdy habits of knights, but the wheels of civilization did not turn upon politeness alone, nor was the teaching of manners restricted to the "muting of drives" that is central to Elias's work. Technology and advances in knowledge are, of course, central to modern civilization, but these could only flourish in contexts that promoted and provided the means for more people to pursue a life grounded in education and culture. As the European aristocracy's actual experience of warfare was gradually replaced by more symbolic contests, many nobles understandably felt compelled to cling to the martial valor that had traditionally defined aristocratic status and privilege in the first place. In a social rather than strictly military sense, the demilitarization of the aristocracy is traceable to the end of the fourteenth century. Once the tensions between France and England abated at the close of the Hundred Years War, young noblemen were increasingly deprived of the kind of wartime experience that would have qualified them as knights and enabled them to possess heraldic arms. Similarly, the number of young nobles with legal rather than military training increased dramatically during this time, weakening the connection between the gentleman and martial experience.[24] If actual (rather than symbolic) military prowess was no longer the essential defining attribute of the gentleman, young nobles needed to acquire more practical skills to go along with the social graces recommended by the court society. Thus alongside the cultivation of acceptable manners, nobles found their traditional martial identities further transformed through a growing emphasis on education as a central attribute of their changing social role.

We must be careful not to overstate the tension between arms and letters, for it is not as if culture and bellicosity were ever completely at odds. As Maurice Keen reminds us, chivalry and learning were clearly interconnected during the Middle Ages, for the patrons of courtly writers were often themselves cultivated men. "Knights and clerks sprang from the same stock and understood each other's worlds, better than is often allowed for."[25] Indeed, the chivalric ideal depended in no small part upon the tales of minstrels and the careful record-keeping of heralds who often accompanied knights on campaign. Nevertheless it remains true that martial prowess remained far more central to aristocratic self-identity than culture or learning. The education of early modern elites also reflected changes taking place in the world of culture itself. The humanists inherited from the ancients a particular understanding of what true virtue was. Concurring with classical writers that reason is what distinguished men from beasts, humanists also contended that this natural reason could be developed through study in order to obtain complete self-control. For them, study rather than combat was the proper activity for the fulfillment of a man's potential, particularly the study of grammar, rhetoric, poetry, history and other "humanistic studies." Like the ancients, moreover, they too emphasized the importance of speech (*oratio*), which, along with reason (*ratio*), was thought clearly to distinguish men from animals. Moreover, rhetoric did not consist merely of elegant or clever speech, but relied as well on persuasive gestures and demeanor, with some rhetoricians contending that a man's gesture is "the speeche of his bodie."[26] Thus orality and performance were central to the formation of the true scholar and the proper gentleman, at least as far as humanists were concerned. While frequently condemning the brutish manners and cultural ineptitude of the traditional nobility, humanists nevertheless retained an interest in martial values, even if only metaphorically. In their schools, as well as in the Jesuit *collèges* of the seventeenth century, the learning of Latin and the art of verbal disputation were cast as adolescent initiation rites that involved physical punishment if not performed correctly, thus constituting a male bonding ritual that structured academic culture well into the modern period. By likening disputation to a form of battle, the rift between valor and learning (and thus between real and symbolic warriors) was imaginatively smoothed over, at least in the eyes of the latter.[27] To the present day, argumentation is most commonly described in our culture as a euphemized form of combat.

This privileging of thought and speech over steel and valor – or, more properly put, of symbolic warfare over direct physical conflict – was a controversial idea in the sixteenth and seventeenth centuries, and likely to elicit scorn among traditional noblemen. In German courts at the end of the sixteenth century, where war-readiness remained a common feature of life for a longer time, horsemanship and the testing of martial skills in tournaments were central to the training of nobles. Nevertheless, in these courts, too, young nobles were expected to adopt the rules of courtesy and culture recommended by Castiglione and della Casa. By the early seventeenth century they even overcame their initial dislike of the humanistic curriculum of universities.[28] In this respect German nobles were ahead of the French, for whom the association of virtue with martial valor remained in currency, even though the opportunities to prove that valor on the battlefield were becoming increasingly rare. With literacy rates for nobles low across Europe, the university-trained nobleman risked being dubbed a "pedant" whose learning caused him to ignore the aristocratic emphasis on lineage, courage and martial virtue. As many early modern universities also admitted wealthy commoners, it was believed that a more suitable education for nobles would encourage distinctive social experiences through travel and attendance at special academies devoted to the training of young nobles in culture, manners and fencing. Hence the rise of the *Kavalierstour* or "grand tour" which could lead young aristocrats from Britain and the German states to Italy and France, which were perceived as being centers of refinement and culture.[29] Although some nobles, like David de Flurence-Rivault, the tutor of King Louis XIII, predicted a moral regeneration of the French nobility if they would devote more attention to learning (and even proposed an Arms and Letters academy at the court), most of these academies failed to combine martial and cultural education to any great degree.[30] The noble encounter with education thus remained rather limited, and a greater emphasis was placed on manners, travel, court and the army than on serious study.[31] It would be left to wealthy commoners of the middling sort to appropriate education and culture (alongside civility) as key aspects of an alternative form of masculinity.

Finally, doubts about the manly credentials of study were not only expressions of an aristocratic identity crisis or a strategy for dealing with social upstarts. Rather, the pursuit of education and culture was also problematic from a medical standpoint. In his well-known *Anatomy of Melancholy* (1621) Robert Burton prescribed study as an excellent cure for melancholy among "those that are otherwise idle, troubled in mind, or carried headlong with vain thoughts and imaginations, to distract their cogitations ... and divert their continual meditations another way." At the same time, however, Burton considered study a principal *cause* of melancholy among students, partly because "they live a sedentary, solitary life ... free from bodily exercise," but mainly because they studied too much, an excess that many authorities believed was conducive to madness.[32] This medical concern about excessive study was usually addressed to males, often in terms that highlighted the gap between scholarly and warrior lifestyles. At once a *noble d'épée* committed to martial valor and an accomplished writer with humanist sympathies, Michel de Montaigne expressed well the tensions experienced between these competing masculine ideals. He too noted that an intemperate approach to study diminished the body and thus undermined the happiness and moral superiority that learning otherwise facilitated. Like many of his contemporaries, Montaigne associated excessive civilization with moral decline. Being able to withstand pain and hardship was central to Montaigne's recommendations for physical as well as spiritual training, but in an everyday as well as a strictly military sense.[33] This belief that excessive study could ultimately ruin manhood would enjoy considerable medical prestige throughout the modern era, especially when it was coupled with related anxieties about luxury and sedentary lifestyles.

LUXURY AND CONSUMPTION

If the adoption of civility entailed a set of practices designed to blunt the otherwise spontaneous eruption of affective drives in social encounters, the discourse of virtue mobilized constraints in an inward manner to act upon desire itself. The contemporary scholarly inclination to reduce desire to sexuality alone artificially brackets sex from the spectrum of sensual pleasures with which it was widely believed to be associated through the early twentieth century. This is why desire may be profitably viewed as a rather broad sensual continuum capable of being awakened by a variety of objects, sensations and services. Sexual expression has always been implicated in a wider context of experiences; it is never "just" about sex.[34] After all, what resided at the heart of what writers like John Milton bemoaned as the "slack effeminacy" of some men was in fact a more generalized penchant for sensual pleasures and an avoidance of austerity and hardness. The effeminacy to which Milton referred reflects the long lineage of the concept and connotations that have changed considerably since classical antiquity. Up until the eighteenth century, the effeminate man was marked by an *excess of heterosexuality* in that he preferred the erotic company of women to the "austerity, resistance to appetite, and mastery of the impulse to pleasure" that characterized the culture of military elites through the Renaissance. Forgoing the brotherly ties of the war band for the sensual pleasures of female company, such men had mastered the art of appearances through the use of perfumes, cosmetics, jewelry and grooming. They had thus cultivated a "soft" style of manhood that was a stark contrast to traditional associations of masculinity with martial virtues.[35] Men termed "effeminate" during the Renaissance thus included those who were so helplessly attracted to women that they dolled themselves up in order to appeal to them.[36] Yet a predilection for sex rather than war was not the only mark of the "soft" man; there was also the traditional idea that the pleasures of the table too might serve to distract a warrior from his bellicosity. For instance, Wolfram von Eschenbach's medieval text *Willehalm* tells the tale of how French princes had quit the battlefield because they preferred the more comfortable life at home, where they would enjoy many feasts.[37] Effeminacy, in other words, implied a penchant for sensual pleasures and refined manners that had little practical or ideological value for the warrior. Because they were said to weaken the body and corrupt the mind, in times of crisis these could be serious liabilities.

The proliferation of material luxuries from the eighteenth century onward thus posed certain challenges to martial images of manhood that focused instead on austerity and abstention. The vexed relationship between sensual indulgence and martial manhood may also be approached by considering the history of the idea of *comfort*, which reveals a shift over time from spiritual and moral referents to a more overt emphasis on physical concerns. Derived from the late Latin term *confortare* (from *con-fortis*, to render strong and, by extension, to alleviate pain or fatigue), the English word "comfort" suggested physical and emotional support, with more of an emphasis on the latter throughout the medieval and early modern periods. When comfort did refer to physical amenities, these were usually of a very modest sort, with most attention paid to hygienic aims that strengthened the body. For instance, in the Middle Ages the physical requirements for a man's comfort revolved around a fire, clean and warm clothes, a well-appointed bed, and someone who could serve him. These basic amenities fulfilled a compensatory function that, in bodily terms, restored the energies consumed by muscular exertion. This tendency to downplay physical comfort persisted into the sixteenth and seventeenth centuries in the concept of *ease*, which usually referred to the absence of pain or distress rather than a positive increase in pleasure, while *comfort* continued to suggest the barest of physical necessities.[38] Excess of physical comfort was not only considered unnecessary, but also unhealthy in that it could result in *dis*comfort. It is not surprising to see that, in the sixteenth century, some would locate the seeds of bodily corruption and illness in the circulation of consumer items that pampered or stimulated the senses, especially if those goods came from abroad. Witness the example of the imperial knight Ulrich von Hutten, whose account of his being cured of syphilis appeared in 1519. Not only did Hutten see merchants as the primary carriers of diseases from foreign lands, but he condemned the very act of commercial exchange that, by importing corrupting luxuries, threatened to debilitate an otherwise healthy country. Syphilis was thus a "French" disease, and any land penetrated by foreign textiles, perfumes and spices thus risked becoming soft, enfeebled and base.[39] This conflation of foreign commodities with sensuality and effeminacy would become a common feature of modern anxieties about consumption and manhood.

Often said to represent the "high" and "low" of human activities, knowledge and consumption tend to be viewed as incompatible in the Western tradition. Ironically, though, the increasing emphasis that Europeans placed on culture and education may have played a role in fostering a greater appreciation for consumer goods and material comforts. After all, if there was one domain in which physical comfort was allowed freer rein during the early modern era, it was in the recent architectural innovation of the humanist scholar's study, which was becoming an essential feature of many elite households. John E. Crowley describes the importance of this new scholarly space for emerging ideas about comfort:

> As spaces designed to store and display items carefully chosen for their style and their accommodation of an individual's highly self-conscious leisure – not just books but desks and chairs, glassware and mirrors, cushions and other textile amenities, facilities for artificial illumination, art objects – the Renaissance study was arguably the initial site of the early modern consumer revolution and of the expression of modern physical comfort.

Thus the humanist scholar, whose profession substituted a more rational and oratorical definition of manhood for that of the robustly physical warrior, may have also been at the center of the growing shift towards more sensual understandings of comfort.[40] Indeed, by the eighteenth century the concept had come to refer more approvingly to material well-being, signaling the "retreat of a climate of austerity and scarcity" and the ascendence of a more consumer-oriented ideal.[41]

By the eighteenth century many of these concerns were subsumed in the concept of luxury, which has been rightly called "the defining issue of the early modern period."[42] For the middling sort in Britain and America, comfort increasingly referred to the satisfaction and enjoyment of physical circumstances. Amidst the consumer revolution that unfolded during this time, it signified a happy medium between luxury and necessity. A similar consumer revolution was under way in France. There it was characterized not only by the extravagant spending of the aristocracy, but by the penchant among commoners for cheap imitations of the luxury goods consumed by the nobility, from jewelry, umbrellas, hats and canes to furniture, earthenware, and tea and coffee accessories.[43] The growing acceptance of luxury, at least in practice if not in principle, revealed that mere comfort was always capable of slipping into more luxurious indulgences that were neutral neither in moral nor physical terms. In Britain and France the controversy that surrounded the publication of Bernard Mandeville's *The Fable of the Bees* (1723/28; French translation, 1740) propelled the luxury issue to national consciousness. Mandeville argued that older forms of social domination had been rendered obsolete by recent economic developments where men eschewed the use of force in favor of the conspicuous display of goods. Dismissing claims that luxury necessarily rendered men effeminate, Mandeville welcomed the search for opulence as a means of stimulating the economy and of fostering civility. Indeed, for him there was no objective way to distinguish comforts from luxuries anyway.[44] Among moderates this utilitarian defense of luxury authorized consumption within certain limits. So long as men and women made rational use of their wealth and did not succumb to excess, luxury and civic definitions of masculinity worked quite well together.

The fear, of course, was that the enjoyment of luxury would not remain contained by any civic spirit, but that it would slip into vice that promoted egoism while diminishing courage, a classical republican argument made by worried moralists in many European countries.[45] And, of course, the male body stood at the center of these concerns. Criticisms of the consumption of commercial goods slipped easily into the language of alimentary consumption, an idea that, when imagined in terms of the body politic, lent itself readily to the alarming imagery of parasitism and vampiric draining by external forces. All manner of dangerous bugbears could be conjured up in this way, of which the bloated capitalist, the parasitic whore and the conniving Jew are merely the best known examples. Yet these figures of "otherness" are intimately related to representations of the "normal," for whom the very act of consumption threatens to turn back upon itself, to consume the consumer. What one scholar has termed (in reference to American history) the "warrior critique of the business civilization" is in fact a recurring discourse of the modern era, a quasi-structural element of the tensions that exist between aggressive masculinity and the softer lifestyles and concerns of modern commercial society.[46] The very concept of consumption thus depends, as Mark Seltzer suggests, upon "a condensation or conflation of bodily and economic states, of the individual and social body."[47]

In this "warrior" critique of civilization, hardship, pain and warfare connect the private body with the demands of the nation in order to strengthen both. Depicted as the special domain of physically active manhood, commercial production is privileged over the consumption of material goods that is said to reduce men to the level of women, children and animals. Eroding the body politic from within, mainly by encouraging personal "happiness" over "virtue," luxury increased the likelihood of foreign invasion or a political seizure of power. According to Vicesimus Knox – and others who shared his view – luxury was but one step on the path towards despotism. "Effeminacy, the natural consequence of vice and luxury caused by defect of moral principle, precludes courage, spirit, and all manly, virtuous exertion."[48] Although often employed by middle-class radicals against the profligate nobility, references to the "manly" virtues of simplicity and modesty were hardly the monopoly of the middling sort. Indeed, by the nineteenth century, working-class men too would bring the language of modesty to bear against the luxury and extravagance of the middle class. "The ideology of masculine sobriety," as David Kuchta rightly notes, "thus remained for all classes of men the terms of political legitimacy."[49] As the following chapters will show, the language of modesty often diverted attention from the reality of indulgence, be it sexual, alimentary or consumer-oriented.

HOMO SEDENTARIUS

Although physical inactivity does not form one of the explicitly touted *benefits* of modern civilization, in the Western world many have considered sedentariness a prerequisite for the formation of human settlements and thus of civil society generally. After all, the deepest historical meaning of sedentariness refers less to a state of the body than to the behavior of human groups, and elements of this idea can be found in ancient cultures. The prehistoric shift from nomadic hunter-gatherer groups to "sedentary" agricultural societies represented perhaps the first real divergence in male identities, at least as they have been imagined after the fact. The myth of the rootless nomad as a male ideal has never ceased to fascinate and haunt more settled versions of masculinity, even though the practical opportunity and need for the hunter has receded as societies have grown more complex, not least due to the differentiation and specialization of tasks that the establishment of settled communities facilitated. From the perspectives of early societies, wanderers often represented a suspicious and even dangerous existence beyond the reach of ordinary civil society. By the nineteenth century the sedentary/nomad dichotomy even contributed to a reinterpretation of world history in terms of what Paul Silverstein calls "a primordial battle between 'man-in-motion' and 'man-at-rest'" that provided an enduring and potent means of framing the relationship between colony and metropole. This privileging of "rooted" communities over itinerant groups and individuals also constituted a common ingredient of modern nationalisms, which often employ a "sedentarist metaphysic" to pathologize such displaced, mobile, and border-crossing individuals as vagrants, "gypsies," wandering Jews, and, in recent years, refugees and asylum seekers.[50]

In the Western world, then, sedentariness is virtually synonymous with civilization, understood in its broadest sense of settled (as opposed to nomadic) human groups. Within this framework, the itinerant stranger is an "other" to those who have more or less accepted the conventions of settled existence.

Yet whereas the appearance of strangers may signal a breach of community boundaries, the fantasy of becoming itinerant oneself has not ceased to captivate the imaginations of settled groups. The spatial difference between the settled and the nomadic is paralleled in corporeal and psychological matters: at heart the difference between the villager or city dweller and the "wild" nomad pertains to vastly different perceptions of the management of bodily urges and comportment. As discussed above, one of the West's most vivid and enduring myths pertains to the wild men (*homo sylvestris, homines agrestes* and so on) whose imagined presence on the margins of civilized society has served as a counterpoint to the customs promoted in the earliest human settlements. Like the physical urges and bodily excesses that had to be channeled or repressed for the sake of sociability and decorum, a continuing fascination with uncivilized and unsettled men has accompanied the civilizing process. As Roger Bartra suggests, "The man we recognize as civilized has been unable to take a single step without the shadow of the wild man at his heel."[51] It is thus hardly surprising that later imperialist representations of non-Europeans (as well as images of whites who broke away from settled life) would be crafted using many of the same ingredients that had earlier applied to the wild man, whose distance from the conventions of "civilized" society could be at once publicly deplored and secretly envied. As the recent popularity of Robert Bly's *Iron John* (1990) suggests, the mythopoetic men's movement owes much to this deep-seated cultural ambivalence about the wild man, whose untamed qualities (when adopted in moderation) continue to be cited as beneficial for more "civilized" men.

Although this rather broad criticism of the sedentary life plays an important role in the modern West, it is perhaps less pervasive than critiques of corporeally inactive individuals residing *within* settled social formations. A decreasing need for strenuous physical effort, either through labor or warfare, is the common bodily denominator of the three faces of civilization outlined above. Historians and anthropologists often claim that the so-called agricultural revolution created the conditions that made possible the specialization of tasks and the creation of leisured and priestly classes as well as their sedentary lifestyles. Yet, as the lifestyles of farmers, artisans and laborers reveal, there is no necessary incompatibility between the rigorous use of the body and the practice of remaining in one place. This is why Jean-Jacques Rousseau thought that the "happiest and most stable of epochs" was not the state of nature, but the simple agricultural societies that balanced primitiveness with sociability.[52] As a problem of gender and body, the danger of sedentariness has pertained more to priestly and social elites than to workers, though this was mitigated to some extent by the nobility's association with martial prowess. The chivalric warrior code was surely an active ideal, and the physical strenuousness of the martial lifestyle was sharpened in the twelfth century by the discovery of classical texts that revealed, among other things, how the

Romans were able to conquer the known world. From ancient writings like those of Vegetius, knights learned the value of discipline and physical training in order to hone their skills and to maintain their bodies in peak condition.[53]

This situation would change as nobles became increasingly demilitarized and wealthy commoners continued to have little interest in martial prowess; moreover, it would be compounded by the gradual spread of overtly physical conceptions of comfort, which also connoted and promoted the passivity of the body.[54] In the sixteenth century, growing concerns about both exercise and inaction were encapsulated in Richard Mulcaster's *Positions Concerning the Training Up of Children* (1581). In addition to his appeal to commoners and limited support for the education of women, Mulcaster was unusual among Elizabethan pedagogues for his insistence on physical education as a necessary complement to mental training, something he wished to see integrated within the academic program rather than dismissed as an extracurricular activity. Knowing his readers would be familiar with stories of extraordinary physical prowess in games and warfare, he assured parents and educators that he had more practical ends in mind for his own students:

> in my exercises, I neither meane to dally with the gamester, nor to fight with the warrier, but to marke which way I may best save studentes, who haue most neede of it: being still assailed by those enemies of health, which waxe more eager and hoat, the more weake and cold that exercise is.

Health seems to have been the main reason for Mulcaster's approval of almost any exercise that promoted "a vehement, and a voluntarie stirring of ones body ... to bringe the bodie to a verie good habit." Relying heavily upon Girolamo Mercuriale's earlier work, *De arte gymnastica* (1569), Mulcaster conceptualized exercise in the context of the reigning humoral physiology of the day, explaining how the dangers of the scholar's sedentary lifestyle needed to be offset by exercise. Indeed, "stilnesse more then ordinarie, must have stirring more then ordinarie ... as quiet sitting helpes ill humors to breede, and burden the bodie: so must stirring make a waie to discharge the one, and to disburden the other." For these reasons Mulcaster even recommended football, one of the sports technically forbidden to the aristocracy due to its association with the common people. "That the exercise of the body still accompanie and assist the exercise of the minde, to make a dry, strong, hard, and therefore a long lasting body: and by the favour therof to have an active, sharp, wise and therwith all a well learned soule."[55]

The belief that physical exercise might temper the ills of the scholarly and sedentary life has been a common claim since ancient times, and persists to the present day. Indeed, early modern physicians like Laurent Joubert recommended regular and vigorous exercise as a means of creating a virile and harmonious body that was an improvement over its God-given form. By voluntarily acting upon themselves, in other words, men could make themselves like grains of wheat purified of any unnecessary chaff.[56] Harmony and proportion were essential to this ideal. Like many humoralists committed to the doctrine of moderation (*mediocritas*), Robert Burton identified "immoderate exercise" as a cause of melancholy; yet by devoting less than a page to this problem he showed that he clearly did not consider excessive exertion to be particularly common. Burton had rather more to say about idleness, which he dubbed "the nurse of naughtiness" as it seemed to foster both physical ailments and moral corruption. As with the problem of luxury, the implications of physical fitness for the body politic were obvious.

> In a Commonwealth, where is no publick enemy, there is, likely, civil wars, and they rage upon themselves: this body of ours, when it is idle, and knows not how to bestow itself, macerates and vexeth itself with cares, griefs, false fears, discontents, and suspicions; it tortures and preys upon his own bowels, and is never at rest.[57]

In addition to its medical implications, the sedentary life was by the eighteenth century often considered downright unmanly, despite that fact that this was the lot of many elites. Always quick to criticize the degradation wrought by civilization, Rousseau was especially hard on men engaged in sedentary pursuits. Thus, when Rousseau broke with tradition to recommend that even upper-class boys should learn a trade, he insisted that these trades should be *active* ones. "Every weak, delicate, and fearful man is condemned by nature to a sedentary life. He is made to live with women or in their manner." Such was the case with tailors, who, as Rousseau saw it, would have never selected such a womanish occupation if left to their natural inclinations. More appropriate for men are hard and dangerous occupations that "exercise strength and courage at the same time." No true man would freely choose a "sedentary and indoor profession which effeminates and softens the body," claimed Rousseau. Any man who did could only be a freak of nature, a male body inhabited by a feminine soul. This is why Rousseau heaped such scorn upon tailors, dogmatically charging that "The needle and the sword cannot be wielded by the same hands." Castration was one means of restoring such false men to their proper female state. "And if there absolutely must be true eunuchs, let men who dishonor their sex by taking jobs which do not suit it be reduced to this condition. Their choice proclaims nature's mistake. Correct its mistake one way or another. You will have only done good."[58] Presumably tailors topped Rousseau's list of the nation's most castratable men.

The tension between activity and sedentariness potentially drove a wedge between different kinds of labor, and thus implicitly called into question the manliness of all non-manual occupations. Usually stopping short of Rous-seau's dramatic solution, physicians concurred that inactive professions were as unbecoming as they were unhealthy. "Sedentary occupations ought chiefly to be followed by women," claimed the physician William Buchan, who was widely read in Britain and America. "They bear confinement much better than men, and are fitter for every kind of business which does not require much strength. It is ridiculous enough to see a lusty fellow making pins, needles, or watch-wheels, while many of the laborious parts of husbandry are carried on by the other sex."[59] From a medical point of view, then, even production could be "unmanly" if it did not enlist a wide range of bodily energies.

* * *

The decline of the battlefield as a realistic arena for proving masculinity altered the self-perceptions of European elites, many of whom found them-selves engaged in bureaucratic assignments that required higher education, culture and refined manners that fostered sociability. This upper-class with-drawal from the relative directness of physicality in both war and everyday life coincided with an increase in sedentariness that distanced them further from the laboring classes, whose physical engagement in their work continued to represent the rough manhood that most elites had abandoned as part of the civilizing process. Yet the fact that, over the centuries, elite manhood has been positioned less and less on the actual field of battle does not signify a loosening of the association of the martial ideal with masculinity. Rather, among elites martial metaphors were mobilized at the same time that formal warfare receded, producing forms of bellicosity that would first be turned inward in order to be directed outwardly in a more controlled manner, often in a world of metaphorical combat in business, politics, or other "civilized" professions. If the medieval knight might experience periods of peace and repose between battles, elite men of the early modern period gradually found their own lives and the world itself transformed into "battles" of a different sort. These everyday conflicts recognized neither boundaries nor clear end points.

A long-term consequence of these developments would be a growing cultural tendency to "remember" the Middle Ages and other pre-modern eras nostalgically as glorious times when men reveled in the unfettered enjoyment of bodily energies and urges. Ambivalence is thus inscribed at the heart of the civilizing process as proscribed bodily processes and emotional expressions come to be viewed in terms of loss and desire. What is often represented as wholeness or authenticity cannot be achieved without crossing the bound-aries drawn by civilization. As Kenneth Lockridge suggests, "The civilized man must transgress, through fear or desire, into the realm of the low, the other, where his sense of the forbidden resides alongside his sense of magic, his emotions, and his desiring body. Transgression becomes a constituent of identity in civilized Western culture."[60] If the figure of the "wild man" reappears in various guises throughout the modern era, it is less because of the "repressed" and "essential" savagery of men than an outcome of our culture's obsessive tendency to align savagery and manhood on the side of "freedom" and "life" as opposed to the restraint and artificiality that is so often elided with femininity. Marianna Torgovnick is thus right to assert that "We conceive of ourselves as at the crossroads between the civilized and the savage; we are formed by our conceptions of both these terms, conceived dialectically."[61]

"In this context," Philip Mellor and Chris Shilling contend, "it is no wonder that modern life may contain a certain nostalgia for the spontaneity and emotional passions often associated with medieval bodies."[62] This would become particularly true by the late nineteenth century, when criticism of refined, sedentary and cerebral bourgeois lifestyles compelled many to seek compensation through action, adventure and physicality, even if such alternatives were available only through fantasy. As the rest of this book will show, nostalgia for a "lost" primitive or warrior heritage is a recurring theme in the history of Western masculinity, not least due to the structuring principles of modern civilization itself. Civilizing processes thus periodically contend with decivilizing processes as part of the internal dynamic of modernity. What Freud said about civilization generally is especially applicable to manhood in the modern world. To the extent that the "liberty of the individual is no gift of civilization ... the urge for freedom, therefore, is directed against particular forms and demands of civilization or against civilization altogether."[63]

2
Balancing Acts: The Paradox of the Gentleman

His qualities may have been lauded, but the gentleman entered the modern world as a somewhat contradictory ideal. By the eighteenth century the complexity of definitions of masculinity was such that no one man could hope to embody all the recommended qualities under the given conditions of modern civilization, with the greatest tension revolving around the contradictions between physical as opposed to moral or mental attributes. German dictionaries of the eighteenth century plot this tension between competing ideals of manhood. For much of the century the *männlich* (an obvious cognate of the English word *manly*) was defined in robustly martial terms and illustrated with adjectives like "brave," "strong," "forceful," "valiant," "resolute," and "unyielding." During the 1780s these ideals were complemented by more "civic" qualities like learnedness, seriousness, wisdom and gravity,[1] thus perhaps reflecting the impact of the Enlightenment on central European gender ideals. By the turn of the nineteenth century, the qualities implied by *männlich* ranged from the aggressive and martial to the civic and moral, even if it was unclear whether men needed to possess all these qualities at the same time.

This instability was also true of the nineteenth-century notion of "manliness" in Britain, which, as John Tosh explains, connoted energy, will, straightforwardness and courage, as well as "bodily associations which were less universally acclaimed," among which he counts physical robustness, self-defense and readiness for combat. As Tosh rightly observes, manliness also had much to do with participation in what were called "manly exercises" (such as cricket, fox-hunting and rowing) as well as physical bearing and sexual potency. It could even imply engagement in strenuous physical activities such as boxing and dueling, which, though generally associated respectively with proletarians and aristocrats, were also described as "manly" activities.[2] This semantic latitude accords with Janet Oppenheimer's description of the idea of manliness before 1850, which she characterizes as a "complex merger of late Georgian and early Victorian beliefs" that generated "a continuation of many late eighteenth-century assumptions and a reaction against them."[3] Broadly speaking, then, what is sometimes mono-lithically described as "manliness" refers to a complex cluster of hetero-geneous qualities, a mixture of emergent and residual cultural elements that could be selectively appropriated depending upon one's age, class and circumstances.

This chapter looks at the gentleman as a paradoxical cultural figure crafted from the tensions between potentially irreconcilable prescriptions for ideal manhood. Compelled to incorporate upper-class behavioral ideals regarding proper comportment, manners and refinement, at various points between the mid-eighteenth and early nineteenth centuries, the gentleman risked being labeled immoral, deceptive or "effeminate" if these qualities were not tem-pered by more direct and even coarse words and deeds. Although the atten-tion to fashion and grooming that these genteel performances demanded necessarily encouraged some engagement with consumption, too much devo-tion to appetites and appearances was widely thought to promote the softness that weakened both individuals and the nation. Thus the manners that were so often said to "make the man" could just as easily *unmake* a man if he became too beholden to the artifice and appetite that these practices required and encouraged. Many middle-class men were keenly aware of the tightrope they walked between the social demand for self-control and the temptations periodically to relax that control. The proper gentleman had to know how to navigate these competing demands.

MANNERS UNMAKE THE MAN

Refinement has always entailed the proper and apparently effortless manage-ment of a wide range of bodily functions and practices, from posture and gait to modes of address, table manners, ways of responding to compliments and insults, and the control of bodily emissions and emotional expression. The ease with which one manifested a mannerly *habitus* was important, for it suggested that the graceful and controlled body was "natural" rather than the result of learning or conscious effort (which, at least in part, it most certainly was).[4] The movement and posture of the body marked a man as belonging to a certain class, and to some extent as having been shaped by a certain pro-fession. The teaching of correct posture encapsulates the tension between physical and moral ideals of masculine uprightness; the one literally embod-ied in a rigidly erect posture and the other represented by resistance to modern culture's siren call to comfort and leisure.[5] Georges Vigarello observes that: "The fact is that the body, just like its uprightness, is 'caught' in a web of categories dominated by moral expectations. Deportment corresponds to the great polarities of behavior, where respect for physical bearing has the same psychological basis as knowing how to be polite." This refinement began at home, manifested through the shaping of the infant body. Considered soft, malleable, and particularly prone to deformations, babies were the target of direct adult intervention. Likened to unformed clay, young male bodies required careful shaping if they were to "harden" into a healthy and socially acceptable shape. The infant son of French nobles was typically wrapped in swaddling bandages that, in addition to keeping his body immobile and warm, were meant to mold it into an "upright" shape. Physical uprightness was the object of constant vigilance and both boys and girls were repeatedly reminded to stand up straight. Correct posture and graceful movement were further reinforced through fencing and dancing, strictly codified activities that discouraged abrupt or coarse bodily motions.[6]

The aim of this early pedagogy was to create a body whose motions and gestures would be performed automatically, without conscious reflection or effort. The alternative would be mere affectation, "an awkward and forc'd imitation of what should be genuine and easy." Thus John Locke praised the free and easy gracefulness of the well-bred man, whose gestures of civility and respect "seem not artificial or studied."[7] This idea was most fully developed in France, whose reputation for being the center and school of European refinement reached its apotheosis with the court society of Louis XIV and persisted through the eighteenth century. With its etymological connection to the word "polish" and phonetic similarity to "police," the concept of *politesse* was thus closely bound up with the notion of *civilisation* as a progressive process of smoothing out the roughness from individuals as well as entire nations.[8] Elites in England, Russia and the German states had for years learned manners by taking cues from France, and the Earl of Chesterfield's famous letters to his son were the widely cited (and just as widely condemned) fruit of this interchange between British and French culture.[9] Such gentility required attention to dress and grooming; it also demanded that one be *au courant* with, and capable of purchasing, consumer goods and the latest fashions. This imperative also migrated across national borders. For example, during the eighteenth century, French and English fashions were disseminated to the German states through *Das Journal des Luxus und der Moden*, which, in addition to providing essential fashion tips to provincial courts, also served as a primer for members of the administrative bourgeoisie who sought to move in noble circles but lacked the necessary training in elegance.[10] Tasteful consumption was thus another essential for the performance of upper-class manhood and for those who aspired to "pass" in such circles.

Although prescriptions for proper behavior were dispensed to both sexes, the discourse of manners seemed to place greater emphasis on the male body, in part because of the demands men faced in professional and political spheres as well as in social and domestic interactions. This was true in Russia, for example, where Peter the Great cemented the association between schooling and civil service as part of his Westernization project. Anyone aiming at high-level posts in the public service was expected to be educated from an early age at one of several elite academies. Sons of the Russian nobility were also encouraged to adopt the rules of civility, first through translations of European courtesy books, later through texts generated within Russia itself. Unlike girls, who often learned manners through family contacts and example, conduct books offered boys more concrete and meticulous advice about table manners, bodily comportment and polite conversation. For example, *The Honorable Mirror of Youth* (1717) discouraged poor posture, drunkenness, gambling and fornication, and in mixed company it proscribed a familiar list of potentially embarrassing activities including coughing, belching, farting, swearing and voracious eating. Building upon cultural exchanges initiated by Peter, Catherine II promoted the adoption of good manners with an intensity and coherence that had not been evident under previous monarchs. Not only were European conduct manuals translated and published at an unprecedented rate during her reign, but, through the network of state-run schools that Catherine established in the 1780s, the educational process became a primary medium for the inculcation of manners. Such ideals persisted through the early nineteenth century, where administrative notions of manhood were marked by the Russian concept of *nravy*, which encompassed the English ideas of manners and morality. Cleanliness and neatness of body and dress revealed the moral worth of the mind. When it came to the training of Russian youths, by the 1830s Western-style conventions of civility were just as highly prized as academic achievement.[11]

However, reflecting Castiglione and della Casa's claims centuries before, there were always fears that the teaching of refinement would go too far, producing men who were so polished, adorned, cunning and narcissistic as to be virtually indistinguishable from women – and herein resides the central paradox of manners that depend upon appearances as the expression of inner qualities. As the attainment of "ease" implied that a person's manners were the effortless result of nature, so impeccable manners were also meant faithfully to reflect the interior qualities of the individual. The discourse of civility that was developed in France optimistically assumed a direct correlation between external appearances and inner reality, which led many to believe they could "read" personal character through the *bon ton*, elegant dress and good conversation displayed by an individual to the world. The *honnête homme* who performed these stylized gestures was, at least in theory, not really *performing* at all, but offering a transparent window onto his virtuous soul. However, as everybody knows, appearances can be deceptive, which opens up the possibility of civility as a mask for immoral intentions. While some seventeenth-century writers worried about a concern with appearances slipping into vanity, others were anxious that civility could be twisted to the purposes of cynical manipulation (which is how Chesterfield's model of the chameleon-like social player was often viewed). The fate of civility as a code of conduct was thus bound up with the problem of refinement itself, and critics took turns either at ridiculing the hidden egoism lurking behind manners, seeking ways of purging civility of this threat, or recommending the nearly synonymous concept of *politesse* as an alternative.[12] Yet even *politesse* was viewed with suspicion, with writers like La Bruyère suggesting that the snobbish affectation of the court could be replaced with a "true" politeness of the mind that valued education.[13]

To some, manners were not only problematic because of the duplicitous potential that lurked within but also because of their close connection with women, whose involvement in polite society would subsequently generate a backlash marked by attempts to return elite women to the domestic sphere by the early nineteenth century.[14] Spending time in female company was widely considered a useful way for males to learn to curb their aggressive tendencies and thus to improve an otherwise unpolished personality.[15] The aristocratic women who hosted the literary salons of *Ancien régime* France were responsible for maintaining decorum among their mostly male guests, whose commitment to argumentation as a form of warfare could produce insults that threatened the cohesion of their "republic of letters." However, in an attempt to remasculinize France and ensure the virtue of the emerging public sphere, by the 1780s men of letters had developed alternative institutions that excluded women – as well as many of the aristocratic standards of polite conversation they had enforced in the salons. Evolving out of Freemasonry, the homosocial sociability of the so-called *musées* not only anticipated the political clubs that proliferated in 1789, but prefigured the republican brotherhood that banned women's political clubs in 1792.[16]

The emotional critique of courtly restraint was also strengthened by the cult of sensibility that emerged during the late seventeenth century. Constructed by John Locke into an influential system, sensationalist psychology placed a premium on the nervous system's capacity to receive and respond to external stimuli. As a means of reworking the overarching desire that male conduct be more refined, genuine emotion promised an attractive alternative to the potential deception of politeness. Although some degree of environmental conditioning was admitted, sensibility was widely considered to be an inborn trait, and the degree of one's sensibility functioned as a marker of rank superimposed over the existing social order. Hence degrees of sensibility were highest amongst the aristocracy, and became increasingly coarse further down the social ladder, with superior status rather paradoxically aligned with greater capacities for weakness and suffering. Indeed, among some writers the slightly built male body was preferred to more athletic or robust types where muscle fibers interfered with the delicacy of the nerves.[17] If politeness threatened to create men who concealed the truth of their inner intentions and feelings, sensibility revealed perhaps more than many wanted to know about the softer side of manhood. The philosophy of sensibility played an important role in the emerging Evangelical view of manliness, which in Britain recommended an equilibrium of moral, physical, emotional and intellectual qualities that was widely promoted during the first half of the nineteenth century. "He is only half a man who can think, but cannot feel," claimed one observer; "who can delight in books but cannot rejoice in friends. Neither is he manly who has the physical, and mental, and emotional powers all in perfect activity, if the moral be lying dormant."[18]

As one might expect, sensibility's unstable relationship with masculinity resulted in rather ambiguous advice about whether, and under what circumstances, a male should give expression to his innermost feelings.[19] Weeping may have been encouraged in some quarters, but in an age when the relationship between masculinity and refinement was being actively debated, the sight of a man in tears hardly met with universal acceptance. The cult of sensibility, as well as demands for balance, were also acknowledged in other countries. As one Dutch observer warned, emotional displays were acceptable but must not be excessive, lest a man "become wholly effeminate, full of apprehension, and the plaything of his imagination and passions."[20] Engagement in the emerging public sphere of politics, business and ideas was cited as one means of keeping a man's emotional nature in check. An active and enterprising profession, it was said, would prevent him from being weakened or enervated by emotional sensations.

As Chapter 5 examines in more detail, the emergence of nationalist ideologies across Europe around 1800 depended upon wresting the refined bodies of male elites from customs and lifestyles that were considered at once physically and morally damaging as well as culturally "French." This was the culmination of a discourse of remasculinization that had been articulated in most countries throughout the eighteenth century and which affected movements in painting, sculpture and music as well as social and political theory.[21] The construction of the nation as a quasi-organic totality thus depended upon the reconstruction of manhood along corporeal as well as moral lines, just as it required the restriction of women's spheres of activity to domesticity and maternity. If France represented the epitome of *civilisation*, for many of the same reasons it also stood at the center of most maps of European effeminacy. German critics, among them Immanuel Kant, agreed that all of this attention to appearances rendered the French national character frivolous and "feminine," and deplored evidence of "Frenchified" habits in their own countries. A similar development was afoot in Russia, where conservatives routinely condemned the vices that seemed integral to the adoption of European values. Prince Mikhail Shcherbatov memorably complained about the adoption of Western manners that: "Coarseness of manners decreased, but the place left by it was filled by flattery and selfishness."[22]

British criticism of politeness focused on its association both with women and with French culture, and some even urged its replacement with the ideal of chivalry, a code of conduct that moderated courtesy while praising the rough, martial education that imaginatively connected modern Britons to their medieval ancestors while suggesting resistance to the excesses of civilization. In the face of over-refinement, chivalry combined the required gentleness with a passion for war, even though few authors of the time used this code as a basis for heroic action. Often connected with the political and social upheavals of the 1790s, sensibility too was emphasized less frequently among men. By the 1820s and 1830s British writers were celebrating a somewhat rougher version of the gentleman, one able to temper his good manners with a more rugged approach to masculinity that bolstered national identity through a successful negotiation of the gendered antinomies of modern life.[23]

Despite these complaints, however, no one recommended the complete abandonment of the basic conventions of manners, which had become so thoroughly embedded in everyday affairs as to be considered the linchpin of social harmony. Indeed, many of the Russian critics who had criticized the adoption of European manners found themselves condemning the falseness of "foreign" manners while fashionably uttering the very French phrases that had become so integral to polite society. What Douglas Smith observes about Russia also holds true for other countries: elites had so "completely internalized the discourse of civility – with its constituent contrasts of coarseness and refinement, rusticity and urbanity, civilization and barbarism – that it had become a permanent filter through which they viewed the world, yet whose presence escaped them."[24] Moreover, no alternative version of manners, however "authentic" it claimed to be, could remain above suspicions of deception. To the British, chivalry may have recommended a seemingly more manly mode of comportment; yet a continuity remained between the courtier's protean performances of the self and the fluid identities of the mid-Victorian city-dweller. "By means of dress, address, concealment and acting," contends Marjorie Morgan, "urban dwellers fashioned themselves in order to convey a carefully selected array of impressions ... Thus, like the courtier, all members of a complex urban society had to be able to switch identities with the grace and promptitude of actors."[25] Whatever the form of manners, self-control and attention to appearances remained central to most understandings of the proper gentleman, while leaving him open to accusations of over-refinement and effeminacy. This tightrope between manliness and effeminacy was walked in every country that fancied itself civilized.

CLOTHING AND CONSUMPTION

Honoré de Balzac observed in the early nineteenth century that "he who says *man* in civilization means *dressed man*." The naked man may indeed be natural, Balzac explained, but from a cultural perspective he is surely "unfinished ... the tailor is called upon to complete him."[26] This accords well with what we already know about the gentleman, for whom all displays of the "raw" (whether of emotion or aggression) needed to be continually refined for the sake of sociability and political peace. Yet if clothing promised to "complete" a civilized man, like most other forms of refinement it also threatened to *supplant* manhood by offering the *appearance* of a well-built body instead of bodily vigor itself. Just as polite manners could conceal a man's inner motives, fashion presented the possibility of concealing the truth about the body beneath layers of finery. This argument was articulated as part of the primitivist fascinations of the eighteenth century. For a writer like Rousseau, "the healthy and robust man is known by other signs: it is under the homespun of the laborer, and not beneath the gilt and tinsel of the courtier, that one will find the strength and vigor of the body."[27] Functioning as a kind of second nature, fashionable clothing threatened to usurp the place of one's actual physique, leading even a dandy like Théophile Gautier to complain that clothes had become "a sort of skin that no man will shed under any pretext. It sticks to him like the pelt of an animal, so that nowadays the real form of the body has fallen into oblivion."[28] These recurring concerns about surface and depth, artifice and authenticity, reveal modern society's ongoing focus on the "natural" body as the location of emotional and psychological depth as well as muscular vigor. Although sometimes criticized for its deceptive potential, fashion nevertheless played a critical role in making sense of the hidden qualities of bodies. After all, the social mores of the era meant that the unadorned body remained inaccessible to the public gaze, so that subjective "interiority could be nothing more than a projection of surface readings."[29]

Evidenced by the rising popularity of trousers and more muted colors, what J.C. Flügel calls a "Great Masculine Renunciation" of color and style is one of the most visible signposts of the gender transformations underway as the eighteenth century passed into the nineteenth. Changes in male dress were linked to complaints about over-refinement and sensibility that placed increasing emphasis on hardness and austerity in the masculine self. Flügel argues that in this context clothing functioned as a kind of armor against moral dangers, wherein the "real protective value of thick clothes" is "unconsciously extended to the moral sphere." If a man's body and character were meant to be free of looseness and flabbiness, so too would his clothing need to be stiff, tight, heavy and "unprovocative in colour." The stiffness of formal clothes not only assisted men in conquering their sensual passions, they were also symbolic of inner character, of the "resistive strength" that was supposed to reside within every proper man.[30] Building upon these observations, Kaja Silverman suggests that clothing renders the body culturally visible while facilitating a sense of self on an intimate level. What one wears "maps out the shape of the ego," she suggests, so that "every transformation within a society's vestimentary code implies some kind of shift within its ways of articulating subjectivity."[31]

Few would dispute the role of fashion in forming a gendered sense of self; yet in many respects this masculine "renunciation" was neither purely bourgeois nor an innovation of the early nineteenth century. As David Kuchta has recently demonstrated, in British culture a preference for sober male styles reflected changing attitudes among the nobility towards consumption since 1688, after which the political power of men was vouchsafed through the public display of manly virtue as opposed to luxury, ostentation and effeminacy. This represented a shift from the sartorial regime of the sixteenth century. By preventing noble clothing from being emulated by wealthy commoners, the sumptuary laws of the time created a hierarchy of dress that promoted conspicuous consumption as an important sign of aristocratic power and status. Moreover, in the age of merchant capitalism, the lavish expenditures of the court on imported goods were thought to promote the creation of wealth at home. Consumption thus proclaimed a man's status, but what one purchased or wore was not viewed as intrinsically masculine or feminine. Insofar as eighteenth-century political culture emphasized the austerity of virtue over the sensual delights of desire and appearances, it promoted a sartorial aesthetic that was in fact an anti-aesthetic. As Kuchta elegantly puts it, this was "a form of display that disdained display, a fashion that denied its fashionability ... This anti-aesthetic was inherently contradictory, precisely because it was still an aesthetic. Since they were still pleasures, manly pleasures always threatened to become mere sensual pleasures" (Figure 2.1).[32]

Herein lies one of the enduring paradoxes of modern masculinity's relationship to fashion and consumerism: an aesthetic defined by a rejection of aesthetics still remains an aesthetic. Fashion and consumption were thus bound up with the same paradoxes that pertained to manners and manhood. In addition to elevating the three-piece suit to prominence as a veritable uniform of male sobriety, 1688 was to "permanently install modesty as a marker of elite masculinity," and thus to legitimate a shared vocabulary for thinking about male consumption whose logic would prove durable enough to outlast the class that initiated it. If defenders of the old sartorial regime saw luxury as a marker of the parvenu, its seventeenth-century critics reversed this logic to depict the aristocracy as luxuriously corrupt, godless and effeminate.[33] In a commercial culture that placed a premium on trade and consumption, this was a source of pleasure that would continually threaten to lead a man from the timeless to the fashionable, and from the rational to the sensual. This is one reason why the many men who actually took quite an interest in consumer goods and collectibles rhetorically insisted that consumption was really a female preoccupation.[34] Writing about the problem of luxury during a

Figure 2.1 James A. Gillray, "How to Ride with Elegance Thro' the Streets" (1800), in *The Works of James Gillray from the Original Plates* (London: Henry G. Bohn, *c*. 1830).

later period, Warren G. Breckman suggests that this teetering between self-restraint and self-indulgence represents "a possibly unresolvable tension" at the heart of the middle-class ethos of production, what others have called the paradox of the Protestant work ethic. By serving as the unavoidable symbol of achievement in nearly every sphere, money was a reward for, and symbol of, bourgeois success; yet "money also threatened the productivist ethos itself because an attainment of wealth might render further work superfluous."[35] The "paradox" of the Protestant ethic is at heart the paradox of a consumer society that encourages both self-discipline and self-indulgence. With elite males historically positioned as the prime movers of capital production (and thus the ones most in need of exercising consumer restraint), the prospect or reality of consumption installs this paradox in the conflicting desires of men themselves.

The relationship between fashion and masculinity was thus inextricably bound up with the gendered tensions circulating around luxury, which was widely thought to be a prime source of "effeminacy." In one of his seminal essays on the history of sexuality, Randolph Trumbach relates the story of a well-known English fop named Captain Rigby, who was tried in 1699 for attempting to seduce a boy. Critics at the time cited Rigby's extravagant cloth-ing – what they called his "effeminate madness" – as reasons why he might have tried to seduce this lad. Was sartorial excess a cause of same-sex object choice or was it a symptom of something deeper? "It is almost certainly the case," Trumbach explains, "that the effeminate manner of a beau like Rigby was seen in 1699 as the cause of his sodomy, only because there had begun to appear a new kind of sodomite who was identified principally by his effem-inate manner."[36] If a passion for fine clothes lay behind Rigby's sodomy, what was it that caused such an "effeminate manner"? Many at the time believed the "cause" of effeminacy was luxury itself, and thus the problem of modern society's material abundance. For them the problem of luxury was explicitly linked to the decline of a warrior ethos that left idle elites to their sensual whims while their bodies atrophied and their courage evaporated. The emer-gence of foppishly flamboyant "macaroni" fashions during the 1760s and early 1770s was depicted as yet another symptom of what could happen to a society enjoying the benefits of both peace and prosperity.[37]

The fact that luxury consumption could be so closely linked to sexuality reveals how sensual pleasures have historically been conceived in terms of a continuum of sensations. Around 1700 "sodomy" itself was a confused cat-egory that included such assorted acts as masturbation, oral sex and anal sex as well as same-sex relations generally. Yet however it was defined, sodomy was thought to be most common in countries where commercial culture was more advanced. In the seventeenth century, the Netherlands had been one of the most prosperous and powerful countries in Europe, clear proof to many that God had smiled upon its citizens' sobriety and modesty. Hence the shock in 1730 at the discovery of a network of sodomites in major Dutch cities. Significantly, this proliferation was primarily explained as the unfortunate consequence of Dutch prosperity, where material abundance promoted frivolous pastimes that hardened into habits and precipitated an inexorable slide into more serious forms of vice. Worried critics mapped out the path along this slippery slope: if left unchecked, what began with misdemeanors like card-playing, indulgence in food and drink and sartorial extravagance eventually led to debauchery and finally sodomy. The "proof" of this was in the fact that same-sex practices simply didn't exist in the Netherlands before this fall into luxury, or so Dutch authorities liked to tell themselves.[38]

While the Dutch shared the English penchant for blaming it all on the French, in France, too, luxury was cited as a cause of same-sex sexuality. There, sodomy was frequently connected to Masonic lodges that, in addition to their secret rituals, were renowned for the rich food and drink enjoyed by their members. This broad-based belief that effeminacy was connected to lifestyle leveled attention less upon the sodomite as an individual than upon the conditions that seemed to produce him in the first place. Although the sexual penetration of the sodomite's body may indeed confirm the abdication of male power observed by some scholars, in the early eighteenth century effeminacy of manners was thought to be the *result* of lifestyles marked by peace, abundance and inactivity. Active or passive, the sodomite was not a model of *homo clausus*, but was in a sense already "penetrated" and softened by the sensual pleasures and habits of the urban world. Sodomy was thus situated on the dark end of a spectrum of effeminate modern behaviors; it was the *effect* rather than the cause of effeminacy.[39]

As consumption was on the rise across the West in the eighteenth and early nineteenth centuries, the charge of effeminacy passed like a hot potato from country to country. Even if the British repeatedly depicted France as the headquarters of international effeminacy, their own virility was hardly beyond reproach, especially among those unruly "children" who populated the colonies and settler societies of the mother country. Colonial Americans seeking to fashion their national identity through a combination of refined gentility and neo-Spartan toughness gleefully belittled what they saw as the over-refinement of the English gentleman, metonymically reducing him to the macaroni fop. Not surprisingly, attention was leveled at fine and expensive clothing as emblematic of luxury consumption. Emphasizing simple homespun as opposed to fine imported fabrics, what had been previously condemned as the tastelessness of the "Yankee Doodle Dandy" was transformed into a virtuous and patriotic simplicity that projected American identity as more "manly" than other countries. Future president John Adams added his voice to the chorus of angry colonists who condemned the "luxury, effeminacy and venality" of the mother country.[40]

Sartorial reform was thus high on the agenda for many countries struggling with the perceived tension between manhood and consumption, and in most

cases a return to austerity in all tastes was the commonly-prescribed remedy
for effeminacy. Among the politically powerless middle classes of the German
states, distinctive clothes facilitated male revolts against the Frenchified habits
of the nobility. This was the case with the perhaps thousands of educated
young Germans who donned the blue jacket, yellow vest and tanned leather
breeches of Johann Wolfgang von Goethe's tragic literary character Werther,
whose well-known sorrows and eventual suicide captured the imagination of
youth. If most young men did not kill themselves in emulation of their literary hero, by rejecting the courtly clothes that signified social status, this
"de rigueur masculine uniform of rebellion" affirmed instead the emotional
core of the private self, even if that sentimentalism had to be carefully cultivated. Against the "civilized" requirements of the bureaucratic state, where
several changes of clothes per day were expected, continuously wearing the
Werther costume affirmed an illusionary masculine autonomy that, when
worn by many others, represented a military code of discipline that was a
negation of ostentation.[41] So important was a more austere fashion to the
recovery of manhood and virtuous citizenship that reformers in France,
Germany and the United States all proposed some kind of national uniform
that would distinguish men and women from both cosmopolitan commercial
trends and the customs of foreign countries.[42]

By the early nineteenth century, a different kind of "uniform", characterized by trousers, would be adopted by male elites across the Western world,
one that tried to reinforce differences between the sexes as well as affirming a
man's distance from effeminate sartorial extravagance (Figure 2.2). In the early

Figure 2.2   French men's fashion (1826–1856). University of Washington Libraries,
Special Collections (UW 27106z, UW 27107z, UW 27105z).

nineteenth century, men who flouted the mainstream insistence on modesty in dress represented an "unrespectable radicalism" that was considered incompatible with the virtue of the public good.[43]

Nonetheless, from the 1830s onward, such a radicalism was represented by bourgeois "bohemians" who employed eccentric clothing as a means of rebellion against the now dominant middle-class culture, thus dramatizing what Jerrold Seigel describes as "ambivalence toward their own social identities and destinies."[44] The dandy was the best known of these rebels against bourgeois conformity. Even though dandies could be likened to the fops and *petit-maîtres* of the eighteenth century, their emphasis on understated elegance was viewed as an austere sartorial strategy. In fact, dandies often cast their struggles for recognition in an almost military light redolent of the old nobility of birth, and their preference for black signified a rejection of the fashionable styles that proliferated between the 1830s and 1850s and that featured an array of colors and patterns, with bright waistcoats, velvet jackets and checked trousers that ranged in shape from the skin-tight to the balloon-like.[45] Yet in his contempt for middle-class conformity and uniformity, the dandy stood outside bourgeois respectability, projecting an aristocracy based on personal taste rather than birth. The dandy presented himself as *déclassé* and thus as not bound to any particular class, a posture that could render him suspect in an age when the bourgeoisie was consolidating its political and cultural self-identity.[46]

MEN BEHAVING BADLY

The dandy and the bohemian were committed to standing apart from typical bourgeois respectability, but their pretensions and protests nevertheless provide some insight into the ongoing tensions existing at the heart of middle-class ideals. If gender is indeed a kind of performance, then attention must also be paid to the stage props and scenery that facilitate that performance as well as the audience and critics who assess a performance's success or failure. The history of material culture provides some clues to how men rebelled against the constraints of the gender order they created. Though widely promoted in conduct manuals, upright posture was more or less enforced through the richly upholstered sofas and chairs that constituted parlor suites in America, and no doubt in other countries. Insofar as the back of each piece was nearly perpendicular to the floor, an erect posture was the only way to achieve a degree of comfort. Such parlor suites also expressed the structured inequality of the sexes that divided American society, which is why the largest chair (significantly called a gentlemen's or "easy" chair) was usually reserved for the male and offered a bit more comfort than the other pieces of the suite.

Whether or not individuals consistently observed this structure when deciding where to sit did not diminish the symbolic force of the code itself, where comfort and gender hierarchy were clearly entwined. Kenneth Ames has provided some very suggestive analyses of male posture in his cultural readings of nineteenth-century family portraiture. In these images fathers are often depicted seated while flanked by standing women and children, whose subordinate position in the family is embodied in their restricted access to comfort (Figure 2.3). Although parlor chairs encouraged "correct" posture, smaller chairs allowed for greater movement on the part of the sitter, even to the point of allowing to the chair to be tilted backward in what was a very common practice for men. While admitting that tilting could signify a range of positive and negative qualities depending upon the context and social status of the sitter, Ames suggests close affinities between tilting and masculinity:

> This male posture of tilting is always literally an act of pulling back, of pulling away ... The preferred posture of tilting backward creates distance, emphasizes separateness, controls connectedness. Tilting backward allows one to survey a situation better, to assume the role of spectator, of voyeur. It allows one to assess, to order, and to render more abstract a given situation. All this is congruent with what we know of conventional male patterns of thought and behavior.

Most important for our purposes is the observation that artistic representations of tilting were consistently set in a world separated from women, in a "male world" presented as less affected by the strictures of gentility so closely

Figure 2.3 Victorian family portraits (Britain, late 1800s). Private collection.

associated with polite society. Tilting may thus be read as a kind of bodily strategy of resistance to that which smacked of too much refinement and female influence. This relaxation of bodily control in all-male company was also echoed in the period's etiquette manuals, where lounging, crossing and elevating one's feet were deemed acceptable only in the "abandon of bachelor seclusion."[47]

However insignificant they may seem, such small retreats from a "feminine" world are common features of masculine identity in most periods, though the perceived need for such lines of flight has surely increased as male and female roles threatened to become blurred in the modern era. In the eighteenth century, Freemasonry and other fraternal orders offered men of the noble and middling sort an escape from the social and economic demands of court culture, a kind of emotional refuge from strict codes of etiquette and self-control.[48] Masonic lodges were especially attractive as spaces where nobles and commoners freely mixed while engaging in pleasurable activities like drinking, smoking, gambling and easy conversation.[49] Fraternal orders were thus similar to coffeehouses and clubs in England, where drinking and conviviality helped to cement male relationships in an emerging public sphere. Yet while the lodges that sprang up across Europe certainly provided alternative opportunities for emotional expression, particularly through their esoteric rituals and notional erasure of social distinctions, these mostly male societies were still structured by their own behavioral codes. Because Masons were encouraged to emulate the luxuries of the rich while never losing sight of virtue, industry and learning, the rules of civility and table manners were insisted upon in most Masonic literature.[50] Freemasonry thus contributed to the formation of gentlemanly conduct while providing a space for the relaxation of other social codes, even, as we have seem, to the point of being viewed as hotbeds of effeminacy.

As Chapter 3 will demonstrate in more detail, the bodies of these male elites usually fell short of the muscular ideals celebrated in the neoclassical art of the eighteenth century. Fascinated by muscular bodies they rarely possessed, nobles and bourgeois alike sometimes compensated for this lack by appropriating the language of muscularity as a way of describing their own rather nonphysical activities. European Freemasonry's odd relationship with the symbols of artisanal manhood is a case in point, especially as these elites rarely had much contact with the professional masons with whom they identified themselves.[51] This did not stop them from valorizing a muscular conception of manliness that, because it had been appropriated by elites and applied primarily to "character" rather than craft, ironically required little physical effort to achieve. Through such organizations gentlemen symbolically donned the identity of skilled craftsmen as part of their ongoing efforts at self-fashioning.[52] A compensatory jargon of muscularity without muscles provided a rhetorical salve for the problematic manhood of social elites whose livelihood did not depend upon physical exertion.

This phenomenon was evident in Russia, whose elites self-consciously existed for centuries on the periphery of European culture. Although often criticized for their secrecy, the more than 140 lodges that spread across the country were important sites for the creation of gentlemanly bearing. Within the walls of the lodge, the rigid social hierarchy instituted by Peter the Great was for a time suspended as men from different estates came together, thus constituting a secret nobility ostensibly based on spirit rather than rank. Here becoming a Mason meant "working the rough stone" of the natural self into a polished, virtuous gem, a process that required the adoption of manners, self-examination and the curbing of base passions. Despite the fact that Freemasonry often presented itself as removed from the outside world, these forms of discipline were also codes for behavior in everyday life. Hence drunkenness at lodge meetings was frowned upon, as were coarse jokes, cursing, rudeness and quarreling, all of which could lead to censure or even expulsion from the lodge. One reason women were generally not admitted as members was fear that their presence would awaken in the brothers the very passions they had hoped to tame, thus threatening to turn them against each other and disrupt both the polishing and bonding process.[53] A similar suspension of social differences between nobles and burghers, as well as a concern with instilling polished manners and refined conviviality, was observed in the lodges that dotted the Germanic states. There too drunkenness, swearing, religious baiting and other forms of misbehavior were strictly forbidden in the interest of fostering more sociable habits among men.[54]

Hypothetically, at least, the same refinement that crafted male respectability through the symbols and rhetoric of artisanal manhood (and that smoothed social divisions between men of different classes and countries) could have been extended to the issue of race as well. This was the aim of Prince Hall, a black artisan from Boston who, with fourteen other free black men, in 1775 established their own lodge after being admitted into the Masonic order. What the Prince Hall Freemasons transformed through their symbolic craftsmanship was less the rough stone of their natural selves than their abject pasts as slaves, which were now rendered irrelevant for the polished and urbane manhood to which they aspired. This transformative ideal was rendered more austere and disciplined through the writings of Martin Delany, who during the mid-1800s recommended a corporeal asceticism not unlike that of the black nationalist Marcus Garvey in the twentieth century. Prince Hall Freemasonry expanded across the country to become an important ingredient in the "road to selfhood" for African-American men, but failed to achieve any profound alteration in the reigning racial stereotypes that situated black males beyond the pale of respectable white manhood.[55]

Lodges may have aimed at cultivating respectability in their members, but they still functioned as reprieves from more formal domestic and public contexts. Their plush interiors, rich meals and atmosphere of camaraderie all conspired to make these male spaces as comfortable as possible, which suggests that, in some contexts at least, manliness could be defined as much by a *right to comfort* as by a *refusal* of it – which should discourage us from too closely associating masculinity simply with explicit codes of self-control, abstention and respectability. As manners seemed always to demand greater formality in the presence of women, it is easy to see that many men would relish all-male company and the freedom to relax in a way that was not deemed incompatible with masculinity, even if, as we have seen, this freedom was not without its own rules and norms.[56] Thus the gentleman's body was not the target of consistent or even wholehearted self-control or self-denial and elite males took advantage of opportunities, however modest, to rebel against the world they had created but whose confines could become oppressive. The ideology of male mastery might prescribe order and self-control, but these little rebellions suggest that a dialectic of control and release attends the lived experience of masculinity, and indeed of any prescribed identity.

While respectability constituted the public face of bourgeois masculinity, it does not provide much of a guide as to how men spent their leisure time. Acknowledging that, as early as the 1840s and 1850s, the ideology of respectability was vulnerable to the pressures of affluence and the attractions of self-indulgence, Mike Huggins takes a more nuanced approach to respectability, suggesting that "there could be different modes of behaviour within a single life style, at different times and in different contexts."[57] Male drinking offers a case in point. In the early modern era drinking offered an opportunity for young males to test the limits of their bodily control while enjoying freedom of association in the alehouse or tavern. Here the inability to remain composed while inebriated threatened to diminish a man's reputation for self-mastery. Despite the persistence in the nineteenth century of "fallen man" narratives that detailed the downward trajectory of those who succumbed to drink, similar patterns of behavior continued into the modern era, where moralistic condemnations of drinking as "unmanly" were hardly a deterrent for those who found in local taverns, pubs and brasseries opportunities for sociability and relaxation.[58] If such breaches of respectability technically violated reigning norms of manliness, there is little reason to believe that men who indulged in such behavior therefore fancied themselves as "feminine" or womanish.

Instead, periodic drunken revelry was clearly aligned with an oppositional style of masculinity that thrived in areas where official moral codes were lax. While there was always the possibility of becoming so beholden to drink that one lost the ability to resist, in many circles it was the abstainer and the prude who risked being considered effeminate. In Russia during the 1830s and 1840s, for instance, the state mandated a gentlemanly ethic of respectability among university students that contrasted with the extracurricular world of tavern sociability, where drinking, comradeship, and even street violence taught different ways of being a man. Navigating between these two worlds was not an easy task; yet in some cases university officials even schooled their young charges in how to strike a balance between conflicting ideals. This was the case with Platon Stepanovich Nakhimov, Chief Inspector of Moscow University, whose well-documented interventions on behalf of rowdy students often consisted of teaching young men the art of taste and discretion in their drinking. Although many others clearly adhered to the letter of the law when they stumbled upon drunken students (or vice-versa!), anecdotal evidence suggests that other inspectors may have also acted in a similarly understanding manner. Being a proper gentleman, it seems, may have meant knowing *when* to be respectable and when (as well as how) to let loose.[59]

Russian ambivalence about gentlemanly conduct was an extension of a deeper ambivalence about the benefits of adopting Western culture, and generated nostalgia for sensations and experiences that had been banished from modern life. As the British romanticized their imagined chivalric past, so Russians romanticized representations of the Cossacks; these rowdy horsemen providing a means of negotiating the tension between traditional Slavic culture and the imposition of models from the West. The Cossacks' reputation for rape, pillage and drunken revelry may have offended the moral sensibilities of elites, but, by symbolically negating state-sponsored attempts at civilized decorum, these figures validated expressions of lust and aggression that, however socially unacceptable, at least had the virtue of being homegrown. "On political, social, and artistic planes," argues Judith Kornblatt, "the Cossack myth helped Russians cope, as it were, 'aesthetically,' with their own repressive reality."[60] In a country where "Western" models had been imposed in a most uncompromising manner, fantasies of oppositional male behavior were appealing due to the freedom they seemed to represent.[61]

Thus explicit codes of conduct provide no more than a partial glimpse into the complicated world of male identity and behavior during the early nineteenth century. To see men behaving badly, one only needed to look beyond the usual sites of respectability, or view these sites with an eye for nuances. For example, male misbehavior was a primary reason that gender-specific facilities and regulations were created in popular French spa towns like Vichy and Aix-les-Bains. At Aix, male bathers were so immodest that in 1832 the wearing of bathing costumes had to be made compulsory; moreover, until separate facilities were constructed, women frequently complained about the "general disorder and abuses" they suffered at the hands of male patrons as they made their way down narrow corridors to their assigned pools.[62] This was also the period in which the city took on new connotations of exoticism and danger that were tempting to well-to-do men seeking escape from convention. In the 1820s upper-class "ramblers" from London's West End might start their day by dressing impeccably before spending the afternoon promenading around St James's Street or Bond Street, home to many barbers, tailors and hatters ready to accommodate the desire of these men for personal display. Like the gentleman stroller or *flâneur* across the Channel, the rambler certainly liked to watch the spectacles of the street; but, like the related figure of the well-dressed dandy, he also liked being *looked at*. Defined as walking without a definite route, "rambling" had the definite aim of consumption and pleasure, which often propelled wealthy men on evening forays into the darkened streets of the East End for the purposes of drinking, gambling or whoring.[63]

The city thus played a double role in gendered perceptions of modernity. Mostly populated by laboring classes who represented the local limits of the civilizing process, the city was imagined as both the center of civilization and the home of its savage others. This dual nature was accentuated by changes in the urban landscape, especially during the 1840s when gas lighting illuminated the streets of major cities and profoundly altered the ways in which urban dwellers came to view their world. With key sites like cafés, shop windows and theaters now cast in light, other parts of the nocturnal city became zones of danger and fascination for bourgeois men seeking a bit of adventure.[64] In this quest for all things "dark," it is understandable that night itself would be conceptualized in feminine terms as a frightening yet exciting domain of desire to be "penetrated." Whether respectable and investigative or pleasure-seeking and illicit, nocturnal journeys into the city depths involved the male's entire body as a penetrating, ideally impermeable force. In these, the early days of "slumming," certain parts of the city itself were imaginatively transformed into a kind of "jungle" with the "civilized" male and his friends acting as its intrepid explorers. This was especially true of dandies who often glamorized lower-class criminality as part of their private revolts against society and who, when descending in groups into this underworld, often modeled themselves on the criminal gang or secret society. Yet, in symbolic terms, these forays into the urban underworld were also explorations of forbidden realms of their own bodies, where encounters with vice were transgressions into the very realm of the "low" proscribed by the whole process of gentility as a means of recapturing "lost" aspects of their impulses and desires.[65]

Nowhere is the perceived tension between the "veneer" of civilization and a submerged "primal" manhood more evident than in the numerous ways in which male elites have been able to rationalize, and in many cases legalize, prostitution. Alexandre Parent-Duchâtelet's 1836 proposal for state-regulated prostitution referred explicitly to the need to provide men of all classes with outlets for their libidinal energies lest they undermine the sanctity of conjugal heterosexuality. The prostitute was thus conceived of as a release valve for pent-up male energies; according to Parent-Duchâtelet, she was a figure "as inevitable in an agglomeration of men as sewers, cesspits, and garbage dumps."[66] Yet if these women were assigned the role of "sewer drain," and thus symbolized the physical and metaphorical "dirt" that men had to disavow, clients still had to "descend" into this sewer, even though many of the *maisons de tolérance* would be equipped with furnishings that would correspond to their income and social habits, thus mimicking the trappings of bourgeois comfort and respectability. The language Parent-Duchâtelet used to describe this situation was tellingly hydraulic, warning of potential "leaks" in bodies otherwise represented as self-contained. For the sake of social cohesion these bodies had to be allowed to "flow," even if only into officially provided and carefully regulated channels (and at the expense of women). Regulated prostitution suggests that respectability and release were quite able to coexist in the representation and experience of elite male bodies, a situation which no doubt generated some confusion for the typical middle-class male, who, as Peter Stearns observes, could "easily grow up wondering whether he best proved his manhood through sexual conquests or through dominance over his own sexual nature."[67]

* * *

Periodic deviations from manners and respectability constituted no necessary departure from masculinity, which, at least in certain instances, was elastic enough to encompass both acts of self-control and self-indulgence. Moreover, the assumption that civilization is a mere veneer covering an essentially bestial male nature remains active to the present. As a Russian conduct manual declared in 1890, the savage within was just waiting for his chance to break free: "A man becomes crude and feral as soon as he stops being polite and attentive."[68] While it is fair to say that the fundamental aims and pitfalls of "civilized" behavior were widely acknowledged by elites, it is equally evident that the persistent need for advice on how to be a gentleman reveals that many continued to find pleasure in flouting these rules and recommendations. Polite manners and respectable dress remained integral to the gentlemanly persona, but so too was the need to affirm "realities" lurking beneath the polished surface of civilized decorum. Toeing the line of respectability in everyday life did not rule out gleefully tripping over that line on other occasions. In some cases, it was downright essential.

These are all examples of the "life of paradox" that, according to Margaret S. Creighton, characterized the situation of men in a variety of societies in the nineteenth century. Many middle-class men found themselves playing both sides against the middle by "celebrating freedom and responsibility, testing social boundaries and reaffirming them, pushing away from the families that nurtured them, and being forever pulled back."[69]

Part Two

Male Bodies in the Eighteenth and Nineteenth Centuries

3
The Armor of Health and the Diseases of Civilization

In 1845 a certain Dr Foy offered this portrait of the healthy man:

> The man who is healthy has a more or less gay hue, a fresh complexion, supple skin, calm and pleasing features, an erect bearing, a graceful stature, a sure and robust step, free and easy labor of body and mind, sweet and replenishing rest, regular bodily functions, a good appetite, quick digestion, proportional excretions, great respiration, regular circulation, intelligence in harmony with his usual occupation, a good character, calm passions.[1]

This picture is remarkable only for its succinctness; otherwise similar portraits appear in health manuals throughout the nineteenth century. Good health signified a variety of aesthetic, physical and moral traits, producing a man who was attractive, pleasing and calm, who held himself upright and walked with an energetic step, and whose internal organs functioned efficiently and harmoniously. Politeness and good manners were nothing without this physical foundation. If champions of the gentleman integrated their accounts of the male body into a more holistic vision of moral, physical and intellectual harmony, physicians understandably paid more attention to men in their corporeal existence. Yet a closer focus on the physical body did not exclude moral and social factors. Through the late nineteenth century medical knowledge linked moral and physical attributes in a manner that was in many respects just as holistic.

Insofar as "manly" qualities such as vitality and action depended upon reasonably good physical health, there is an obvious consonance between active manhood and robustness. Sociologists who consider men and health often do so from the perspective of potentially dangerous substances, like alcohol or illicit drugs, that, aside from being common denominators of male violence against women, children and other men, are often physically damaging to the individual involved. By approaching the body as a bounded entity as well as a

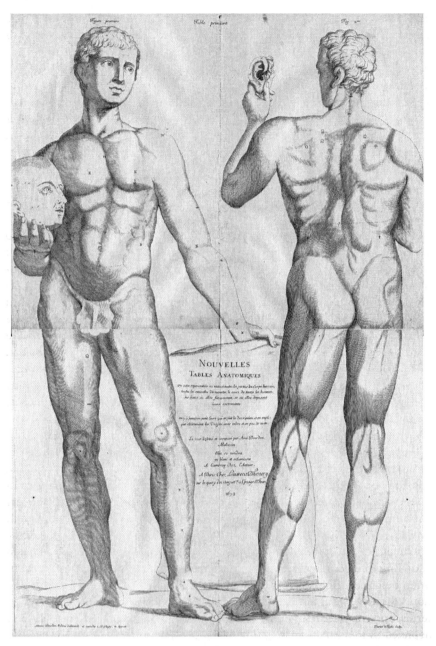

Figure 3.1   Amé Bourdon, *Nouvelles tables anatomiques* (Paris: Chez Laurens d'Houry, 1678). Courtesy of the National Library of Medicine.

quantum of force, however, it becomes clear that health is also a critical aspect of the formation of male bodies and boundaries. Kaja Silverman's analyses of masculinity provide some useful ways of approaching this problem. Using battlefield experience as a key example of trauma, Silverman theorizes how such ordeals compromise a man's psychic and somatic boundaries. "It is not surprising, then, that when the male subject is brought into a traumatic encounter with lack, as in the situation of war, he often experiences it as the impairment of his anatomical masculinity." For Silverman this anatomical dismembering is less of an issue than the *psychic* disintegration it also entails: "the disintegration, that is, of a bound and armored ego, predicated upon the illusion of coherence and control."[2] In psychoanalytic parlance "lack" suggests an inability to live up to the "dominant fiction" of male superiority; and a similar phenomenon may be observed in the case of illness and disability, where the diminishment or impairment of the body may also generate doubts about a man's authority, autonomy and integrity. Thus, in the Victorian era, Bruce Haley observes, the state of health denoted constitutional growth and development "in which the bodily systems and mental faculties interoperate harmoniously under the direct motive power of vital energy or the indirect motive power of the moral will, or both." Moreover the integrity, wholeness and completeness of the healthy body was something that was experienced kinaesthetically as an inward sense of "wholeness and unencumbered capability" and manifested outwardly through useful and productive labor or, in other cases, military fitness. The ultimate aim, and thus the implicit meaning of male health, was oriented toward mental or manual labor and military service. As the old dictum went, a sound mind had to be firmly anchored in a sound body.[3]

We are not far from the image of the self-contained and disciplined body promulgated in conduct manuals and reinforced in practice through the approval and opprobrium of polite society. In the modern era health and manliness were frequently conceptualized in the parallel terms of somatic integrity and firm ego boundaries, allowing health to function as a form of moral and physical "armor" that could be breached in the event of illness or bad habits. The image of health as a kind of armor made particular sense in the world of allopathic medicine which, by treating diseases as foreign or enemy forces, often described illness in the spatial terms of "penetration" and "contamination." Moreover, this armor was usually understood in moral as well as physical terms, and the potentially unhealthy temptations of the external world were depicted as seeping into men whose bodies and minds were supposed to be insulated from these solicitations. Indeed the entire outside world, particularly the modern city, was sometimes likened to a contaminating ocean filled with enervating and seductive elements threatening to infiltrate and destroy the weak or the unwary. Any vulnerable organism would clearly benefit from the armor that good health might provide, although it was clear that this bounded entity would not be female: considered anatomically and emotionally unsuited to such a public existence, the consensus was that women possessed weak bodies that rendered them less healthy and thus less capable of withstanding outside influences. That such views have amounted to the image of female bodies as inherently more porous and "leaky" than men has been rightly observed in feminist scholarship.[4]

This picture is complicated if we move from representations to experience. Insofar as the body often takes seriously the metaphors that describe it, as Pierre Bourdieu suggests,[5] one might expect this biomedical language of armor and penetration to have consequences for the ways in which men experienced their bodies. Just what did good health *feel* like in an age when illness was widespread and pain was very much a fact of life? In the nineteenth century this feeling of wholeness and vitality seems to have been fleeting at best, and was often defined in negative terms: the experience of health meant *not* being conscious of the body's workings. Well known for his celebration of robust heroes, Thomas Carlyle was himself plagued by health problems from youth. "Oh, it is an earnest tussle this Life of ours here below; and if a man's *body* fail him, and he get continual grinding misery of ill-health to encompass him for thirty and odd years, and drag down every step of his poor limbs – But let me not complain."[6] Still, complain he did, as did many other educated men and women whose mental acuity and refined sensibility condemned them to a heightened awareness of their inescapably vulnerable embodiment.

This and the following chapter consider a range of issues pertaining to the health and ill-health of the male body, and probe the relationship between these bodily states, ideas about vitality and boundedness, and the pitfalls of civilization. To the extent that poor health had an obvious and direct impact upon one's ability to master appearances and opinions, the healthy body represented the core of the gentlemanly ideal. Similarly, despite the fact that good health was ideally meant to be enjoyed by all, when applied to men it had important implications for the state of the body politic, especially in terms of its capacity for work and war. Moreover, at the heart of the struggle for health lurked recurring anxieties about the very civilization that was so frequently cited as the hallmark of Western male superiority and the rationale for its global reach. From the perspective of medicine and anthropology, the modern male was uncomfortably situated along temporal and geographic axes where he risked being unfavorably contrasted to men from days of yore as well as to so-called "primitive" peoples, whether they were found in other countries, at home among the peasantry or in the distant past of ancient heroes. Seen in this context, gentility and sensibility were potential liabilities signaling the diminishment of male vitality over time.

"NATURAL" MANHOOD

Several historical trajectories must briefly be mapped if we are to understand the evolving relationship between masculine ideals and medical notions of health in the modern era. First, there is the important shift in biological thinking about men and women that occurred during the eighteenth century. Second, we must consider how the *homo clausus* that conduct manuals sought to create through disciplined self-control was simultaneously being brought into being in new medical models of the body, so that the male body was conceptualized as more self-contained and resistant than the female body, even though this corporeal closure also needed to be continually reinforced through vigilance and bodily techniques. To this end, finally, we must account for the role of lifestyle and agency in the lived experience of health. In the face of unhealthy modern lifestyles, traditional "hygienic" precepts were still widely disseminated as the keys to physical and mental well-being.

Before the late eighteenth century, it is probably fair to assert that the "male body" did not exist in the medical imagination as an organism radically different from the female. In his influential book *Making Sex: Body and Gender from the Greeks to Freud*, Thomas Laqueur argues that, for much of Western history, male and female bodies were viewed as broadly similar, with the female representing an inversion of the male. When pre-modern doctors examined the womb and ovaries they saw an inverted penis and testicles; they even maintained that both sexes secreted semen. While this "one-sex" medical model hardly guaranteed equality among the sexes, it remained firmly in place until two sexes were "discovered" in the late eighteenth century in a development that paralleled growing anxieties about gender roles. The shift to the now prevailing medical belief in sexual dimorphism functioned partly as a means of grounding an emerging ideology of "separate spheres" in the bedrock of incommensurable biological difference.[7] Several historians have questioned the location of the shift to a two-sex model of the body, citing evidence from the sixteenth and seventeenth centuries of earlier beliefs about bodily differences or even a persistence of old views about homologies between men and women.[8] Cultural practice is of course far too slippery to be neatly contained within period-based categories; but, at least in medicine, a two-sex model seems to have been firmly in place by the end of the eighteenth century.[9]

If the rise of a two-sex model seemed to foreclose the troubling potential in the early modern era for fluidity between male and female bodies, new scientific models sought to supplant older ideas of the fluid and the "open" with an idea that emphasized closure and solidity for men as well as women. Among historians it is now commonplace to assert that neither the medical advice nor social customs of the pre-modern era evince the same preoccupation with bodily closure that marks most modern societies in the West. As Barbara Duden remarks, in traditional medicine "the skin does not close off the body, the inside, against the outside world. In like manner the body itself is also never closed off; it is composed of material that is no different from the world surrounding it ... The 'body' as a discrete object of social control ... had not yet taken shape."[10] This is not to imply that most people were especially *comfortable* with this openness. One aim of traditional hygienic practices was to insulate the organism so that it would be better able to cope with un-predictable external factors such as climate, temperature and air quality. Pre-modern Europeans conceptualized the body as a house that was susceptible to attack because unwanted substances were able to penetrate its exterior. Hence the belief in the value of a constant layer of dirt and sweat to protect the vul-nerable body, and the corresponding aversion to removing this layer through full-body bathing. For many peasants, mud, soil, sweat and excrement were even seen as *part* of the body whose boundary they formed.[11]

The new understanding of the body as solid and bounded accompanied the gradual abandonment of humoral notions of physiology. 'Fluids' were replaced by muscle and nerve fibers in an entity which, as Michael Stolberg explains, "was more self-contained, whose physical boundaries were more sharply defined, and whose fibers and nerves guaranteed its inner cohesion and strength."[12] Coupled with evolving ideas about self-control, this "new" body functioned as a psychosomatic envelope within which the fantasy of self-containment could be kinaesthetically *sensed* as well as thought – even as repeated effort was required to approximate the desired state and at times such efforts failed altogether. While both sexes were capable of pos-sessing delicate sensibilities, most doctors agreed that men were gener-ally made of firmer stuff, physically as well as morally. The intrinsically gendered nature of the firm and bounded body is evident when we consider the numerous connotations of its opposite, as in the case of the French word *lâche*. When defining this term the *Encyclopédie* glided effortlessly from an adjective meaning "loose" to a noun denoting a "coward," addressing along the way a spectrum of corporeal, moral and mental qualities. That which is *lâche* is:

> the opposite of taut ... It is the opposite of firm, and a synonym for flabby [*mol*] ... It is the opposite of active ... It is the opposite of compact ... It is the opposite of compressed; one has a flabby stomach [*le ventre lâche*]. Figuratively it is the opposite of brave; he is a coward [*un lâche*]. It is synonymous with the abject and shameful; he has done a cowardly deed [*une action lâche*]. Someone guilty of cowardice is commonly more despised than someone who has committed an atrocity. It is better to inspire horror than pity. Treason is perhaps the most cowardly of all actions. A writing

style is *lâche* when it is laden with useless words, and when those employed do not vigorously elaborate the main idea.[13]

In this entry the physical and the moral become virtually indistinguishable as the cowardly man is implicitly lax and "flabby" on just about every level. Underpinned by the new ideas about sexual dimorphism, during the eighteenth century good health also signified a difference in boundaries between males and females, once more suggesting that *homo clausus* was not considered an ideal to which women could realistically aspire. As Anne Vila explains, doctors defined the normative male body in part by its natural ability to "resist or overcome unwelcome irritants and obstacles, whereas women cede involuntarily to the multiple stimuli to which they are subject because they have no more power to resist than do children."[14] Finally, the male's more pronounced solidity implied greater energy and longevity for men than for women. As Christoph Wilhelm Hufeland contended in his widely-read *Macrobiotics, or The Art of Prolonging Life* (1796), women may frequently grow old, but it was intrinsic "male strength" that made it possible for men to become very old.[15] This normative association of physiological manhood with optimal health and vitality persisted throughout the nineteenth century, establishing a stark contrast to artistic and literary depictions of invalid and consumptive women whose physical ailments served to confirm the belief in the inherent frailty of femininity.[16]

The radically different anatomies of women meant that they could never achieve the strength, robustness and bodily closure of which men were said to be "naturally" capable. However, the two-sex model, with its reduction of gender differences to a bedrock of biology, was in itself unable to guarantee that male bodies would also be masculine bodies. Rather, from the mid-eighteenth century and persisting into the nineteenth, medical notions of gender were based largely on the interaction between one's lifestyle and the organism taken as a whole. Thus how one *lived* as a man was just as important as the possession of anatomical maleness, which accounts in part for the divergent health advice given to males and females during this time. One may thus concur with Ludmilla Jordanova that ideas about gender – that is, assumptions about how different sexes were supposed to inhabit the world – were built right into medical images of the body. Because neither men nor women always lived up to their physical potential, doctors and patients alike wrestled with the fact that men of the noble and middling sort often deviated considerably from the powers and capacities implied by their anatomies.

Two examples from the eighteenth century demonstrate the sexed nature of the body at that time while implicitly conceding just how frequently "nature" required assistance. The first are the wax anatomical models used in medical schools for depicting the bodies and bodily zones of males and females.

As Jordanova observes, female models are almost always presented as recumbent, with special care taken to beautify their hair and skin, while the odd erect female model displays the nervous system, thus illustrating the close association of women with nervous sensibility and even hysteria. In contrast, most of the erect anatomical models are male, and display, not the nervous system, but the muscles when flexed and relaxed, all of which certainly reinforced medical views of the nervous system as "feminine" and of muscularity as "masculine." A second example comes from the world of art. The eighteenth-century admiration for the bodies and morality of the ancients helped to fuel the art historian Johann Joachim Winckelmann's celebration of the male bodies idealized in Greek sculpture. George Mosse has indicated the importance of Winckelmann's writings for establishing an ideal male body that would resonate throughout the modern era. Sculptures and medical drawings of youthful athletes revealed strong, muscular and proportionate bodies unmarred by fat or contorted by fierce emotions, bodies that illustrated the classical ideas of exercise, balance, moderation and calm (Figures 3.2 and 3.3).[17] Both the wax models and Wincklemann's idealized images propose the healthy body as an exemplar of a natural or ideal masculinity, and therefore as a profoundly physical foundation for gender differences and, in the latter case, symbols of the nation.

While this gender distinction seems straightforward enough, a gulf still separated these images from the lived experience of most male elites throughout the modern era. As Jordanova reminds us, those who designed the anatomical models did so by drawing upon class-based ideas about gender. Viewing nervous sensibility as an especially "feminine" attribute allowed them to naturalize qualities that were considered germane to middle-class women rather than proletarians, who were often viewed as singularly lacking in sensibility. Conversely, the male models naturalized muscular qualities that were, by and large, the result of lifestyles centering around physical work and exertion. Such attributes were notably *lacking* in both noble and middle-class men, who in the eighteenth century were much more likely to be aligned with the very nervousness and sedentariness considered "natural" among bourgeois women. Matters weren't helped by the fact that many conduct manuals recommended that the gentleman's body be slight, and therefore a testimony to the more exquisite quality of his sensibility.[18] Despite the importance of "work" to middle-class views of masculinity, the non-manual labor on which such men typically prided themselves did not produce the bodies that physicians and worried social commentators held up as exemplars of robust manhood. Male elites were thus separated from the natural muscularity celebrated by both medicine and art. Lamentations about the weaknesses of modern man often claimed that the physical robustness attributed to men in the past lay dormant within the contemporary individual, just waiting to be awakened

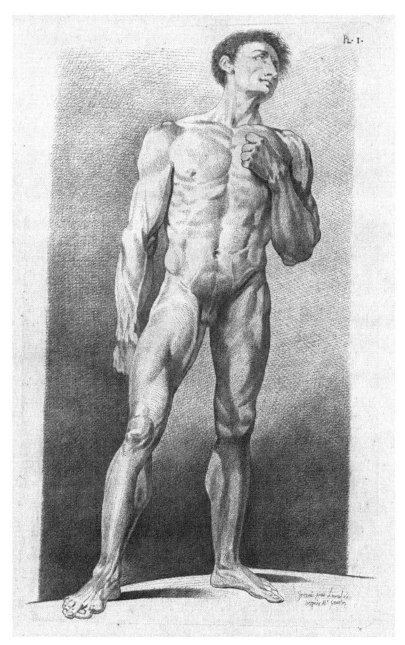

Figure 3.2   Jacques Gamelin, *Nouveau recueil d'ostéologie et de myologie* (Toulouse, 1779). Courtesy of the National Library of Medicine.

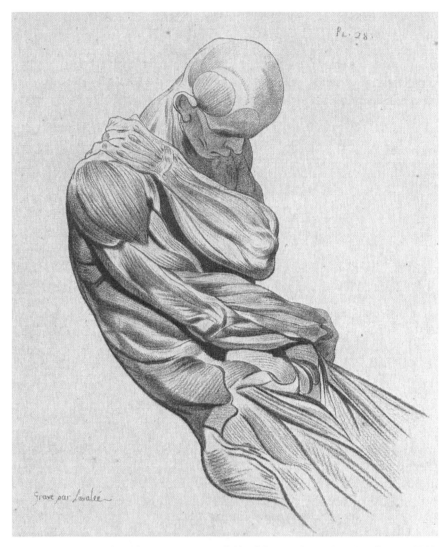

Figure 3.3   Jacques Gamelin, *Nouveau recueil d'ostéologie et de myologie* (Toulouse, 1779). Courtesy of the National Library of Medicine.

and put to work. What the health reformer J.F.C. Gutsmuth described as "our slumbering powers," for instance, was an appeal to the lost, but hypothetically recuperable, strength of Germanic warriors that remained in the bodies of his contemporaries, whether as a residue of racial commonality or the sheer fact of maleness.[19]

Medical and artistic ideals reinforced what doctors had been saying, and would continue to say, throughout the modern era: due to a combination of education, profession and lifestyle, elite male bodies could not stand as models of manhood in its natural (which is to say, its desirable) state. If the "natural" male body offered a propensity for beauty, action, endurance and exertion, then male elites were at odds with their organic potential. As the rest of this chapter will show, this situation produced at least two consequences. On the one hand, the actual bodies of male elites were thought to be so far from either of these ideals that polite society was able to valorize physical weakness and even illness as markers of refined manhood. On the other hand, this embrace of physical weakness could only function within the rarified circles of noble and middle-class existence; it became much more problematic when these same men were faced with male bodies (whether from other classes or other races) that seemed to come closer to these more hardy ideals. This disjunction between (ideal) body, lifestyle, class and gender would continue to haunt middle-class masculinity up to the present, constantly threatening to undo whatever "armoring" good health was supposed to provide.[20]

DISEASES OF CIVILIZATION

Modern physicians and patients were under few illusions about the mixed blessings that civilized life brought to the human body. While most marveled at the diseases that Western doctors were able to cure, or at least prevent, they also admitted that the peculiar circumstances of modern life generated a host of new disorders for elites, sometimes called "diseases of civilization." The disjunction between elite and popular bodies has often been remarked upon, though the inherent instability of this hierarchy has received somewhat less attention. Enjoying greater material abundance, better sanitary conditions, and improved access to doctors and hygienic literature, social elites had a vested interest in distinguishing themselves from peasants and workers on bodily grounds. They also had more free time to devote to reading about and caring for their bodies. It is therefore unsurprising to learn that elites did not suffer from epidemic diseases or other health issues to the same extent as the popular classes, suggesting that in many respects these were privileged bodies indeed. Surely more than a few of those living in poverty and squalor would have traded their own ailments for just about any of the diseases of civilization.

Yet elites suffered in other ways. The nervousness that George Cheyne dubbed the "English Malady" in the early eighteenth century was a common feature of life among sedentary and luxurious elites, whose material consumption was mirrored in the "wasting" disease of the same name.[21] In the mid-nineteenth century the French alienist Jean-Etienne-Dominique Esquirol could describe insanity as a "disease of civilization," and even claimed that "the number of the insane is in direct proportion to its progress."[22] Masturbation was also seen as a special vice of the civilized, one partly traced to a sexual appetite precociously awakened in urban environments. Homosexuality too was cited as being more or less a result of urban lifestyles, as was constipation, which would be described by more than one Victorian doctor as the "scourge of civilization." Christoph Hufeland was certainly not alone when he allowed himself "one melancholy remark, which is, that the enemies of our life have, in modern times, dreadfully increased; and that the degree of civilization, luxury, refinement, and deviation from nature in which we at present live, by so highly exalting our intensive life, tends also to shorten, in the same proportion, our existence."[23]

Being vigilant about health and maintaining a lifestyle that might sustain it have been central elements of the ethical self since ancient times, when proper regimen demanded attention to the six "non-naturals," that is, environmental factors that affected the individual's humoral complexion: air, food and drink, sleep and wakefulness, motion and rest, evacuation and repletion, and the passions of the mind. As Michel Foucault explained of ancient Greek hygiene, "the practice of regimen as an art of living was something more than a set of precautions designed to prevent illnesses or complete their cure. It was a whole manner of forming oneself as a subject who had the proper, necessary, and sufficient concern for his body."[24] Entailing a reflexive approach to the body that made matters of health, cleanliness and morality the personal responsibility of the individual, classical hygiene reinforced bodily boundaries: it was a means of bolstering frail elites against the sensory overload of the modern world. Thus *homo clausus* was crafted through attention to hygiene as well as manners.[25] Elements of this classical notion of hygiene remained prominent in the West, to be invoked as a corrective to the luxuriance of elite lifestyles. "The only useful part of medicine is hygiene," declared Rousseau; "And hygiene is itself less a science than a virtue."[26] This hygiene, then, was a form of self-knowledge stemming from introspection, and manifest as a set of bodily techniques it did not fall by the wayside like the old humoral physiology with which it was associated. Rather, it continued to be promoted, and apparently widely embraced, well into the twentieth century.[27]

From the late eighteenth century to the mid-nineteenth century, German physicians looked to hygiene and dietetics as means of allowing men and women to maximize their store of "life force," a fixed quantum of energy that was imagined as something to be carefully managed, not unlike a bank account, to cover the entire life curve from youth to old age. Poor diet, sexual excess, extended periods of physical labor without rest, and (for women) excessive child births expended the life force more quickly and thus caused one to age prematurely. Here traditional advice regarding basic hygienic principles was extended to include the bourgeois principles of self-discipline and personal responsibility as techniques for maximizing vitality into old age.[28] None of this was unique to the German-speaking world.[29] In France the hygienic self-surveillance that Réveillé-Parise recommended in the 1830s resonated for at least the next century. In all that concerns hygiene, he counseled, one must "direct oneself according to the knowledge one has of oneself, of one's organization and habits." A lack of vigilance in this realm redounded upon the individual and personal character: "In the final analysis, a man is only the result of his habits, that's what makes him what he is."[30] This emphasis on personal responsibility yielded increasingly negative views of the elderly, whose physical or mental failings could be uncharitably chalked up to a profligate youth or mismanaged adulthood. In American society images of old age acquired an increasingly unfavorable aura from the mid-nineteenth century onward, not least because – in a culture that had come to value autonomy, success and health – bodies in decline were an unpleasant reminder of the limits of self-control.[31]

Health, as the subjectively realized sense of wholeness, remained the medical ideal of middle-class manhood. Certain diseases of civilization impacted directly upon the personal boundaries that were being encouraged from the early modern era onward. Melancholia, which, under the name "hypochondria," persisted as a disease category into the early nineteenth century, is a good example of this. Widely known as the "disease of the learned" because it afflicted men devoted to scholarly and sedentary pursuits, melancholia counted among the primary disorders of civilized life, and threatened any man whose livelihood depended on mental rather than manual labor. Its effects on a man's sense of his own body were striking, and included the sensations of extreme fragility reported in the seventeenth century by the Dutch physician Caspar Barlaeus, whose preoccupation with his own health is evident throughout his correspondence with friends and family. The melancholic Barlaeus could feel as though he were made of glass and, afraid that he might shatter, grew very anxious about people standing too close to him. At other times Barlaeus thought he was made of butter or straw, and thus feared melting or bursting into flame.[32] These and other bizarre symptoms were widely reported in descriptions of melancholia. Accounts of the glass delusion tell of men who believed their entire bodies were urinal flasks or oil lamps, or that certain body parts (particularly their heads, chests and buttocks) were made of glass. Such perceptions of fragility were accompanied by fears of cracking or breaking and releasing whatever liquid substance the body was thought to contain. At other times the central obsession was with the *transparency* of the glass body, which was thought to lay bare one's thoughts and feelings along with organs and bodily fluids (which accounts for the fear of sunlight manifested by some sufferers).[33] These sensations of shattering, melting or transparency revealed melancholia's particular tendency to affect the lived experience of the substance and boundaries of the body, and would have been particularly distressing in an age when bodily boundaries and the concealment of emotions were becoming essential to conceptions of the properly bounded and self-regulating individual.

Madness and civilization, as Esquirol had suggested, seemed to many to go hand in hand. Surveying the relative lack of mental disorders among "savage" peoples, Scipion Pinel also concluded that madness was the "privileged affliction of peoples who think" and "the thermometer of their state of advancement, it rises or falls with it."[34] Therein lies the rub: as a result of modern lifestyles and professional habits, the ideally self-contained individual often seemed caught in the process of coming apart. Most physicians insisted upon the damage that cerebral, sedentary and luxurious lifestyles were doing to the bodies of elites, and by extension, to the future of the nation. In addition to its other dangers, excessive bookishness was thought to deform the body through the bent posture that reading encouraged, thus producing stooped profiles that were not only morally and aesthetically questionable, but compromised the individual internally through the harmful squeezing of abdominal viscera that could cause dyspepsia.[35] The Swiss physician Samuel-Auguste Tissot, whose translated works were popular in Britain and Germany, spoke for many when he condemned the hygienic carelessness that characterized many men of letters, whose health problems so clearly called into question their claims to physiological manhood. "It is necessary to be a savant without ceasing to be a man," he asserted, and male scholars ever since have tried to find ways of accomplishing both.[36] Others, however, could see no way of reconciling the apparent contradiction between scholarship and manliness. Tissot's German contemporary, Johann Christian Ackermann, even recommended that scholars abandon their books for the battlefield, while his colleague, Johann Christian Reil, condemned educational practices that transformed the sons of "ancient, iron-hard Teutons" into Frenchified and hysterical fops who were "thin as locusts, with no backs and calves."[37]

If many elites took these medical warnings to heart, others were able to endorse, in the name of masculinity, the very ailments that diminished their bodies. Despite the implicit boundary problems that hypochondria posed, by borrowing the rhetoric of martial valor it was possible for scholarly men to embrace its symptoms as part of a rite of passage and even as a badge of honor. To be sure this was an uncomfortable ordeal, but it was also capable of bringing a man to a higher level of culture and learning. For the physician Herman Boerhaave, whose theories about vital forces were critical for the development of sensationalist psychology, these symptoms were nothing less than a form of masculine validation for scholars, an emotional compensation for those who could not compete physically with more robust kinds of men. As Boerhaave saw it, the so-called "scourge of scholars" (*flagellum eruditorum*) was comparable to "the scars of soldiers."[38] By the eighteenth century it was becoming clear that philosophers and men of letters had no monopoly on the sedentary or contemplative life, which seemed to be a common trait of most well-to-do people. No doubt a good measure of the fashionableness of nervous disorders and other ailments sprang from similar beliefs in the validation that certain illnesses might confer. Like the battle wounds borne by warriors, health problems could be embraced as proof of a man's willingness to endure physical distress in the name of some higher ideal.

Other battle scars, however, could be incurred from far less demanding activities. The well-fed and sedentary men of business, law, medicine and letters who most often suffered from gout could gain a measure of compensation in seeing their affliction as a kind of "luxury tax" on their elite status. Often considered capable of warding off other, more serious maladies, in the eighteenth century gout was an illness that, ironically, suggested health (although Figure 3.4 shows it as part of a seasonal selection of ailments). The historian Edward Gibbon, while subject to an array of potentially embarrassing health problems, saw in his gout something to be proud of. Short, fat, and suffering in his later years from a swollen testicle (or varicocele) the size of a melon, Gibbon welcomed gout both as evidence of gentility and as a promise that it might counteract one of his other afflictions. In the context of his refined and inactive lifestyle, Gibbon's gout could be rationalized as a badge of virility. Gibbon's case was not an anomaly in the eighteenth century. As Roy Porter suggests, many male invalids took great pride in being incapacitated: "being wheeled around in their bath chairs with their feet heavily bandaged, sufferers would flaunt, in a phallic way, the magnitude of swelling."[39]

If sometimes size *did* matter, not every disorder was quite so validating, or as easily flaunted. Although a cultural history of hemorrhoids is yet to be written, piles must have counted among the less glamorous diseases that civilization could generate. Long considered an easy way to purge oneself of excess humors (thus obviating the need to pay a physician to do the honors), hemorrhoids were sometimes praised as a cost-saving "golden vein." Many physicians even approved of hemorrhoidal bleeding as a healthy male counterpart to menstrual flux, perhaps as a sign that men could withstand losses of blood just as women did every month. This was good news for the penny-pinching patient, but a mixed blessing when viewed against the background of anxieties about modern life. In probing the causes of piles, German doctors like Franz Anton May and Johann Kaspar Stunzer cited a range of predictable sources, including frequent bloodletting, lack of exercise, and studious pursuits as well as warm drinks and rich foods. Whereas gout could be embraced by the well-to-do, hemorrhoids were condemned as a punishment for slothful, gluttonous and otherwise decadent lifestyles. If this were not feminizing enough, more than one physician associated a bloody anus with "pederasty," thus implicating "unnatural" sexuality within the

Figure 3.4 "The Compliments of the Season!!!" Colored etching by J. Cawse, after G.M. Woodward (London, 1809). Wellcome Library, London.

continuum of civilized vices.[40] With its obvious similarity to menstruation and hints of sodomy, the bleeding anus further undermined ideals of masculine self-containment by revealing a man's capacity to be just as "leaky" as a woman.

With frazzled nerves, sensations of melting, and maybe rectums leaking blood or foul vapors to boot, men suffering from the diseases of civilization were hardly models of self-contained manhood. Nevertheless, in the decades around 1800 elites continued to find ways of embracing their health problems as evidence of refinement and even virility. The early American diaries that circulated among a small, literate elite suggest the importance of illness as a formative experience requiring resignation and endurance for men and women alike. Men were expected to suffer in silence as proof of their capacity to control their passions, and excruciating pain could render a man powerless and leave him unmanned.[41] Of course the road back to health could also function as virilizing narrative that, as Elizabeth Green Musselman suggests, "foregrounded a weakness in order to display one's strength in subduing it."[42] In other cases, playing the "sick role" could yield certain social and personal dividends. Illnesses like consumption provided British invalids with an excellent excuse to seek cures and distractions in other countries, notably at one or more of the numerous health resorts situated along the Mediterranean coastlines of France and Italy.[43] Throughout the nineteenth century, the middle classes of Europe and North America would set aside several weeks each year to visit spa towns renowned for their mineral waters, and often subject themselves to rigorous treatments at the hands of specialists in hydrotherapy – all so they could reconstruct the healthy sense of wholeness that modern life had destroyed.[44]

Many male invalids who were uncomfortable about the gender implications of their condition found ways of compensating for their prostration, usually by clothing their sufferings in the language of courage and sacrifice. Of course there were other benefits to be reaped as well. The writer Charles Lamb fondly recalled his time in the sick bed as a "regal solitude" that allowed him "to enjoy monarchical privileges." Indeed, when compared to the kingly luxury of being waited on hand-and-foot by worried relatives and patient servants, the convalescent's recuperation of health surely represented a kind of "fall from dignity, amounting to a deposition." Writing in the 1830s, the popular writer Edward Bulwer-Lytton would have concurred. One of the "consolations" Bulwer-Lytton found in being ill was that "we are less subject to ungenial interruptions – to vulgar humiliations – to the wear and tear of the mind – the harassment and the vanity" that come from immersing oneself in "the world."[45] If being ill allowed a man to opt out of the daily struggle for public honors and advancement, then perhaps illness functioned as a strategy of resistance to some of the demands of normative masculinity.

Taking on the sick role, in short, may be likened to a line of flight. That such apparent emasculation could bring pleasures bordering on the masochistic is certainly conceivable. Hence, perhaps, the perverse joy of Fyodor Dostoyevsky's fictional "underground man" at the thought of "a cultured man of the nineteenth century" suffering from a toothache and filling his normally serene household with anguished groans.

> Well, the pleasure lies in all this conscious shamefulness. "I'm disturbing you," he seems to say, "I'm lacerating your feelings and preventing everybody in the house from sleeping ... I'm not a hero to you any longer, as I used to try to seem, but only a worthless good-for-nothing. All right, then! I'm very glad you've seen through me."[46]

For Dostoyevsky, who was no fan of civilization, the toothache lays bare the pretenses of the enlightened men of the nineteenth century. It occasions a catharsis that springs from a bodily defect whose sensations rip through the carefully constructed layers of self-restraint and denial to reveal a kind of truth. The pleasure of which he writes is at once the masochistic joy of a man finally stripped of his civilized veneer and exposed before his loving family and the sadistic glee of one who enjoys sowing discomfort in others. If in some circles the loss of health suggested a drift away from the full bodily capacities of manhood, in others it could be embraced either as an alternative form of masculinity or as a holiday from the duties and pretenses that patriarchy entailed.

SEDENTARINESS AND DEGENERATION

> There has been a pastoral age, and a hunting age, and a fighting age. Now we have arrived at the age sedentary. Men who sit longest carry all before them, – puny, delicate fellows, with hands just strong enough to wield a pen, eyes so bleared by the midnight lamp that they see no joy in that buxom sun (which draws me forth into the fields, as life draws the living), and digestive organs worn and macerated by the relentless flagellation of the brain.

So, at least, wrote Pisistratus Caxton to Albert Trevanion, Esq., MP, in Bulwer-Lytton's *The Caxtons* (1849). For Caxton this sedentary world was a prison whose walls were constructed from row after row of books, all of which constrained and sapped the strength and vitality of his body:

> All the professions are so book-lined, book-hemmed, book-choked, that wherever these strong hands of mine stretch towards action, they find

themselves met by octavo ramparts, flanked with quarto crenellations ... Where can these stalwart limbs, and this broad chest, grow of value and worth, in this hot-bed of cerebral inflammation and dyspeptic intellect? I know what is in me; I know I have the qualities that should go with stalwart limbs and broad chest.[47]

Bulwer-Lytton's mid-Victorian complaints probed the intersection of the cerebral world of the bourgeois professions with a romantic model of manhood based on action and fully supported by the medical community's repeated warnings about the dangers of sedentary lifestyles. After all, sedentariness was the common denominator of most "diseases of civilization," and, even when it was not cited as the *cause* of an illness, an inactive life was widely thought to aggravate pre-existing conditions. Unlike such things as gout, hemorrhoids or masturbation, which were associated with self-indulgence and over-stimulation, sitting or standing in one place for long periods of time was an essential *pre-condition* of the kind of mental, non-manual work increasingly required by modern society. Honoré de Balzac, a keen observer of modernity, insisted that civilization was a process of using up manhood, of "expending oneself more or less quickly."[48] Physicians were able to show exactly how this happened. In his popular book *A View on the Nervous Temperament* (1807), Thomas Trotter depicted the civilizing process as a movement from a "savage" condition marked by strength and endurance to an "effeminate" present where physical weakness, excessive sensibility and other "unmanly" traits seemed to predominate. Children in civilized society, he charged, were raised to marvel at external sensations while their bodies were weakened by luxuries and lack of exercise. Their physical weakness and heightened sensibilities made them appear "feminine" in comparison to the stronger and insensate "savage." The result of this softness was everywhere: in the nervous and weak bodies of businessmen and in the "pale and sallow, soft-fibred and ... slender" shop clerks who, in both appearance and manners, seemed to resemble the women they served every day.[49] Trotter was one of many physicians who called into question the manliness of civilized society, and helped to promote the idea that "true" manhood could only be approached by incorporating into oneself certain aspects of the "primitive."[50]

Concern about the "movements of the body" had long been a feature of the traditional concept of hygiene: in Western culture exercise has always been acknowledged as an indispensable element of physical and moral well-being, even if elites often resigned themselves to relatively inactive lifestyles. Yet because visions of the proper manner of employing the body were bound up with changing notions of class and gender, the ways in which "movement" was understood could vary considerably. As we have seen, from the early modern period onward, coarse or direct expressions of bodily force were rarely deemed acceptable for elites, among whom grace and elegance counted for much more, even when displays of strength and violence were required. When noble children did participate in so-called "manly exercises," such as wrestling, boxing, swimming and the discus (as French nobles were taught by the Jesuits), these were more straightforwardly recreational games that allowed nobles to avoid being labeled tender or "effeminate" due to their book learning. More pedagogical intent was invested in fencing and dancing, which exercised the body while instilling the habits of control and elegance that were essential in polite society.[51] Men of the middling sort, who had no military heritage to live up to, often shared this noble disdain for inelegant bodily movements, not least because adopting a graceful carriage might offer a degree of social acceptance in aristocratic circles. If we take medical self-help literature as a guide, most elites seemed happy to do the bare minimum to keep their basic functions moving. Coach-riding, cold baths, having one's body brushed, and even vomiting, were just some of the rather passive "exercises" that George Cheyne recommended in order to improve the circulation and perspiration of his well-to-do patients without coarsening their bodies through more vigorous activity.[52]

As we have seen in both Rousseau and William Buchan, the paradox this posed for traditional images of active masculinity had been apparent for years. Similar concerns exercised physicians across Europe, where a sedentary existence was typically described as denoting an unmanly life. And if sedentary lives diminished corporeal manliness, they also impacted upon male generative power. Indeed, many observers in the early nineteenth century detected some dire consequences in the data gathered on birth-rates and occupation. Some even claimed that male births were lower among the commercial and manufacturing professions (which "tend to enervate bodily forces") than among the agricultural jobs that "develop physical qualities."[53] Matters were not helped by the increasing popularity of coach travel in the eighteenth century, a convenience that discouraged elites from walking and even riding, and thus further contributed to the physical deterioration of men.[54]

The double threat of sedentariness and study continued to haunt the medical and national imaginations, and no "civilized" country was spared the health problems posed by its own lifestyles. As the bourgeoisie consolidated its power during the early nineteenth century, its economic and political success was qualified by lingering worries about the physical price-tag that came with such dominance. In America the usual complaints about mothers who indulged their sons' every whim became a chorus warning against mental training without some form of bodily discipline to balance it. Similarly, fathers who saddled their developing boys with too many ambitions necessarily put undue stress upon their minds, which was only exacerbated if their bodies were not sufficiently developed.[55] In France Réveillé-Parise observed that the nervous temperament of men engaged in intellectual professions was necessarily aggravated by immoderate mental work, lack of exercise, solitude, late hours and the neglect of basic hygienic precepts. His advice pertained to a range of men whose work was primarily cerebral rather than physical – from artists, writers and scientists to administrators, businessmen, politicians and functionaries. From this medical perspective, lofty works of genius and complex affairs of state sprang from a common condition of intellectual fatigue and muscular inaction.[56] Finally, as the complaints of Pisistratus Caxton reveal, sedentary occupations were quite often seen as dull and monotonous, and thus worlds apart from the adventurous and daring exploits depicted in popular novels. The writer Charles Lamb described the tedium that made him come to resent "the irksome confinement of an office" in a counting house that seemed to sap his spirit and diminish his health. "I had grown to my desk, as it were; and the wood had entered my soul."[57]

Such concerns about the bodies of elites reveal the role of class tensions in competing definitions of manhood. Imagining the city as a kind of jungle may have provided a compensatory fantasy that allowed middle-class men to pretend to be the adventurers and explorers they could not be under everyday conditions. Bourgeois gentlemen may have relished their nocturnal forays into the darkened streets, but the natives of these domains were not always happy to play along. The caricatures of Honoré Daumier and Charles Philipon were said to depict the physical features that proletarians attributed to the Parisian bourgeoisie, who they saw as greasy, pot-bellied or emaciated, lecherous and ugly. Perhaps hyperbolically, Louis Chevalier even suggests that some of the apparently random violence visited upon middle-class visitors may be explained by this basic physical revulsion, with "bourgeois ugliness inevitably provoking the rough word or blow."[58] Middle-class physicians bolstered the pride of their patients by underscoring the peculiar burdens under which they labored. The difference between men whose livelihood was based on contemplation and those who relied on manual labor was critical: unlike manual labor, where exertion ceased once the muscular work ended, mental work was not so readily put aside. However validating it might have been to reveal the mental worker as someone who worked and risked more for his profession, most doctors warned that this potentially flattering situation was really just a recipe for disaster: "The mind always active, the body always at rest, is there any surer way of drawing to oneself a multitude of woes?"[59] As a precondition and facilitator of cerebral and consumer habits, the sedentary life eroded elite masculinity from within, thus revealing the worm at civilization's core.

Worries about the eventual decline of the male body inevitably prompted cross-cultural comparisons, both within the West and across the globe. Like many of his contemporaries, the physician Johann Christian Ackermann saw some value in combining primitive simplicity with civilized lifestyles.

> We should surely not see so many degenerates and unhappy people ... if our customs were less refined, our tastes less developed, our love of comfort less strong, in other words, if we had retained the commendable elements worthy of imitation of the half-civilized peoples, and combined them with the good elements of our century.[60]

Believing their own countries to be buckling under the weight of effeminacy, eighteenth-century scholars and travelers looked hopefully to other lands as a means of measuring their nations' actual state of health. Not satisfied with having "effeminate" France at their doorstep, the British looked for signs of manliness and weakness in other countries. Reiterating the platitude that the luxuries of "polished nations have effeminated them," one traveler to Scandinavia took careful note of the degrees of effeminacy of the various regions he visited. The Norwegians he met were particularly impressive. Unlike other northerners, they did not bury themselves in furs, but assumed a more defiant stance in regard to the cold: "to shew their hardiness, [they] will even put snow into their bosoms. A warm dress is considered as effeminate." For this Briton, enjoying the simple pleasures amidst a life of hardship was most commendable. "The luxury of a Laplander is, to be wrapped in furs during winter, to scorch some favourite part of his body at the fire, to eat bears' flesh, and to drink whale oil: as these luxuries do not increase his diseases, nor shorten the period of his existence, I should, for my own part, esteem the Lapland luxury the best."[61]

If somehow the Laplander definition of the good life failed to catch on in other parts of Europe, perhaps it was a sign of the depths to which the elites of most "civilized" nations had fallen. Was civilization inversely proportional to strength? This was the pressing question that led amateur anthropologists like François Péron to test the muscular power of Australian Aborigines in the early nineteenth century. Using for his tests the notoriously unreliable dynamometer – a portable device used to measure the strength of arms and legs – Péron proudly concluded that higher levels of civilization in fact produce greater muscular force. Despite occasional warnings that such devices ought only be applied to individuals from similar backgrounds and with comparable physical habits, tests like these were conducted regularly in the nineteenth century, often reaching the flattering conclusion that white Europeans were on the whole more muscular than the indigenous peoples of Africa, Australia or New Zealand. Such claims nevertheless flew in the face of anthropological reports and travelers' accounts which maintained that, thanks to their closer proximity to "nature" and lack of luxuries and refinements, the "noble savage" was the white European's physical superior in almost every respect. As dismal reports about the connection between civilization and physical degeneration mounted in the nineteenth century, they ultimately drowned out such defensive assertions to the contrary.[62] This mixture of envy and disdain for non-Europeans' corporeal abilities extended to eyesight in the case of the Bushmen (or San) of Africa, that most noble of senses that seemed to become less acute among well-educated Westerners.[63] How could white European civilization serve as a beacon to the world if it carried such self-destructive mental and physical consequences? The paradox this posed for the supposed racial and cultural superiority of the West is nicely summed up by Steven Shapin, who rightly observes that those elites described today as "Dead White Males … were generally Sick White Males."[64]

Even the act of exploration that was needed in order to get first-hand knowledge of overseas effeminacy was sometimes viewed with ambivalence. Captain James Cook's eighteenth-century voyages to the Pacific seemed to affirm the enlightened use of tolerance, civility and tact when persuading indigenous peoples of the benevolent superiority of the British empire (as well as the scientific project of data and specimen collection). Early accounts of island peoples thus often turned up the usual accounts of suspect gender, as in the case of the Society Islanders, who were contrasted to the warlike Maoris as "an effeminate race, intoxicated with pleasure, and enfeebled by indulgence." In other cases, the superior physiques of indigenous peoples were aligned with raw animality, the surest proof of their inferiority. This was the thinking of Christian Meiners, who concluded that the muscular superiority and relative insensitivity of black Africans predestined them to a life of menial servitude and forced labor. Of course the views that indigenous peoples had of Europeans could be just as gendered. Polynesians had serious doubts about the virility of British explorers, whose all-male company and refusal of sex with island women raised a number of eyebrows.[65]

Western scientific discourses about race and class were thus generated by an intellectual elite whose claims to masculinity were implicitly fractured by the physical and moral effects of their own lifestyles. A harmony between physical fitness and mental prowess was a masculine ideal that was continually frustrated by the conditions of life wrought by modern civilization. The "beauty of form" that Meiners thought distinguished Caucasians from Africans represented a cultural ideal to which few whites ever approximated,[66] and this idealized figure could be used as a yardstick to measure the degree to which civilization caused the health and physiques of men to degenerate.[67] The primitive or the "savage" were exploited in attempts to save civilized males from themselves, often by drawing attention away from the less salubrious elements of modern existence to ponder the elemental qualities that all men might share. In keeping with the eighteenth-century tendency to valorize the primitive, German civic and health reformers heaped praise upon peoples who had not been corrupted by the civilizing process, from the "Californian, black Africans and Greenlanders" to the hardy ancient Germans. Renowned for their strength, fitness, courage and martial prowess, the Teutonic "fore-fathers" praised by reformers like Johann Peter Frank enjoyed wholesome diets and wore simple clothing, they braved the elements and led rugged lifestyles that rendered their bodies hard and strong.[68] In most countries, though, it would be left to novelists, painters and sculptors to produce fantasies of male heroes who embodied the best of both worlds, as in James Fenimore Cooper's novels *The Last of the Mohicans* (1826) and *The Deerslayer* (1841), where in the character of Natty Bumppo civilized manhood is mediated through ties with Native Americans who represent a near-animality that perhaps enables more "authentic" versions of untamed masculinity.[69]

The "superiority" that many Europeans claimed over Africans was implicitly qualified by the glum admission that, when it came to their own medical standards of masculinity, white men often fell short. To the extent that corporeal defects were widely believed to undermine whatever intellectual and cultural pre-eminence Europeans possessed, this inability to measure up on a bodily level threatened to diminish these accomplishments as well. In some cases, though, one had to assert difference in the face of uncomfortable *similarities* between cultures. Among Jews, who were reputed to be especially devoted to scholarship and speculation, the risks of sedentary professions and excessive study were similarly cited. Just as non-Jewish elites had been warned about their unhealthy lifestyles, Jews were also told that excess in such activities would surely result in nervousness, weakness, illness and cowardice. In his reformist work *On the Illnesses of the Jews* (1777), the Jewish physician Elcan Isaac Wolf applied much of the reigning medical advice about exercise, diet and other hygienic matters to the Jews as if defects in these areas were somehow germane to them alone. Regenerating the Jewish body, especially among more traditional communities, might allow them to conquer their own ailments and perhaps enjoy wider acceptance by their Gentile neighbors. Not surprisingly, Gentile observers made similar comments about how health reform might enable the "regeneration" of the Jews and promote their successful integration into the nation, despite the fact that many of the nation's non-Jewish elites were widely thought to suffer from virtually identical problems. Regardless of how often Gentiles insisted upon the *otherness* of Jews, the Jewish body was also problematic precisely because of its disavowed *similarity* to those of European elites.[70]

Discomfort about sameness was also evident in the British encounter with India, where, from the eighteenth century onward, the qualities associated with the "effeminate" Bengalis bore a striking resemblance to those already identified in Britain as well as other Western countries. What were the sources of the Bengali "cowardice" and "effeminacy of character" that seemed to justify their loss of independence to the British invaders? The answer was a combination of climate and occupation: if the Punjabi Sikhs of the north could be praised by one officer as "a fine martial race," the tropical heat of the south rendered people there "soft" and "lazy." When accounting for Bengali effeminacy, Thomas Macaulay provided a list of the usual suspects that owed nothing to European civilization: peaceful employments, sedentary pursuits, slight musculature, aversion to physical exertion, and lack of a warrior spirit. "The physical organization of the Bengalee," he wrote, "is feeble even to effeminacy ... Courage, independence, veracity are qualities to which his constitution and his situation are equally unfavourable."[71] The rather defensive tone of this comment becomes evident when situated in the wider context of anxieties about British manhood: such disparaging remarks might have been equally leveled at Trotter's feminized shop clerks and businessmen. Health reformers and muscular Christians would hurl similar charges at the effete upper classes throughout the nineteenth century. No wonder that colonialists like Cecil Earle Tyndale-Biscoe sought to "grind some grit into Kashmir" by compelling Brahmin schoolboys to overcome their delicacy through sports and physical exercise, for a similar process of masculinization through sport was by then well under way in England as well.[72]

* * *

Idealized images of the male body provide important insights into the physical and moral qualities that many elites attributed to the perfect man, but they also reveal how far short of this ideal most men fell in their everyday lives. This also illustrates how the discourse of civilization generated paradoxes for men who embraced sensibility and refinement as hallmarks of superiority while being regularly reminded how inferior they were in other respects. Further, the relationship between men and women hinged on this more fundamental problem of the male body. This is why Gérard de Nerval was able to state in 1851 that Europeans should look to the East for a land of patriarchs where women were still kept in their proper place: "In Europe, where our institutions have suppressed physical strength, woman has become too powerful."[73] The next chapter shows how the armor of health was further compromised on the dietetic front, where the refined practice of gastronomy represented the epitome of civilized manhood while setting the stage for a host of ailments that threatened that manhood in physical terms.

4
A Diet of Pleasures? The Incorporation of Manhood

By most accounts, Rakhmetov was an extraordinary man. Though by no means a weakling as a boy, at seventeen he decided to develop his body as much as possible through gymnastics and by engaging in tasks normally reserved for common laborers, including carrying water, chopping firewood, felling trees and cutting stones. As different tasks allowed him to develop different muscles, he changed jobs frequently and set off on travels across Russia to maximize his physical prowess. By the age of twenty he was hauling barges on the Volga, and on one occasion he stunned onlookers by out-pulling several sturdy men. His astonished comrades quickly dubbed him "Nikitushka Lomov" after a legendary barge hauler renowned for his impressive strength. But physical development was not the end of Rakhmetov's journey toward self-perfection. So as to be as well-rounded as possible, Rakhmetov also developed his mind by immersing himself in French and German philosophy and literature. At twenty-two he was back in St Petersburg living an austere existence, avoiding women and alcohol and eschewing luxuries. He even refused himself the comforts of a straw mattress, sleeping instead on a strip of felt. Along with these ascetic habits, his dietary regimen was central to the maintenance of his physical, moral and spiritual health:

> To become and remain Nikitushka Lomov, he needed to eat beef, a great deal of beef. So he did. He regretted every kopek he spent on any other kind of food. He ordered his landlady to purchase good quality beef, the very best cuts for him, yet everything else he ate at home was the cheapest. He gave up white bread and had only black bread at his table. For weeks at a time he never put a lump of sugar into his mouth [as was the elite Russian custom when drinking tea]; for months at a time he ate no fruit, no veal, and no poultry. He would buy nothing of the

sort with his own money. "I have no right to spend money on luxuries I can do without."[1]

Such were the virtuous qualities the writer Nikolai Chernyshevsky gave to the "extraordinary man" he described in *What is to be Done?* (1863), easily the most influential novel in Russian history. Imprisoned for his radical views, Chernyshevsky was the best-known representative of those men and women situated outside the various ranks of the nobility, a group of radicals known as the *raznochintsy* ("estate outsiders"). Perhaps the closest thing nineteenth-century Russia had to an educated middle class, this radical intelligentsia was known for the swipes it took at the decadent and "effeminate" habits of the nobility. As one who conspicuously abstained from luxury and vice, Rakhmetov was Chernyshevsky's model of the "new man," an ascetic professional revolutionary whose efforts and example might help to remake the world, but only after he had first remade himself.

As eighteenth-century critics contended that the slippery slope to effeminacy and sodomy was lubricated with rich food and drink, so Chernyshevsky's model man observes a range of sensual luxuries that need to be avoided in the name of preserving strength and virtue. For Rakhmetov sexual and alimentary restraint are integral to the rejuvenation of Russian manhood and society more generally. Hunger for sex and for food were not imagined as radically separate urges; women, food and alcohol were located along a spectrum of potentially "softening" temptations that the city had to offer and which challenged the hardier and more stoical manhood that Rakhmetov created and that he wished to sustain. In *What is to be Done?* "appetite" is an expansive concept that unites the sensual pitfalls of modern civilization under a single heading. For all their references to gustatory pleasure, Chernyshevsky's understanding of the appetites remained sexual as well as alimentary, and the management of these closely bound appetites demonstrates yet another way in which an idealized masculine body that contains the seeds of a future regeneration can be counterposed to a corrupt present society.

While the study of food and food cultures has a long history, scholars have only recently begun to investigate critically the intersection between food consumption and social identities structured around gender, sexuality and the body. This chapter demonstrates that the consumption of food and other ingesta was thought to have considerable consequences for the masculinity of Western elites, whether aristocratic or bourgeois, in a manner that promoted the cultural construction (literally, the "incorporation") of manhood both as a social representation and an embodied experience. It discusses the role attributed to eating and digestion as quintessential processes for crafting manhood through the literal incorporation of cultural ideals about gender. Special attention is accorded the problematic position that gastronomy played in the social construction of elite manhood: as a science of good taste that celebrated culinary refinement and sensual pleasure, the art of fine eating promoted the social distinction of male elites while encouraging many of the "vices" of civilization that threatened to diminish male bodies. The chapter concludes with a closer look at how the gastronome's mismanaged diet challenged manhood on the bodily level. Not only was the correct functioning of abdominal viscera pivotal to manhood, but long before "guts" were metaphorically recommended as the foundation of courage, certain ingesta were thought to offer mixed blessings to male elites, notably coffee, tea, tobacco, alcohol and meat.

MANHOOD INCORPORATED

Historians of the body have not always been attentive to the impact of ingesta once they pass through the mouth to be materially incorporated (that is, *embodied*) in the digestive process itself. To the extent that the digestive tract is the site of the chemical transformation of food into flesh, the stomach, bowels and other viscera merit attention as critical domains for self-fashioning. Even the modern reliance on nerves did not release the stomach from its central role in the bodily economy; rather, many observed that nerves merely extended the stomach's domain.[2] The continuing debate in medical circles about the pros and cons of various ingesta, not to mention the considerable influence that medicine had upon everyday life in the modern era, suggests that food, drink and other substances did not simply construct masculinity on the representational level of distinctive or conspicuous consumption. Rather, by impacting upon the nervous, digestive and reproductive systems, these substances were thought to craft the very materiality of manhood itself, thus illustrating the potential of cultural practices to serve as forms of literal incorporation.

The stomach and the organs of the lower abdomen have long been pivotal to Western conceptions of masculinity. In Georgian England, for instance, the bowels were widely cited as the anatomical location of courage, "pluck" and "bottom." Around the late nineteenth century this cluster of ideas connecting courage and organs would be united under the rubric of "guts" in English and "cran" in French, and by the early twentieth century an American football coach would coin the phrase "intestinal fortitude" as a further elaboration of this ancient belief.[3] This location of courage and morality in the viscera was more than just a residue of pre-modern ideas, and received considerable support from physicians who worried about the effects that culinary extravagance could have on the body. Among the most common of these effects, at least for elites, was hypochondria, a disorder we encountered in Chapter 3. So named by Galen due to its seat in the organs of the upper abdomen (such as the liver, gallbladder and spleen), hypochondria was marked by an excess of "black bile" (melancholia) that upset digestion and produced "vapors" that wafted upward to disturb the mind. The symptoms and etiology of hypochondria survived the medical turn away from the humors around 1700, and this gut-based nervous disorder would be viewed as the male equivalent of hysteria until the early nineteenth century ("spleen" would continue to serve as a synonym for melancholy throughout the century). Shielding men from the potentially feminizing diagnosis of hysteria seems to have been a courtesy of physicians, even though most agreed that the symptoms in both sexes were uncomfortably similar. If healthy and strong viscera were a precondition of certain masculine qualities, organs that had been weakened or corrupted through rich diets or lack of exercise logically generated the opposite qualities; hence the widespread conclusion that hypochondria rendered men effeminate.[4]

Lifestyle and dietary choices were therefore essential for the creation of healthy organs, and the state of one's viscera impacted, and was affected by, other parts of the body, not least the brain. Despite the fact that some rationalized hypochondriacal symptoms as battle scars for scholars (as we have seen), the disorder was disturbing due to its capacity to unsettle, and even overturn, the hierarchical relationship that was typically observed between the stomach and the brain, with the body clearly being described as an internal polity.[5] Even milder abdominal complaints were viewed with concern. In describing the potentially dire consequences of indigestion or "dyspepsia," for instance, the *Encyclopédie* drew analogies between private and public bodies. Insofar as dyspepsia necessarily led to "a new generation of putrid humors," it threatened to disrupt general health. At the heart of the problem lurked the mismanaged life: "There is in the animal economy, as in the political economy, a series of diseases born of a first vice in principles, whose force seduces everything."[6] Brains and bowels were thus closely related in medical views of the body, constituting in some cases a kind of "cerebrodigestive" axis connecting the body's "higher" and "lower" functions.[7] Trouble was brewing when the stomach's demands overrode the dictates of the brain, but so too when mental disturbances upset digestion. Christoph Hufeland, who considered proper digestion to be central to longevity, contended that the good stomach was one that functioned imperceptibly, without drawing attention to itself. "Whoever feels that he has a stomach," the founder of macrobiotics pronounced, "cannot have a good one."[8]

This connection between brain work and digestion has retained its power throughout the modern era. In the early nineteenth century, Réveillé-Parise explained how men with nervous temperaments often suffered from an "unequal distribution of vital and sensitive forces" that made them especially prone to disequilibrium and ill-health. Envisioning the body in economic terms, he contended that excessive study diverted the nervous energy meant for digestion, nutrition and circulation to the brain, thus leaving the other organs depleted and unable to perform their functions efficiently. "The continual excitation of the brain," he observed, "has a direct and immediate influence on the stomach." This observation, which more or less repeats that made by Samuel-Auguste Tissot nearly a century before ("the man who thinks

Figure 4.1   James A. Gillray, *A Voluptuary Under the Horror of Digestion*, 1792. Color etching on paper. Gift of Frank and Eleanor Gifford. Courtesy of the Samek Art Gallery, Bucknell University.

the most is the one who digests most poorly"), extended the eighteenth-century concern about men of letters to any man whose livelihood depended more on brains than brawn. The widely-held contention that muscular and mental prowess were physiologically at odds was here applied to the matter of "digestive power," which is "almost always in inverse proportion to intellectual power." Men who digest poorly suffer in a variety of ways, and as their bodies become weak and lifeless their nervous sensibility is augmented: such men are either neuropaths "or quickly become so." If there was a positive side to this dire prognosis, at least the sufferings of such men might be mercifully brief: "Whoever digests badly can hope neither for stable health nor a long life" (Figure 4.1).[9]

For physicians who held to these ideas the immoderate exercise of the mind clearly interfered with the functioning of the digestive organs; yet the problem could also move in the opposite direction. Tissot had considered indigestion to be bound up with most of the body's other systems and the source of countless ills, including madness and premature death. Decades later, P.-J.-G. Cabanis too observed that disorders of the lower viscera played a central role in determining the moral outlook of an individual, even claiming that autopsies revealed intestinal disorders to be the cause of various forms of insanity. Such disorders "transform, disturb, and sometimes completely invert the usual order of sentiments and ideas ... Thus in this way cheerful or gloomy ideas, sweet or distressing feelings, follow directly from the manner in which certain abdominal viscera exercise their respective functions."[10] The followers of Cabanis made similar observations, sometimes using their own experiences as evidence. Identifying the stomach as "the source of my ill-ease and my habitual concentration," Maine de Biran confided to his journal in 1816 that "gastritis can help make me more somber, more fearful, more discontent with myself."[11] Such views of the importance of digestion to the health of body and mind were widespread, and when François-Joseph-Victor Broussais argued that a great many diseases could be traced to the irritation of the gastrointestinal tract, physicians and patients in France and abroad took heed.[12]

Maine de Biran's personal reflections revealed the often unspoken connections between the depths of inwardness and the political world, potentially dangerous liaisons that had also been observed during the early modern period. As we saw in Chapter 3, melancholy could generate delusions of extreme physical fragility that would have challenged the period's tendency towards the creation of more sharply defined bodily boundaries. Consequently there is some irony in the idea that the social ideal of psychosomatic "closure" ultimately depended upon a body that "flowed" properly. As melancholic Caspar Barlaeus was advised by a friend: "adhere now to a stricter diet and in food and drink to avoid anything that causes dark vapours and waste products and prevents the body being what according to your rules it ought to be: with good bowel motions and easy, deep breathing."[13] A "good" bowel movement, however, was not an excessive one, which is why John Locke observed that "people that are very loose, have seldom strong thoughts, or strong bodies."[14] Despite the cultural value accorded to notions of firmness and closure in the West, medical advice usually touted the healthful benefits of regular but moderate flow, a fact that compels us to qualify our view of *homo clausus* in light of the widespread view that moderate flow was essential for mental and physical health.[15] Something of this clearly persists in modern anxieties about constipation and "regularity" that have preoccupied Westerners since the nineteenth century.

Contending that digestive problems could upset the polity of the personal body, many shuddered to think of the broader implications such disorders might have for the body politic. Some even suggested that many of history's greatest tragedies might have been avoided had world leaders paid more attention to their bowels. Voltaire, who took his own flagging intestinal health very seriously, had one of his literary characters link the constipation of Oliver Cromwell and Charles IX, respectively, to the beheading of Charles I and the Saint Bartholomew's Day Massacre.[16] Had he lived long enough Voltaire might have applied a similar analysis to the French Revolution, but as it happened others would look to digestion to get to the guts of the matter. Some physicians in the early 1800s argued that the Reign of Terror had much to do with the state of Robespierre's colon, which was revealed after his death to have been severely constipated.[17] A proper gentleman's emotional composure thus relied heavily upon his inner life, and for those in positions of power the results could have broad implications. Herein lay a not entirely fanciful basis for classifying human types: claiming that digestion is "of all the bodily operations the one which has the greatest influence on the moral state of the individual," the famed gastronomer Jean Anthelme Brillat-Savarin even proposed dividing the entire civilized world into the three categories of the regular, the constipated and the diarrhetic.[18]

Brillat-Savarin's association of digestion with temperament may have been jocular in tone, but as noted in the previous chapter constipation was widely cited in the nineteenth century as a "scourge of civilization" that could afflict anyone wallowing in the overfed and inactive lifestyles of the city. Representing what the American physician Samuel Thomson called a "clogging of the system," constipation would be linked to just about every degenerative disorder the nineteenth century had to offer, and when post-Pasteurian physicians added the specter of bacterial poisoning to the mix, the "auto-intoxicated" colon became a continuing source of anxiety in most Western countries.[19]

Yet as bad as constipation was, it was rivaled by that other scourge of civilization that troubled the sleep of the moralistic Victorians: masturbation.

As both were connected to the living conditions of urban modernity, the two phenomena were bound up with each other. In his broad cultural treatment of the West's obsession with masturbation, Thomas Laqueur demonstrates how anxieties about solitary vice were intermeshed with concerns about a rising commercial society that offered greater opportunities for sensual pleasure. The crux of Laqueur's argument is that anxieties about masturbation were by-products of the emergence of modern civil society and the commercial order it fostered. "If I were pressed to come up with one sentence to explain why masturbation became a problem," Laqueur claims, "it would be, 'Because it represented, in the body, some of the deepest tensions in a new culture of the marketplace; solitary sex was to civil society what concupiscence had been in the Christian order.'" Laqueur observes that the new commercial culture, with the attention paid to the imagination, privacy, solitude, excess and addiction, generated misgivings about luxury and appetite, which were only reinforced by print culture and pornography, all of which seemed to be concentrated in masturbation and its debilitating mental and physical effects (Figure 4.2).[20]

Masturbation was indeed antisocial, but, like sodomy, it also remained closely associated with civilization and was frequently cited as one of its most common and unsavory consequences. Tissot and Rousseau both agreed that boys were more likely to succumb to solitary pleasure in modern urban contexts where sedentary, studious and overstimulated lives were common.

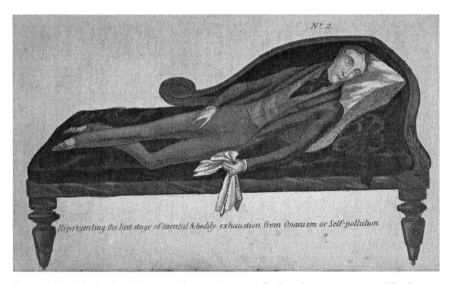

Figure 4.2 R.J. Brodie, *The Secret Companion, a medical work on onanism or self-pollution, with the best mode of treatment in all cases of nervous and sexual debility, impotency, etc.* (London, 1845). Wellcome Library, London.

German health reformers seconded this opinion, and linked the increasing sensitivity of modern youth to the practice of masturbation. Gotthilf Salzmann and other physicians recommended that boys be toughened up through manual labor (especially gardening) as well as through dietetic regimens that would reverse the softening tendencies of modern lifestyles. A healthy dose of adult supervision was also prescribed.[21] By the early nineteenth century medical dictionaries often stated that the frequency of masturbation in any given society was proportional to the level of its social, economic and cultural development, rendering it, like madness and suicide, another dubious yardstick of civilization. Even though the Victorian era devised many new and interesting ways to combat the masturbatory urge, key preventative strategies continued to include dietary and digestive vigilance.

While, as we will see below, spices, condiments and meat were thought to stimulate appetites while fatiguing the body, the retention of urine and feces were similarly linked to the awakening of sexual passion. American physicians including William P. Dewees counseled parents not to allow boys and girls to linger in their beds after waking. Along with the bed's warmth, "the accumulation of urine and faeces, and the exercise of the imagination, but too often leads to the precocious development of the sexual instinct."[22] Years later, Dioclesian Lewis told the sad tale of Mr D., a man blessed with a strong constitution and stomach who had the good fortune to marry a woman with "remarkably good digestion." Unfortunately this recipe for reproductive success was undermined by Mr D.'s excessive masturbation, which, according to Lewis, resulted in all six of their children suffering from dyspepsia. "I have taken pains to investigate many cases where the father had been addicted to self-abuse, and have arrived invariably at similar results."[23] Even if some physicians would later condemn masturbators as exercising a contaminating influence that made them "destroyers of civilization,"[24] the factors that most believed to be *causes* of solitary sex were invariably related to the lifestyles promoted in the modern era.

What was true of masturbation applied as well to other proscribed forms of sexuality. We have already seen how closely sodomy was associated with the corrupting influence of modernity, and was often thought to be caused by an advanced commercial culture. This was particularly the case with France and the Netherlands, where an abundance of good food and drink was a symptom of a softness that was believed to make just about any form of vice possible. As critics had insisted centuries before, sexual precociousness of every sort seemed to breed out of the "softer" and more stimulating conditions of urban life. The city was also closely associated with homosexuality because only in urban contexts did one find networks of sodomites grouped together in distinct subcultures. When Heinrich de Haan published his *Psychopathia Sexualis* in 1844, he too considered sexual deviance as symptomatic of individual and social conditions rather than the expressions of a pathological personality.[25] As long as modern lifestyles were considered the primary *causes* of effeminacy, differences between straight and gay men remained one of gender and environment rather than biology. In other words, homosexuality continued to be seen as the consequence of upbringing, lifestyle and choice, not the expression of an unchanging essence.

If masturbation and what was often termed "sexual inversion" revealed the effects that soft lifestyles could have upon elite bodies, obesity was the most tangible sign that a man enjoyed the abundance that others could not. Stoutness had certainly been no social sin in Georgian England, where upper-class men and women were expected to display a certain embonpoint as a sign of health. Nevertheless, as George Cheyne made clear in his discussion of the "English Malady," becoming fat was just one of the many pitfalls of living in a consumer-oriented society, where wealth rarely seemed synonymous with health.[26] This scenario became more complicated by the early nineteenth century: after all, a fat belly may have signified status, but so too did the graceful and elegant carriage of the body. As fashion at this time began to pay more attention to slender waistlines, prominent chests and muscular calves, well-dressed men had to include diet as a technique that helped them present an acceptable silhouette. Slenderness, then, was becoming increasingly important for the sake of appearances rather than simply health, which partly explains why, as a young man, Lord Byron boxed and fenced regularly to keep his weight down and improve his mental outlook.[27] It is also why the dandy Beau Brummell was able to humiliate the Prince Regent "in his physical person, his *véritable moi*," by disdainfully inquiring aloud: "who is this fat man?"[28] Nevertheless, a large belly still symbolized prestige among the grande bourgeoisie while excessive slenderness remained a sign of poverty.[29] While gastronomes like Brillat-Savarin discouraged becoming fat through fine cuisine, Brillat himself sported considerable girth, as did many other well-fed men of his day. Maintaining, in accordance with reigning fashion codes, that the sinews of his legs remained as solid "as those of an Arab horse," Brillat admitted that he had waged a thirty-year battle with his paunch in which he had "beaten it and reduced it to majestic proportions." Here too was a dubious badge of civilization. Obesity, he declared smugly, "is never found either among the savages, or in those classes of society in which men work to eat, and eat only to live."[30] Hence what Dostoyevsky's "Underground Man" noted sarcastically of the wealthy and complacent fat man corroborated a common view of how status and abundance were viewed as embodied qualities: "'Now *he's* somebody! That's a man who positively has something!'"[31]

Doctors always sketched the flip-side to this picture. For them the special "something" that distinguished the fat man could range from congestion,

Figure 4.3   Boniface's visit to the doctor. "Do you think I shall die, doctor?" "Yes, of repletion" (nineteenth century). Wellcome Library, London.

constipation, muscular weakness and weak willpower to low sperm count and impotence (Figure 4.3). It is no wonder that some doctors identified the onset of obesity as one of the bodily signs that *l'âge virile* was coming to an end, both in the sense of old age and a decline in manly powers.[32] Nevertheless, physicians disagreed about the causes of obesity: while some pointed to the traditional culprits of immoderate eating and lack of exercise, others connected fat to related digestive problems like constipation. Among physicians who insisted on the benefits of physiological flow, fat was a "disease" that was related less to excessive nutrition than, as the American physician Russell Trall put it, to "deficient excretion."[33] Whatever the cause of obesity, excess at the table was increasingly depicted as the undoing of any cultivated man. "From gaiety of heart, the most spiritual in the world, one contracts frightful illnesses, the least of which is the exhausting obesity which numbs the faculties and darkens the soul by making its corporeal envelope more dense and coarse." Overeating and obesity disturbed the harmonious functioning of bodily systems, causing the alimentary to dominate mental powers: "A fat belly [*le gros ventre*] makes for coarse [*gros*] understanding."[34] Other doctors warned of the menace that obesity posed to proper sexual functioning, where, even if the spirit was willing, a man could still suffer from impotence on physical grounds. "Among men frigidity often accompanies obesity," claimed one physician; "one sometimes observes the complete absence of spermatozoa in the seminal fluid."[35] Regardless of how much money and power his corpulence might suggest, the fat man could be unmanned through self-indulgence and care-lessness about his own health.

DISTINCTIVE TASTES

Food and status have always gone hand-in-hand as distinctive signs and tastes, markers of social and cultural difference that divide as much as they define. Writing at a time when the concept of physical comfort still referred to the barest minimum, John Locke complained about elite society's growing obsession with the well-fed child. In the houses of the well-to-do, he observed, "eating and drinking are made so much the great business and happiness of life, that children are thought neglected, if they have not their share of it." Such concerns with good food and drink always risked going to extremes, where solicitous parents encouraged eating even when children were not hungry: "every body's invention is set on work, to find something luscious and delicate enough to prevail over [the] want of appetite." What took place in one household was echoed throughout a whole social stratum that prided itself on the ability to enjoy what others could not. Locke argued that this pretense only encouraged gluttony, for the "commendation that eating well has every where, cannot fail to be a successful incentive to natural appetites, and bring them quickly to the liking and expence of a fashionable table."[36] Thus the artificial stimulation of "natural" appetites would inevitably instill in children a taste for the "unnatural," which most moralists agreed would not remain restricted to alimentary pleasures. Locke's concerns more or less mirrored complaints being made about the gluttony, idleness and perverse tastes that had become closely associated with elites since the end of the sixteenth century, and anticipated the connection between luxury and effeminacy that circulated widely in the eighteenth century. As we have seen, the moralists of that era found in material abundance the seeds of unnatural urges that ran the gamut of vices from gluttony and sedentariness to sodomy at the dark end of the spectrum.

The relationship between manhood and food is further illuminated through a brief sketch of changing Western approaches to diet and medicine since the early modern era, during which period the social basis for understanding food and drink changed considerably. The fifteenth century recognized few foods that were considered appropriate only for specific classes, with the exception of the belief that certain coarse foods were more easily digested by laborers who possessed more robust constitutions (and thus more digestive "heat"). Conversely, lighter fare was recommended for the more delicate physiques of leisured people, though such foodstuffs would do laborers little good. What was central to this regimen was the hygienic matching of diet to temperament and lifestyle, with strict social considerations taking a back seat to dietetic wisdom. As society underwent considerable changes during the sixteenth century, the class connotations of certain foods were correspondingly sharpened in European dietary texts. Thenceforth whole categories of hitherto acceptable foods were discouraged primarily because of their association with the lower orders, though little dietetic evidence was marshaled to support these class-based proscriptions. Moreover, it was largely the rising middle class who embraced these dietary rules. Struggling to separate themselves from decadent aristocrats and coarse laborers, middle-class people distanced themselves from foods that seemed at once to cause and symbolize the shortcomings of these other groups.[37]

For centuries the preparation of food had been firmly grounded in the dietetic advice linked to humoral physiology, with "taste" conceptualized mainly in terms of what naturally appealed to one's personal humoral make-up (complexion or temperament). From the seventeenth century onward, however, two important new developments began to change this view: scientific advances in chemistry and physiology that chipped away at the ancient humoral view of the body, and the emergence of the concept of "good taste" to account for a new elite appreciation of works of art, literature and music. The effect of these changes, on cooks and diners alike, was to undermine the traditional medical reasoning behind the preparation and consumption of food, gradually replacing it by an emphasis on the intrinsic qualities of the dish itself. Of course there were still certain foods considered most appropriate for this or that class, but culinary preparations were coming to be seen as objectively good or bad, regardless of a person's individual temperament.[38] In fact, the origins of the modern restaurant may be found at the crossroads of these competing concerns with dietetics and good taste. Pitched as a boon to the "weak-chested" city-dweller, male or female, the strength-restoring bouillons or *restaurants* that were marketed to health-conscious Parisian elites satisfied both the quest for rejuvenation and the dictates of good taste. They also appealed to this group's tendency to find personal validation in illness: publicly sipping a cup of broth was a form of conspicuous non-consumption that proudly displayed one's delicate constitution and refined spirit.[39] From a broth for the weak and the ill which achieved a refined status, the restaurant became a place for the service of food, and one of the emerging public sphere's numerous male meeting places. Another among the proliferation of new sensations made possible by the consumer revolution of the eighteenth century, new habits of dining celebrated gustatory refinement to an extent that would have been impossible in earlier ages and that reflected, above all, a new abundance of food. The age of gastronomy had well and truly arrived.

Freeing cuisine from the medical yoke paved the way for a valorization of eating that also celebrated the refined (usually male) eater, although it necessarily left him open to charges of luxury and over-indulgence. After all, one of the criticisms leveled at Masonic lodges in the eighteenth century was their reputation for conspicuous and excessive dining habits, a clear flouting of the anti-luxury concerns of the period. Depicted as wallowing in sensuality, it was said of such men that "their stomachs are their God."[40] In the eighteenth century gourmandizing remained connected to the Christian sin of gluttony and both epithets were employed to describe the dining habits of the aristocracy, the favorite target of anti-luxury discourses. The physician James Graham even claimed that the supposedly diminishing population of Britain was due to the sexual appetite being eclipsed by competing appetites for food and drink.[41] Others insisted that things were far worse overseas. Was the fecundity of the French affected when the famed gastronome Grimod de la Reynière insisted in his *Almanach des Gourmands* (1803–12) that the enjoyment of good food was far superior to dallying with women?[42] Although few British tourists vilified refined cuisine as either cause or consequence of the alleged vice and weakness of the French (a theme repeated *ad nauseum* in caricature and on the stage), many were taken aback at the culinary differences across the Channel (with frogs' legs and *escargots* receiving special mention).[43] Others, however, got some polemical mileage out of exploring the gender implications of such differences. Disputing the claim that the English were a "luxurious nation" (which would have ranked them among the "effeminate"), John Andrews insisted that "Plain, simple, substantial Nourishment is yet in the greatest Request among us." Not for the English, he claimed, was "that effeminate Fondness for Culinary Niceties" that afflicted elites in other countries (that is, France).[44] Thus substantialized through cuisine, the "manly" virtues of plainness and simplicity were celebrated as Britain's most distinctive national traits.

Gastronomy's masculine credentials were therefore aligned with a cultured refinement that distanced itself from mere gluttony and corporeal excess. Contrasted to the near bestial sensuality of the gourmand, the writings that celebrated the cult of good taste presented the gastronome as a paragon of discipline, discernment and moderation, a rational man who sought only the best and most refined culinary experiences. The recent innovation of the restaurant provided a new public space in which gastronomes could display their distinctive taste, and thus their elite status, in a way that also classified the non-diner as non-elite. Finally, the cultural experience of gastronomy achieved coherence and constructed a community through a culinary discourse disseminated through gastronomical journalism, culinary treatises and cultural commentary as well as broader cultural products such as novels and even works of political theory.[45] The ideal-typical gastronome was a man whose finely-honed taste was enabled both through economic means and a cultured engagement with texts that mediated his encounter with food.

There is much in the gastronome's lifestyle that might have validated his masculinity in the wider social world. Gastronomy was the almost exclusive preserve of well-to-do and educated men, and thus functioned as a homo-social reprieve jealously guarded against incursions by women and proletar-ians. In this sense gastronomy represented "the public pursuit of sensory pleasures, not the private satisfaction of physiological needs," as Priscilla Parkhurst Ferguson has nicely put it.[46] By signaling such refined tastes, culi-nary discernment was an essential ingredient of the bourgeois gentleman, flavoring his character and sensibility in a way that set him off from the lower orders. There is a continuity here with earlier periods. We have seen how the Masonic lodge, where food and drink were refined and plentiful, fulfilled this dual role as all-male preserve and school of distinction. Yet insofar as they remained closed to the uninitiated, the lodges were more or less private enclaves rather than public venues for the display of conspicuous consump-tion. From the nineteenth century onward the restaurant and dining club served this public function, though this exclusivity would decline with the growing acceptance of women patronizing restaurants around the 1890s.

The exclusion of women from the scene of dining was based as much on sensation as on homosociality. After all, a woman's allure, many claimed, threatened to distract a man from the sensual pleasure of the dish at hand. Since the delights of sex and of food were clearly of a similar caliber, one needed to make some hard choices. Decades after Grimod de la Reynière explained why good food was better than sex, one etiquette manual dis-approvingly described the gastronome as a man who raised his love of food above all other passions, especially any "feminine element."[47] The man who loved food more than women was hardly a stable masculine exemplar, and was the frequent butt of satirical humor. "Where to begin?" ponders an epicurean in a print by Philibert-Louis Debucourt as he chooses between a bare-breasted beauty reclining on his sofa and the food on his table.[48] This connection between gustatory and sexual appetites is reinforced in an 1805 caricature in which a gastronome, menu in one hand, digs deep into his front pocket with the other, either to scrounge around for cash or to pleasure himself (Figure 4.4). Gustatory and sexual needs were thus enmeshed in the broader concerns with sensual pleasure and material abundance that were generated by an increasingly consumer-oriented society. "How can one resist the clever seductions in this city?" Balzac wondered. "Paris has its addicts, whose opium is gambling, gastrolatry or sex [*la courtisane*]." For Balzac, even the physiological process of incorporation was intimately related to sexuality: "Digestion, by using human forces, constitutes an inner battle which, for gastrolaters, is the equivalent of the greatest climaxes [*jouissances*] of love."[49]

Gastronomy was thus a rarified homosocial practice that combined civilized refinement with the trappings of more robust styles of manhood. On one

Figure 4.4 Unknown French artist, "Der Gastronome nach dem Mittagsessen," *London and Paris* (Volume 15, 1805). Br 38.11.5* Houghton Library, Harvard University.

hand, it constituted a disciplined and moderate indulgence in food worth eating, something akin to the disinterested appreciation of art; it was thus carefully distinguished from the artless self-indulgence of mere gourmand-izing or gluttony. As one might expect for such a refined pursuit, proper eti-quette at the table remained important, and indeed essential when appetite might tempt a man to take more than his fair share of each course. On the other hand, the rituals of the meal as set out in gastronomy manuals were replete with military language: from the creation of a guest list and the issuing of invitations to the preparation, serving and consuming of food, metaphors of strategy, skirmishes, attacks and ambushes abounded, with the host described as a valiant general leading his stalwart troop of privileged guests. Once again the refinements and luxuries of middle-class existence were under-written by compensatory fantasies of warfare, where the "weaponry" consisted of tasty delicacies and fortitude was measured by one's ability to keep up the pace. Through such rituals, Jean-Paul Aron observes, "the middle classes dis-cover at table that fine spirit which the aristocracy had discovered in war."[50]

As was the case with many other attempts to validate the manhood of sedentary and cerebral elites, the spirit of warfare fostered by fine dining remained a poor surrogate for actual combat and risk. It is perhaps fitting that, when Samuel Johnson reportedly claimed that "Every man thinks meanly of himself for not having been a soldier," he did so while enjoying a dinner with friends.[51] As with many bourgeois customs, that which seemed to establish a strictly social basis for manhood in luxury, refinement and status also threatened to undo it when it came to the consuming body itself. The reality of such culinary adventures, at least as reported by doctors, revealed the difficulties gastronomes often encountered in striking a workable balance between pleasure and restraint. However, if health concerns as encapsulated in the 'non-naturals' were no longer paramount for chefs and gourmands, dietetics persisted as a body of cautionary medical literature, and even gained momentum as the gastronomic heyday of the early nineteenth century faded into the dour concerns of the fin de siècle, where repairing exhausted digestive systems became the focus of special attention. Medical appraisals of the bourgeois body thus seemed to regret the disconnection between cuisine and dietetics as doctors implored men and women to temper their eating habits with good hygienic sense. If men in general eat and drink too much, noted one physician, this excess was surely "awakened by refined culinary art."[52] Doctors and chefs thus waged a running battle for the bodies of elites.

APPETITES FOR DESTRUCTION

While doctors warned both men and women of the ill effects of certain foods, beverages and condiments, some ingesta were singled out for their especially deleterious effects on masculinity. Stimulating substances – including a range of different kinds of foodstuffs, from spices and condiments to caffeinated drinks and alcohol – were particularly frowned upon. Paradoxically, some of these substances were being discouraged by medical opinion at the same time that they were becoming significant in some social circles for the constitution of male identity. Coffee and tea, for example, were closely associated with the masculinist public sphere that gradually emerged during the eighteenth century, especially with the coffeehouses that sprang up in Paris and London around 1700 (each city had around six hundred of these establishments). Coffeehouses were the venues for discussions of weighty matters of trade and politics; to the chagrin of some, however, many men came to drink their coffee and to chat about frivolous things like fashion or scandal. As well as tea and coffee, coffeehouses also sold chocolate, perfumes, and (in France) spirits. Some even offered merchandise for sale, from juices, tobacco, coffee beans, and packages of tea to medicines, tooth powders, lottery tickets and West Indian citron water.[53]

One of the factors that contributed to the success of the coffeehouse was the perceived effects of the non-alcoholic drinks consumed there on men's behavior. In the early eighteenth century, broad generalizations about the medicinal benefits of coffee and tea abounded, and there was some agreement that, at least for the purposes of business and politics, the moderate use of caffeinated beverages was preferable to imbibing alcoholic drinks. While alcoholic beverages had long been an important component of male conviviality, not to mention an enjoyable means for testing the limits of one's bodily control,[54] where business was being conducted, it was felt that wine, ale and spirits might cloud the judgment and arouse the passions, thus leading to poor decisions, gambling and heated arguments. In some circumstances strong drink could perhaps even propel one into the arms of loose women. The milder stimulation of caffeinated drinks sharpened the wit and allowed one to focus on the matter at hand. Hence any disagreements that arose could be dealt with rationally and soberly. On the other hand, there were critics of coffee who felt that this curb on passion went too far and questioned the manliness of those who spurned stronger libations: during the Restoration era coffee was thought to sap a man's sexual drive and reduce the habitual drinker to effeminacy. Poised between rationality and sexual potency, masculinity was in a predicament. Whatever their effects on virility, at least in the long run coffee and tea were more cost-effective than liquor. Unlike ale or wine, which could lead to more and more drinking, the desirable effects of coffee and tea were achieved more quickly and with less danger of succumbing to debauchery. None of this means that coffeehouse patrons were necessarily teetotalers or that they avoided taverns on other occasions. Rather what these men sought in the coffeehouse was the means to achieve the mental and physical comportment proper to the conduct of business and the discussion of politics in a rational and civil manner. In other words, male rationality emerged only through carefully managed circumstances and the ingestion of the right substances.[55]

The value of coffee and tea as stimulants of body and mind was also acknowledged by intellectuals and writers, although few were as ruthless as Balzac in his experiments with stimulants in the 1830s. Balzac settled upon "a brutal method that I recommend only to men of excessive vigor," namely, drinking cold, concentrated coffee at night on an empty stomach. Noting the profound impact this method had on his creativity, Balzac described the mental effects of caffeine as primarily martial in nature: "Ideas quick-march into motion like battalions of a grand army to its legendary fighting ground, and the battle rages." For Balzac, caffeine served as a performance-enhancing drug that allowed him to transcend the ordinary limits of his body and mind, arguably to explore the full potential of his masculine creativity. Coffee taken in such a concentrated form and in such vast quantities as recommended in Balzac's recipe for creative success did not exactly promote the calm and rational sociability more associated with the coffeehouse: "one's voice rises, one's gestures suggest unhealthy impatience; one wants everything to proceed with the speed of ideas; one becomes brusque, ill-tempered, about nothing." This was hardly proper behavior, and Balzac was forced to the conclusion that the jittery "man of spirit must therefore avoid going out in public."[56]

Caffeine was thus a tricky substance for the construction of masculinity. Fostering sociability and self-control when consumed in moderation, it could drive a man to nervous and emotional excesses that disrupted fellowship and destroyed self-possession. Restoration critics of caffeine had predicted that it would lead to impotence, but it was also condemned for its ability to awaken sensuality. The over-stimulating potential of coffee and tea was reported most frequently among health reformers of the early nineteenth century, whose cautionary tales about the depths to which caffeine addicts could sink were repeated by subsequent generations of reformers well into the twentieth century. The American health evangelist Sylvester Graham cautioned against the use of almost all of the stimulants that were becoming so readily available in cities of the 1830s, not least because they were thought to enhance venery. This advice was perpetuated decades later by the popular reformer Dioclesian Lewis, who, being particularly worried about the effects of coffee and tea on sexual desire, issued to his readers "A Special Warning: Tea and coffee are directly unfavorable to sexual cleanness. Coffee is perhaps the one thing above all others that, taken into the human system, gives rise to ungovernable salacity."[57]

As well as coffee and tea, tobacco, alcohol and opium were also commonly used by professional men to enhance their productivity or creativity; any of these could be frowned upon by physicians for the fatigue they brought in their wake and the damage they wrought upon the body, especially among men with sedentary and cerebral habits.[58] Tobacco consumption, like the drinking of coffee and tea, was also a common, and problematic, element of male conviviality in the modern era. Whereas earlier images of smoking were associated with adventure and wildness, beginning in the eighteenth century an alternative image was established through medical claims that tobacco promoted the kind of emotional stability that was essential for the exercise of rational manhood. Sherlock Holmes is iconic in this context. Tobacco was an essential tool of his deductive trade, and his was one of the earliest of the many images in Western culture that associate long draws on a pipe, cigar or cigarette with the act of contemplation. The older and more adventurous connotations of tobacco were not subsumed by this image of rationality, but assimilated into a more respectable figure of the mature, sober and rational male, lending him a whiff of a more robust virility that subtly suggested transgression (but of a rather domesticated sort). Tobacco might enable a businessman to reinforce the illusion that commercial ventures are in fact "real" rather than surrogate adventures. Expensive tobaccos and smoking paraphernalia counted among the few consumer passions in which Victorian men could

indulge without any risk of appearing "feminine" in the eyes of contemporaries; and a definite social hierarchy existed between the pipe and cigar,
which suggested tasteful retreats from the world, and the mass-produced ciga-
rettes of the late nineteenth century, which were bound up with the hectic
nature of modern urban life. Finally, much as gastronomes frequently compared gustatory and sexual pleasure, tobacco connoisseurs liked to feminize
their drug as "Lady Nicotine." They too liked to debate the relative merits of
smoking with the gents or suffering the company of women.[59]

As the case of Rakhmetov illustrates, consumption of meat has had very
strong masculine connotations; as such, it too was sometimes targeted as an
area of potential reform. Despite refinements in the preparation of meat
dishes that distanced sensitive diners from the unpleasant facts of bloodshed
and killing, a carnivorous diet still echoed the violence of less civilized times.
The persistent appeal of hunting in some circles no doubt represents the
appeal of the (real or imagined) connection between manhood, violence and
meat that reinforces the masculinist allure of the carnivorous diet.[60] Perception of this connection is one reason why, around 1800, the radical vegetarian
Joseph Ritson could link rejection of a carnivorous diet with the abolition of
blood sports and slavery as part of a plea for a broader reformation of male
manners.[61] Claiming that "all vice" sprang from meat eating, the poet Percy
Shelley even claimed that the French Revolution would have been far less
bloody had Robespierre and Napoleon eaten their veggies.[62] (It might have
improved Robespierre's congested bowel as well.) For these reformers a lust for
animal flesh was, quite literally, an appetite for destruction. Yet it represented
an appetite for sex as well. For the intrepid hunter in urban jungles, woman
was meat pure and simple. As Lord Tennyson pronounced in 1847, "Man is
the hunter; woman is his game." No wonder that the term "tenderloin"
evolved out of its reference to the most employed part of a prostitute's trade.[63]

Yet meat-eating had more overtly material implications for man-building.
Especially in France, whose diminishing birth rate would generate considerable controversy later in the century, meat was also implicated in sexual
reproduction. Arguing that the health of the sperm and egg depended on the
amount of nitrogen that resided in each, advice manuals of the period advised
women to follow a regimen rich in nitrogenous foods, with generous help-
ings of meat coupled with regular exercise, while white meat, vegetables, and
longer periods of rest were recommended to men. Not only should a man
perform exercises such as swimming or sea-bathing that would "augment the
activity of the nutritive functions," but during the act itself he had to deploy
"all of his combined moral and physical forces, and [like his partner] fix his
thoughts on the sex of the child he wants to procreate."[64] That a carnivorous
diet (with a generous helping of wishful thinking) might promote the conception of boys was certainly intuitive, at least in light of the close connection

of meat-eating with male vigor and sexuality; but – as has been the case with most other beliefs about the powers of certain foodstuffs – there were others who condemned the excessive meat-consumption of elites, which in France was denounced by some vegetarians as being partly responsible for the nation's falling birth rate.[65] By the end of the century those we might call "muscular vegetarians" insisted that their lifestyle was conducive to the restoration of bodily force. As one pro-vegetarian study observed, "the word *Végétarisme* traces its etymology not to the substantive 'vegetal,' but to the adjective *vegetus*, strong, vigorous."[66]

The ability to engender offspring was just the beginning of the alimentary construction of masculinity. Inadequate food, both in terms of quality and quantity, was found to be as important in the sorry health conditions of undersized and underweight proletarians as were all other lifestyle factors, including physical activity and residence in the city or the country. The poor living conditions of proletarians generated widespread concerns on a number of fronts, not least the social one, where a poor diet was considered a breeding ground for popular unrest, strikes and even revolutionary activity. Both concern for the health of the poor and the aim of undermining potential unrest were among the rationales offered for vegetarianism and other dietary reform movements during the late nineteenth century, though meat continued to be fed to boys, not least due to its association with muscle and strength-building properties. The "sexual politics of meat" is thus a widespread and enduring phenomenon.[67] If maintaining a well-fed (and thus pacified) populace was one of the aims of food reform, military demands formed another, especially among army doctors frustrated by large numbers of workers deemed unfit for military service. Unlike the elites, theirs was a problem of food scarcity rather than abundance. According to Alphonse Quetelet, the development of physical force depended to a considerable extent on relative ease, abundance of nutritious food and moderate exercise, and negative factors like poverty and excessive labor worked against the creation of powerful men. This point was corroborated by other researchers, who claimed that "poorly nourished children can acquire neither a favorable stature nor a robust virility" and recommended greater attention to matters of nutrition, work conditions and housing as a means of rehabilitating proletarian manhood.[68] Alimentation thus remained central to the social reproduction of soldiers and industrial laborers, for whom a robust and healthy body was essential.

* * *

All bodies are literally materialized through alimentation and dietetic principles, which is why food consumption and dietetic strategies must be considered critical sites for understanding how bodies are culturally constructed.

As this chapter has shown, the incorporation of manhood was a complex and fraught business. Throughout the modern era, physicians dispensed dietetic advice aimed at weaning men from the indulgent lifestyles that threatened their health and rendered them unfit for the active life that is an enduring component of masculinity, including physical labor and military prowess. Like the other diseases of civilization, dietetic mismanagement also threatened to generate or aggravate a host of sexual disorders, from masturbation to impotence, that spelled disaster even for the most hardy of men. As the following chapter shows, when combined with the other health problems of modern life, dietary issues raised questions about warrior manhood at the very moment that modern nations began to emerge.

5
Building Bodies: Violence, Pain and the Nation

One of the ironies of the gendered discourse of civilization is that, despite the terror, torture, warfare and domestic violence that is perpetuated in the world, it is the capacity to enact and endure violence that is often represented as one of the most unjustly *repressed* aspects of male experience. Yet if violence and warfare are so often celebrated for their "regenerative" potential, it is perhaps because the more positive ideals of sacrifice and self-denial that defined the warrior code have, since the early eighteenth century, been systematically challenged by developments that emphasize the value of self-indulgence and softer lifestyles. While peace has been celebrated throughout modern history, it has also been criticized for its tendency to make individuals and societies complacent and weak. "Just as the blowing of the winds preserves the sea from the foulness which would be the result of a prolonged calm," wrote G.W.F. Hegel, "so also corruption in nations would be the product of prolonged, let alone 'perpetual,' peace."[1] This concern about corruption as the inevitable result of perpetual peace was a reply to Immanuel Kant's celebrated 1795 essay on the topic, and reveals Hegel's own anxieties about the negative effects of an emerging commercial society on morality and, implicitly, manhood. Intimations of this position were evident years before in the *Phenomenology of Spirit* (1807), where Hegel envisioned life-and-death struggle as a precondition of full self-consciousness. In this hypothetical primal scene of abstract individuality, one self-conscious being can only actualize its transcendent potential by proving that it "is fettered by no indeterminate existence, that it is not bound at all by the particularity everywhere characteristic of existence as such, and is *not* tied up with life." For Hegel this could only be achieved by seeking the death of another self-consciousness whose very existence poses a threat to freedom and individuality. True freedom can thus only come about by risking one's life, which would prove that "self-consciousness is not bare existence … The individual, who has not staked his life, may, no doubt, be recognized as a Person; but he has not attained the truth of this recognition as an independent self-consciousness."[2]

As Hegel only saw males as being truly capable of "self-consciousness," we might reformulate his statement in less abstract terms: unless a male has risked his life struggling on equal terms with another male, he has not really actualized his masculine potential. In this scenario only the male who is willing to risk it all emerges as the "master," while the one who yields by choosing life over death is placed in the subordinate, implicitly "feminized" position of a slave or bondsman. That the master is in turn rendered a slave to his appetites through his distance from the self-actualizing labor performed by the slave does not undermine the life-and-death struggle as a precondition for selfhood. Rather it merely underscores how, for Hegel, choosing life, comfort and consumption negates the fullest development of manhood.[3]

To be anything other than feminizing and corrupting, then, civilization must periodically refresh itself through violence, daring and rigorous physical effort, either in labor or conflict. In the civilizing process, pleasure and pain are bound up with one another, and despite liberal philosophical claims that humans naturally seek pleasure and avoid pain, in practice people have responded in more complex ways. If traditional Christianity viewed sacrifice and resignation to pain as important parts of life, in eighteenth-century Europe new approaches to medicine, consumer goods and the cult of sensibility stigmatized both the sensation and spectacle of pain as barbarous, cruel and unnecessary. A number of key developments punctuate the modern history of pain relief: the use of nitrous oxide gas (1773), the isolation of morphine (1808), the use of ether as an anesthetic (1847), the chemical synthesis of aspirin (1899) and so on. In many areas of modern life pain and violence were roundly condemned, from the beating of children to the violently punitive practices of the armed forces. Nevertheless painful sensations continued to exercise a hold on the imagination, even as they were gradually removed from everyday experience. Spectacles of torture and violence not only became commonplace in the pornographic texts of the eighteenth century, but they also played an increasing role in the Gothic fiction and sensationalist crime stories that proliferated throughout the nineteenth century. Even humanitarian efforts to reduce suffering unwittingly eroticized pain through titillating language that encouraged readers to imagine scenes of torture and punishment for themselves. Thus, as elite culture came to redefine pain as forbidden and even obscene, the capacity of violence and suffering to shock and stimulate increased, contributing to what Karen Halttunen calls a "new pornography of pain: a heightened awareness of the close relationship between the revulsion and the excitement aroused by pain."[4]

The significance of pain went beyond feverish readers and their vicarious experiences. Pain also played an important role in attempts to reconstruct a masculinity that seemed to have been corrupted by too much peace and prosperity. After all, for many observers there was something intrinsically problematic about a life lived mostly for pleasure and ease. Criticizing the "moral effeminacy" of the gentlemen of his day, John Stuart Mill remarked that it was refinement in general that compelled these men to steer clear of "not only actual pain, but all that can be offensive or disagreeable to the most sensitive person." Though generally defending civilization as a boon to humanity, Mill also saw effeminacy as "a natural consequence of the progress of civilization [that] will continue until met by a system of cultivation adapted to counteract it."[5] If some observers regretted the way in which refinement promoted a delicacy unbecoming to men, others proposed the related idea that it was modern consumption that caused more and more people to abandon hardship and sacrifice for lives of indulgence and comfort. In German history the notion of "pain" has typically been contrasted to "prosperity," which draws attention to advances in material life whereby bare necessities have been provided for, diseases have been cured and greater numbers of people can expect longer lives relatively free of scarcity and the need for sacrifice. The opposite of "pain" was thus not some abstract "pleasure," but a much wider range of sensory experiences connected to modern advances in medicine, consumption and rising standards of living.[6] Through such disciplinary techniques as military training, sports and other forms of physical fitness, measured doses of "pain" are welcomed (or at least tolerated) as *productive* and even *empowering* experiences that bring into being things that were not there before, at least not in the same way. The roots of the slogan "no pain, no gain" thus extend at least back to the early modern period, in which classical ideals were updated for a new era and prescribed to the West's enfeebled elite.[7]

Concerns about manhood were common in any country whose rising standards of living made life more peaceful and enjoyable while threatening to render men soft, weak and cowardly. Edifying tales of men who could silently bear extraordinary hardships circulated as counter-narratives to the standard accounts of how weak and effeminate elites had become. For example, claims that British bodies and morality had grown soft through good living and the sartorial extravagance of "macaroni" fashion were rife during the late eighteenth century, which is why some cultivated the mythology of the common sailor whose loyalty and virility, supposedly untainted by luxury or sedentariness, was proven through feats of martial prowess and military discipline.[8] Other branches of the military told similar tales. According to a British soldier who lost a finger at Waterloo, one of his comrades was able to chew stoically on a tobacco plug while having his forearm amputated. A wounded Frenchman nearby was unable to muster such self-possession, and when he cried out at having his wounds probed by a surgeon, the stoic Briton used his own amputated arm to strike the man, shouting at him to "stop your damn bellowing."[9] Apocryphal or not, this tale illuminates how the enduring of pain served as one means of differentiating peoples and nations in terms of manliness around the beginning of the nineteenth century. Often considered a quintessentially masculine capacity, the ability to endure and even invite pain was also an inverted yardstick of civilization (even if at such times the vitality of the nation rested upon non-elite bodies).

Given the recurring claim that civilization was at best a mixed blessing for masculinity, this chapter argues that exertion, aggression, violence and the risk of injury or even death were central to the kinds of male bodies deemed most useful to emerging concepts of the nation around the turn of the nineteenth century. Viewing the duel as a microcosm of the boundary-building potential of violence, it investigates the complex interplay between this convention-laden custom and concerns about the effects of civilization. It then analyzes how many of the functions attributed to the duel were subsumed by the emergence of new notions of the nation that, in official discourses, depended upon disciplined and hardened men capable of furthering the interests of the nation through military service. The chapter then considers the relationship between military ideals and masculinity in the emerging emphasis in the nineteenth century on gymnastics and sport, which were often proposed as means of recuperating or preserving the robustness of the male under civilized conditions. Common to all of these practices is not only the presumption that hostilities among men can and will break out at any time, but a belief that violence and sacrifice contain a rejuvenating and productive potential that creates as much as it destroys. Faced with the softening tendencies of modern civilization, effort, pain and violence became ways of constructing boundaries around the male body that replicated the boundaries of the nation as a kind of superorganism.[10]

THE FUNCTION OF DUELING

Dueling is a custom that at once facilitates and mitigates the civilizing process. Formulated and practiced in Italy in the sixteenth century, dueling codes migrated to other countries as an important component of elite manners, and through colonial expansion they even made their way overseas. They were disseminated to the same circles that also consumed conduct manuals, and were thus closely bound up with the kinds of male bodies required by the court society. Nonetheless, the relationship of the duel to civilization was an ambiguous one. In many ways the practice was a bona fide *instrument* of civilization, a convention-laden series of steps that intervened between the shock of the initial affront and the necessary response. Dueling demanded that a man possess enough self-control to postpone any direct riposte to an insult in order to follow the prescribed steps of honorable combat: issuing a challenge, naming seconds, deciding on the proper location for the duel, selection of weapons and so on. In the earliest dueling codes,

challenges needed to be delivered in writing (and always in courteous language), while the duel itself had to be conducted in an orderly and gracious
manner that compensated somewhat for the breach of social harmony it
represented. The theatrical aspects of dueling allowed men to "perform" their
masculinity under decidedly extraordinary circumstances, requiring complete
control of the body, and the projection of an air of imperturbability and self-
mastery that signified *sang froid*. Dueling with a sword required a combination
of grace, skill and courage, qualities that were integral to the self-perception of
the nobleman as well as to the bourgeois who sought admission to his world.
Fisticuffs, which often erupted immediately following an insult, were usually
frowned upon by elites because they encouraged the direct and often brutal
expression of physical force in ways that were deemed antithetical to the
elegance, control and grace of proper gentlemen. In practice, of course, these
gentlemanly codes were not always observed. In nineteenth-century Russia
some of the *raznochintsy* seemed to *prefer* direct physical force to the formalities of dueling, so that attacks upon honor might just as easily be answered
with immediate punches, slaps, or blows with walking sticks as with the string
of formalities that proper dueling required.[11] Despite these unfortunate
breaches of etiquette, the assumption was that indecorous behavior would be
minimized by observing the niceties of convention.

However "civilized" a form of fighting dueling was, though, it still represented the persistence of male aggression and courage that many embraced as
an essential counterpoint to the softening potential of civilization. A willingness to duel was evidence that a man retained a core of untamable bellicosity
and courage, even if that wildness at heart was mediated by social considerations and softened through manners. This affirmation was especially important as the state began to consolidate its control during the early modern era.
While dueling challenged the government's presumed monopoly of the use of
violence and was thus generally illegal, these acts of violence confirmed that
there were spaces in a man to which the civilizing process did not extend.
As Ute Frevert observes, the German duel was regarded as "a test of true,
unalloyed masculinity" that became especially significant in an age of constraints: "The more the concept of rugged masculinity was in danger of forfeit-
ing some of its validity during the course of the eighteenth century, the more
necessary did such a test appear to become."[12] An innovation of courtly
conduct, dueling was also its compensation: it was a concession to the need
for rules and decorum, and a rejection of the softening effects that refinement
was thought to entail. On the European continent, dueling would fulfill this
double role through the early twentieth century. By then it offered the
middle-class student in Germany what Kevin McAleer calls a "martial compensation for the softening effects of book-study, of the merely intellectual
life," and thus injected into a man doses of "chivalry" that would offset the

effects of over-refinement. In this sense the duel gave men access to a more bellicose (yet imaginary) past.[13]

In addition to these functions, dueling also influenced the ways in which upper-class males came to perceive their own bodies in everyday life. Early modern concepts of aristocratic honor reveal the centrality of the noble body in a way that was not evident in the Middle Ages. If medieval honor codes referred mainly to a nobleman's worldly goods (which included his wife), the emergence of courtly culture placed a premium on individual reputation that shifted honor's reference from possessions to the person. This was a world in which beauty, elegance and character were the most important indices of social standing and thus of personal honor. Honor was more than a posses-sion, it was a matter of conduct, comportment and demeanor: it described the intrinsic qualities of a man, which, when manifested outwardly, were deci-pherable to those literate in reigning honor codes.[14] The connection between noble honor and courage is well illustrated in early modern France, as is the idea that a sense of honor had to be cultivated in boys from an early age. In aristocratic households fear was thought to be normal among younger chil-dren, and it was not uncommon to allow young boys to lie with adults in order to help them sleep. At around the age of six or seven, a boy received his breeches, and more effort went into encouraging him to confront and master his fears. Adults employed a range of tactics to instill courage in boys, includ-ing praise, blame, and even taunts and provocations. Such techniques were reinforced by a shift in disciplinary measures from corporal punishment to various methods of shaming, a change that ingrained in young nobles a keen sense of honor.[15] If the young noble were to subdue his fearful impulses, he would have to become sensitive to all that might call his honor into question, suggesting that the very techniques that aimed at "hardening" the nobleman also had to result in what some might see as a "thin skin." While being con-sidered a quality inherent in the person, honor still had to be experienced at the level of the body and its boundaries as well as through interactions with others. In many respects the duel provided men with a means both of crafting and policing their fragile sense of personal boundaries.

As an exclusively aristocratic practice, the early modern duel was a weapon of social distinction that separated those who were considered capable of "giving satisfaction" from those who were not. Yet as the duel was most fully developed in countries where the person rather than the clan took center stage, the custom also had an undeniable *individualizing* effect that sharpened attention to the peripheries of the self. This individuation was an experience that was becoming less and less a condition of modern battle. Over the cen-turies, developments in military technology had brought about a profound change in the physical experience of combat. In the Middle Ages knights and archers would have been trained for years in the arts of wielding a broadsword, fighting on horseback, or taking careful aim, so that the whole body was engaged in the skills and experience of fighting. The development of firearms altered this experience significantly. Requiring little physical prowess, guns also created a new sense of physical detachment from the fight itself (along with the virtual elimination of any individual achievement amid the storm of steel that would increasingly characterize modern battle). The withdrawal of the body from the act of combat was accompanied by a heightened awareness of the body's vulnerability: cannonballs and bullets rendered most forms of material armor useless and left little room for individual greatness.[16] Despite the occasional violent intervention of overzealous seconds in the seventeenth century, dueling placed the individual combatant back at the center of things. A man's ability to display bravery and self-command was much more in evidence when pitted against a single opponent.[17] The duel thus individualized a man while implicitly equalizing the credentials of those willing to step onto the field of honor, even if by the nineteenth century bravery in battle was eventually replaced by courage to withstand assaults (Figure 5.1).

The duel's individualizing effect was enhanced through the heightened awareness that it promoted of bodily boundaries, both within men and in their perceptions of others. As an extension of the stylized behavioral codes propounded in polite society, the prospect of unwittingly provoking a duel by bumping into

Figure 5.1   Jean-Léon Gérôme, *Duel after a Masked Ball* (1857). Oil on canvas. 68 × 99 cm. Inv.no. GE-3872. The State Hermitage Museum, St Petersburg.

another man or treading on his toes entailed a different manner of conducting oneself, both on the street and in society at large. This boundary-building aspect of dueling persisted throughout the nineteenth century, but seems to have varied depending upon context. Irina Reyfman explains this in terms of the increasing importance of the ideal of physical inviolability among the Russian nobility. "While making a gentleman open to the violence of ritualized combat, [the duel] guaranteed his physical inviolability in other contexts of civil intercourse. In fact, the duel's existence signaled society's readiness to recognize a person's right to private space and physical inviolability."[18] This was a particularly sensitive issue for Russian nobles, whose sense of honor could be infringed if subjected to unwarranted physical punishment or abuse. Nobles who organized themselves into a ruling class in accordance with European models "began to assimilate the Western notions of personal autonomy and sanctity of private space," as well as the idea that the boundaries of that space should be legitimately policed through the threat of violence. Such practices, moreover, were not exclusive to the nobility. Although they had acquired an education, the sons of the socially-mixed *raznochintsy* were still commoners who usually had no training in manners, dancing or fencing, a fact that put them in an awkward position in relation to their aristocratic betters. While they might insist in their writings upon the importance of inner virtues rather than superficial social convention, the assumed link between dueling and courage made it virtually impossible for such socially ambiguous (and ambitious) men to reject the practice outright. More often than not, striving for equal status with the nobility meant that educated commoners insisted on their equal right to fight duels. For them dueling represented a form of social acceptance as well as a tacit admission of male equality.[19]

Even if the emphasis in dueling shifted over time from concrete displays of martial ability to the demonstration of the willingness to risk pain and even death, the violence implicit in it continued to perform a number of functions for aristocratic and middle-class men. In many circles the mere fact of the duel was evidence that a man had not become so used to refinement and comfort that he had lost the capacity to make the "ultimate sacrifice," whether for honor or his country. As a social custom, moreover, dueling prompted men to pay greater attention to their own conduct and bodily peripheries, thus fostering a sense of corporeal enclosure that was policed by the threat of violent reprisals. Finally, such risk-taking and boundary-building were techniques for integrating men into larger homosocial groups, thereby facilitating the passage of youths into manhood and, in some cases, the assimilation of men from marginal groups into the mainstream of national manhood. The boundaries of these larger groups were, by the same token, means of excluding those considered incapable of risking their lives in the same manner. Whether as threat or reality, enduring pain and inflicting violence were thus productive techniques that constructed men through the creation and reinforcement of individual and collective boundaries. These were qualities that the duel shared with military training and warfare, which the Prussian military theorist Carl von Clausewitz described as "nothing but a duel on an extensive scale."[20]

THE WORLD'S ONLY HYGIENE

Having long served the interests of states, from the time of the French Revolution through the era of realpolitik, militarism and warfare have been among the principal means through which nations have been formed as imagined communities as well as geographical entities.[21] Of course women as well as men played a role in constituting the nation; yet the techniques that aimed at integrating people into this collective body differed for each. "Women are typically constructed as the symbolic bearers of the nation," notes Anne McClintock, "but are denied any direct relation to national agency."[22] Yet this symbolic role in nation-building did not erase the very real physical and emotional pain women were expected to bear for the sake of the nation, from the suffering of childbirth and the endurance of privations during times of war to the horror of having their children die in combat or while under siege. Moreover, the nation may be gendered as feminine during states of emergency which authorize depictions of a passive or prostrate body politic capable of being "raped," "amputated" or even "castrated" by enemy forces. For men, though, nationalism has often been understood in more active terms, with a premium placed on physical endurance and the capacity to forge the nation through warfare.

Many commentators adopt a moral understanding of civilization to suggest that a state of war represents a descent into barbarism; yet because such a view does not consider the productive capacities of controlled violence as veritable *techniques of civilization*, this analysis is not very satisfactory. What Michel Foucault says about the many manifestations and functions of "power" can be applied to the no less provocative issues of violence and pain: from the perspectives of many elites, the blatantly *negative* effects of combat (death, dismemberment, trauma, disease, malnutrition) were worth risking in order to benefit from the many *productive* uses to which preparations for war could be pressed. The historian Alain Ehrenberg sees no tension between the "docile bodies" created through often strenuous and restrictive pedagogic disciplines and the freedom of the individual so vocally promoted since the eighteenth century. This is what Foucault referred to as the military dream of the perfect society: "its fundamental reference was not to the state of nature, but to the meticulously subordinated cogs of a machine, not to the primal social contract, but to permanent coercions, not to fundamental rights, but to indefinitely progressive forms of training, not to the general will but to automatic docility."[23] As

Ehrenberg explains, this military dream "represents the will to create a con-crete economy of individual liberty in which the autonomy of each person constitutes the measure of his obedience."[24]

Conceiving of war as a large-scale duel, as Clausewitz did, highlights the ways in which concepts of male honor and personal boundaries could be subsumed into emerging ideas about the nation. Described in increasingly organic terms since the eighteenth century, the nation-state was not approached as a simple geographical or administrative unity. Rather, the nation was often described as a living being whose growth was intimately bound up with the physical and moral identities of its citizenry. It was at once an "imagined community" that allowed strangers to acknowledge a common identity, and a cultural and geopolitical macrocosm that (ideally) reproduced itself imaginatively in the microcosm of the person. This convergence of the personal and the national presupposed a psychosomatic integration of the male into the social whole, the creation of "an entirely new self" whose personal boundaries might be exper-ienced as coextensive with national boundaries, as Johann Gottlieb Fichte proposed in his *Addresses to the German Nation* (1808).[25] In this way the nation would ideally become a community so intensely "imagined" that assaults upon it would reverberate in the bodies and minds of those who sought to actualize it. The numerous duels fought for patriotic reasons throughout the nineteenth century suggest that affronts to the body politic were often exper-ienced as virtual infringements of a man's private body. In this way national dishonor could be tantamount to a personal affront and shame.[26] By the early twentieth century this psychosomatic identification with the nation had become so urgent that F.T. Marinetti could even claim that "To deny the fatherland is the same as to isolate, castrate, shrink, denigrate or kill yourself."[27]

Overtly corporeal images of the nation were reinforced by the plethora of medical terms that were used to describe it. Since the late seventeenth cen-tury, illnesses of the private body had been considered to impact dangerously upon the health and vitality of the body politic, so that the very term "consti-tution" referred at once to the legal and corporeal state of the nation. Imagined as an island fortress that needed to be protected from the contaminating influence of foreign customs, Britain was represented in much the same way as the male bodies that inhabited and defended it: as a fragile entity whose borders required reinforcement through practices of austerity.[28] Similarly, the rigorous working of male bodies seemed to sharpen the boundaries of the nation, not least because it entailed (at least theoretically) the elimination of "soft" and "corrupting" habits so often associated with the influence of foreign cultures. In this way, the strengthening of a sense of "Englishness" was facilitated through the rejection of French customs and commodities, not only in the protectionist terms of trade but on the level of the desires that stimulated that trade in the first place. Yet England's tension with other cultures was often manifested in military terms that also reinforced a sense of common identity. Being at war at various points throughout the eighteenth century, and culminating in wars with France during the revolutionary and Napoleonic eras, it was as if British national identity had been forged in the heat of battle. As Linda Colley suggests, Britain is a culture that is "used to fighting and has largely defined itself through fighting."[29]

The British case is hardly unique. Warfare has been a central means through which many nations have consolidated themselves in the modern era, and under such circumstances the need to remake male bodies became especially urgent.[30] The rigorous military drill that formed European armies during the early modern era was an important technique for the nation-building projects of the late eighteenth century. By adapting ancient military practices to the peculiar demands of gunpowder weapons, in the late fifteenth century Prince Maurice of Orange developed training methods that instilled in soldiers the ability to perform, upon command, stylized movements efficiently and simultaneously. With constant repetition these movements became almost automatic, and produced infantrymen who could march together, load, aim and fire their weapons more efficiently than before. The manual that Prince Maurice published on the topic, with illustrated plates to demonstrate each motion appeared in 1607 and was translated into other European languages throughout the century (Figure 5.2). In addition to mechanizing the movements of the body, this method of training soldiers is a key example of what William H. McNeill calls "muscular bonding," or the "euphoric fellow feeling that prolonged and rhythmic muscular movement" induces through such collective activities as dancing, calisthenics and marching in time. A loss of personal boundaries and feeling part of the group are among the most frequently cited perceptions reported by those participating in these activities. Whether or not one accepts McNeill's transhistorical claim for the "primal" nature of these experiences, it is easy to see how muscular bonding functioned as a key technique for the substantialization of the nation. Through such practices an *esprit de corps* was cultivated among men from different social backgrounds whose devotion to their fellows allowed them to eagerly defend their nations on the field of battle.[31] This reduction of men of different backgrounds to a shared maleness is evidence of the "deep, horizontal comradeship" that is central to most conceptions of the nation.[32] When combined with the representational work of creating a nationalistic culture based on collective symbols, images and texts, military training was integral to the process of masculinization as a concomitant of nation-building, a method of creating people who would both embody and serve the interests of the state. The well-trained body is an example of what Ana María Alonso describes as "the fusion of the ideological and the sensory, the bodily and the normative, the emotional and the instrumental, the organic and the social, accomplished by

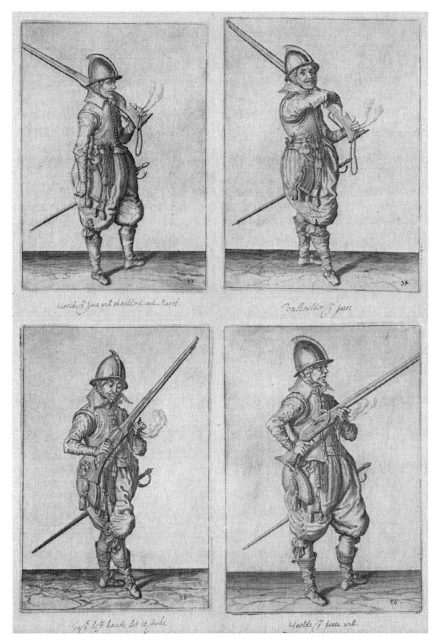

Figure 5.2 Jacob de Gheyn, *The exercise of armes for caliures, muskettes, and pikes after the ordre of his Excellence* (Amsterdam: Hage, 1608), plates 33–36. By permission of the Folger Shakespeare Library.

these tropes and particularly evident in strategies of substantialization by which the obligatory is converted into the desirable."[33]

If military training aimed at constructing bodies whose movements could be shaped, calculated, coordinated and deployed at will, its success varied according to the quality of the raw materials at hand. As we have seen, stories abounded of the remarkable strength and endurance of common sailors and soldiers, but this had not always been the case. British military setbacks in the early days of the Seven Years War (1756–63) generated considerable anxieties about how the country's expanding commercial culture had weakened its fighting men.[34] Around the same time Rousseau expressed similar comments about the French army being corrupted by men who were unaccustomed to hardship: "With what courage ... can it be thought that hunger and thirst, fatigues, dangers, and death, can be faced by men whom the smallest want overwhelms and the slightest difficulty repels? With what resolution can soldiers support the excessive toils of war, when they are entirely unaccustomed to them?"[35] If comfort had once suggested the capacity to make one strong (*con-fortis*), measured doses of *discomfort* were increasingly prescribed in the midst of the consumer revolution. It was only through rigorous hardening practices that men who were morally and physically slack (*lâche*) might be prevented from becoming cowards (*lâches*) when the nation needed them most. This was precisely what military and, as we will see, gymnastic training promised to deliver. Removed from comfortable lives and thrust into harsh conditions, hitherto soft males might be hardened through physical ordeals that taught them how to conquer fear and pain as well as to inflict violence upon others. The military uniform played an important role in the formation of military masculinities. In addition to enforcing a certain bodily shape, it performed the same negation of ostentation and indulgence that the three-piece suit was meant to signify in civilian life. "By presenting a blank surface," explains Daniel Purdy, "uniforms drew attention to the operations performed below the first level of sartorial signification. Muscular stature, athletic performance, and practiced execution were foregrounded by the refusal to locate identity on the level of garments."[36] Finally, just as the duel implied an equality of status and manhood for its participants, so the field of battle performed a similarly equalizing and masculinizing function: here too men fought together as men, and thus partook in a kind of transcendent brotherhood regardless of which side they supported. Nation-building and man-building were coextensive processes, and the rigorous and even painful working of the body was the cement of each.

The case of France at the end of the eighteenth century illustrates many of these developments. There the problems of civilization were so thoroughly identified with the corruption of the *Ancien régime* that the latter's eradication could be imagined as, among other things, a step towards a brave new world for men who had become weakened by despotism, luxury and idleness. In France as elsewhere, the problems of modern society were not to be solved by a return to the primitive, but through the selective incorporation of "savage"

Figure 5.3 Jacques-Louis Pérée, *L'homme régénéré* (1795). Bibliothèque Nationale de France.

elements that would consolidate a new social order. Shifting from meanings that were narrowly theological (rebirth through baptism and resurrection) or medical (the regrowth of tissue), the concept of "regeneration" expanded throughout the course of the eighteenth century to encompass all manner of "rebirth," moral, physical and political. The modern French nation was crafted juridically through the revolutionary extension of rights to all men; yet this was also accomplished palpably through the call for men of all classes to take up arms in defense of the nation.[37] If, as Rousseau had alleged, aristocratic women threatened to turn men into women through the teaching of refined manners, then the revolution logically represented a remasculinization of French manhood. This corporealization of the nation required bodies of a particular type: removed from comfort and subjected to effort and pain, they were molded into shape and accustomed to perform arduous new tasks through rigorous (albeit hasty) training. Such bodies were understood as being part and parcel of the "new man" inaugurated by the revolution itself, one who had been regenerated morally, physically and politically (Figure 5.3).

Given the contempt that was often heaped upon the impotent, bloated and luxury-ridden bodies of the aristocracy and the king, revolutionaries understandably turned to classical images for examples of how the ideal male should look and act. The neoclassical paintings of Jacques-Louis David in the years just preceding the revolution represented men as classical heroes, muscular, upright and heroic. Free of any softness or sentiment, their muscularity attested to lives of action and war. These bodies were moreover highly individuated, with strict and rigid boundaries suggesting enclosure and impermeability, thus perhaps approximating the boundaries of an emphatically masculinized body politic. Finally, the impermeable nature of these bodies was "proven" through their stoical endurance of pain and punishment, precisely what the previous French elites had been thought incapable of doing.[38] What was inscribed on the canvas was thought to be possible in the flesh. As the mayor of Paris, Jérôme Pétion, prophesied in 1789, "the men of the free nation will be physically larger, more handsome, more courageous; morally they will be more virtuous and better." In keeping with the Janus-faced nature of nations, such corporeal regeneration represented at once a utopian dream for the future and a return to the idealized uncorrupted Gauls or Franks, thus fusing with the bodies of revolutionary men the glory of the ancestors and the freedoms of a perfected political order. Destroying the Old Regime was more than the fact of the overthrow of a corrupt political system, it also represented, in the name of a new society, the transcendence of many of the excesses of civilization itself. As Jean-Joseph Pithou enthused:

> Frenchmen, you have reconquered your liberty, that liberty of which the first Franks, your ancestors, were jealous; you will again become like them,

strong and healthy, like them you will let your beard grow, and you will wear the long hair that they favored. Goodbye hairdressers, beauticians and merchants of fashion, now you will cover yourselves with cotton or home-spun. From now on you will scorn all the ornaments of luxury, and you will make use of all your physical and intellectual faculties.[39]

What, if any, concrete effect did these robust symbols have on the actual bodies of men, especially those whose muscles didn't magically begin bulging after the fall of the Bastille or the execution of the king?[40] Some looked to Rousseau for a solution, claiming that, under a proper republican government, young boys would ideally be bathed twice a day in icy water while older ones would include swimming among their daily physical exercises. After all, it was claimed, since practices like these had helped Sparta to defeat the "effeminate Asiatics," in republican France they would surely forge men with "souls of steel, in bodies of iron."[41] Others argued that classical sculpture faithfully conveyed a lost bodily reality that present-day men could approach by radically reforming their own lifestyles. Facilitated through selective breeding and a rigorous hygienic regimen, the regeneration of France was as much a physical ideal as it was a moral program. With an awe-inspiring name that might be equally at home on the cover of a bodybuilding guru's latest tome, Dr L.-J.M. Robert proposed what he called "mega-anthropogenesis" as a process aimed at producing great men cut in the classical style.[42] The military meaning of such impressive bodies if anything increased with the ascendance of Napoleon and his empire. When traditional military discipline was reinstated during the Napoleonic era, the drill was at once a process of training the body to respond to external orders and a means of internalizing those orders. The effects of such training for the embodiment of the nation would be profound, both in material bodies and in their representations. "The body is no longer leased to the state," Norman Bryson suggests, "it *is* the state; the state emerges as a new kind of biopolitical entity, and by virtue of gender the male body belongs to the state, as state property. Hence the need to glorify that body: In post-Revolutionary France the state is no longer figured in the king, but in the male body itself, and the body's destiny for glory or defeat is that of the nation as a whole."[43]

What was true of French nationalist symbolism may also be observed in central European states, where conquest and annexation by Napoleon's army inspired the re-creation of Germanic manhood along military-nationalist lines. In Prussia the humiliating defeats of 1806–07 inspired a nationalist movement that asked hard questions about the physical and moral qualities of its men. Along with most countries in the eighteenth century, the German states too deplored the sheltered and sedentary lives of noble and middle-class men, and made it clear that this emasculation was legible in their weak bodies and frazzled nerves. When Christian Meiners had praised the superiority of the Germanic people above all others, like most of his peers he wasn't thinking of the well-fed and lazy weaklings he observed all around him; rather he had in mind men and women from earlier times. Coupled with a lack of physical exercise, culinary and sexual excess had resulted in the physical degeneration of the once powerful Germanic warrior, a decline that Meiners thought could be reversed only through vigorous military training.[44]

Regardless of these concerns, few German reformers of the period actually promoted martial behavior as the model of proper masculinity. Even when military exercises were incorporated into gymnastics, martial prowess was not the main concern: as middle-class reformers noted throughout the early nineteenth century, the recommended sphere for the well-built man was civilian rather than military, with individual self-cultivation or *Bildung* often cited as the chief educative aim. Reformers nevertheless insisted that the fullest understanding of self-cultivation had to include a physical component.[45] Identifying civilian life as the proper aim of male physical development was a contentious issue for ardent nationalists. In Prussia some military reformers sought a means of reconciling military service with bourgeois trepidation. Acknowledging that middle-class men were, by and large, reluctant (if not physically unable) to serve in the military, these officers recommended allowing members of the "more genteel classes" to hire replacements instead of forcing them to submit to compulsory conscription. Not only would this quell potential unrest among these groups, they argued, but it would allow burghers to demonstrate their love of country while permitting the army to gain more robust and able-bodied recruits, presumably from the lower orders. This proposal was nevertheless shot down by others on the reform commission, for whom personal duty to one's county was a paramount concern, as were the presumed benefits of military service for "commercial and academic classes" who tend to manifest "unwarlike and cowardly" attitudes.[46]

Military reformers and nation-builders wanted to infuse this civic definition of masculinity with martial values. Enacted in 1813, just as the Prussian army was preparing to expel the French, the law for compulsory military service performed the function of gender therapy for burghers who were distanced from a warrior lifestyle. Like the patriotism that enlistment in the army was supposed to reflect and create, ultimately the manliness of elites had to be forcibly crafted. As a technique of man-building, the forceful working of the body prepared the individual for his part in the collective experience of the nation. Locally this took place through the muscular bonding of troops through drill, but in terms of nationalist discourses drill was meant to bring about in the male a physical condition approximating that of the nation's ancestors, thus revealing a bodily continuity with the past that would revitalize the nation's present and prepare it for the future.

A century before the Futurists provocatively dubbed war "the world's only hygiene," compulsory military service in Prussia was proudly celebrated as a form of regeneration through violence.[47] Prussian reformers, like their counterparts in France and Britain, believed that comfort and luxury counted among the main enemies of the fit soldierly body. "Hence, the noble-minded man will be active and effective," explained Fichte, "and will sacrifice himself for his people." Fichte added that

> Life merely as such, the mere continuance of changing existence, has in any case never had any value for him, he has wished for it only as the source of what is permanent. But this permanence is promised to him only by the continuous and independent existence of his nation. In order to save his nation he must be ready even to die that it may live, and that he may live in it the only life for which he has ever wished.[48]

Compelling all men to submit to military training and to face the prospect of combat would have considerable and long-lasting effects. "In this way," declared the propagandist Ernst Moritz Arndt, "we'll produce a handsome, strong, and magnificent sex, protected from effeteness and lasciviousness by the ultimate appeal of manliness."[49]

Military training and combat were conceived as hygienic measures for the nation as whole, especially a nation engaged with a modern culture of commerce and consumption. However much Clausewitz would later insist that warfare was a tool of state policy, he too agreed that it was also a method of gender hygiene for advanced nations. "By it alone," he claimed, "can that effeminacy of feeling be counteracted, that propensity to seek for the enjoyment of comfort, which cause degeneracy in a people rising in prosperity and immersed in an extremely busy commerce."[50] For many men the daunting prospect of universal conscription was sweetened by the creation of a national cult of heroism: whereas the ancient myth of the "death for the fatherland" had valorized only fallen nobles, now every man of military age was deemed qualified to sacrifice himself for the country and, if necessary, to die in its name. In addition to the introduction of the Iron Cross, a badge of honor which allowed commoners to be rewarded for their service, militant Prussians promoted the cult of heroism through widely circulated monuments, songs and poems. The construction of the nation and the regeneration of bodies thus went hand-in-hand as part of what George Mosse has called the "militarization of masculinity."[51]

Comfort, pleasure, domestic ties and even life itself were things that had to be sacrificed for the sake of the nation. Moreover, if the threat of armed conflict were to remain permanent, some argued, so too would the physical and moral readiness of the nation's men. Just as combat could function as a form of therapy for softened bodies and flagging resolve, its transformative potential also made it a rite of passage, as much for adolescents entering adulthood as for ethnic minorities seeking membership in the nation. The history of European Jews provides a useful case in point. In France inquiries into the Jewish question had been made just before the revolution, and even the most well-meaning observers concluded that Jewish men needed to reform themselves in order to be accepted into the national body of men. In the late 1780s the Abbé Henri Grégoire famously observed how an outer layer of "burlesque traditions," "physical degradation," and "odious practices" distracted most people from the shared qualities that qualified the Jews as members of the "universal family" of humanity. By improving their weak bodies and "effeminate temperaments," Grégoire proposed, Jews could be completely assimilated into the nation, which he implicitly cast as a strong and masculine entity.[52] Bellicosity and physical robustness were thus cherished as potentially transformative qualities that created the conditions under which men could engage with each other on an equal footing that promised to render differences of race, ethnicity and class irrelevant. Just as wealthy Russian commoners valued the duel as a means of affirming their ability to mix with the aristocracy, so too did Jewish men insist upon their right to duel and to serve in the military. These were strenuous and violent examples of what Grégoire termed "regeneration."

  Thus when Napoleon introduced his so-called "Infamous Decrees" in 1808, he insisted that all Jews conscripted into the army had to perform military service themselves. Jews were not allowed to hire replacements as wealthy non-Jews could do. However inequitable this double standard was, arguably the emperor felt he was furthering the regeneration of the Jews through mandatory schooling in physical toughness and male codes of civility. Moreover this was very much in keeping with the Jewish enlightenment project known as the Haskalah, where assimilationist Jews agreed that adopting the robust warrior ways of Gentiles was an indispensable step toward full membership in the nation (even though Gentiles too fell short in these areas).[53] In German-speaking countries many Jews valued military service for precisely these reasons: it was what Ute Frevert calls a "ritual masculinizing" that affected Jew and Gentile alike.[54] Nevertheless, in Prussia the presumed unfitness of the Jew for military service was often taken for granted, and treated as a hereditary defect that no amount of military training could overcome. For some the alleged shortcomings of the Jew's body were at the heart of the problem. Johann David Michaelis, for example, had insisted in 1783 that Jews as a race were much too short to meet the standard height of European soldiers (5 feet, 2 inches).[55] Despite the fact that many Jews were conscripted and acted bravely in the wars of liberation, the assumption of Jewish effeminacy persisted in military circles, and after the French were expelled many

Prussian Jews were ousted from their civil service jobs and banned from the armed forces. According to the Jewish writer Gabriel Riesser, among Jews during the 1830s an accusation of effeminacy represented the "most defamatory of all slurs" that could be answered only with a challenge to a duel. When more liberal political currents caused Prussia to reinstate mass conscription in 1845, Jewish enlistment was encouraged because it might improve their physical prowess, foster a sense of patriotism and prompt them to convert to Christianity.[56]

If Jewish men were charged with effeminacy due to their close association with civilized practices, black masculinity has been historically positioned between the poles of cowardice and savagery, both of which have been cited in order to disqualify African men from equality with white men. African slaves in colonial America were widely viewed as being naturally cowardly and docile, despite ample evidence to the contrary in the form of rebellions and enlistment on both sides in the war of independence.[57] The Civil War offered another opportunity for black men to take their place alongside whites as brothers in arms, and perhaps in society at large. In fact, many black men were convinced that their service would finally qualify them as "men" in a way that put them on equal footing with whites. Around 186,000 black men were recruited by both sides of the conflict, often with promises of equal pay and better treatment, but the equality they anticipated never materialized.[58]

Within this Janus-faced nation, a product of the developmental and forward-looking outlook of the eighteenth and nineteenth centuries, which nevertheless keeps its gaze fixed upon its mythical past and the kinds of men and women who supposedly thrived there, nationalism may be seen as a quintessentially modern phenomenon. This temporal tension is deeply gendered, with women usually situated on the side of ancient, even atavistic elements of the nation: even when they become engaged with modern developments, women continued to be associated with what McClintock calls the nation's "conservative principle of continuity."[59] Yet a look at the corporeal requirements for nationalism suggests that middle-class men were not as securely located on the side of "forward-thrusting, potent and historic" elements of national progress as might be assumed. Given the importance of the military to nationalist representations, in order to be effective agents of the nation men were repeatedly implored to draw upon bodily habits and experiences more closely associated with the past than with the soft conditions of contemporary society. Of course, none of this disrupted the broader hegemony of white, middle-class/aristocratic men over women, proletarians and ethnic/racial others. Rather, by laying down these state-sponsored rules for able-bodied manhood, the militarization of citizenship placed demands upon men's bodies in times of peace as well as war. The bodies most recommended for national service would thus need to be composed of a balance of modern and pre-modern elements, and, in order to be proper citizen-soldiers, men had to retain this hybrid nature in peacetime as well as at times of war. As the urgency of the military-national project increased towards the end of the nineteenth century, so too did the practical difficulties of living up to this almost impossible ideal.

CIVILIZATION'S CURE?

The risks, rigors, and deprivations of wartime promised to keep male bodies in fighting trim, but how was one to craft and sustain men capable of switching efficiently from civilian peacetime activities to the more demanding regimen of military service in times of crisis? Businessmen and professionals may have enjoyed describing their world as combative and brutal and some may have fancied themselves "warriors," but their bodies told a different story. In fact, not even soldiers could be counted upon to remain active and fit in peacetime; they too had to be monitored closely lest they lapse into indolence and vice.[60] Whether manifested in gymnastic regimens or team sports, compulsory physical exercise offered experiences of violence, discomfort and pain that might prevent men from becoming slack in peacetime. Far from being considered degrading to male elites, such exercises functioned as yet another form of hygiene, an armoring prophylaxis against the conditions of the modern world and an important means of nation-building.

Around the turn of the nineteenth century rigorous physical reform was widely recommended as an antidote to the sedentary lifestyles of elites and the myriad of diseases perceived to be the outcome of civilization. An especially influential method of exercise, developed primarily as a means of negotiating the perceived tension between elemental masculinity and the problems of modern life, came from Sweden, which, like other nations, felt the existence of a gulf between its ancient warrior heritage and the less glamorous realities of civilized society. As early as 1794 the Swedish economist Johan Fischerström bemoaned, in an address to the Royal Academy of Science, the decline of Swedish manhood due to the twin scourges of excessive luxury and a lack of physical exercise. The soft men of his day, he declared, were pale reflections of the men of old, whose hardened bodies would scarcely succumb to such modern softness.[61] The earnest implementation of reforms, however, would have to wait several years. By the early nineteenth century, the growing bureaucratization of economic and political life was bringing considerable change, offering some benefits while closing off other avenues of personal satisfaction. As we have seen in other parts of Europe, these changes promoted interest in an idealized warrior past – in Sweden this took the form of "gothianism," a nationalistic celebration of the country's Viking heritage that was accompanied by the denigration of the luxurious, refined and superficial "civilization" of southern Europe. Before launching his unique brand of gymnastic exercises in the early nineteenth century, Per Henrik Ling had written poetry celebrating this warrior ideal, which he came to believe was necessary to the creation of a world in which the raw strength of the Vikings would be regained through exercise, yet shaped and held in check by the bourgeois values of obedience and discipline. Ling gymnastics were promoted in Swedish schools until the mid-twentieth century, and adopted throughout the nineteenth century in other countries as well.[62]

In Germany, J.F.C. Gutsmuth's *Gymnastik für die Jugend* (1793) provided another important basis for the future practice of physical exercise. Harking back to classical aesthetic ideals, like those celebrated by Winckelmann, Gutsmuth promoted exercises that would develop strength and health as well as beauty. Concerned less with bellicosity and the martial side of chivalry, he instead recommended adjusting chivalric ideals to the requirements of middle-class culture. Hence compassion and integrity played more important roles than military training in his writings, a tendency that would have surely appealed to many members of the *Bürgertum*. However a firmer connection between gymnastic exercise and military training was made by Friedrich Ludwig Jahn, whose ideas were well-received amid the nationalist sentiments inspired by the Napoleonic wars. Jahn too connected gymnastics, or *Turner*, with German medieval knights, whom he claimed employed terms like *Turnen* and *Turnieren* for the tournaments that brought fellow knights together in competition. Thanks to Jahn's efforts, gymnastic exercises were integrated into the newly-reformed Prussian school system as part of an attempt to create more patriotic boys, and were fully incorporated into the military training that had become mandatory for men of all classes.[63]

The use of gymnastics as a means of recreating warrior masculinity in opposition to the conditions of civilization was reinforced by spatially distancing the body-in-training from the noxious influences of the city. Thus rural rather than urban locations have been most often presented as ideal sites for crafting athletic and military bodies. Rather than the enclosed indoor gymnasiums, fencing halls and ball courts of the early-modern nobility, reformers like Gutsmuth and Jahn recommended exercises that would be performed outdoors, often while wearing casual and loose clothing that flouted the prim and proper codes of noble dress. This process bound the concept of bodily "freedom" to physical (and psychological) distance from urban life, thereby cultivating a more direct experience of "nature."[64] The forging of the athletic and military body in a rural environment instituted an enduring connection between soldiers and the countryside and established an essentially rural image of the land for which they fought or in which they adventured. We see this in the iconography of the British empire and nineteenth-century representations of the "homeland," as well as in the poetic imagery of the First World War. In countless modern representations of the military, it is the countryside that is depicted as the soldier's natural home, reflecting the essential process of becoming a soldier; extensive work on the body (often in country locales) tantamount to the stripping away of layer after layer of civilian habits, many of which would have been acquired through the less physically demanding lifestyles of the city.[65] From this perspective only a hard life in the country – or the creation of its simulacrum – could create the kind of men needed to defend a national homeland constructed around largely rural imagery. In both military training and gymnastics male bodies did not need only to be subjected to greater discipline and challenges, they also needed to be resituated spatially if they were to embody nature and nation.

Despite these early attempts to build men along with the nation, the nationalist drive was experienced by many Western countries later in the century. Prussian authorities may have sought to redeem the flagging robustness of middle-class men, but after 1815 nationalistic militarism was considered unnecessary in civilian conceptions of manhood. Of course, men needed to be ready to defend the fatherland in the event of a crisis, but until the 1870s domesticity and sensibility were cited as the principal civilian male virtues.[66] This is explicit in Johann Jacob Sachs's 1830 description of the purpose of male fitness: "The male body expresses positive strength ... sharpening male understanding and independence and equipping men for life in government, in the arts and sciences."[67]

Gymnastics, however, grew in respectability over the coming decades, and its practice was increasingly shifted from the open air to newly-built enclosed gymnasiums, thus moving away from the models established by Gutsmuth and Jahn. In cities including Berlin, Stuttgart and Hamburg, gymnastics evolved toward greater emphasis on rational control, moderation and self-restraint, increasing their appeal to a largely bourgeois clientele. Developed by Adolf Spiess in the 1840s, and later altered by Otto Heinrich Jäger, so-called "free and order" exercises were practiced without apparatus and in groups, usually in response to a leader's commands. The body was to be trained and strengthened, not for the purposes of stunts, acrobatics or other vulgar displays, but to cultivate willpower and promote moderation in the appetites and emotions. Although sedentary work left merchants and educated men prey to physical and emotional weaknesses, raw muscular force was frowned upon as coarse and "craftsmanlike," as something that connoted a loss of control that, for many, called to mind the revolutionary events of 1848/49. Moderate gymnastics aimed at producing a dignified and strong middle-class body that was as distinct from the effete nobility as it was from the coarse proletariat.[68] The resurgence of interest in Jahn's gymnastics at the end of the century represented a backlash against the negligible effects of such moderate attempts to reform bourgeois bodies.

If gymnastic exercises had a somewhat limited impact upon the bodies of elites on the European continent, in Britain athletics were at times avidly pursued by young men determined to overcome the negative effects of brain-work on sedentary bodies. At Cambridge University undergraduates preparing for the grueling mathematics exam known as the "Tripos" regularly sought exercise as a means of strengthening their constitutions for prolonged and intense periods of study. After 1815, and before competitive games had become a main-stay of English public schools, rowing, running and long-distance walking were embraced as just the sort of strenuous activities the "hard-reading" man needed to test the limits of his physical capacity. This coupling of mental and physical training remained integral to shaping the ideal manly character at Cambridge for decades – until the end of the century when performance in sport became a more persuasive index of masculinity than academic success.[69] Despite the dis-similarities between this hygienic program and the aggressively anti-intellectual team sports that would come to dominate British educational culture, these approaches share a distrust of study without a corresponding increase in cor-poreal exercise and endurance. In each instance the rigorous working of the body is seen to be essential for building the masculinity of the student.

This same anxiety was evinced in the early days of the public school move-ment. English fathers were concerned about the softening effects of domestic comforts and maternal influences upon growing boys, and sought to have them educated in environments that would toughen them up for the increas-ingly immoral and cruel realities of public life. As all-male environments enforcing a physical distance from women, boarding schools were favorably looked upon as builders of toughness and endurance: not only were most utterly lacking in the basic comforts of home, even to the point of being dan-gerous to health, but they were places where cruel treatment at the hands of students and teachers alike was considered commonplace.[70] To be sure, the Evangelical ideals of "godliness and good manners" were officially touted as the main benefits of a public school education; yet many parents appreciated the extent to which their sons would be plunged into a harsh, but ultimately edifying, world. Before the advent of organized and compulsory team sports, physical toughness was instilled negatively through the removal of most ordinary comforts while continuing to promote manners and education. More "positive" means of character-building would proliferate from the 1850s onward as team sports became compulsory features of public school life and the style of manhood crafted therein. It's not surprising that, as exam scores fell towards the end of the nineteenth century, many advocates of competitive sport would praise its potential for training males for war.[71]

* * *

If the rhetoric of martial and athletic man-building emphasized the ways in which their techniques developed and harnessed all that was "natural" about manhood, the constructed qualities of such bodies remained hard to deny. Foucault reminds us that, contrary to earlier periods when a soldierly bearing reflected the nobleman's "bodily rhetoric of honor," by the end of the eighteenth century

> the soldier has become something that can be made; out of a formless clay, an inapt body, the machine required can be constructed; posture is gradually corrected; a calculated constraint runs slowly through each part of the body, mastering it, making it pliable, ready at all times, turning silently into the automatism of habit.[72]

What connects these various practices is the common endorsement of strenuous effort and discomfort, if not outright pain, as methods of hardening the bodies of noble and bourgeois males. In the masculinist discourses of national greatness, pain and violence were (and continue to be) prescribed as a form of therapy, a means of constructing and reinforcing boundaries around the self while affirming commonalities among men who submit to the rigors of combat, training or exercise. Dueling, warfare and sport thus not only reinforced distinctions between men and women; rather they were also important means of distinguishing between different kinds of men. What also emerges from these developments is a new emphasis upon the military fitness of men as an index of the vitality of the nation, the kind of measurement that would abound in early anthropological accounts of national strength and weakness. The anthropologist Paul Broca was just one of many who argued that, because "the man who is fit for service is also fit for peacetime works," military aptitude provides a sense of the productive capacities of a nation.[73] By the end of the nineteenth century, as the following chapter demonstrates, most Western countries expressed further doubts about the fitness of their men, and the need for still more concerted efforts to alter their bodies.

Part Three

The Twentieth Century and Beyond

6
Modern Primitives: Manhood and Metamorphosis around 1900

"To be a man just once before death" was one of Henri-Frédéric Amiel's fondest hopes. This quote from Rousseau appears frequently in Amiel's twelve-volume *Journal intime*, which records in painful detail just how much this dream eluded him. For instance, in a typical entry from 1869, the forty-eight-year-old Swiss philosopher berates himself for his aversion to wild animals: "A man should be more brutal and coarse than that ... A man should know how to eviscerate and kill ... What you lack is a bit of ferocity; having neither gone hunting nor camping, you are decidedly too soft; you are too much of a woman." Distressed by his own effeminacy, the bookish Amiel sought the advice of a friend about how to improve his sorry state. Amiel fully concurred with the counsel he received: "I should make my delicateness, my character and my style a bit more *brutal*, dip my feet in the river Styx for a little while, that is to say to *masculinize* myself, and to virilize myself ... to become someone and something."[1] Although Amiel probably never did anything of the sort, he shared with many men the feeling that the path toward remasculinization led away from the comforts and conveniences of the city toward more dangerous locales where death lurked at every step.

Previous chapters have demonstrated how this belief in the hygienic and therapeutic value of pain, violence and hardship has functioned in the West as a method of preserving men from the conditions of a civilized existence that, if left unchecked, threatened to render them soft, cowardly and effeminate. Of course the prescribed dose of primitivity needed to "inoculate" men against modern softness has varied considerably since the eighteenth century, and in some periods the emphasis on instilling more "civilized" habits into middle-class boys and men has taken precedence over competing calls for austerity. This was especially true during the first few decades of the nineteenth century, when an ascendant middle class sought to distance itself from corrupt nobles above and "bestial" proletarians below. Along with "godliness and good manners," education and commercial acumen were hallmarks of the civic definition of manhood that was touted in many countries during these decades. This vision of masculinity enjoyed considerable popularity among elites, but was never stable enough to ward off persistent claims that neglect of the body could be just as dangerous as neglect of the mind, perhaps even more so when the defense of the nation was at stake. By the last quarter of the nineteenth century, the virtues of adopting a harder, coarser approach to life would be emphasized across the Western world.[2]

This chapter examines three different but interconnected metamorphoses that impacted directly upon the male body from the late nineteenth century through the 1920s. First, it considers the complementary discourses of evolutionary progress and physical degeneration that marked social and medical thinking in the second half of the nineteenth century. Despite the self-congratulatory rhetoric that characterized much Social Darwinist thinking, the supposedly superior white male body that emerged through the process of becoming civilized was a particularly vulnerable entity. Second, this discussion is illuminated by an examination of changes taking place in the social composition of the middle class itself, which from mid-century onward swelled with men and women from more modest origins laying claim to bourgeois status and privileges. Edifying tales of rags-to-riches financial transformations were undermined by the starker realities of the emerging corporate world, which rewarded some while relegating many others to the realm of perpetual clerkdom. As we will see, consumption and fashion provided social climbers with essential props and costumes for the successful performance (or even parody) of the respectable gentleman, and thus of acceptable images of masculinity. Finally, this chapter examines the attempts made in various countries to counter the prospects of negative metamorphosis by promoting a whole-hearted engagement with the "primitive," a loaded concept that promised to many worried groups a means of overcoming modernity's impact upon bodies and minds.

EVOLUTION AND DEGENERATION

Metamorphosis is at the heart of evolutionary biology, and one result of the work of Charles Darwin and his champions was to set many of the hitherto "stable" bases of human nature more or less into motion – though toward *what* exactly remained a mystery. Although some feminist and egalitarian thinkers were able to use Darwinist ideas to advance their schemes, evolutionary thought was more generally used by men to promote patriarchal and racist agendas.[3] After all, the values and institutions that Darwin saw as integral to "civilization" included reason, self-control, morality, marriage, monogamy and domesticity (and, implicitly, heterosexuality). Evolutionary ideas also appealed to sexologists from Richard von Krafft-Ebing and Havelock Ellis to

Sigmund Freud, who tried to accommodate the relatively genderless humanity that dominated Darwinian theory to the sexual dimorphism that had been a predominant assumption of medical science since the Enlightenment. Evolutionary biology allowed sexologists to theorize the development of sex in terms of an ever-widening gap between men and women, a "natural" process that was theoretically tantamount to a long-term "virilization" of the Western world. As women became more "womanly," it was suggested, men would necessarily become more obviously masculine in body and mind. Along with heterosexuality, sexual differentiation was thought to march in step with civilization and could be viewed as a mark of progress. In contrast, "primitive" peoples were often viewed as less sexually differentiated and thus lower on the evolutionary ladder.[4]

Physical anthropology and the other sciences that have informed and reinforced evolutionary arguments have devoted much attention to measuring the material facts of human life and less to consideration of social and cultural factors. Many of the observations used to reinforce the superiority of white Westerners over black Africans were also employed as a means of distinguishing white men from white women, with the latter usually aligned with other "lower" human types. Craniology was a key area for these overlapping observations, and while some discussion of the virtues of the cephalic index (the ratio of skull length to skull breadth) took place, far more credence was given to the size and weight of the brain as a sure sign of intelligence.[5] Comparing skulls from the twelfth and nineteenth centuries, Paul Broca concluded that the cranial capacity of Parisians had increased considerably, thus seeming to prove a correlation between brain size and civilization. Nevertheless Broca was equally concerned with height and military fitness as evidence of national strength and prosperity, and thus promoted muscular development and dietary reform as important elements of education.[6] The description of women as more emotional, impulsive and weak-willed than men allowed them to be aligned with just about every counter-type to the white male mental ideal – which is why they were just as likely to be associated with children as with "savage" peoples both at home and abroad.

Studies such as these asserted the uniqueness and superiority of white men over women as well as men of other races and classes, thus positing Western civilization as the fruit of a "natural" evolutionary development. Obviously these brain-based indices of white male superiority had been formulated by white male scientists and embraced by middle-class professionals, men for whom employment, status and promotion in their respective fields depended upon cogitation and sociability far more than muscle power. For such men status and power were found in modern political institutions, social customs and mental pursuits. Evolutionary writers may have also encouraged the development of a man's strength, beauty and charm, but intellectual abilities were almost always foregrounded as the most striking differences between men and women, and between the West and "the rest."[7] Even the secondary sexual characteristic of facial hair, most notably an ample "philosopher's beard," was offered as tangible proof of the superior virility of elite white men.[8] For men whose lifestyles distanced them from manual labor and martial effort, what we might call "muscular intellectualness" offered an important, yet nevertheless unstable, way of affirming manhood.[9]

Arguing that "endurance," "courage," and "heroic struggles" are required for success in the world of ideas has proved an attractive strategy for many men, in particular for those whose lives actually involve little physical challenge.[10] But, despite the smug self-confidence that science seemed to confer upon white manhood, the muscular intellectualness that counted as "superiority" in some circles could just as easily be construed as a weakness in others. Physical strength remained an important factor, just as it had been in the eighteenth century; yet if eighteenth-century elites often fell short of this standard, were their Victorian counterparts any better off? Contemporary Western societies struck many people as "artificial" and as working against evolutionary processes towards biological and mental superiority and sexual dimorphism. Darwin himself warned that, because "highly civilized" nations had largely reduced the "struggle for existence" through welfare schemes that assisted the mentally and physically disadvantaged, the result might be a diminishment of the biological value of their populations.[11] Although Darwin defended such humanitarian interventions, proponents of eugenics accused welfare programs of encouraging the survival of the unfit, whose numbers seemed to be multiplying at an alarming rate around the turn of the century. Showing compassion for those who would otherwise have died off was further evidence that civilized people had lost both the capacity to suffer and to see others suffer, the consequence of which could be the decline of the nation and its defeat at the hands of more robust countries.

Welfare and charity schemes for the underfed and unemployed were just part of the problem, for there was also the matter of women increasingly demanding greater, if not necessarily equal rights. However modest and "familial" the claims of many feminists were during this period, the mere fact of women's seeking some measure of equality signaled a shift away from the strict sexual differentiation that was supposedly the mark of advanced societies. While the popular press responded with gender-bending caricatures of mannish women and effeminate men, even a relative feminist like Havelock Ellis observed that recent social tendencies towards sexual democratization risked minimizing the differences between men and women. If allowed to continue, Ellis suggested, this trend threatened to produce "masculine" women and return Western humanity to a "primitive" level.[12] When viewed in light of this devolutionary trajectory, it is easy to see how demands for women's rights could be imagined as exercising an impact upon male bodies similar to the medical version of "feminism," which referred to arrested development in males, just as feminist ideas were widely thought to "virilize" the women who held them.[13] Any alteration of the sexual status quo was understood as exercising a potentially detrimental impact on male bodies.

As we have seen, the idea that civilized societies breed moral and physical decline was not new, and the notion of "degeneration" has been around since ancient times. Traditional concepts of degeneration referred broadly to a diminishment over time of the morality, hardiness and manliness of society. Inherent in this largely social and cultural definition was the idea that civilization was an implicitly feminizing force that threatened to reduce men to the level of women in their dress, demeanor and behavior. The fear was always that advances in the material abundance and conveniences of civilization would lead to a gradual eradication of sexual differentiation and a diminution of physical and moral fitness. This received a biological rationale with the work of Bénédict Augustin Morel, who cited the interplay between environmental and hereditary factors in the etiology of mental illness, claiming that modern society made excessive demands on the nervous system. From Morel's Lamarckian (rather than Darwinian) standpoint, there was no clear distinction between innate and acquired characteristics.[14]

Degeneration was thus perceived as a pathological process through which unhealthy environmental factors produced offspring with a range of defects, from criminality and insanity to sexual perversions and sterility. Whether proletarian or bourgeois, it was city-dwellers on whom modern life had the greatest effect. Degenerate individuals, over-stimulated by the stresses and temptations of modern civilization, were considered less capable of controlling base impulses through the use of their "higher faculties," and were thus increasingly left slaves to their more "primitive" physical urges. Degeneration could effectively transform men into "women" or "savages," and women would become more mannish and dominant than their weakened male counterparts. It threatened Western society with a reversal of hierarchies of race, gender and class.[15]

If interpretations of evolutionary theory placed a premium on the steady progress and superiority of Western civilization, theories of degeneration plotted a very different trajectory. By the mid-nineteenth century, worries about the decreasing robustness of men received empirical support from a number of statistical surveys of the size and health of those recruited into the army. French experts lamented the declining height of recruits over the past 150 years as disturbing evidence of the physiological degeneration of Gallic manhood, with lack of exercise topping the list of contributory causes.[16] Similar worries plagued British physicians around the time of the Crimean War (1854–56), and with recruitment of men for the Boer War (1899–1902) more serious questions were raised about British manhood. Between 40 and 60 per cent of volunteers for the Boer War were rejected by the military as being physically unfit for service, a figure that would change little by the First World War.[17] Misgivings about the state of French and British men were exacerbated by the Prussian military victories of the 1860s and 1870s, triumphs that focused attention squarely on the link between nation-building and the creation of strong male bodies. What was the secret of this troubling Teutonic success? In Germany the educated middle class chalked military prowess up to the triumph of *Kultur* in their own ranks, and boasted that it was German schoolmasters who had really won these battles.[18] Others were less convinced, and emphasized instead the pivotal role played by physical education and military service in fostering both strong bodies and a sense of national solidarity.[19] Whatever the reason, the threat of further German triumphs loomed in the country's rising birth rate, which generated alarm in France and, to a lesser extent, Britain, where falling populations and anxieties about national decline elicited more demands for health reforms.

Degeneration discourses implied that the conditions of modern civilization created obstacles to the "natural" differentiation of the sexes that evolutionary theory promised. Through its very refinement, modernity seemed to promote a reversion to earlier stages of existence, whether through the narrowing gap between men and women or the physical debilities of elites. Although Darwin himself claimed that civilized men seem to be "physically stronger than savages," he also agreed that, among Westerners, bodily evolution was far less developed than intellectual and moral development.[20] Mental training that neglected the rest of the body was never viewed as a satisfactory condition, especially when the evolutionists' view of sexual difference seemed to be restricted to the brain. Many celebrated the superior intelligence of white men while bemoaning the fact that their bodies seemed to have gotten stuck on one of evolution's lower rungs. The founder of eugenics, Francis Galton, warned his readers about the "deleterious influences" that "modern civilisation" had upon the race, and thus urged greater attention to eugenic techniques for preserving society's health. Having had a nervous breakdown while studying at Cambridge, Galton had a first-hand appreciation of the consequences of overwork. "A powerful brain is an excellent thing," he conceded, "but it requires for its proper maintenance a good pair of lungs, a vigorous heart, and especially a strong stomach, otherwise its outcome of thought is likely to be morbid."[21] Galton also thought that raw muscle power had its uses, and in 1885 he even tried to measure it by setting up an Anthropometric Laboratory at the International Health Exhibition. Using a padded rod that, when punched, would measure the force of the blow delivered, Galton was disappointed at what he found. "It was a matter of surprise to myself, who was born in the days of pugilism, to find that the art of delivering a clean hit, straight from the shoulder, as required by this instrument, is nearly lost to the rising generation."[22]

Still, Galton was not known for his boxing, nor was his cousin Charles Darwin. The weaknesses of Darwin's own aging body exemplified both the boon and bane of Western civilization. Emphasizing moral over material factors as evidence of the march of civilization, the sedentary naturalist was himself afflicted with some of the typical ills associated with professional men in modern societies, which in his case mainly consisted of gastrointestinal disorders like indigestion, constipation, flatulence and frequent vomiting. Although occasionally using poor health as an excuse for abstaining from undesirable social engagements, these illnesses also reflected longstanding medical beliefs about the lifestyles of modern men. Darwin himself was equivocal about his sorry physical state, sometimes acknowledging that too much study tended to bring on his illnesses, while at other times claiming that mental pursuits allowed him to distance himself from these physical ailments.[23] In his own way, Darwin embodied the internal contradictions between the supposed evolution of masculinity and the detrimental tendencies of the civilizing process.

Among those who saw masculinity (and thus human superiority) reflected in a large brain and that cluster of mental powers subsumed under the heading of "ability," outspoken and intelligent women were easily caricatured by showing them with comically enlarged heads; yet the same could be done for those men whose physiques were not as developed as their minds. A modern Parisian might have a larger brain than "savages," explained one alienist, but as this brain became perfected over the generations it also became "more fragile, more impressionable, and thus more susceptible to the causes of disorganization ... the history of madness is the history of civilization."[24] Such claims exercised educational reformers across the West. During the 1880s, the strict regimen to which French schoolboys were subject provoked an outcry about intellectual overtaxation (*surmenage intellectuel*) that left boys mentally exhausted while depriving them of physical exercise. Although medical experts and pedagogues alike called for greater attention to gymnastics and sport to offset the strains of excessive study, attempts to promote physical fitness were thwarted for years by institutional limitations as well as parental resistance. Thus in his book *La Vie éléctrique* (1892), the French illustrator Albert Robida could present his darkly comic vision of the eventual "physical degeneration of overly refined races" by depicting a degenerate family gathering around an infant's crib (Figure 6.1). Not only does everyone in the scene wear eyeglasses (vision was widely thought to diminish as civilization progressed), but all possess comically enlarged and conical heads that are stark contrasts to the slightness of their arms and chests. Moreover they are all avidly engaged in the very activities that had caused such physical transformations over time: reading and debating. Looming on the wall behind them is a portrait of a hale and hearty army officer, presumably some ancestor whose

DÉCHÉANCE PHYSIQUE DES RACES TROP AFFINÉES

Figure 6.1   "Physical Degeneration of Overly Refined Races," Albert Robida, *La vie électrique* (1892).

closer acquaintance with physical exertion, endurance and combat has little place in this dubious future age. Mental development without a corresponding muscular development was less of an advance than a monstrosity.[25]

Robida's coneheads may have come from France, but their physiognomies reflected international fears of intellectual advancement at the expense of physical development. Such anxieties circulated widely around 1900, producing many more images of figures with enlarged skulls and puny bodies as caricatures of the cowardly weaklings being produced by schools. Among the educated elites of America, claimed one writer, the "natural" instincts toward action and pugnacity had been "stifled" by logic and ideas: "Such a man has cast off the restraints of nature."[26] The point that Esquirol had made decades earlier about madness and civilization was reinforced by specialists in other countries. One physician attributed 11 per cent of American insanity to excessive study, while doctors in Germany, Britain and France all condemned the unhealthy practice of "cramming" in which many students participated around examination time. The nervous exhaustion or "neurasthenia" described in the 1870s by George Beard as a distinctively American malady was widely cited across the Western world. To offset Beard's nationalist description of this disorder, more than one physician instead dubbed it a "disease of civilization."[27]

The modern world was most often conceptualized as a matrix of hyperstimulus that few urban men could escape. "Every man actively engaged in the world's business to-day is a microcosm," claimed an American observer. "The world's pulse beats within him, and he is sensitive to its throbbings; he burns with its feverishness, and faints with its languor."[28] Far from being masters of the world, in medical and psychological terms urban elites were bound by its ever-expanding webs, the content of which was described in dizzying terms by one French alienist:

> It's at every instant and at every step the noise of carriages which roll noisily across the cobblestones, the whistling of locomotives and other steam engines, tram horns, the cries of merchants, the roar of public meetings and the various sounds of the crowds that constantly deafen the ears. It's the sight of the most diverse objects, of the most gaudy colors, of the strangest forms, of the almost perpetual movement of men and things, of electric lights, of dazzling shop windows, etc., as much as luminous sensations that tire the eyes and give them no rest. Finally, for the senses of smell and taste, it's the multiple excitations of the most varied and heady perfumes, the most heavily spiced and refined dishes, the most exquisite and intoxicating liqueurs and tobaccos.[29]

Such pervasive overstimulation reinforced fears that the civilizing process was accelerating to the point of decadence, decline and impotence. The pleasures of overstimulation reduced the willingness to endure pain, whether from illness, the elements, or deprivation. From the mid-nineteenth century onward, men and women were targets of competing discourses that promised deliverance from pain and castigated them for succumbing to consumer comfort. While many physicians celebrated release from pain as a boon of civilization, others feared that doing so left people less able to cope with any kind of suffering. As the American physician Silas Weir Mitchell observed, "Civilized mankind has of will ceased to torture, but in our process of being civilized we have won, I suspect ... intensified capacity to suffer."[30] Once again the presumed insensibility of the "savage" was juxtaposed to the acuteness of modern man's sensitivity. Others had arrived at largely the same conclusion. "The civilized man both enjoys and suffers far more keenly than the savage," insisted one critic, "and this increased delicacy of organization, this quicker sense and broader range of feeling ... is only too likely to produce youths who will lack the old hardihood which has made our race what it is."[31]

For many the proof of civilized man's growing sensitivity was found in the trials he was unable to endure. Soldiers were declared less and less fit by the end of the century, and gone too was the fabled stoic soldier of the Napoleonic wars. So, at any rate, lamented the journalist G.W. Steevens, who blamed society for modern man's apparent inability to cope with pain, a weakness that was made plain when so many soldiers in the Boer War requested anesthetics during surgery. However impressive public-school athleticism might have been, it could not guarantee the kind of men Steevens had hoped to find at the front: "Already our gentler civilisation has weakened us physically. We make bicycle records, but we are not prepared to converse cooly while having our legs cut off, as was the way of our great-grandfathers." This was but a symptom of a more general softening of English sensibilities throughout the nineteenth century. "If civilisation is a conspiracy for the preservation of puny life, lowering the physical standard of the race, then civilisation may be no blessing, but a curse ... Civilisation is making it much too easy to live."[32] However, M.G. Mulhall felt that in one respect civilization made it easier to die. So great was the demand for easy and comfortable lives, he claimed, that any thwarting of the desire for material goods generated profound dissatisfaction, a fact that was felt even more keenly as literacy rates rose throughout the century. Thus, Mulhall could claim that suicide was a particularly civilized deed, the "crime of intellectual peoples. ... the strength of the tendency to self-killing may almost be regarded as an index to a people's civilization."[33]

As we have seen in earlier chapters, sexuality was the subject around which many wider anxieties about the effect of civilized lifestyles upon body and mind crystallized. This contributed, as Harry Oosterhuis observes, to a "widespread belief ... that the higher evolutionary development of humanity had made sexual activity more dangerous than it ever had been before."[34] Mental strain remained bound up with a range of related diseases of civilization, including masturbation, with which it shared a number of symptoms.[35] So deeply ingrained was this association that one French doctor described the habit of blaming civilization as something that had been "accepted without question and reproduced, like a tradition, by the majority of physicians and moralists."[36] At perhaps the darkest end of the spectrum, civilization threatened to make sexual reproduction impossible: one of the most frequently cited causes of male suicide – sexual impotence – was widely perceived as an effect of over-civilization.[37] Sexual inversion, which had often been associated with a range of "effeminate" personal traits and habits, represented a more extreme example of male weakness as a consequence of modernity. As Vernon Rosario writes, "the diagnosis of inversion consolidated numerous disorders and dreads: immorality, effeminacy, degeneration, mental illness, genital 'abuse,' national decay, and genocide."[38]

If some distinctions between men, women, and what some physicians described as a "third sex" of homosexuals began to be made in the name of promoting tolerance for differences in sexual orientation, we must consider the kind of cultural "work" that distinctions like this may have made possible. Distinguishing homosexuals as a third sex was likely to have been comforting to many heterosexual men, not least because it meant rejecting the belief that sodomy and other "effeminate" behaviors were an outcome of modern social conditions. If the distinction between "manly" and effeminate men had previously been drawn in discomforting shades of gray, biological determinism promised divisions in stark black-and-white. The biologically-determined sexual invert was not a threat, because he was nothing at all like a "normal" man, whose virility need not be challenged by modern life.[39] Just as anxieties about Jews and blacks were hardened through biological notions of race during the late nineteenth century, so this "racializing" of homosexuality allowed straight men to imagine their otherness as absolute.

However, if the "invert" was often viewed as a distinct personality and morphology, as Michel Foucault famously observes, third-sex claims were not the rule in sexological writing, and medical discourses (especially those based on degeneration theory) never completely divested themselves of environmental analyses when trying to explain sexual orientation. Indeed, attempts to draw lines between "acquired" and "innate" inversion usually failed or were quickly contradicted by other studies.[40] From the Lamarckian perspective that characterized much degeneration theory, what would have been considered a *congenital* sexual proclivity for an individual, when considered over several generations, was really more of an *acquired* tendency for a particular bloodline. "Degenerate" sexuality might have been associated with primitivity, but this was a regression intimately bound up with the advances of modernity.[41] Even Krafft-Ebing, who often developed biological accounts of sexual orientation, echoed eighteenth-century associations of urban life with a higher frequency of vice. "Those living in large cities, who are constantly reminded of sexual things and incited to sexual enjoyment, certainly have more sexual desire than those living in the country." For Krafft-Ebing the problem reached beyond mere opportunities for temptation to the condition of the urban body itself. "A dissipated, luxurious, sedentary manner of life, preponderance of animal food, and the consumption of spirits, etc., have a stimulating influence on the sexual life." Conversely, Krafft-Ebing noted, "primitive" peoples may have lacked shame but remained more or less free of the "perversions" created by civilization.[42] Even after August Weismann's studies on the continuous existence of germ plasm of the 1890s, the notion of an absolute distinction between inherited and acquired traits did not attract widespread credence until the 1920s.[43]

Images of the city as a breeding ground for vice continued to gain wider currency as the pace of urbanization accelerated. Where else could one expect to find "unnatural" love except in this most artificial of worlds? The closing decades of the century were thus rife with campaigns aimed at protecting boys and adolescents from the corrupting influence of the city. Dancing, tobacco, alcohol, dime novels and pornography were all thought capable of inciting a heterosexual excess that, if left unchecked, could lead to homosexuality.[44] The scandals provoked by the Oscar Wilde trials during the 1890s heightened fears about the sexual pathologies of modernity. Amid defensive claims about the effeminacy of the aristocracy, according to the *British Medical Journal*, the usual suspects of luxury and excessive study were at the heart of Wilde's same-sex attraction: "The intellectual development of man has destroyed the pristine balance between the various functions of the body, and civilization, with its artificial conditions of existence, has [stimulated] the growth of perverted tendencies."[45]

Variations on this theme were to be widely found. Across the Channel Charles Féré concurred that sexual inversion was a form of hereditary degeneration that would necessarily increase as society became more civilized, a view vividly captured in J.-K. Huysmans's *A rebours* (1884), the ultimate decadent novel, where the sensation-addicted protagonist experiences homosexuality along with most other vices as he spirals downward.[46] In Germany Iwan Bloch considered homosexuality to be, like masturbation, a vice acquired through the circumstances of urban life, while Max Dessoir contended that all sexual orientation was culturally acquired.[47] These environmental explanations persisted throughout the twentieth century, though always in dialogue with competing interpretations based on psychoanalysis, endocrinology or genetics. By the 1940s, the belief that the proliferation of homosexuality "paralleled the growth of civilization" was apparently still respectable enough to be cited in the *American Journal of the Medical Sciences*.[48]

All of these anxieties reveal a continuing ambivalence about civilization, even from the perspective of evolutionary biology. The widening gap between different social strata only seemed to accentuate these degenerative traits. As the poor sank deeper into animality, the wealthy seemed to become ever more emaciated, weak and timorous, a scenario that, if imaginatively projected into the future, could easily result in the dismal world H.G. Wells described in *The Time Machine* (1895). The Time Traveler's encounter with the meek and gentle Eloi, whose emaciated bodies bore few traces of sexual dimorphism but all the signs of hot-house flowers, got him thinking about how this might have occurred developmentally. Before encountering the bestial Morlocks, the Time Traveler reckoned that such weak beings were "an odd consequence of the social effort in which we are at present engaged," where the conquest of necessity had deprived elites of the need for struggle, strength and endurance. "The work of ameliorating the conditions of life – the true civilizing process that makes life more and more secure – had gone steadily on to a climax." Under such circumstances, certain traditional male traits would surely become obsolete: "Physical courage and the love of battle, for instance, are no great help – may even be hindrances – to a civilized man." His later discovery that the bestial Morlocks had been feasting on this feminized "elite" destroyed whatever compensation he might have found in the Eloi's pathetic status. "The too-perfect security of the Upper-worlders had led them to a slow movement of degeneration, to a general dwindling in size, strength, and intelligence." As bad as things were for the Eloi, things would get even worse for a virtually genderless humanity that had little use for the body. Having escaped the brutal Morlocks, the Time Traveler speeds into the distant future to witness the end of the world. With the sun eclipsed, he spies hopping about a shoal "a round thing, the size of a football perhaps, or, it may be, bigger, and tentacles trailed down from it." Although he does not say what it was about this creature that made him faint, its similarity to the caricatures of his own day may provide some clues. This being composed of mostly head with thin trailing limbs may have easily suggested the sad future of modern people whose brains seemed so much more developed than their muscles, ready to be reclaimed by the amniotic blood-red sea.[49]

SLAVES WITH WHITE COLLARS

The metamorphosis that seemed to diminish the gap between men and women, which the Time Traveler observed as already under way in his own time, was reinforced by the accelerating expansion of desk-bound "white-collar" professions from the end of the century onward, a change that in part reflected the growing porosity of class divisions and the rise of the lower middle class. Better educated than their proletarian parents, this upwardly-mobile lower middle class moved into formerly middle-class contexts, but without the social and cultural capital that would have made their ascent in the world smooth and natural. A refugee from the proletariat and a parvenu among the solidly bourgeois, the office clerk was a stigmatized figure who crystallized many of the anxieties about modern society's impact upon male bodies. Yet the circumstances that threatened to diminish the clerk's corporeal masculinity also held out the promise of potentially liberating metamorphoses as well.[50]

Clerkship has never been a secure site for modern masculinity. In the early nineteenth century being a clerk or a member of the state bureaucracy constituted a form of apprenticeship that usually led to an increase in responsibility, income and prestige, but it was nevertheless a profession with a low degree of status and autonomy. Thus while it shared many of the conditions one found in other bourgeois professions, notably cerebral and sedentary labor, it lacked the financial compensations and social status of, for example, being a lawyer or a doctor. Nevertheless, as business boomed in London from the mid-nineteenth century onward, the number of commercial clerks expanded at a faster rate than any other profession, with many coming from the skilled working class or from migrant groups. The already dubious manhood of the clerk was worsened by the influx of women into clerical professions. Although most female clerks occupied positions of low pay and even lower status with little hope for advancement, their presence appreciably diminished the manliness of such work while increasing competition in an already unstable job market. Some contended that female rivalry was the main cause for their own lowly status, while others worried more abstractly about the fate of feminine beauty and domesticity with so many women seemingly intruding into a man's world. Whatever the complaint, in most Western countries the influx of women into clerical positions continued unabated throughout the twentieth century, and as men were edged out the status and income of these jobs declined accordingly.[51]

The nature of clerical work was symptomatic of larger changes in the economic world. The emergence of large bureaucracies and corporations in the United States dealt a serious blow to traditional ideals about the self-made man and independent entrepreneur. Whereas prior to the Civil War 88 per cent of American men were either independent farmers or businessmen, this percentage had declined precipitously by the end of the century. Yet this development did not necessarily signal the end of the breadwinner ethic that had validated economic manhood in the nineteenth century. In fact, many corporations took steps to create a form of "white-collar manhood" that promised progress up the corporate ladder to hard-working and enterprising young men. Dreams of entrepreneurial success were thus able to coexist with emerging corporate ideals. Many firms promoted sales as the yardstick of manly achievement, and thus cultivated a competitive atmosphere in which leading agents were rewarded with such incentives as vacations, bonuses and write-ups in the company newsletter. Although in this scenario the successful man was still subordinated to the company's bureaucracy, an ethic of individual achievement approximated the traditional entrepreneurial ideal. After all, none of the heroes of Horatio Alger, the best-known example of heroic boot-strapping in the nineteenth century, were actually independent entrepreneurs, but employees who worked their way up the ladder. The "manliness" of this corporate path was also promoted through the differential treatment of female employees, whose accomplishments were often unacknowledged, and through the more or less complete absence of men from non-Anglo-Saxon backgrounds.[52] The emergence of corporate manhood thus represented a negotiation of old ideals of commercial manhood in the context of changing economic conditions and employment opportunities. In America this ethic was supported by popular magazines, including the *Saturday Evening Post*, the *American Magazine* and *Collier's*, which continued to celebrate the Victorian entrepreneurial ideal through the 1920s.[53]

While corporate culture tried to sustain some trappings of entrepreneurial manliness, it also insisted upon a refinement of manners that seemed antithetical to traditionally masculine qualities like aggressiveness and competitiveness. Of course such energies were still valued and rewarded in the workplace, but, in the interest of fostering teamwork and *esprit de corps*, they needed to be channeled away from the individual towards the organization as a whole. Although woefully underpaid and poorly-treated, women were still considered ideal, even superior, workers in a context where cooperation and sensitivity were valued more than potentially divisive aggression and self-reliance.[54] The apparent softening of corporate manhood was further exacerbated by stories of the many who would simply never amount to much in this new environment. If men in middle and upper management represented the success stories of the corporate world, popular culture represented those in entry-level positions as among the most demoralized and stigmatized. The structure of modern business had transformed clerkship from an apprenticeship into a potentially permanent condition.[55] It was in these lowly jobs that large firms vetted their most promising employees while stripping them of status and authority, thus ensuring a rapid turnover rate as clerks sought better positions within the same corporation or by shifting to another. These jobs were also frequently singled out as especially unhealthy, and the weak, pale and nervous clerk was a common target of ridicule in texts that worried about the connection between degeneration and modern urban professions. An *Atlantic Monthly* report on a survey of college men revealed that white-collar work ranked among the least desirable career paths, a gloomy view that was reinforced in a 1926 survey of office workers in which only slightly more than half ever expected to be promoted, and that those who did entertain such expectations already held advanced positions in their respective departments.[56] Both the low-paid clerk and the better-off "organization man" thus remained internally-conflicted male figures, and would become more so as an increasing number of family-owned firms shifted towards managerial capitalism after 1945.

Among white-collar workers consumerism clearly provided one means of achieving worthwhile change, but one that was fraught with gender pitfalls.[57] When in Germany members of the *Bildungsbürgertum* expressed concern about the effects of luxury on the nation, they usually traced the problem to the socially-ambiguous *Angestellten* or "new" urban middle class of white-collar employees. For these men and women, social mobility was partly facilitated by spending money on new fashions and other lifestyle-related goods and activities. From the perspective of the educated middle class, such luxury was a form of effeminacy usually associated with female spending, the popularity of French fashions, and the perceived dominance of "feminine" influences in society.[58] In nationalist circles it was also downright un-German. The distinction that economist Werner Sombart sketched during the First World War between "heroes" and "merchants" summarized many conservative accounts of Germany's relationship with the commercial cultures of Western Europe and North America. Claiming that German culture privileged Spartan warrior values over the mediocre and effeminate *Komfortideal*, Sombart turned a blind eye to the broad appeal of comfort in his own country. By the 1920s and 1930s more and more Germans were seeking to enhance their experience of comfort by having fewer children, seeking better housing, a more varied diet, and more leisure time. This was set against the backdrop of medicalized and racialized depictions of the flagging health of the body politic and of the feminizing potential of social security measures that discouraged courage, strength and the virtues of hard work.[59]

Criticisms of white-collar workers for their desire for social mobility and preference for "soft" consumer lifestyles were widespread during the early twentieth century. Yet one thing that lower-middle-class men did *not* buy was the claim that consumerism necessarily undermined their manhood. In Victorian London it was not uncommon for single clerks and shop workers to compensate for their gray working lives with flamboyant displays of color in their clothing, and in their free time many manifested an effete sartorial style as fashionable "gents" or "mashers" at music halls or even as aspiring "bohemians" in the drinking dens of Soho. Music-hall bachelors had constituted a significant market for ready-made clothing and other products from the 1860s onward. By modeling themselves in part on stage performers, they took advantage of commercialized popular culture as ways of forming their identities. Ready-made suits with detachable shirt-fronts, cuffs and collars allowed men of modest origins to approximate acceptable standards of male appearance and propriety, making at least one irritated Briton snort that nowadays anyone wearing a linen shirt could count as a "gentleman."[60]

Despite this smug contempt for store-bought respectability, there is ample evidence that consumption appealed to men from other sectors of society as well. If the rhetoric of the American labor movement placed greater emphasis on muscularity in the decades following the Civil War, it also insisted upon the working man's right to a certain standard of living that would allow him to meet "civilized needs," thus initiating a reorientation of proletarian male identity away from production towards consumerism.[61] Mark A. Swiencicki has inquired into the commodities that American men of all classes consumed during this period. By counting such things as tobacco, wine, toiletries, lodge paraphernalia and sporting equipment as bona fide consumer items, Swiencicki's research suggests that, between 1880 and 1930, men consumed twice as many recreational and leisure goods as women, and that they spent around 30 per cent of their disposable income to do so.[62] Consumerism thus continued to play its conflicted role in the production of modern manhood, functioning as a crucial means of achieving status and respectability while generating doubts about masculinity.

THE CALL OF THE WILD

In his 1913 study of the "New Man," the British author Philip Gibbs condemned the emergence of soft sensibilities connected to the politically and sexually aggressive "New Woman" as well as the changing material conditions of modern life. In a gesture common among the solidly middle class, Gibbs depicted the social-climbing clerk as a man subjected to the tyranny of women. Experiencing his office as a cage and working only to fulfill the material demands of his wife and daughters, the white-collar slave had become a victim of a feminized world. "The fibre of his nature has been weakened by the loss of his mastery over women," charged Gibbs. "He has been made less of a barbarian by contact with the New Woman, but his manhood has been emasculated." Nevertheless Gibbs also observed a profound dissatisfaction at the heart of this pathetic New Man, who was himself "a victim of the microbe of restlessness and discontent which is biting into all our brains. At times as he adds up a row of figures a ray of sunshine straying upon the blotting pad stirs in him a sense of rage against the narrow cage of his city office." Hearing "the call of the wild, and the faint, far-off echoes of nature music," he yearns "to get away to 'a man's life,' as he calls it, under the open sky, to harden his muscles, which are going flabby, to put some new red corpuscles into his blood."[63]

Rage against the machinery of modern life is a common theme in twentieth-century culture. To Gibbs, the clerk experienced most acutely the "discontent which is biting into all our brains." Subject to the demands of polite manners, deadening routines, sedentary professions and the profligate spending of their wives, the "domesticated" clerk was viewed as especially prone to fantasies of escape and metamorphosis. Throughout the early twentieth century, proletarian and lower-middle-class men were avid readers of adventure and true-crime stories, "hard-boiled" novels and science fiction that provided vicarious routes to robust (if not outright criminal) manhood. Others became involved in, or more often merely enthusiastic followers of, the organized team sports that became popular across the West around the turn of the century.[64] Although such examples of "spectatorship masculinity" have been the subject of a great deal of scholarly inquiry, in what follows I explore some of the more proactive steps people have taken to alter their bodily experiences.[65]

For some men escape from the mundane took tangible form, such as migration to more primitive locations where economic opportunities were matched by the possibilities of physical and moral rejuvenation. As early as the 1850s, an Englishman named Charles Hursthouse wrote and lectured widely about the benefits of migration to Australia or New Zealand. Such a move, he claimed, could do for other men what it had done for Hursthouse himself years before: "to achieve a happy escape and good deliverance from that grinding, social serfdom, those effeminate chains, my born and certain lot in England." As a rule, he explained, the "feeble-minded, the emasculate, the fastidious, the timid, do *not* emigrate; they bow their necks to the yoke, ply the distaff, and spin wealth for the great at home. It is the strong and the bold who go forth to subdue the wilderness and conquer new lands." To the many manual laborers who made their way down under in the nineteenth century, life in the bush demanded a physical strength and dexterity that validated their manhood while underscoring the distinctiveness of their new home in gender terms. Although some claimed that all men could be transformed through such an experience, others suggested that clerks and shop men would simply be unable to cope as sheep-shearers or gold-miners, a hardy life that, as E.W. Elkington revealed in his own experience of felling trees, was inescapably corporeal: "it makes the life-blood tear through my veins and I feel that there's something in me, after all."[66]

The imperial manhood that thrust itself upon indigenous peoples and colonial territories was an implicitly reciprocal category that gave as much as it received. As Anne Windholz observes, "British manhood would bring civilization to the hinterlands of the world; in turn, the hinterlands of the world would save British manhood from civilization."[67] It made sense that a hard life in the colonies would be promoted as a way for metropolitan men to redeem their flagging virility. After all, like the physically robust masculinity with which it was so often elided, "real" life was always elsewhere for the malcontents of civilization. Gail Bederman suggests that, as Americans gazed with ambivalence upon the modern commercial society that emerged in the second half of the nineteenth century, many proposed inoculating themselves with small doses of "savagery" against the physical and moral pitfalls of modernity.[68] This is what Brooks Adams had in mind when he called for "the infusion of barbarian blood" as a means of regenerating a modern industrial civilization grown corrupt and materialistic through commerce.[69] The metaphor of inoculation is not only useful for understanding the American scene, but it also applies to other countries facing the tension between manly vigor and over-civilization. Human progress, averred the British sexologist Edward Carpenter, "has only been restored again by a fresh influx of savagery."[70] Of course, in an age of escalating racism, infusions of "savage" blood did not usually mean the peaceful coexistence of people from different cultures; rather it meant the rediscovery of the "primitive" aspects of white masculinity that had been concealed by the veil of civilization. This is one reason why European colonialism was so often presented as the story of virile supermen with bodies hardened from muscular exertion and, in tropical climates, libidos enhanced as a result of the heat.[71]

The virtues of outdoor life that had been celebrated around 1800 were more forcefully articulated around 1900. Carpenter, who dubbed civilization a form of "disease," conceived of modern metamorphosis as both a regressive and progressive development, a point clearly made in his arguments in favor of adopting an outdoor life. "Man has to undo the wrappings and the mummydom of centuries," Carpenter declared, "by which he has shut himself from the light of the sun and lain in seeming death, preparing silently his glorious resurrection – for all the world like the funny old chrysalis that he is ... Nature must once more become his home, as it is the home of the animals and the angels."[72] This call was heeded by many British men and women, not only those who ventured to the seaside for holidays from the turn of the century onward, but also by those of the much maligned lower-middle class who participated in hiking or "rambling" during the early twentieth century. For white-collar workers, rambling represented a means of reclaiming bodies that were normally submitted to the daily routine of the commute and confined to offices and desks, activities that were sometimes described as a form of "slavery." From this perspective long walks in the country, which on average covered distances of fifteen to twenty miles, taxed the body in a way that represented for many a form of emancipation. It should come as no surprise that pain and suffering were central to the appeal of rambling, without which the feeling of reclamation might not have been quite so pronounced. Much like the *Wandervögel* movement in Germany, which from the 1890s took young people away from the noxious influences of city life to the rejuvenating countryside, British rambling took on spiritual dimensions as walkers communed with nature and with each other. The practice expanded dramatically in both countries during the 1920s and 1930s as suburban rambling organizations promised "exercise and companionship" as alternatives to the sedentary and impersonal environment of the modern city.[73]

This desire to "reclaim" bodies that were otherwise subjected to routine activities and sedentary work was manifested across the Western world, especially in countries that had modernized at a later date and at a faster pace. German industrialization was among the most rapid in Europe, resulting in an increased population and urban expansion along with the usual negative consequences of poverty, slums and criminality that accelerated earlier ambivalence about modern society. As a partial response to these factors, the classical body ideal was enthusiastically endorsed in the loosely-knit *Lebensreformbewegung* (life reform movement), which was buoyed in part by a resurgence of interest in open air gymnastics that prompted many to forsake enclosed gyms for the experience of the great outdoors. Whether it involved nudism, vegetarianism, natural therapies, physical culture or sunbathing, life reform appealed especially to members of the middle and lower middle classes, people who subscribed to the nineteenth-century idea that social change must begin with personal reform. Life reformers thus promoted self-disciplined and ethical lifestyles as means of ameliorating the social divisions and unhealthy conditions generated by the modern city.[74]

Among many life reformers, the sun-drenched, well-developed and naked body was viewed as an exemplar of health and racial beauty. Closely connected with vegetarianism, social reform and racial hygiene, nudism or *Nacktkultur* was a loose constellation of subcultures that often pursued quite different social and political aims.[75] With his book *Der Mensch und die Sonne* (1924) selling 250,000 copies in its first year, Hans Surén was by far the country's most popular and influential proponent of nude culture. Recommending nudism to men as well as women, Surén was clear about the rejuvenating effects of fresh air and sunlight on men's bodies. Exposure to all of the elements was salutary for rebuilding manhood: "The sensation of virile primitive manhood becomes even stronger if one achieves the will and the fortitude to expose one's body naked to storm and wild weather."[76] Within this approach to the body, the skin was readily likened to marble that could be shaped and polished, although by the 1920s the color of this ideal statue had changed from the classical white praised during the 1890s to the bronze that accorded well with modern views of sunshine. The effect of these practices was the creation of bodies whose hardened and uniformly-bronzed appearance made them seem almost metallic, thus underscoring both the appearance and function of impermeability (Figure 6.2). The most militaristic proponent of *Nacktkultur* was Richard Ungewitter, who made much of his own transformation from a "weak and sickly child raised by the milk bottle to a healthy muscular man" through the adoption of exercise and a vegetarian diet, thus overcoming his unpromising social origins through sheer force of will. Although not all nudists subscribed to Ungewitter's preoccupation

Figure 6.2   Hans Surén, *Man and Sunlight* (1924).

with Aryan racial purity, many would have concurred with his denunciation of what modern life had done to the body.[77]

Nudism and other practices broadly associated with physical culture insisted on revealing the strength and form of the body without the deceptive veneer of clothing, and in the process challenged many bourgeois conventions about respectability. This class dimension is important for understanding the growing fascination with muscular display around 1900, which seems to have been most pronounced among lower-middle-class men. Unable to enjoy the social prestige of a *Gymnasium* or university education, clerks and shopkeepers in Germany found in the highly developed body an alternative form of social distinction. There was thus a significant element of class antagonism within the life reform approach to muscularity. If, as we have seen, the *Bildungs-bürgertum* condemned lower-middle-class consumption habits as "effeminate," white-collar health reformers responded by interpreting the cerebral and well-fed lifestyles of middle-class intellectuals as signs of degeneracy, which they summed up in the caricature of the fat and bloated *Bierphilister* (beer philistine), whose alcoholism, sexual debauchery and dueling scars revealed his inadequacy for the general cause of social advancement. Outspoken critics such as Ungewitter even connected homosexuality to this refined and educated world, where he claimed that drinking, debauchery, nightlife and mental over-exertion inevitably resulted in a host of decadent habits. As a striking contrast to these elites and their modest attempts at reforming their lifestyles, bodybuilding and other strenuous activities were much more popular among lower-middle-class life reformers, such as Lionel Strongfort, whose physical culture enterprise thrived in Germany and quickly expanded to other countries as well (Figure 6.3).[78]

Figure 6.3   Lionel Strongfort, *Lebensenergie durch Korperkultur* (1928).

Physical regeneration was also high on the agenda for many German Jews, who had been barred from the military and excluded from dueling clubs. In the case of Jewish men, however, the emphasis on physical regeneration sprang not only from the unhealthy conditions of modern life, but from racial stereotypes that alleged, among other defects, a close association between Jews and the ills of modernity itself. Max Nordau's strident appeals for the development of "muscle Jews" during the 1890s echoed across the Zionist world in the next decade, and encouraged quite a few Jewish men to develop their muscles and fighting prowess. As an expression of hyper-assimilationism, self-hating Jews like Walter Rathenau even called for the "conscious self-education and adaptation of unathletic Jews to the expectations of the Gentiles."[79] E.M. Lilien's illustrations of classically-endowed muscle Jews circulated widely as postcards from 1915 onward, providing a stark contrast to traditional negative stereotypes of weak, ill and cowardly Jewish males (Figure 6.4). Excluded from the increasingly antisemitic *Wandervögel* movement, many Jews formed their own hiking clubs, and in 1912 a Jewish rambling society emerged with the "Blau-Weiss"(Blue-White) youth movement, which was devoted to scouting, fitness and Jewish nationalism. During the 1920s gender therapy continued to be on the agenda of Jewish boxing clubs in Germany, while in Austria the call for muscle Jews resulted in the founding of the SC Hakoah Wien, a sports club whose purpose was to showcase Jewish physical development to the general population.[80]

Figure 6.4   E.M. Lilien, *Die Erschaffung des Menschen* (postcard, *c.* 1915).

Whereas Jewish men sought in muscular development a means of refuting assertions of their intrinsic effeminacy, African-American men looked to athletics as a way of gaining social respectability. This was by no means an uncontroversial strategy. During the nineteenth century a significant number of African Americans joined all-black Masonic lodges that emphasized similar definitions of gentlemanly respectability to those encouraged in white lodges. Moreover, during the nineteenth century black universities like Howard and Fisk sought to instill the virtues of thrift, hard work and character into their student bodies, even if at times they resorted to quasi-military techniques in order to do so.[81] At the same time, however, a growing emphasis on more aggressively physical ideals of black manhood had emerged since the 1850s to promote the values of "living men" as opposed to those who seemed "dead" in life.[82] Of course this emphasis on "life" demanded considerable negotiation with the tenets of respectability. The sporting achievements of the champion cyclist Marshall "Major" Taylor were enhanced by his cultivation of sportsmanship, clean living, and gentlemanly deportment, though such qualities were often acknowledged only overseas. Given the longstanding reduction of black Africans to raw physicality, the line between respectability and physicality was a difficult one to toe. Boxer Jack Johnson's famous victories over several white opponents were thus met with ambivalence by black community leaders and journalists, many of whom deplored the savagery of boxing while appreciating the significance of Johnson's achievement. In this pugilistic realm, Johnson's victory seemed to indicate the superior masculinity of African-Americans, and thus, for many, reinforced pre-existing anxieties about the sorry state of white bodies.[83]

Muscularity thus served a number of functions for men around 1900. It affirmed an elemental masculinity in the face of the growing number of women in the workforce, and it provided a means of countering the feminizing effects of modern society, and of bolstering the self-esteem of men whose backgrounds excluded them from integration into socially dominant groups. Large muscles could be concealed beneath clothes, but, as the famed bodybuilder Eugen Sandow demonstrated in his many public appearances across the West, they could also be dramatically unveiled as proof that willpower and vitality throbbed beneath the surface of respectable fashion and manners (Figure 6.5). While the spectacle of unveiling was widely applauded and emulated (Figure 6.6), this new emphasis upon the display and use of large musculature did not eclipse older bodily ideals emphasizing proportion, balance, grace and health. Middle-class reformers retained these traditional concerns through the early twentieth century, and continued to share a physiological vision that was centered on the "normal" man and his usefulness to society, rather than with those who aspired to break records.[84] Moreover, despite the spectacular muscular displays that they promoted, most of the era's best

Figure 6.5   Eugen Sandow (1894). Private collection.

Figure 6.6 Richard Andrieu, Untitled ["Le Terrrrible Rrrrempart"], in *La Culture physique*, 2, no. 16 (June 1905): 94–5.

Left: **The Terrible Rrrrempart [Terrible Fortress].** – You make me laugh with your Physical Culture and Desbonnet Method. I don't practice such nonsense, and look how well built I am: I weigh 240 lbs, young man! Nevertheless I am at your service to give you a lesson!
The Young Man who Practices Physical Culture – With pleasure, I am always happy to learn.
Right: **The Terrible Rrrrempart,** *when he sees the young amateur in his training clothes.* – *???? !!!!*
The Young Culturophile. – I am ready to receive your advice and your lesson.

known bodybuilders themselves emphasized the need for a balanced concern with all aspects of physical health. The call of the wild was not meant to lure men away from civilized comportment altogether. Rather it was to remain a voice in the back of men's heads reminding them that, however mundane and domesticated existence might seem, real life was elsewhere.

* * *

In the decades before 1914, warfare represented for many the perfect example of a rejuvenating adventure that would wrest men from their domesticated softness. In a tract dedicated to opposing the drift of European nations towards war, William James nonetheless praised militarism as "the great preserver of our ideals of hardihood, and human life with no use for hardihood would be contemptible." Echoing the sentiments of Hegel and Clausewitz, James averred that the great task of modern commercial society would be to find a way to enjoy peace without slipping into complacency.

A permanently successful peace-economy cannot be a simple pleasure-economy. In the more or less socialistic future towards which mankind seems drifting we must still subject ourselves collectively to those severities which answer to our real position upon this only partly hospitable globe. We must make new energies and hardihoods continue the manliness to which the military mind so faithfully clings. Martial virtues must be the cement; intrepidity, contempt of softness, surrender of private interest; obedience to command, must still remain the rock upon which states are built – unless, indeed, we wish for dangerous reactions against common-wealths fit only for contempt, and liable to invite attack whenever a centre of crystallization for military-minded enterprise gets formed anywhere in their neighborhood.[85]

Remaining in a perpetual state of combat readiness would not only make actual war less likely, James suggested, but it would force nations to keep their citizens tough and strong. Without this virilization, human life would be "contemptible."

Many men agreed with this view, at least in principle. If some embraced the early days of the Great War as an opportunity for adventure, even a kind of game, others predicted a rejuvenation of Western culture that had been under way in other social and cultural domains for years. Still others, especially men in white-collar professions, heard in the call to arms an irresistible challenge to prove their mettle as men. Contrary to claims that clerks and other white-collar suburbanites were unpatriotic luxury-seekers, men from commercial and financial professions represented around 40 per cent of all those who enlisted in the British military between August 1914 and February 1916, the largest percentage of any employment group. Stigmatized as weak, nervous and hollow-chested, men from clerical professions were nevertheless found to be more able-bodied than their working-class counterparts, not least due to their better nutrition, healthier work environments and opportunities for fitness in sports clubs and gymnasia. For a time, at least, war allowed white-collar workers to cast doubt upon their social reputation, thus revealing that sometimes the ultimate metamorphosis must take place on the level of perceptions.[86]

According to some accounts, many men encountered "life" only vicariously through adventure stories and films or in relatively mild activities like camping trips, dude ranches and spectator sports. Yet none of the adventurous rhetoric stopped men from getting married, having children, and working at dull jobs. One might agree with Margaret Marsh that the rhetoric of action and adventure complemented the subtle *reinvestment* of men in family matters, particularly once middle-class women began to expand their own roles outside the home and some fathers felt compelled to take a more active role in child-rearing. "One might hypothesize that men, as their behavior within the family became less aloof (or patriarchal), and more nurturing and companionable, would develop a fantasy life that was more aggressive. The rage for football and boxing, and the reading of adventure novels, might have provided that vigorous fantasy life, masking but not contradicting masculine domesticity."[87] Marsh's analysis suggests that the lure of adventure rarely called for a wholesale "flight from domesticity," but something more complex. As Martin Francis reminds us,

> Men constantly travelled back and forward across the frontier of domesticity, if only in the realm of imagination, attracted by the responsibilities of marriage or fatherhood, but also enchanted by fantasies of the energetic life and homosocial camaraderie of the adventure hero. If there was a "flight from domesticity" in the late Victorian and Edwardian periods, it was unable to claim a monopoly over the masculine imagination, which was characterized by contradictory patterns of desire and self-identification.[88]

7
Men of Steel: Technologies of the Male Body

Echoing hygienic advice delivered at the end of the eighteenth century, a therapeutic recourse to "nature" promised to restore masculinity through an escape from the city. Many men who took to the outdoors did so in order to wrest themselves from the real and metaphorical machinery of modern life. As one Italian mountaineer put it, modern men were "no longer so much men as robots laboriously pressed by the thousands of tentacles of marvelous machines."[1] Ironically, though, technology often provided the vocabulary through which people conceptualized such "natural" things as the body and its apparent release from the mundane. By adopting the most natural methods imaginable, for instance, German nudists prided themselves on the creation of hardened and bronzed bodies that shone like metal. "Radiant bronze skin mirrors the light of the Olympian sun," observed one enthusiast in 1927, "with the same pure sobriety as the sparkling pistons of clearly formed machines."[2] A similar conflation of flesh and machines characterized the famed Tour de France, whose tireless male racers seemed so much a part of their bicycles that they defied any easy separation between the natural and the technological.[3] In a gesture that was common to the modernist aesthetic of the twentieth century, the new man would be both organic and machine-like, a heady amalgam of flesh and metal in which male regeneration incorporated both the distant past and the near future (see Figure 7.1).

Yet the machine does not provide a stable model for the heroic re-creation of male bodies. As the fruit of scientific knowledge applied to the development of practical technologies, the machine has had a long and troubled relationship with the self-image of Western people. Since the seventeenth century European scientific and technological developments have been upheld as exclusively male domains that to many were proof of the intrinsic superiority of modern civilization. This celebration of the machine depended upon technology remaining the creation and instrument of men who could control, but ultimately stand apart from, their creations. Yet the very devices that

169

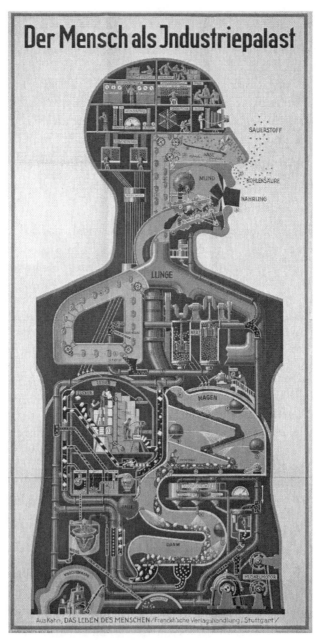

Figure 7.1   "Man as Industrial Palace," from Fritz Kahn, *Das Leben des Menschen* (1926). Courtesy of the National Library of Medicine.

supplement and extend the body's capacities (crystallized in Freud's description of technologically-enhanced man as a "prosthetic god") also threaten to diminish, constrict or supplant those capacities, manifesting what Hal Foster aptly calls the "double logic of the prosthesis."[4] In its relationship to representations of the male body, the contradictory logic of machines is an extension of the double logic of modern civilization. The irony of a machine-civilization that promised to advance humanity while threatening to undermine its corporeal foundations was not lost on George Orwell, who probed this paradox in *The Road to Wigan Pier* (1937): "In tying yourself to the ideal of mechanical efficiency, you tie yourself to the ideal of softness. But softness is repulsive; and thus all progress is seen to be a frantic struggle towards an objective which you hope and pray will never be reached."[5]

This tension is further complicated by the fact that, throughout the modern era, the body has always had something of the machine about it. The materialist world view of the eighteenth century had already conceived of the cosmos as a vast clockwork, and if nature itself was seen in terms of integrated and functional component parts, then even animals could be said to operate in a machine-like manner. The development of thermodynamics in the nineteenth century shifted the dominant metaphor from a machine composed of parts to a motor that, much like the steam engine, converted energy into labor power, a view that became widespread by the second half of the century. If physicians had earlier conceptualized illness in terms of "imbalance," by the 1850s "inefficiency" had become the operative term. As machine culture became an increasingly inescapable feature of modern life, the language of machines pervaded even those domains of psychological and corporeal experience considered to be "natural." By the early twentieth century interest in efficiency and a corresponding distrust of "waste" extended to a spectrum of corporeal activities, allowing for images of the well-functioning machine to be mixed with economic metaphors that spoke of vital energy as a form of "capital" that could be saved or squandered depending upon how it was invested. Health reformers may have emphasized the "natural" aspects of the lifestyles they promoted; yet their conception of the efficiently-functioning body remained tied to the machine imagery that had saturated scientific and popular conceptions of the world. Machine culture thus dreamed of bodies without fatigue.[6]

As Mark Seltzer suggests, what sustains these conflations of the natural and the technical is the distinctly modern notion that bodies and even persons are things that can be *made*, a concept that draws liberally from the language of industry. This is how the leaders of the Boy Scouts, for instance, could condemn the artificiality of modern lifestyles while contending that their organization functioned as a "character factory" that processed the raw materials of masculinity.[7] While the "steel-like romanticism" praised by Joseph Goebbels was the perfect expression of the German combination of organicism and mechanism that has been dubbed "reactionary modernism," conflations of nature and technology were common features of modernist and anti-modernist sentiment in most Western countries.[8] The vocabulary used to describe a man's "natural" qualities thus borrowed freely from primitive as well as mechanical registers, and often slipped from one to the other. This tendency may have even become more pronounced after World War I, where men who killed were often likened to mindless machines while those who returned with missing limbs had to rely on prostheses in order to function at all.[9] However complex and contradictory, the postwar reconstruction of manhood was inextricably bound up with the logic of machines.

This chapter examines some of the more prominent interfaces between men and machines, literal or figurative, in the first half of the twentieth century, with special attention to the fantasies and nightmares that accompanied these projects. While many Westerners became fascinated by the seemingly infinite extension of human capacities through new technologies, others yearned for a return to the natural and the unadulterated. Getting back to nature promised them a means of rescuing their bodies and minds from the pitfalls of an increasingly technological world. These dual approaches to modernity could both be served through the development of what we might call "primitive machines": whether they pointed toward the distant past or the speculative future, man-machine fusions positioned the male beyond the limitations and trivialities of present-day civilization. This is why, in the cultural imagination, new technologies such as the car and the airplane could depict their operators as ancient gods and medieval knights or as futuristic fusions of flesh and metal, both of which promised a technological rejuvenation of manhood in the face of the corruptions of modern life. Through such identifications with shining steel and turning wheels, male bodies achieved a fantasmatic compromise with a machine society that had less and less practical use for raw muscular power. It is through such alchemy that one could dream of "men of steel" who expressed the ideals of both nature and culture.

MACHINE MEN

Concerns about the dehumanization or even emasculation of workers subjected to machines are traceable to nineteenth-century critiques of factories as dark Satanic mills. Given longstanding anxieties about the poor health and diminishing powers of men, Westerners had cause to be worried about the long-term implications of industrial expansion. H.G. Wells's *The Time Machine* (1895), as we have seen, warned of the dangers of mechanization eventually outstripping muscular exertion to result in the bifurcation of humans into bestial subterranean machine-tenders and emaciated, enfeebled elites. The rationalization of the labor process presented yet another facet of the mechanization of bodies in the early twentieth century. Rejecting the notion that the march of industry necessarily entailed "a world of metal machines and human machines," Henry Ford conceded that repetitive labor held few attractions to certain kinds of men. "It is terrifying to me. I could not possibly do the same thing day in and day out." Yet Ford was also confident that this was not the case for "the majority of minds, [for whom] repetitive operations hold no terrors. In fact, to some types of mind thought is absolutely appalling."[10] The rhetoric of mechanization had some contradictory effects for workplace masculinity. As embodiments of modern efficiency the assembly line and scientific management promised to remasculinize the workforce, partly by overcoming those all too "human" aspects of the productive process that interfered with efficiency. Such features were distractions that corrupted body and mind. Ford himself wondered about the manliness of "the poor fellow who is so soft and flabby that he must always have 'an atmosphere of good feeling' around him before he can do his work."[11]

The doubt that Ford cast on the manhood of such "soft and flabby" fellows was often shared by factory workers who struggled to sustain a sense of identity on the increasingly rationalized shop floor. Historically, industrial workers have been able to appropriate aspects of difficult and unpleasant conditions for their sense of manhood: pitting themselves body and mind against machines and harsh working conditions has been a powerful basis for the assertion of a muscular proletarian manhood, both for individual men and as a basis for comradeship. Set by others to work the machines, proletarian manhood was still asserted through the successful control of these technologies.[12] However, along with Frederick W. Taylor's methods of "scientific management," Fordist approaches to industrial labor removed brawn as well as brains from the workplace, and redefined skill in terms of the ability to perform repetitive and monotonous tasks with speed and dexterity. Deprived of status, income and the physical understanding of work that had long been central to working-class manhood, proletarians had reasons to feel that the modern workplace was emasculating. Hence, as Stephen Meyer suggests, workers' attempts to remasculinize the shop floor through fighting, drinking, coarse language, and the "general degradation and dehumanization of all women" through pornography, pin-ups, lewd jokes, and harassment.[13]

As an expression and extension of a modernist emphasis on efficiency, which often contained a disdain for "feminine" elements that privileged ornamental form over function, new industrial techniques were explicitly cast as "masculine" innovations even as they challenged the corporeal manhood of workers themselves. This disjunction could be imaginatively overcome by fusing these workers with the strength and efficiency of their machines. American-style technological innovations held considerable appeal overseas

during the early twentieth century, where the emphasis on efficiency and toughness resonated with ongoing European interests in adopting a more sober
approach to modernity. Often looking Westward for inspiration, Russian
reformers employed the language of steel, machines and hard labor as ways
of expressing "natural" masculinity, especially after 1917. Partly inspired by
the asceticism of Chernyshevksy's vision of the "new man," Russian leftists
often harbored negative attitudes toward the sensual aspects of their bodies,
and admired the self-denial of Chernyshevksy's creation Rakhmetov. Such
concerns crossed ideological lines: in the decades before 1917, the physical
culture movement also aspired to this ideal by promising to build men with
zakal or "backbone" through rigorous exercises (as well as hardening practices like cold showers) that would temper male bodies like steel. In the hands
of Bolsheviks these techniques were also a means of discouraging men from
engaging in suspiciously individualistic and "softening" activities like masturbation and premarital sex.[14]

This hygienic transformation assumed even greater symbolic importance as
the revolutionary process was imagined as either an alchemical transformation
of flesh into metal or a purifying metamorphosis of iron into steel. As a means
of celebrating distinctive physical traits as well as bolstering the view that
social revolution was really a man's work, the language of hardness pervaded
radical discourses of the early twentieth century. Himself a devotee of physical
fitness, V.I. Lenin approved of being considered steadfast and "rock-like" by
his opponents, and encouraged Bolshevik activists to keep a tight rein on their
emotions and to resist any spontaneity or enthusiasm that might distract
them from their transformative social aims. Lenin's austere and unassuming
life was notable among his contemporaries for its utter disregard for luxury
and comfort. An approving Leon Trotsky claimed that such self-discipline
would one day create new people who would be stronger and wiser with more
subtle and rhythmic bodies.[15] Even the selection of revolutionary pseudonyms
reflected a preoccupation with hard and metallic qualities. Not only did Trotsky's
brother-in-law, Lev Rosenfeld, choose for his moniker the surname "Kamenev"
(from *kamen'*, meaning "stone"), but Joseph Stalin himself changed his surname
from Dzhugashvili (*dzhuga* meaning "iron" in ancient Georgian) to the Russian
word for "steel," suggesting the further refinement and strengthening of an
already tough character.[16]

Of course the revolutionary rank-and-file was not excluded from this process. During the industrial utopianism of the early 1920s, the machine became
an emblem of progress, harmony and control. This merging of worker and
machine was concretized when, under the directorship of the metalworker
and erstwhile poet Aleksei Gastev, the Central Institute of Labor propagated
"Taylorism" as a means of revamping the productive process along with the
psycho-physical make-up of workers themselves. Indeed, scientific approaches

to industrial efficiency promised to extend the machine further into the lives of workers. Heroic proletarians were depicted as "parts" in a greater whole and admired for a hardness that allowed them to become almost machinelike: not only was "mastery of the body" celebrated in the context of factory work, but everyday life too was meant to be "mechanized" through the propagation of a hygienic approach to personal cleanliness, diet, and sleep.[17] Such transformations accorded well with Gastev's poetic visions of the future man whose mechanical and metallic qualities were raised to lyrical heights. "I have merged with steel" is uttered by one such proletarian hero in Gastev's best-known prose-poem, "Out of Iron We Grow" (1918). This is a man who feels "iron blood" pour into his veins as his entire body becomes erect and enlarged: "I have grown bigger yet,/shoulders of steel and immeasurably/ mighty hands grow on me."[18] In such poetry the indisputably masculine proletarian becomes a kind of super-man forged out of hard discipline, work, and revolutionary utopianism, a towering metallic phallus capable of incredible feats.[19]

Although machine metaphors had fallen out of official favor by the late 1920s, Soviet admiration for productive bodies working at rates that exceeded the norm was widespread and enthusiastically promoted. Named after Aleksei Grigorievich Stakhanov, the "model Soviet worker" renowned for his quota-breaking production, the Stakhanovite workers of the 1930s comprised those unskilled or semiskilled laborers who, with little education or political clout, had counted among the "little men" of an earlier period. Among such heroes physical strength was complemented by courage and daring to push themselves beyond normal production quotas, whether this daring was said to flow spontaneously from within or, as many Stakhanovite biographies claimed, to have been inspired by one of Stalin's speeches. Drawn in the colorful hues of the *bogatyr'*, that rebellious hero of folk literature, the Stakhanovite found his enemies in the bureaucrats and scientists whose red tape and knowledge set obstacles in the way of his transcending conventional limits.[20] Although likened to Hercules, Prometheus, and the warrior knights of Russian epics, the Stakhanovite was not meant to be simply a model of brute strength, but a harmonious blend of physicality and intellect, the latter considered a trait most visible on the face.[21] This cult of the individual hero became central to Stalinist official propaganda, and finally resulted in Stalin himself being elevated to the level of a superman in Soviet photography by the end of the 1930s.[22]

As the automation of factory work continued, the need for muscularity in the labor process decreased, thus perhaps fueling fantasies of metal-like bodies as a form of compensation. "Masculine corporeality had been structured to signify strength and energy," notes Maurizia Boscagli, "in the very period when physical strength was being appropriated by machines – hence the modernist desire to signify the body as a mechanical apparatus, to not simply emulate and challenge technology but instead to identify with it."[23] Meanwhile, the masculine imagination often soared high above the repetitive drudgery of the workaday world. The same year that Fritz Lang's film *Metropolis* (1927) was first screened in Germany, with its robot-like workers and fembot rabble-rouser, wildly enthusiastic crowds greeted Charles Lindbergh's plane after it touched down in France, welcoming a man who seemed to embody the best of two worlds. One was the old world of the nineteenth century, where character and effort enlisted machinery for the conquest of nature. In this world machines were extensions of human mind and muscle, compensatory yet still safely external. The other world that reveled in Lindbergh's achievement was a more resolutely modern one, where heroic deeds might reveal a glorious *assimilation* of men and machines that might allow them to transcend human limitations.[24] In this world it was the fusion of flesh and metal that captured the imagination and seemed to liberate masculinity from its earthly shackles.

HUMAN PROJECTILES

"The twentieth century was born yearning for a new type of hero," observes Robert Wohl: "someone able to master the cold, inhuman machines that the nineteenth century had bequeathed and at the same time capable of transforming them into resplendent art and myth. Unknown to themselves, the Western peoples secretly desired an epic poetry of technological deeds."[25] Responding in part to exciting new machines like the automobile and airplane, the Italian Futurists offered the most euphoric celebrations of machine culture and speed in the years just before World War I. In his 1909 manifesto, F.T. Marinetti had insisted upon the role of speed in the heroic male body. "We believe in the possibility of an incalculable number of human transformations," Marinetti had proudly declared, "and without a smile we declare that wings are asleep in the flesh of man."[26] This was an ideal of man as a kind of bullet or missile, what Benito Mussolini would later celebrate as the "human projectile."[27] Fantasizing about a transformation of men themselves was a common feature of this techno-fetishism, which is why Wilbur Wright's dazzling flying successes in France earned him the title "birdman." Celebrating this fusion of men and machines, Marinetti even feverishly predicted "a bodily development in the form of a prow from out the outward swell of the breastbone, which will be the more marked the better an aviator the man of the future becomes."[28]

As with any machine that amplifies the body's powers while compensating for its limitations, airplanes are available for use by women as well as men; yet persistent stereotypes about the limitations of women prevented the transformation of aviation into a gender-free pursuit.[29] As the most potent symbol of technology's triumph over nature, aviation also took on a special symbolic significance in the countries experimenting with fascist or communist utopias, not least because it was perhaps *the* emblem of modernity at this time. In fascist Italy dreams of metallic men were fulfilled in the person of the aviator-soldier Italo Balbo, whose long-distance aerial feats captivated the world in the 1920s and reinforced fascism's embrace of daring and speed. The mass aerial cruises that Balbo planned and executed between 1928 and 1933 spanned oceans and expanded the image of fascist heroism from the solitary aviator to the collective. Described as a "falcon," the best known Soviet aviator of the 1930s, Valerii Chkalov, was embraced by Stalin as a prototype of the new Soviet man. Such celebrations of aviators as machine-men were nevertheless often tempered through their association with more "ancient" imagery, such as that of the virtuous knight whose mystical aura retrieved him from too close an association with mechanical technology. In the Soviet Union the superhuman powers of aviators were described with references to Russian folk-lore, where princes from Kiev and Muscovy were also called falcons and where mythical heroes frequently transformed themselves into birds. Insofar as all aviators struggled against the forces of nature and endured harsh conditions, Stalinists emphasized their warrior qualities, often with reference to the myth-ical *bogatyri*.[30] And while aviation captivated the imagination of Germans generally, the steel body of the man/plane amalgam especially appealed to German Jews. Countering racist stereotypes of Jewish effeminacy, the flying prowess of Jewish pilots was proudly celebrated as evidence that the virile blood of the ancient Maccabees still ran in their veins.[31]

Airplanes surely captured the imagination of the early twentieth century; yet at the end of the day they remained chariots of the gods rather than vehi-cles for Everyman. The vast majority of men who never once climbed into a cockpit had to content themselves with the symbolic trappings of speed and daring, perhaps with a clean-shaven face that enhanced youthfulness and brushed-back hair in the "aviator-style."[32] Fortunately, though, for men with neither the training nor the means to become pilots, the automobile provided a much more affordable way of enjoying the liberating interface of man and machine.

By now the privileged role of men in relation to cars is so culturally ingrained as to be almost parodic; yet the not-too-subtle association of automobiles with the male body itself also merits attention, not least because of the compensa-tions that might be provided by a hard shell moving through space. If office jobs left men few opportunities to express themselves through handiwork, the automobile elevated mechanical skill to a central place in male identity. It became an attribute of gender rather than of class. In the early years of motor-ing, technical mastery and muscular prowess went hand-in-hand: upper-body strength was needed when turning the crank and replacing tires, and often made car ownership seem like man's work.[33] The association of male bodies with cars was thus made at the very beginning of the automotive age, and for a time driving was even counted alongside other sports as a form of "physical culture": it increased respiration and promoted circulation, thus making motoring a novel addition to a rich man's daily regimen.[34] The enthusiasm that Futurists showed for airplanes was similarly lavished upon the automobile. Marinetti praised "the man at the wheel, who hurls the lance of his spirit across the Earth, along the circle of its orbit."[35] Although Marinetti envisioned literal human-machine fusions in the future, most motorists were content with metaphorical equivalences between men and this new technology. This was evident in early advertisements for the storage battery, which typically conjured up images of limitless masculine energy through carefully chosen names, such as the single-cell "Samson" of the 1890s, or through provocative tag lines like that penned for the Exide battery, a.k.a. "The Giant that Lives in a Box."[36] At other times the car itself was likened to a tough male body, such as the Oldsmobile Viking, which was described in 1929 as if it were a Nordic youth raised to endure cold and other hardships in order to test his leadership capacities.[37]

Gendered advertising copy was one thing, but it was the exhilarating experience of driving that gave men (and women) a visceral sense of empowerment that turned the automobile into a kind of surrogate body. This feeling of mastery was widely reported. Acknowledging the weakness of being a mere pedestrian, the Swiss architect Le Corbusier found in motoring the "simple and naive pleasure of being in the midst of power, of strength."[38] This theme made its way into literature as well. George F. Babbitt, the eponymous hero of Sinclair's Lewis's 1922 novel, was one of the first fictional characters to find compensatory power in his automobile. A successful but unhappy real estate salesman, Babbitt found in driving a sensation of mastery that made him feel like a human projectile. "He felt superior and powerful, like a shuttle of polished steel darting in a vast machine."[39] A columnist for the British magazine *Autocar* made much the same point a few years later when he declared that "manhood is restored by swinging into the seat of something one can drive with precision and dexterity."[40] Images of the car as a rejuvenator of manhood attested to modernity's persistent need to carve out new spaces for authentically "masculine" experience in the face of shrinking opportunities in other areas. Yet the car could also be imagined in different ways, less as therapy than as catharsis and expression. An ad for Vauxhall (Figure 7.2) emphasized the expressive potential of driving a fast car by tapping into medieval imagery. Even though the good old days of feudalism were long gone, among modern men the warrior heritage lived on in "the combative spirit, the competitive in man, [which] is as strong as in the days of joust and tourney." Here this eternal competitive spirit was sated, not through "the thundering charge" or "the splintering lance," but through "a thrill as we catch, and hold, and pass our fellows on the road." A fast car appealed to a hydraulic model of

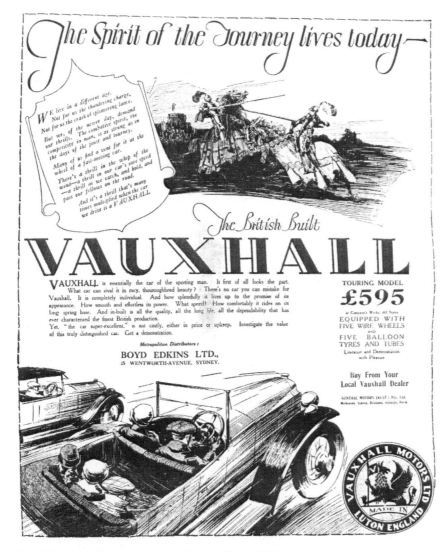

Figure 7.2 Advertisement, *Sydney Morning Herald* (1927).

masculinity in which skillful driving tapped an indomitable urge to defeat other men. "Many of us find a vent for it at the wheel of a fast-moving car." A product of modernity, the car offered a compensation for its emasculating tendencies by encouraging men to entertain conspicuously mechanized pre-modern fantasies.

The car provided armor for the male while allowing him to revel in the powerful sensation of speed; yet by discouraging walking as a means of transport, automobile use meant that drivers did not use their bodies for anything other than steering, switching gears and pressing pedals. Automobiles thus ended up diminishing the very physical powers they artificially amplified, threatening to leave men even more debilitated than before. Concerns about the double-edged nature of technology were registered in a number of areas. In his 1928 short story "The Revolt of the Pedestrians," the science fiction writer David H. Keller imagined a world where the machine has entirely triumphed over the body, whose movements are largely rendered superfluous in a society where "Nothing mattered in a man's body but his brain ... machinery had replaced muscle as a means of attaining man's desire on earth." This development had even extended to the domestic interior, where most people used personal-sized vehicles for indoor use, thus living "within metal bodies, which they left only for sleep." Extrapolating from contemporary trends towards mechanized mobility, Keller more or less anticipated the Segway® Human Transporter (HT), the two-wheeled, self-balancing electric walking machine that was introduced in 2002, apparently with the aim of making walking obsolete while minimizing car use.

Keller's story continues over many centuries as this reliance on technology at the expense of muscle power produces marked changes in the human body, with most people's legs devolving into pitiful shrunken appendages, even in rural areas where machinery performed all agricultural labor. Although a small number of people failed to adapt themselves to the general trends of civilization, in time legislation was passed to exterminate the "miserable degenerates of our race" who refused to advance "towards a state of mechanical perfection" along with everyone else. As only the strongest had been able to survive attempts to exterminate them, pedestrians pursued a similarly eugenic policy in hidden colonies where, "deprived of the so-called benefits of modern civilization," boys and girls were raised with clean bodies and clean minds. "Occasionally a child grows up to be abnormal – degenerate. I frankly say that such children disappear." The revolt of the pedestrians occurs with the aid of a device which "separates the atomic energy which makes possible all movement, save muscular movement." By activating this device all electrical machinery becomes useless, and thus all motorists are forced to rely upon their own feeble muscle power for survival (Figure 7.3). Of course millions of the unfit die. Purged of the decadent specimens of excessive civilization, this post-apocalyptic scenario promises a eugenic solution for human decay and a future society where machines do not supplant muscle.[41]

The automobile was to the early twentieth century what the coach had been to worried doctors of the eighteenth: a mechanical device that enhanced speed, convenience and status at the expense of bodily vigor. "When a man earns his bread by the sweat of his brow [nature] maintains him in good physical condition," explained one health reformer. "When he rides in a motor-car

Figure 7.3 David H. Keller, "The Revolt of the Pedestrians," *Amazing Stories* (1928).

instead of walking she atrophies the muscles of his legs, hangs a weight of fat around his middle, and labels him 'out of the running.' If he persists in eating and not physically exerting himself, she finally concludes that he is cumbering the earth, and she takes him off with Bright's [disease] or diabetes ... she simply pushes him off to make way for a better man."[42] Sex reformer Marie

Stopes even included the stresses of motoring among the modern causes of sexual impotence.[43]

Fears of a totally mechanized world robbing the human being of muscular and sexual power preoccupied many who shuddered to imagine what the future might hold. "Even now it needs far less nerve and skill to drive a car ordinarily well than to ride a horse ordinarily well," George Orwell remarked; "in twenty years' time it may need no nerve or skill at all. Therefore, one must say that, taking society as a whole, the result of the transition from horses to cars has been an increase in human softness." Technological advances thus threatened to produce a "paradise of little fat men," where courage had drained away along with any need for physical effort.[44] However distressing this could be on a personal level, the national implications of this "paradise" were even more worrying. As a writer for *Harper's Magazine* warned in 1940, America's reliance on the automobile for just about everything was a glaring symptom of how the country had been rendered "soft" through modern conveniences. This was precisely the kind of softness that had recently transformed countries like France and Britain into veritable women at the hands of Germany, only to discover their ability to fight "when locked in the ravisher's arms." According to this author, one index of this weakness was the fact that automobile use was high in those countries, whereas prewar Germany, "with sixty-six million people – the greatest technicians of modern times – had fewer passenger motor cars than the State of Pennsylvania." The solution proposed was an old one indeed: "For our civilization to survive it must turn its democratic energies toward strength and away from comfort."[45]

CARING FOR THE MALE MACHINE

Modern people have been well aware of the double logic of the machine's relationship to the body. While industrial and domestic machines promised to ease the burdens of life, men and women were reminded to invest more time and care in maintaining their own bodily machines, sometimes with analogies drawn directly from the automotive world (Figure 7.4). Revelations of the machine's troubling tendency to eliminate the need for bodily energy refocused attention on the unsavory facts about modern lifestyles. Yet it is equally clear that fascination with the disciplined creation of muscular and fit bodies made room for more positive visions of men whose bodies functioned with machine-like strength, efficiency and precision, a kind of compensation for being subjected to the mechanistic operation of modern bureaucracies. Whether articulated in academic, military, sexual or sporting domains, the twentieth century gave birth to what John Hoberman aptly calls "an ideology of uninhibited performance" reflecting "the sheer ambition to improve performance in the absence of any restraints upon this ambition."[46] For men as well

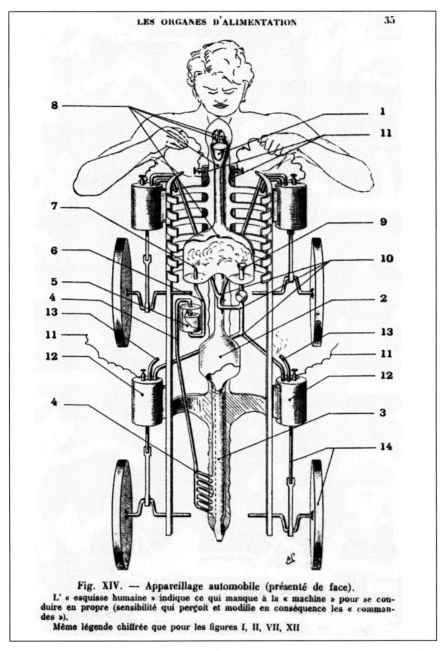

Fig. XIV. — Appareillage automobile (présenté de face).

L' « esquisse humaine » indique ce qui manque à la « machine » pour se con-
duire en propre (sensibilité qui perçoit et modifie en conséquence les « comman-
des »).

Même légende chiffrée que pour les figures I, II, VII, XII

Figure 7.4   Louis Chauvois, *La machine humaine enseignée par la machine automobile* (1926).

as women, the modern culture of machine-like efficiency promoted a bodily ideal of boundless energy and expert performance in many spheres of life.

"Faster, higher, stronger": Pierre de Coubertin's influential motto for the burgeoning Olympic movement conveys many of the machine-like aspirations held for the male body around the turn of the twentieth century, when record-breaking performances in sport captured the popular imagination across the West. With roots extending to the late nineteenth-century fascination with English team sports and the resurgent interest in gymnastics, the sporting craze achieved new heights during the 1930s as football, soccer, rugby, cycling, swimming and boxing elicited dreams of national greatness delivered by extraordinary and tireless bodies. The drama and spectacle of male bodies crashing into each other enthralled spectators across the West, who often rallied behind their teams on the international stage.[47] Whether located on playing fields or in stadiums, fantasies about the body as a kind of "human projectile" hurtling through space received considerable support from the domains of eugenic engineering and industrial design, each of which borrowed the rhetoric of the other in their mutual celebration of "streamlined" bodies and products during the 1930s and 1940s. Streamlined bodies moved easily through water or air without producing a resistance or "drag." Curved surfaces, epitomized by the teardrop form, were proposed as the most efficient shapes for maximizing flow and speed. Here the division between nature and culture was blurred as vehicular shape was increasingly guided by the movements of animals through their environments, thus emphasizing the priority given to "organic" principles of design in terms of both function and aesthetics. The rhetoric of streamlining was also central to the eugenic discourses of the 1930s, which in the United States confidently predicted a world of scientifically engineered "supermen," a new race of physically fit and aesthetically formed geniuses who one day would be expertly produced like cars or houses. Brilliant, powerful, and faster than a speeding bullet, Jerry Siegel and Joe Schuster's comic-book Superman was born where adolescent fantasies and scientific aspirations converged.[48]

The legions of supermen-in-training who participated in this cultural dream needed to acquire bodies capable of surmounting the dysgenic effects of modern life.[49] The famous Charles Atlas ads that began to appear in American pulps during the 1920s memorably replayed the drama of the 98lb weakling shamed into bodybuilding by a sand-kicking bully and a mortified girlfriend. Yet the Atlas Dynamic Tension System was more than a simple celebration of brawn over brains, and Atlas balanced its more spectacular aspects with traditional hygienic principles pertaining to diet, sleep and excretion. The criteria for the right kinds of foodstuffs did not differ appreciably from those employed by health reformers throughout the nineteenth century: unrefined food was best, while stimulating substances like coffee and tea were strongly discouraged. Atlas also drew upon technology and the rhetoric of streamlining in order to impress upon students the need for dietetic awareness, explaining how high-speed airplanes required the right kind of fuel to "hurl themselves from New York to California, shrieking through the air with enormous power and terrific speed."[50] Why should the human projectile be any different?

Above all, man-building food needed to be easily digestible so as to avoid constipation, the still infamous "scourge of civilization."[51] Afflicting most modern people at some point or other, constipation was deemed especially problematic for men because it diminished their pep and spirits, placing them at a disadvantage both professionally and romantically. What health reformer John Harvey Kellogg had dubbed the "civilized colon" was a sluggish mass transit system for the toxin-filled substances that passed for food in the modern world. To illustrate this point, Kellogg sketched a timetable for the transit of food through "the alimentary subway" with special attention to those "stations" where the "train" often faced delays and other obstructions. Combining the language of machines and nature, Kellogg promised that the "efficiency" of the "digestive machine" would be ensured through the adoption of "natural" ways of living to some extent borrowed from "savage" and "primitive" peoples. While women also suffered from constipation, among men the disorder was made more problematic because of its tendency to diminish the vitality and mental acuity they needed to be successful breadwinners. By exercising and incorporating roughage into their diets, men would themselves become tougher, firmer and more efficient.[52] Excrement, too, needed to move through the system with all due haste, though (thankfully) at a somewhat slower pace than a speeding bullet.

The road to "perfect manhood" thus passed, as to some extent it always had, down the throat, through the stomach and bowels and out via the anus. However "closed" the modern body may often seem, the model of the through-put system has remained relatively intact as a means of conceptualizing the way in which the body processes food and generates waste, thus drawing attention to the amount of energy produced by the body in relation to the amount of food eaten. Concern with the body as an eating, acting and defecating machine had been on the rise since the late nineteenth century, and reached a crescendo by the early twentieth century. Horace Fletcher's famous method focused on chewing as the first and, for him, the most important part of the digestive process. Recommending that diners chew each bite until it involuntarily slipped down the throat and left the non-nutritious fibers behind, Fletcher not only promised taste sensations hitherto unknown to those who bolted their food, but assured that proper mastication would fuel the body while producing very little waste (just a bit of "ash" instead). If less vigilant eaters were digging their own graves with a knife and fork, Fletcher saw in efficient and economical digestion the surest path to "supermanhood" for men and women alike.[53] It is worth recalling that the Ohio State football coach, John W. Wilce, innovator of the expression "intestinal fortitude," was also a professor of Clinical and Preventive Medicine.[54] In this case the acquisition of "guts" was thus hardly metaphorical!

As anti-obesity discourses reveal, male machines that consumed more fuel than they required risked becoming far less than supermen. Such bodies were emblematic of inefficiency and "waste" that rendered them suspect in the eyes of many. British weight-loss manuals of the 1930s waged an ongoing war against the expanding waistlines of middle-class men, predictably contrasting neo-Spartan stoicism and hardness to the softness of sedentary clerks and fat businessmen. Although women were rarely targeted at this time, they could still be blamed for causing the softness of men.[55] Because "every wife" knows that deep down "all men are schoolboys," one author observed, it was only logical that fattening foods like steak-and-kidney pudding and jam roll would appear frequently on the dinner tables of England. Though these were clearly the dishes their husbands preferred, women who worried about their men not eating enough might cause them to eat beyond their capacity. With nervous women heaping on helping after helping, over-indulgence was ironically depicted as a sort of sacrifice, a new kind of white man's burden: "we gobble up the stuff for the sake of domestic peace." Nevertheless men could not avoid responsibility for failing to exercise, repeatedly consuming fattening alcohol at the club, and generally overeating. The irresistible lure of domestic comfort seemed to crystallize all of these causes, where, "after the usual satisfying evening meal, man wants nothing better than the thrill of a comfortable easy chair."[56] As F.A. Hornibrook indicated in his popular text *The Culture of the Abdomen* (1934), overweight was a "disease of civilization" that literally embodied the softness of domesticated men lolling about in well-fed bliss (Figure 7.5).

Such dietetic issues were widespread in the interwar years. In France the popular reformer Paul Carton saw in refined white bread the first step on the path toward the "over-consumption" that plagued the well-off, leading them to addictive stimulants like tobacco, coffee, spices, tea, condiments, sweets and even morphine. Like many others, Carton saw in modern lifestyles a "fever of material, immediate and easy enjoyment" that possessed men as well as women, making them "drunk by their new powers."[57] Yet dietetic antimodernism could also promote conformity to the modern cult of appearances. Appearing side-by-side on the same page, two advertisements from a 1926 issue of the French men's magazine *Adam* juxtapose two possible trajectories for the management of the body in the twentieth century (Figure 7.6). On the left youthful slenderness triumphs over aged obesity in an ad for the physical culture studio of G. Lerousseau, where a winged, barbell-wielding ephebe descends to crush a prostrate and fearful fat man. Here the cultural denigration of obesity is conflated with the strenuous, even violent body-work needed to lose weight, and suggests

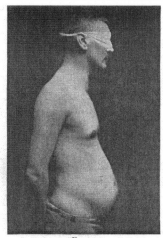

Fig. 3

Here we see a man of early middle life whose abdomen has become pendulous and protuberant, due to excessive local fat deposit and faulty posture.

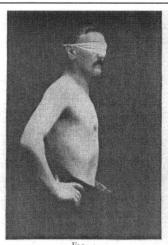

Fig. 4

Shows the same subject after a course of treatment. Note the striking change in general contour and condition.

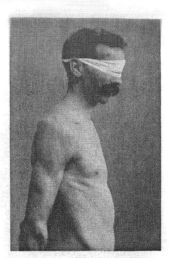

Fig. 5.

Shows the general external appearance of the body in faulty attitude, with dropped internal organs (*Enteroptosis*).

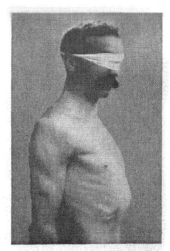

Fig. 6

Shows the same subject with the errors corrected after a course of training by myself. Note the improved musculature and pose.

Figure 7.5 F.A. Hornibrook, *Culture of the Abdomen* (1934).

Figure 7.6   Advertisements, *Adam: Revue de l'homme* (November 1926).

Left: "You will be another man thanks to Physical Culture!"

Right: "Dr Namy's anatomical belt. The secret of masculine elegance!"

that, through such measures, "You will be another man!" The advertisement on the right proposes an alternative path toward a more slender profile with Dr Namy's anatomical belt, "the secret of masculine elegance!" Recommended for all men who dress properly, and described as "peerless for those who are beginning to 'acquire a belly,'" this girdle fitted around the waist, underneath the clothes, to allow men without the time or self-discipline for exercise to retain a slim and youthful silhouette. If the apparently fit male in the ad looked as if he had scant need for such aids, "special models" of the belt were available for the frankly obese (just in case the fellow on the left balked at the rigors of exercise).

   These two ads illustrate a similar ideal about the size and shape of the body in the 1920s, and leave no doubt about the aesthetic purposes of attaining that ideal. Developing physical strength for any practical reason is not the primary aim of the bodybuilding advertisement, and strength certainly plays no role in the girdle ad either. Rather in both cases it is youthful beauty that is promised above anything else, albeit by very different routes. Venues for the display of physical beauty had multiplied by this time. As Charles Atlas made clear to millions, the seaside was the perfect place to show off one's trim new body, and as beach culture expanded in many Western countries during the early twentieth century, so bathing suits shrank to reveal more flesh than ever

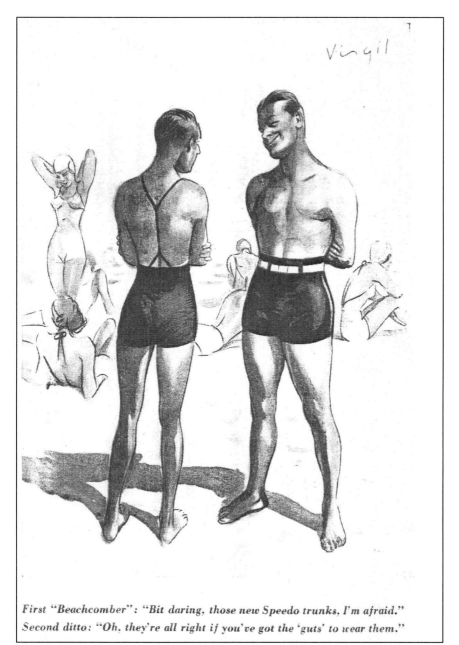

First "Beachcomber": "Bit daring, those new Speedo trunks, I'm afraid."
Second ditto: "Oh, they're all right if you've got the 'guts' to wear them."

Figure 7.7   Advertisement, *Man: the Australian Magazine for Men* (1937).

before. By the 1930s two-piece bathing suits for women and trunks for men had become commonplace, thus focusing attention on the shape and tone of the abdomen. A 1937 ad for Jantzen's strapless swim trunks capitalized on this anxiety by playing on the moral, heroic and aesthetic connotations of a trim abdomen (Figure 7.7). "Bit daring, those new Speedo trunks, I'm afraid," observes one beachcomber, his back to the reader and arms folded discreetly across his stomach. "Oh, they're all right," replies his taller smiling friend, arms crossed behind his back as he proudly reveals his toned abdomen to both the reader and his bashful companion: "if you've got the 'guts' to wear them." The smug exposure of chest and stomach illustrated here became an act of "daring" as seaside pleasure took on grandiose connotations of adventure and risk. Achieving this kind of physique became an ideal of beach culture, and the firm, toned abdomen emerged as a sign of beauty, strength, and discipline. Conversely, the fat or scrawny abdomen was a potential source of ugliness and shame for all. Realizing that many middle-aged men simply did not have the "guts" to pull off this kind of performance, thankfully the Jantzen's people were there to help members of "the tummy tribe" with specially made trunks for "the slightly bay-windowed gentleman whose figure on the beach no longer looks willowy."[58]

While the great outdoors was widely promoted as an ideal locale for overcoming the pitfalls of modern life, there were other ways of recovering a therapeutic wildness. Disaffected members of the middle classes could selectively appropriate primitiveness as a means of catching glimpses of freedom from the everyday without needing to leave the city. From around 1900 celebrations of the wildness of boy culture circulated widely in American culture, from the adolescent psychology of G. Stanley Hall to the popularity of fictional characters such as Peter Pan, Tarzan and others who combined boyishness with benign primitiveness. If the boy was to the man what the "savage" was to the civilized adult, then doses of this boyish savagery were useful ways of coping with modern refinements without losing one's inner "core" of masculinity. The early films of Douglas Fairbanks, Sr, dramatized for many men the tightrope that stretched between refinement and primitivity, morality and muscularity, maturity and boyishness, with Fairbanks often energetically demonstrating how to strike a balance between these extremes.[59] Those seeking less vicarious experiences could delve into the numerous mass entertainments that were on offer during the 1920s. Jazz was seen as an especially "primitive" form of music due to its African-American provenance and its fans – black and white alike – reveled in the freer bodily movements that it encouraged. Citing a quickening pulse, spasmodic movements, and the loss of ordinary emotional control as the effects of this visceral music, both defenders and critics acknowledged jazz's potential to diminish psychic and bodily boundaries. While some welcomed the "primitive transfusion" that African-

American culture seemed to promise, others relished this emotional and gestural release as a kind of safety-valve for life in the machine age, a rejuvenating "balm" or "tonic" offering a space of freedom in a world of constraints and conventions.[60] Those Europeans who eagerly consumed American popular culture in the 1920s concurred. "We have been civilized for too long," gushed a French enthusiast, "and this primitive music ... gives us once again for a moment the simple souls of children."[61]

A tonic whose origins extended into the nineteenth century, mass culture offered therapies for modernity drawn from the popular classes of the city, whose "savage" potential has always challenged its reputation as the center of civilization. Jazz thus represented a primitiveness made possible by civilization itself, and for many people the urban jungle provided all the wilderness they needed. This was a sensual form of "nature" that depended upon machine culture for its very possibility. Interest in the erotic potential of machines, whether of the human motor or of direct interfaces of bodies and machines, had been a preoccupation of modernist art and literature since the early 1900s.[62] The idea of performance thus assumed a double valence in the 1920s, coming to suggest role-playing in the service of dating and seduction as well as the carrying out of a task, in this case a spectrum of sexual acts. This notion was well supported by Hollywood films, such as Buster Keaton's *Sherlock, Jr* (1924), where a movie projectionist copies the gestures of the romantic lead on the screen in order to woo his girlfriend. There is also evidence that the much-publicized sex appeal of the era's most popular male stars, Rudolf Valentino and Douglas Fairbanks, was deliberately emulated by young men from a variety of backgrounds, many of whom carefully studied the on-screen seduction techniques of their heroes in order to enhance their own performances in the real world.[63] Women were well aware of this form of emulation, and some British women who frequented the cinema agreed that they now had a more discriminating view of dating and love-making, which one young clerk had come to see as "more of a technique than as an outcome of emotions."[64]

This knowing competence in the relatively new world of dating reveals the growing importance of female pleasure during this period, at least when safely contained in matrimony. Although surely downplayed, women's sexuality was not always categorically denied in the nineteenth century, and at least in France, marriage manuals advised that men give adequate attention to the clitoris and recommended climax for both partners, ideally at the same time.[65] In the twentieth century the science of sexuality resulted in a greater rationalization of coitus, as pleasurable sensation and, above all, as a potential act of reproduction. The writings of influential sexologists such as Havelock Ellis, Marie Stopes and Theodoor van de Velde changed the way in which men approached their performance of sexuality, which now called for greater attention to the techniques of foreplay and consideration for their partners' pleasure. This had an impact throughout the West. For instance, frank and public discussion of sexuality was popular in Weimar Germany, where many young men and women looked to science as a means of debunking old myths about sex and marriage. Increasing openness about sexuality in the 1920s and 1930s resulted in the publication of a number of manuals aimed at improving the love lives of married couples. German sex reformers embraced a conception of the body as a machine whose functioning could be made more efficient and reliable, thus attuning it with the contemporary rationalization of industry. Sex therapists, including Dr Ludwig Levy-Lenz, urged men to employ both tongue and finger in their efforts to overcome female "frigidity" and to achieve the ultimate goal of simultaneous orgasm. None of this would have made much sense if women's bodies and arousal patterns had not already been "scientifically" mapped out and readers supplied with step-by-step instructions on how to operate the female machine. The sex advice that Max Hodann addressed to working-class men underscored the need for skill in such areas. "There is no such thing as a frigid woman," Hodann declared, "only incompetent men." If at the workplace industrial machinery threatened to make the body redundant, male expertise might still be validated by acquiring a different kind of manual skill: "The sexual personality of a woman unfolds only under the hands of the man."[66]

Thanks to the rationalization of sexual pleasure, the modern husband was transformed into a technician of love, sensitive to the intricacies of the female machine and capable of coaxing from it ever greater quantities of pleasure. Women's bodies became sites for the kind of male technical competence that had already been applied to automobiles (which were often described in tellingly feminine terms). Yet the male role in this relationship was hardly unproblematic. Unlike an ordinary mechanic working on an inert piece of machinery whose personal happiness is not at stake, the male sexual technician could not assume an external position to the female machine; rather his competence remained bound up with the performance of his own body as a mechanism similarly saddled with the goals of efficiency and endurance.[67] Performance in the bedroom thus became an important means of preserving marriage and promoting compulsory heterosexuality. If a century earlier self-control might have compelled men to refrain from sex, by the early twentieth century the site of restraint seems to have been relocated within the act itself, with a man's ejaculation ideally postponed until his partner achieved orgasm (or at least pretended to).[68] When applied to the bedroom the performance principle required every man to be a self-maintaining mechanical mechanic, in many respects just another machine that needed energy, tune-ups and practice in order to function efficiently.

To make matters worse, becoming a sex machine could be hard work. Many married men found it difficult to stave off climax for the full twenty minutes recommended by Marie Stopes; yet these feelings of physical ineffectiveness were nothing compared to the problem of impotence, complaints about which seemed to be on the rise throughout the century. Through the work of Wilhelm Stekel, psychoanalysis extended the old belief that civilization occupied a central place in the etiology of male impotence, but shifted the emphasis from the hyperstimulus cited in the late nineteenth century to modern society's tendencies toward sexual repression. What older medical theories saw as the diversion of energy from the genitals to the brain or stomach was now reinterpreted as the sublimation of sexual energy into mental tasks, themselves chosen due to a "secret sexual aim which is not attainable." The sexual defects of the brain-worker were just some of the discontents that modern society generated. "Among civilized people, the sexual athlete is a rarity; while the sexual weakling and the semi-potent individual are almost the rule." Therapies that had once aimed at maximizing energy in the body were now retooled to teach patients how to overcome inhibitions.[69]

For the next several decades, psychoanalysis would exercise a formidable influence over the psychology of sexuality in a number of countries; yet when it came to the rejuvenation of male potency, psychoanalysis was not the only show in town. Rather, men seeking the keys to health, vitality and longevity have long looked toward chemical solutions that would maximize their sexual desire and performance. Above all, it was the emerging field of endocrinology that offered hope for many male performance issues. Serge Voronoff's famous "monkey gland" procedure attracted many men to Paris to have the testicular extract of monkeys grafted onto their own testes, just as Eugen Steinach later lured others (including such luminaries as Freud and W.B. Yeats) to his Viennese clinic with the promise of bodily rejuvenation through a simple vasectomy.[70] As an extension of the dubious rejuvenation therapies of the early twentieth century, hormone pills were increasingly prescribed as the answer for middle-aged men desiring to recover youthful energy for sex, work or everyday pleasure. While glands generally were described as "small chemical factories" and even "spark plugs" that manufactured and distributed secretions throughout the body, the gonads were often singled out for their ability to energize both men and women. Care was taken to minimize the specifically sexual aspects of male and female hormones by drawing attention to their more general importance for the body, especially their role in regulating bodily systems and secondary sexual characteristics.

This attempt to distance the "male hormone" from narrowly sexual functions remained a common aspect of medical discourses of testosterone through the 1950s. Despite considerable public interest in synthetic testosterone as an aphrodisiac, the lingering prudishness of many physicians postponed the explosion of interest in male sexual rejuvenation until the 1970s.[71] Of course none of this stopped popular magazines from crowing that the laboratory synthesis of testosterone might offer a "cure" for homosexuality as well as a means of rejuvenating aging men.[72] Popular texts on endocrinology not only assured readers that "your life is in your glands," but also attributed "the entire masculine outlook" to the male hormone, even arguing that "cultural factors are much influenced by it." Here was proof of modern man's chemical link to his primitive ancestors, whose very survival depended upon the vital and robust traits that androgens seemed to deliver. "Although civilization has tended to make virile attributes less indispensable," conceded hormone popularizer Herman Rubin, "we still retain them. The interstitial cells haven't 'heard' of civilization."[73]

The discovery and eventual laboratory synthesis of androgens and other hormones may have offered a chemical means of extending male energy, but it also undermined the strict sexual dimorphism that had been central to the description of gender differences since the eighteenth century. Complementing the claims of some sexologists that humans are basically bisexual and that each sex contains aspects of the other within it, endocrinologists argued that "the sexes were organized according to a fluid system of internal secretions that could be influenced by factors within and outside the body."[74] As a result, the notion of an antagonism between male and female substances was hotly contested. Scientists reported the cooperative and synergistic relationships of different hormones in the development of secondary sexual organs in men and women, and hypothesized that interrelations between sex hormones were regulated by a feedback system between the gonads and the brain. Although biochemists and biologists disagreed about the proper terminology for such substances, these findings promoted the idea that sexual differences between men and women are, chemically speaking, relative at best.[75]

A logical consequence of viewing bodies in terms of machines and chemicals is the possibility of remaking them entirely, which is what endocrinology and new surgical advances helped to make possible. Along with aesthetic surgery, which had gained in popularity since the First World War, endocrinology reinforced the image of the body as a machine with parts that could be altered or interchanged almost at will, making possible the first steps toward transsexual surgery in the 1920s. In the 1940s Laura Dillon would undergo a mastectomy, phalloplasty and hormone treatments to become Michael Dillon, thus demonstrating the possibilities of transsexual alternatives to the corporeal status quo.[76] This is how a largely male-dominated medical profession gained the ability to correct "errors of nature," consequently undermining the primacy of the body at the very moment when it became the object of obsessive attention.

MEN OF STEEL

Years before he formed Le Faisceau, France's first fascist movement, Georges Valois proposed a radical rethinking of the founding fiction of the body politic. In the beginning, his story goes, men (sic) lived like animals in a sort of primal horde, and huddled together in fear of bears and tigers that prowled in the forest. One man found this situation intolerable: "This is not the existence of a man! This is not living! I want to live." He thus addressed the rest of the group: "Gather your fruit for me; I will go kill the tiger." After some time he returned from the forest "a strong man, with solid fists [and] a quick mind." Brandishing a whip fashioned from the slain tiger's tail, he ordered his fellows to work and they obliged him. In Valois's social vision the very possibility of society and manhood hinged on pain and force; the man with the whip, this first aristocrat and "initiator of civilization," at once transformed his siblings into slaves and "*liberated* them from animality through the labor that he imposes." Yet the memory of this originary pain was not enough. Rather pain must be periodically reinflicted in order for the social world to remain intact, just as repeated doses are needed to prevent a man's relapse into a pre-social savagery. Physical pain was thus not only expedient but desirable, a hygienic measure that also served as a sign of the master's love. Indeed, the men in this tale are thankful for what the master's violence has done for them. "Blessed be thy name, o victorious one, for the whip in your hand is like the desire we have to rise above ourselves. Strike us then, master, if you love us, and do not abandon us, so that we do not become like feral dogs again and do not return to the laziness of animals. Strike us so we that remain men."[77]

This is brutality as therapy and hygiene, the kind of regenerative violence that has frequently been prescribed in both fascist and non-fascist discourses of masculinity, both individually and collectively.[78] At the heart of Valois's vision is the modernist ambition of effecting an "anthropological revolution" as a solution to the many problems facing Western civilization.[79] Rather than plotting the emergence of fascist images of masculinity, this section shows how fascist representations of manhood proposed "men of steel" as explicit correctives to the "soft" men who seemed to thrive under consumer-oriented democratic regimes. Putting aside the matter of explicit political ideology, what is most important for our purposes is the degree of *continuity* that exists between fascist and non-fascist approaches to the male body, approaches that flirted with images of both pre-social primitiveness and the hardness of machines. If "hardness" was a recurring concern to men enjoying the material benefits of modern society, it was virtually an obsession of fascist ideologues, and a common denominator of most other fascist ideals. Virility, Barbara Spackman explains, "is not simply one of many fascist qualities, but rather ... the cults of youth, of duty, of sacrifice and heroic virtues, of strength and stamina, or obedience and authority, and of physical strength and sexual potency that characterize fascism are all inflections of that master term, virility."[80] However, the male body imagined by fascists did not differ markedly from the ones that liberals and republicans dreamed about in other countries: images of active and energetic male bodies hardened against external seductions, consumer conveniences, and the sensuality of the flesh abound throughout the early twentieth century. The fascist strongman was in many respects a variation on a broader theme that has recurred throughout this book: the forging of physical hardness as a means of forestalling the softening tendencies of modern civilization.

Only recently have scholars begun to explore the continuities between fascist and non-fascist approaches to muscularity, an inquiry that would need to incorporate a critical analysis of sport and physical exercise. As John Hoberman points out, few have explored "the relationship between fascism and a 'sportive' male style, the degree to which sportive values coincide with fascist values, and how a sportive style featuring quasi-athletic self-dramatization in the form of the self-inflicted ordeal became a special province of the fascist imagination. This is an example of ideological differentiation, and it is in this sense that sport may be said to be 'haunted' by fascism." Nevertheless there remain important differences between athletic and fascist conceptions of corporeal hardness. "'Hardness' is ambiguous in that it may be directed inward or outward," Hoberman explains:

> that is to say, its demands may be inflicted on the self or others. In the case of the athlete, the martyrdom of hardness is suffered alone; interaction with others takes the form of competition rather than annihilation. In the case of the SS warrior, hardness means submersion in a suffering which legitimates the cruelties inflicted on others. Here we encounter the intoxicated sadism which does not belong to the athlete's emotional repertory.[81]

Many forms of fascism viewed athletic hardness as a preparation for more militant expressions of force. In Britain, whose liberal institutions supposedly offered a bulwark against fascism, there was an obvious continuity between the public school sporting ethos and the active and aggressive masculinity most valued by Oswald Mosley and the British Union of Fascists (BUF). This continuity was fully acknowledged by the fascists themselves, who embraced Baden-Powell's celebration of exercise and the outdoor life and praised the Scouting movement as a means of countering modern tendencies toward softness. The ideal fascist male was hardened through exercise and effort, and Mosely, himself an avid boxer and sportsman, was often revered for the splendid physique and fighting nature that seemed to epitomize fascist manhood. Laziness, according to one fascist, was at odds with Mosley's "creed of Steel" in that it allowed bodies to be "softened to putty." So too was excessive mental exertion, and if intellectuals weren't effeminate enough in the eyes of Mosley's blackshirts, leftist thinkers were seen as virtually homosexual in that they combined "the Pink and the Pansy." Against this decadent intellectualism and aestheticism, the BUF prescribed the usual remedies of sport and self-discipline. For many fascists sport was the logical method of instilling in men an "ordered athleticism" whose discipline extended to every aspect of life. Rugby, which one Blackshirt called "a real Fascist game," was particularly conducive to this ideal: in addition to cultivating a sense of teamwork, it was "a hard game, and those who play it must be prepared to give and take hard knocks, but always with a grin." As a form of male therapy, British fascism extended and transformed the ethos of the public schools into a formal political program.[82] And, of course, the ideal British fascist was forged through direct engagement with industrial society. As Mosley himself declared, such a man was an "instrument of steel" for an "iron age."[83]

If the BUF was never popular or powerful enough to seize political control, its idealized image of the male body nevertheless transcended ideological lines. After all, Americans and Britons had no monopoly on the "warrior critique of the business civilization," elements of which shaped many conservative accounts of Germany's relationship with the "soft" commercial cultures of Western Europe and America.[84] This was an example of the kind of toughness that impressed German industrialists and artists alike during the mid-to-late 1920s, a period broadly associated with the *Neue Sachlichkeit* (new objectivity or sobriety), a cultural tendency that sought to end the sentimental and "feminine" ornaments of the past in the name of a sober, cool, tough approach to life that was implicitly understood as "American" in tone and "masculine" in expression. During the interwar period sport, and boxing in particular, was often seen as the epitome of this tough and sober way of life. Like many of his contemporaries, the Austrian writer Hermann Bahr sharply contrasted the hard world of sport with the feminine sensibilities of the Wilhelmine era: "In Sport we find the path out of the realm of sensitivity into the realm of action; out of the tender and clinging world into one – if you will – that is brutal and ruthless … and real."[85] In the face of consumerism and material comforts, as well as a welfare state that was accused of sapping the virtues of hard work, courage and strength, a rhetoric of self-sacrifice was widely promoted as a means of regenerating what many viewed as a sick body politic.

With the Nazis this ethos of regenerative sacrifice became organized along military lines.[86] If in other domains of Nazi ideology the health of the body politic was to be preserved through the quasi-surgical removal of its soft and "cancerous" parts (Jews, homosexuals, "gypsies"), then individual men would need to overcome their personal tendencies toward weakness, comfort and cowardice by eradicating the "softness" within. "The weak must be hammered away," declared Adolf Hitler. "I want forceful men, majestic, awesome, and fearless; able to withstand pain; without weakness or gentleness." This would be accomplished through rigorous exercise and training, including boxing.[87]

As we have seen, these were widespread preoccupations in the early twentieth century. The arduous, outdoors ethos celebrated in America and Britain
was also readily adopted by many Italians, who, long before the fascist era, had
put sports high on the list of man- and nation-building techniques. For instance,
when in 1904 Theodore Roosevelt's *The Strenuous Life* was translated into Italian
as *Vigor de vita*, nationalists applauded Roosevelt's ideals as being capable of
transforming "cowardly and miserly Italy" into a more virile nation. Roosevelt's
program of personal transformation through exercise, sport and endurance, it
was believed, might foster a similar metamorphosis of the Italian body politic,
but only if individual men earnestly submitted themselves to more strenuous
living.[88] This was a period in which Italians had experimented with techniques
for curing themselves of the consequences of over-civilization through moun-
taineering and other outdoors sports. Sport thus extended into an essential component of Italian fascism, and was associated with a celebration of the hardy and
robust bodies of peasants who were said to be uncorrupted by city life. Benito
Mussolini would later be repeatedly compared to the American rough-rider, not
least due to his own self-transformation from a weak and nervous intellectual
into a brawny, fascist strongman after the Great War. He thus became a perfect
fusion of civilization and manhood, a "modern barbarian" who was an example
to all.[89]

Differences in style distinguished the way in which Italian and German
fascists depicted ideal masculinity: after all, Mussolini and Hitler represented
very different kinds of men. Nevertheless the overarching tension between
city/domestic life and manhood was shared by both. Among Italian fascists
crucial experience was to be gained by having served in the military during
the Great War, especially in the famous black-clad shock troops known as the
Arditi, or in the numerous paramilitary *squadristi* led by Italo Balbo, whose
carefully orchestrated violence against socialists, striking workers, and ethnic
minorities did much to further the cause of fascism in the early 1920s. Balbo
himself quickly became an icon of Mussolini's regime: here was an aviator and
warrior who lived the ideal fascist life of adventure and daring. As in Nazi
Germany, where storm troopers had to choose between family life and rough
street-fighting values, the myth of the *squadristi* was founded on their critical
distance from what modernity had made of most other men.

A recent study of eighteen novels written by former *squadristi* shows how some
early adopters of fascism described their espousal of a hard new lifestyle as a profound transformation that was not unlike a conversion experience.[90] Regardless
of their social origins, most *squadristi* heroes were depicted as having wallowed in
material pleasures and unheroic professions before transforming themselves into
fascist warriors. They chose *squadrismo* out of love of country and, above all, a
fascination with the *Arditi* who seemed to personify virility itself. Acknowledging
their previous habits and lifestyles as essentially "feminine," these writers

described the process of becoming fascists as a form of masculinization otherwise thwarted by ordinary society. In the novels of *squadristi* who origin-
ated from the urban middle classes, fascist redemption is usually framed as
a transcendence of bourgeois existence that finally gives birth to the "new
man."[91] These texts bear striking similarities to the novels, memoirs and auto-
biographies of the Freikorps famously studied by Klaus Theweleit, though
their anxieties about modernity prompt a more nuanced reading of the relationship between masculinity and the civilizing process.[92] In both cases "fascism"
represented as much a way of life and a structure of feeling as an explicit ideology that stripped from a man all that was "feminine" in society and in himself.
The fascist man of steel thus merely extended deeper and broadly shared misgivings about the effects of modernity on the body. He differs from many non-
fascist male ideals only in terms of degree.

* * *

"There has been much attention lavished on Germany's *Sonderweg* to nation-
hood," observes Roger Griffin,

> but perhaps not enough to the bigger *Sonderweg*, the 'special,' dysfunctional
> path of Western civilization in which Germany's history was embedded.
> It is indeed important to see *völkisch* nationalism emerging as a response to
> the particularly liminoid conditions created by the impact of moderniza-
> tion on Wilhelmine Germany combined with its 'belated' nationhood. But
> it is no less important to see this crisis in turn as one permutation of a phe-
> nomenon that was taking place throughout the Western world wherever
> fault lines opened up between modernity and 'traditional' culture once the
> combined scientific, capitalist, technological, liberal revolutions gathered
> pace.[93]

What Griffin calls the palingenetic drive to create "new men" and "new
women" is common to many social and aesthetic modernisms, but the widespread tendency among fascist movements to depict the flaws of modernity in
feminized terms of decadence and disease and explicit "effeminacy" lends an
implicitly masculinist cast to attempts to imagine new modernities shorn of
these qualities. Fascist gender politics is thus a particularly noxious version of a
general cultural dream of male rebirth predicated on a strategic rejection of
modernity's most softening tendencies.

In the Western cultural imagination physical development may be likened
to a form of alchemy in which abject bodies become purified through rigorous
and sometimes painful effort that transforms the corporeal whole into something better. Despite the modern tendency to describe bodily attributes by

way of machine metaphors, the cultural relationship between the muscular and the mechanical became tighter around the end of the nineteenth century, just when the human body was becoming less essential for the labor process. Yet it was during the post-1945 era that consumption began to definitively outstrip production in Western societies, both as the basis for national economies and, implicitly, as a touchstone of masculine identity. As the industrial order gave way to the information society, the factory worker heroically engaging with his machines was now becoming an endangered species as the "brain worker" continued his (and, increasingly, her) ascendence. Both in terms of work and war, the muscular body was becoming ever less critical for everyday life in the West.[94] By the 1950s even the once heroic aviator now seemed to have been replaced by the less impressive jet pilot, whose feats of speed depended less on courage than on weight, diet and mores as the man himself was reduced to mere ballast, a "reified hero" who was more robot than man.[95] As the next chapter will show, the postwar era renewed concerns about a decline of manhood in the Western world.

8
The Last Men? Consuming Manhood since 1945

"It's like people, uh, had a choice a long time ago between havin' all those nice things or, uh ... freedom. Course they, uh, chose comfort." Thus spoke Jonathan E., the less than eloquent protagonist of the 1975 film *Rollerball*. At the center of *Rollerball* is the social function of a hyper-violent team sport in a comfortable and refined future society dominated by corporations. Admired by society ladies for being "quite beautiful in a wild kind of way," rollerball players are so tough in comparison to ordinary men that they are jokingly dismissed as androids who have been "made in Detroit ... the whole game is played by robots!" A "horrible social spectacle" created by corporations to "demonstrate the futility of individual effort," rollerball provides vicarious violence for the masses and decadent elites, but it is "not a game man is supposed to grow strong in." This why the game's current star, Jonathan E., is being asked to retire, lest he encourage others to believe that resistance is anything less than futile. Choosing to risk death instead of the future comfort that quitting would ensure, Jonathan is the last man standing in the bloody championship final, much to the chagrin of the worried corporate executives. Yet Jonathan's victory is purely personal, for the crowd chanting his name seems happy to continue enjoying spectacles of savagery while remaining safely enmeshed in pacifying comfort.

Visions of a future society populated by well-fed and complacent people immersed in an ever-expanding array of consumer pleasures and labor-saving devices have haunted the Western cultural imagination since at least the eighteenth century, and show no sign of abating in the twenty-first. Friedrich Nietzsche's "last men" were those who, in the face of the great upheavals of world history, would one day opt for comfort rather than struggle, and conformity rather than individuality. "'We have invented happiness,' say the last men, and they blink. They have left the regions where it was hard to live, for one needs warmth ... Everybody wants the same, everybody is the same: whoever feels differently goes voluntarily into a madhouse."[1] Aldous Huxley certainly had this vision in mind when he penned *Brave New World*, where the soma-soaked denizens of a dystopian future enjoy a comfortable "civilization that has absolutely no need of nobility or heroism." This was after the Nine Years' War, which was so cataclysmic that people were "ready to have even their appetites controlled then. Anything for a quiet life."[2] In the eyes of many, the so-called Age of Affluence that followed the Second World War seemed like a troubling realization of Huxley's vision. To be sure, male fantasies of regenerative violence were widely discredited after 1945, along with the strutting fascist strongmen who had put such fantasies into practice. Yet did lifestyles devoted to consumption and appearances represent palatable alternatives? For those concerned about the future of men, appliances, televisions, domesticity, status-seeking and organizational structures all added up to what the playwright John Osborne dubbed a "Brave New-nothing-very-much-thank-you," a pacified world in which consumer goods abounded but noble causes worth dying for were few.[3]

Confronted with a society in which people are routinely expected to assume layer after layer of new "needs" and ever more refined tastes and roles, it is easy to see why "primitivity" (implying a spectrum of qualities from the raw, simple and unrefined to direct expressions of aggression and sexuality) would exercise considerable allure for the therapy or even liberation it might promise. After all, both Nietzsche and Huxley wondered about the therapeutic potential of wildness, whether in the "chaos" that Zarathustra said still lurked within the people of his time, or in the example of John, the "Savage" that Huxley transplanted for a time into the heart of his future world. If Nietzsche was more optimistic about the transformative potential of instinctual drives, Huxley suggested that savage spectacles merely encouraged a conformist search for new sensations, the commodification of primitivity as the semblance of "true" liberation. While agreeing with Marianna Torgovnick that the commodified primitive had become "an essential fact of urban life" during the last decades of the twentieth century,[4] this chapter suggests that the commercialization of savage transgression was becoming firmly established in the 1950s as a popular means of negotiating the tensions between manhood and modern life. The chapter thus presents a very broad mapping of the postwar world to reveal a number of paths to the present. The mass consumerism that threatens to "consume" masculinity by encouraging men to indulge their appetites and impulses also provides "primitive" methods of release from constraining rules and conventions.

THE INCREDIBLE SHRINKING MEN

American manhood has received considerable attention in masculinity studies, with much interesting work being devoted to the distinctive gender traits and relationships of specific periods. Yet, as the previous chapters suggest, painting on a broader canvas has the value of revealing the interplay between continuity and change at any given time, both within and across national borders. For instance, Susan Jeffords has persuasively shown how the Vietnam War effected a crisis of national identity that demanded a "remasculinization of America" evident in mass culture and political discourses since the 1970s. To be sure, the warrior dreams wrought by the Vietnam experience reflect very specific fears and anxieties; yet some of the reasons offered for the American defeat reveal deeper anxieties about manhood and modernity, such as the claim that, at least at the leadership level, in the modern world warrior values had been replaced with technocratic and managerial ones that undermined the efforts of fighting men.[5] As we have seen, this concern that male elites have become too detached from their warrior heritage in a way that threatens the strength and vitality of the nation has recurred throughout the modern era.

What is rarely questioned in post-Vietnam warrior discourses (that is, besides the legitimacy of the war itself) is the fighting prowess of soldiers who, in a striking variation on the "stab-in-the-back" theory of the Weimar Republic, had been betrayed by their cowardly leaders. Yet we know that a diminishment of combat ability has been an ongoing concern in the Western world, with the blame often attributed to the softening potential of modern life itself. Twentieth-century wartime experiences only seemed to reaffirm this concern. In the two world wars, the long-range weaponry that delivered death while keeping the enemy out of sight fostered a sense of confusion and isolation that could have an unnerving effect on enlisted men, many of whom failed to fire their weapons without being ordered to do so (and who would cease firing once their commanding officer had moved on). Between 1939 and 1945 soldiers died in alarming numbers and horrific ways, and for every example of bravery there seemed to be at least a dozen cases of men who simply couldn't cope with the experience of modern warfare. Reluctance to engage with the enemy was often traced to the changing social composition of the military, which by the Second World War included greater numbers of older and better-educated middle-class recruits. Because they were civilians first and soldiers only temporarily, these men seemed to lack the killer instinct that would have rendered them more active combatants.

Such "passive" soldiers reinforced concerns about how "soft" civilian life had made these men, and why military training had to adopt strict new measures to toughen them up. In addition to the training rituals of brutalization that sought to desensitize men to the horrors of combat, so-called instinct therapy proved an enduring psychological technique for recalling to men their supposedly hereditary passion for killing. By systematically ripping the "veneer" of civilization from these men, one army psychologist claimed, "the polite bank-clerk strips down, not to a peaceful individualist, but to a soldier born." Nevertheless, many of these born-again warriors failed to overcome their civilian distaste for killing, and at the end of the war only one-third of those entitled to medals ever bothered to claim them.[6] Others came home horribly disfigured or as amputees, or suffering from deep psychological wounds, as illustrated in John Huston's long-suppressed documentary about shell shock, *Let There Be Light!* (1946), and in Hollywood films like *The Best Years of Our Lives* (1946) and *The Men* (1950).[7]

Concerns about the state of manhood persisted throughout the period of the Cold War, focusing attention on the benefits of hardened and stoic bodies even as ordinary men seemed to be growing ever softer.[8] This theme was appropriated in American political rhetoric of the late 1950s, especially in references to the "New Frontier" promised by John F. Kennedy.[9] Drenched in gendered rhetoric explicitly drawn from Theodore Roosevelt, Kennedy's 1960 presidential campaign underscored what many Americans felt about the consumer conformity associated with the Eisenhower era. At the time that Richard Nixon famously celebrated America's many household appliances as a sign of national superiority over the Soviet Union (a domestic compensation for lagging behind militarily), Kennedy invoked more Spartan ideals, arguing that modern conveniences also threatened to soften America when compared to a more disciplined and austere Soviet society.[10] Kennedy made this fear of softness-through-consumption explicit in the physical fitness initiatives he launched after becoming president, where he warned that "our growing softness, our increasing lack of physical fitness, is a menace to our security."[11] Such statements extended earlier claims about the gender-bending capacity of civilization, a point more clearly articulated by the essayist Herbert Gold: "consumer culture devours both the masculinity of men and the femininity of women."[12]

Between the late 1940s and the 1960s, then, the male body was regularly reminded of its warrior potential even as it seemed to dip even further into pampered softness and inactivity. The 1950s image of the responsible male breadwinner enjoyed undoubted social and professional dominance, secured in large part by the domestication of women and the exclusion of men from lower-class and non-Anglo-Saxon origins. Yet the so-called "man in the gray flannel suit" also generated considerable misgivings among men whose social power seemed to have been purchased at the price of masculinity itself. Just as the clerk of the 1890s elicited concerns about status and manhood in an increasingly corporate society, the organization man represented both power and weakness. Sociologist C. Wright Mills captured this sense when, as early as 1951, he famously dubbed the white-collar man "the hero as victim, the small creature who is acted upon but who does not act, who works along unnoticed in somebody's office or store, never talking loud, never talking back, never taking a stand."[13]

Many men would have recognized themselves in Mills's grim portrait. The middle-class man whose autonomy was jeopardized through his role in corporate culture was also at risk through the lifestyle he led. Despite periodic claims about the "natural" strength and endurance of male bodies, in the late 1950s men were told that, in terms of longevity and health, they were in fact the weaker sex. In earlier decades, both men and women could look forward to living for relatively equal periods of time, but by the 1950s men were living four years less than women, largely, it was said, due to the demands of the modern workplace.[14] At the same time, coronary heart disease, which in America afflicted men far more often than women, was being cited as the number one killer of the developed world. Considered an "epidemic" by some, for others it was yet another "scourge of Western civilization," evidence of the damage that modern society sowed in the bodies of men. By pathologizing the middle-class work ethic, the threat of an early grave was a wake-up call for many, especially those men now diagnosed with a success-driven "Type A personality," whose behavior was marked by an obsession with success and recognition as well as a tendency to take on multiple tasks subject to time restrictions. Yet even those who were not especially ambitious or "driven" could also succumb to heart attacks, a fact that other cardiologists began attributing to "stress" as a more or less constant feature of hurried modern lives (despite the fact that stress cannot be measured or detected in any of the usual ways of assessing medical problems).[15]

If stress and the Type A personality seemed to pathologize both modern men and the world they had created, these warnings hardly prompted the wholesale restructuring of either men or society. As the home was widely considered an emotional haven from feelings of powerlessness at work, stress could be viewed as the legitimate risk of leading a "manly" life as an organization man, just as the hyperstimulus of the modern city a century before contributed to "wear and tear" that was as lamentable as it was validating. As in the nineteenth century, modern stress was manifested in variety of corporeal and mental symptoms. "Show me a man who has to drink milk instead of wine with his meals," quipped the humorist Art Buchwald years later, "and I'll show you a titan of American industry."[16] As we have seen, enduring pain and bearing "wounds" have long been integral elements of white male bodies, forms of suffering that have been to some extent validated through the production of some kind of satisfactory outcome: in corporate terms, securing that lucrative contract, a job promotion, a new house or car, all of which allowed some men to retain social and political privileges over women and men from other classes and ethnic groups. Even the man who developed the concept of stress, Hans Selye, did little to discourage it in his readers. For him stress was "the spice of life," and "the absence of stress is death" (though he later distinguished between "good" and "bad" stress).[17]

Home, it is widely acknowledged, played an important role in the identities of these middle-class men of the 1950s. The joys and comforts of the domestic interior provided a barrier between the world-weary (white) male and the workaday world, and thus acted as a kind of container for sexual passions as well as a womb-like therapeutic realm.[18] Unfortunately, men ensconced in this domestic world seemed to be padding their own personal boundaries with a layer of fat that increasingly characterized suburban bliss. For middle-class men the central problem was in fact an old one: how to remain fit and vigorous without ceasing to enjoy the comforts of modernity? According to diet and exercise gurus, the consuming male had to find moderate ways in which to enjoy the good life without succumbing either to seductive advertising or his own appetites. Several weight-loss writers employed military (and negatively gendered) language to describe the fat belly as the symbol of a feminine "surrender." Such metaphors pervaded Elmer Wheeler's popular writings about weight loss, enabling men to transform their personal diet narratives into war stories in which they heroically conquered their own appetites. Insofar as Wheeler and other reformers situated the regeneration of manhood within marriage, they relied upon the "housewife" and the domestic life that she created to contain the male's waistline together with his gustatory (and sexual) passions. After all, didn't poor eating habits begin at home, where doting mothers risked indulging their sons' appetites instead of schooling them in self-control?[19] "Softness" was what most threatened to corrupt the typical middle-class man, whether it sprang from a lack of physical fitness, an attachment to domestic comforts, or the smothering influence of wives and mothers (hardly a new idea when Philip Wylie nastily coined the term "Momism").[20] This is why the many experts who engaged with the troubling findings of the Kinsey reports tended to link homosexuality, widely regarded as the epitome of male softness, to the myriad effects of modern living.[21]

In the face of the threat of nuclear annihilation and/or Soviet invasion, popular culture articulated traditional complaints about the diminishment of modern manhood while offering attractive fantasies about men who refused to be softened. One did not need to venture far to find opportunities for hardness. The urban jungle was the natural habitat of fictional tough guys like Mike Hammer, Mickey Spillane's wildly-popular private eye whose wartime experiences had exposed him to the "muck and the slime" of real jungles where he had "gotten a taste of death and found it palatable to the extent that I could never again eat the fruits of normal civilization."[22] This interpretation of Hammer's trademark violence, initially delivered by a hostile judge at the beginning of *One Lonely Night* (1951), is finally accepted and even celebrated by Hammer by the end of the novel. Hammer's difference from ordinary men is noticed by the psychiatrist Charlotte Manning, who confessed to spending her days treating repressed and obsessed "little men" who tell her their "pitiful stories." This is what sent Charlotte hunting for a "real man" like Mike: "when you constantly see men with their masculinity gone, and find the same sort among those who you call your friends, you get so you actually search for a real man." Hammer was precisely the sort of man she was looking for, "a man who was used to living and could make life obey the rules he set down. Your body is huge, your mind is the same. No repressions."[23]

Such pop-psychoanalytic interpretations of a repressive civilization and less inhibited male types permeated American culture during the 1940s and 1950s. Indeed, the men who consumed Spillane's novels may have also read the "true adventure" magazines that flourished from the late 1940s through the end of the 1960s. Here aggressive male fantasies and lurid misogyny were served up as a reactionary counterpoint to the ruling image of domesticated and corporate manhood (Figure 8.1). In these pages men grappled with the peril, pain, violence and death that had been increasingly removed from daily life.[24] In many cases, though, a rapprochement between refinement and toughness was presented as the most palatable solution. Crime dramas of the 1950s often played down hard-boiled loners in favor of breadwinners who, despite being family men, still proved capable of defending their territories, as the home-invasion film, *The Desperate Hours* (1955), vividly illustrates.[25] A tension between the softness of consumption and a more warlike society was also a recurring theme in science fiction, which, building upon earlier models, came into its own as a mainstream literary and cinematic genre during this time. Robert A. Heinlein's controversial *Starship Troopers* (1959) offered a militant critique of the culture of comfort set against the backdrop of the Cold War. Supposedly inspired by a proposed moratorium on nuclear arms, *Starship Troopers* unfolds Heinlein's objections to a world gone soft. In this vision of the just society, only those who have served two years' military service are eligible to vote, and while women are technically qualified to serve in many capacities (for instance, as starship pilots), this remains an over-whelmingly masculinist vision where men fight to protect women and where service itself builds manhood. "I had at last found out what was wrong with me," explains Juan Rico's once resolutely anti-militaristic father, who decides to enlist after the "Bugs" (that is, the alien arachnids of Klendathu) attacked Earth, killing his wife: "I had to prove to myself that I was a man. Not just a producing-consuming economic animal ... but a *man*."[26]

Framed by Cold War anxieties about gender and military fitness, Heinlein's critique of *homo economicus* is a variation on an old theme. So too was the "warrior critique of the business civilization" described three years earlier by John Mallan, who also doubted that modern Americans were really up to the Soviet challenge. Given the "materialist complacency" that was rampant in the 1950s, Mallan regretted that "few men can wish to think seriously about a world of permanent violence and the sacrifices it will entail."[27] Although

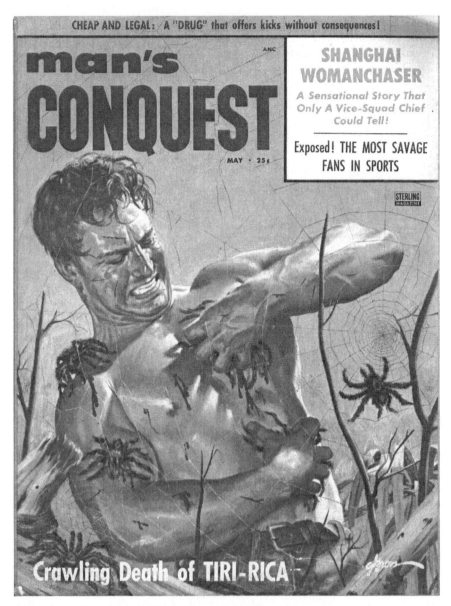

Figure 8.1 *Man's Conquest* (1957). Private Collection.

imagined only on a personal level, a "world of permanent violence" is precisely what Richard Matheson offered in his science fiction novel *The Shrinking Man* (1956). In this book, which was quickly made into a feature film as *The Incredible Shrinking Man*, Scott Carey's radiation-induced shrinkage brings to the surface just about every conceivable form of male inadequacy, not least in relation to his wife's obsession with financial "security" that made him don his white collar in the first place. Ironically, though, it is Carey's desperate struggle for survival that leads to his remasculinization. Trapped in the cellar and forgotten by his now giant-sized family, he reverts to instinct and physical prowess in order to find food, to scale the mountainous terrain of discarded furniture, and eventually to kill the black widow spider that has been hunting him. Seeing his surprisingly relaxed reflection in the shiny surface of a thimble revealed the change that had taken place in him: "Perhaps jungle life, despite physical danger, was a relaxing one. Surely it was free of the petty grievances, the disparate values of society. It was simple, devoid of artifice and ulcer-burning pressures. Responsibility in the jungle world was pared down to the bone of basic survival ... There was only to be or not to be."[28] Eventually freed from his prison, and getting smaller still, our tiny savage anticipates with glee the challenges and dangers that await him as he enters the realm of the microscopic. It is at the vanishing point of civilized life (and of visibility itself) that "true" masculinity can fully assert itself. "To a man, zero inches mean nothing. Zero meant nothing" (p. 200).

As Scott Carey plunged into the "wonderland" of less-than-zero life, males who weren't actually shrinking found that release from the "feminizing" constraints of corporate culture was provided by modernity itself. The same culture that encouraged men to adopt the role of domestic provider was also quick to disparage that role as a form of entrapment. The young, educated urban bachelors who were repeatedly cited as the primary readers of *Playboy* magazine saw little tension between predatory sexuality and an explicit interest in consumer goods (especially if the latter assisted the former). If the dejected organization man retreated to his suburban home at the end of the day, the fun was just beginning for the bachelor, whose high-rise apartment (according to the stereotype) was decked out with modern conveniences tastefully selected and capable of bolstering his manhood. The bachelor thus enjoyed the best of both worlds: while his impeccable taste in food, music, clothes and furniture rendered him even more "civilized" than women, he enjoyed a freer approach to sexual passions than his more domesticated mates.[29] "Historically, the bachelor apartment marked the single man's marginal position with the domestic ideology of the period," notes Steven Cohan, "but it also indicated his recuperation as a consumer whose masculinity could be redeemed – even glamorized – by the things be bought to accessorize his virility."[30] As marginal figures that were sometimes associated with immaturity and even homosexuality (why else did such men want to remain single?), bachelors nevertheless represented for many an attractive alternative to the already fraught identity of the ordinary breadwinner.

If commodity culture facilitated the tasteful refinement of the bachelor and his predatory sexuality, for others it fostered a kind of wildness that challenged both the bachelor and the breadwinner. It was in America that teenagers first formed a new market for consumer goods that provided ways of rebelling against Cold War culture and the gender roles it promoted. During the 1950s many young white males donned zoot suits as a means of asserting their difference from mainstream values. The zoot suit was a garment of excess that mocked middle-class sartorial codes: jackets with extra-wide lapels and strikingly wide padded shoulders were worn over pleated trousers that were baggy at the leg but tapered around the ankle. Inspired by the look of Mexican dandies of the previous decade, whose self-conscious abstention from wartime American values incurred the wrath of servicemen during the Zoot Suit Riots of June 1943, the garment reinforced an oppositional masculinity that was at once "tough" yet obsessed with appearances. Essential to the look was the greased pompadour that often concealed a switch-blade or two, deadly symbols of rough masculinity that, by being employed like bobby pins, also functioned as quasi-feminine accessories.[31] Transgressive in terms of style, the zoot-suiters cultivated a reputation for delinquency that combined flashy clothes with a distinctly tough, and proudly unrespectable, masculine image.

If zoot-suiters and other teen rebels found a validating primitivity through consumer items, the Beat writers appealed to stereotypes about African-American, Native American and Latino men whose non-white "savagery" might rejuvenate the blocked virility and libidos that seemed to plague white males. Becoming "white Negroes" allowed such men to project themselves imaginatively into the kind of primitiveness that was marginalized in respectable white society and repressed within white men themselves. David Savran's analysis of the Beats reveals how such efforts to incorporate non-whiteness suggested to the white male "a fantasmatic recovery of that which he has lost, of that otherness which he so desperately desires, and which is instantiated as a sense of community, ecstasy, the body, sensuality, the primitive, the authentic, the paternal." Needless to say, neither of these stock male figures – the responsible husband/father and the rebellious son – represented stable masculine types: the authority of the former was diminished both at the office and at home, while the latter's expanded sensual freedom was compromised by his flirtation with sexual dissidence and his largely aesthetic and/or consumerist lifestyle.[32] Consumption may have offered men new ways of propping up their virility, but without some violent potential, it always risked consuming the consumer.

COCA-COLONIZING MANHOOD?

What worried Kennedy and other critics about the growing softness of American bodies was registered across the Western world, but in distinctive ways.[33] For centuries "America" existed in the European imagination as a place of both wildness and novelty, a cultural wasteland that has doubled as a land of innovation. It was thus associated with both the productive and progressive and the disorienting and destabilizing aspects of modernity. Commerce and consumerism have been central to perceptions of American life. Indeed, the middle-class obsession with physical well-being that Alexis de Tocqueville observed in the 1830s has remained an integral ingredient of European stereotypes about America. This perception expanded during the 1920s: while many agreed that American men displayed aggressive business traits, others suggested that this was largely due to their unnaturally assertive wives and girlfriends. According to this stereotype, American economic power was really just a reflection of the weaknesses of men unable to control their domineering women.[34]

Such stereotypes may have flattered European self-esteem and legitimized traditional gender identities, but what was a nation to do when large numbers of its own (presumably more virile) population happily manifested similar traits? After all, what made Americans seem less than manly were the same flaws that the British observed among the lower-middle-class clerks who were so ubiquitous around 1900 (see Chapter 6). Viewed in socio-cultural terms, the presumed "otherness" of America illuminated European anxieties about where their own societies were headed, thus projecting "scenes of a possible European future" that exacerbated pre-existing anxieties about modernity.[35] Indeed, when de Tocqueville observed the importance of material comfort in the United States, he also acknowledged that something of an "analogous character is more and more apparent in Europe," a qualification that conceded the broader appeal of consumer goods and physical ease.[36] Of course legitimate grievances have been registered against America's political and economic dealings in the world since 1945. Yet if "America" also stood for the disconcerting implications of modernization, then to some extent anti-Americanism provided European elites with a convenient embodiment of everything they found troubling in their own countries' movements toward modernity: the rise of the masses, a rush toward distracting sensual experiences, the collapse of morality ... and the list goes on. Although the fear of cultural colonization by America had been expressed during the interwar years, by the 1950s it seemed to many a *fait accompli*. "Thus in the beginning all the world was America," observed John Locke.[37] Nearly three centuries later, many wondered whether the world would end that way too. "Perhaps all our children will be Americans," muses Cliff in the film adaptation of *Look Back in Anger* (1959). "That's a thought, isn't it?"

To some extent, then, becoming "American" and becoming modern were synonymous, and both seemed unavoidable during the postwar period. The boom conditions that Americans enjoyed immediately after the war did not hit war-ravaged Europe until some years later, but when prosperity did arrive it was widely welcomed as the beginning of a new era of comfort and well-being. In France the postwar world was marked by three decades of prosperity commonly known as *les trentes glorieuses*, in Italy these years witnessed an "economic miracle," and in Britain it was the dawn of the Age of Affluence where Britons were assured that they "never had it so good." And so it seemed. In many countries the economy was growing, unemployment was low, welfare services were expanded, and many more consumer items became available at affordable prices. Despite being cautioned to curb their spending in order to keep inflation low and to increase provisions for publicly-funded services, Europeans exuberantly spent their money on cars, homes, clothes and domestic appliances, including television sets, which became commonplace after commercial broadcasting was developed in the mid-to-late 1950s.[38] Unsurprisingly, postwar reconstruction ran along gendered as well as ideological and economic lines, providing a domestic definition of woman as an ideal housewife surrounded by labor-saving appliances. America's new ethos of domesticity resonated with the issues faced by Europeans, for whom, as Mary Nolan suggests, the (not always voluntary) "retreat *into* the home in the 1950s and 1960s was a retreat *from* nationally and culturally specific problematic pasts and threatening presents."[39] The reconstruction of the economies and infrastructures of combatant nations thus entailed a parallel attempt to reconstruct masculinities for the brave new world that was upon them.

One effect of these changes was that European men were targeted as consumers as never before. Launched in the 1930s as an answer to *Esquire* (and supposedly a favorite among troops during the war), the first British men's lifestyle magazine was *Men Only: a Man's Magazine*. Despite the sexist cartoons, "artistic" female nude photography, humorous short fiction and articles about cricket that filled most issues, *Men Only* was framed front and back with ads for products that would enable well-to-do men to care for their bodies and display their good taste. The pride of place that *Men Only* accorded fashion reflected postwar developments regarding male consumption patterns. Dramatic changes in the menswear industry during the early 1950s included new approaches to marketing and salesmanship as well as a pronounced emphasis on the superior taste of British men, all of which sparked the ongoing tendency towards a constant cycle of innovation that emerged in the mid-1950s and reached its apotheosis in the "swinging London" fashions of the 1960s. One factor in this new approach to menswear was the entrepreneurial desire to persuade men to take a real interest in their appearance.[40]

Such concerns elicited anxieties that we have encountered before. Memories of wartime deprivation and sacrifice were reasonably fresh and could be invoked as a counterpoint to the consumerism and domestication that now seemed to characterize middle-class men. A cartoon from *Men Only* concisely illustrates the predicament of warrior manhood in peacetime, with a man who had recently been in the European theater now taking stock of himself in the mirror as he washes dishes at home, his wife conspicuously shown reading contentedly in the living room. "Surely you remember yourself, Bill Rawlinson? The man who stormed across Europe just a few short years ago?" (Figure 8.2). As if this feared reversal of prescribed gender roles were not bad enough, British bodies were not much better off than American ones. In his rather provocatively entitled book, *Be Fit! or Be Damned*, one health reformer reminded his readers of their pre-historic heritage: "It now appears evident that civilised man, by virtue of his brain, and his belief in it as to the rightness of his way of life, has departed from the natural needs of his body and its functions, even to losing the capacity for reasonably healthy survival."[41] The campaign against male obesity waged in Britain during the 1930s was thus renewed in the 1950s, and for many of the same reasons. "The amenities of civilization, the creature comforts that may undermine vitality have come to be regarded as a natural heritage," warned one exercise text, which recommended moderation rather than absolute abstention and personal vigilance rather than hypochondriacal obsession with health. "We are compelled to accept these consequences of modern existence and, since they cannot be prevented, the problem of fitness is largely concerned with the provision of antidotes."[42]

Never having had it so good clearly had its flip-side. In fact, if consumerism displaced men once again from any warrior experiences, it also, once again, threatened to undermine heterosexuality. Members of the Wolfenden Committee, who met between 1954 and 1957 to debate the matter of homosexuality (and who eventually recommended its decriminalization), assumed that same-sex desire was an acquired and distinctly modern problem somehow connected with the growing consumerism of British society (and thus a falling away from the productive work, savings and sacrifice that had been celebrated in earlier decades). If heterosexuals worked hard and sacrificed for the sake of the next generation, the committee reasoned, homosexuals, who were less likely to have children, spent their disposable income on consumer pleasures and promiscuous sex. Thus freed from any curb on their consumer-oriented and promiscuous lifestyles, free-wheeling gay men went about "contaminating" impressionable youths and thus threatening Britain with eventual collapse.[43] The explanatory power of the slippery slope from consumer indulgence to effeminacy and same-sex vice retained its influence well into the twentieth century.

Anxieties about the future of British manhood were also expressed in high-brow culture. Riding the wave of social criticism that surged after the Suez Crisis of 1956 (proof to many that Britain's days as a world power were over), the phenomenon of the "Angry Young Man" represented another engagement with the presumed effeminacy of the affluent society, a working-over, as

" Surely you remember yourself, Bill Rawlinson ? The man who stormed across Europe just a few short years ago ? "

Figure 8.2   Men Only (1948).

John Hill suggests, of "a more generalised cultural anxiety around the question of male identity."[44] So what were these young men so angry about? The note of discontent sounded in John Wain's *Hurry on Down* (1953) reached a crescendo with John Osborne's popular play *Look Back in Anger* (1956), and a year later with the works of Colin Wilson, the best-known "philosopher" of the group. Although a great deal of resentment in these works was heaped upon women, whose changing social status threatened to rob men of traditional roles in the workplace, the real target was a more amorphous "effeminacy" that seemed to characterize the nation's postwar affluence and decline as an imperial power. Cultural snobbery, superficiality, pettiness and materialism were just some of the ingredients of this perceived effeminacy, the antidote for which sometimes seemed to be suggested in a validation of manual labor and a directness of expression that seemed out of place in a world devoted to consumerism and surfaces. As well as being the focus of complaints in relation to their changing role in the workplace women also served to focus these diffuse anxieties about effeminacy, in some cases becoming explicit targets of the protagonists' rage, as vividly portrayed in *Look Back in Anger*.[45]

Despite these critiques of postwar affluence and conformity, others found ways of asserting oppositional forms of manhood through consumption.[46] The so-called "Teddy Boys" are a case in point. By 1950 the nostalgic "New Edwardian" look, which called for bowler hats, polished shoes and rolled umbrellas, had migrated from the affluent West End to the working-class neighborhoods of South London. Here, as youth cultures had done for decades, proletarian dandies appropriated elite styles for the less refined purposes of gang identification and rough, street-fighting values. With fancy hair-styles, drape jackets with flaps and velvet collars, boot-lace ties, flowery or plain waistcoats, and tight trousers, the Teddy Boy ensemble would have cost around £20, which was an unusual amount for working-class males of the time to spend on themselves. By the mid-1950s, the Teddy Boys had become associated in the public eye with delinquency and aggression, especially after widely reported instances of gang fighting, vandalism (notably during the rock and roll movie *Rock around the Clock*), and even murder.[47] While their working-class parents dismissed the Teddy Boy look as "effeminate," worried elites associated the flamboyant yet violent style more with Hollywood movies and mass consumerism than with the upper-class dandyism it had obviously appropriated. As a result, media accounts of youthful destruction and theft were often framed with reference to sartorial transgressions and consumer-driven exhibitionism.[48]

Similar misgivings about the impact of consumerism on manhood were voiced across Western Europe. If Germans were not prepared to come to terms with the infamy of their Nazi past, many were quick to lament the decline of manly vigor that seemed to mark the entire nation following the defeat. In the immediate postwar years, West German officials complained that women and children comprised 67 per cent of the population and that only 23 per cent of people belonged to the middle class, facts that suggested a feminization and proletarianization of an already defeated country.[49] Nevertheless, by the 1950s many Germans found themselves immersed in the new world of technological conveniences and consumer comforts. Economists and policy-makers endorsed the introduction of a market economy as a means of regenerating the nation, thus displacing energies that might have been directed at nationalism into the project of creating what economics minister Ludwig Erhard called "a free nation of consumers."[50] "Catching up" was the key phrase in West German society. When surveys asked people which goods they had to acquire in order to be doing well, refrigerators, washing machines, vacuum cleaners and (later) televisions topped the list.[51]

Things were somewhat different across the border, where East Germany lacked a burgeoning consumer culture. Rather than seeking to recast men as husbands and fathers, as was the case in West Germany, East Germans tried to craft the "New Socialist Man" through a militarized link between manliness, sacrifice and the state.[52] However, despite these differences, both East and West Germany found the project of remasculinization hampered by unruly working-class youths whose predilection for American culture seemed to transform them into males of ambiguous gender. On the one hand, with consumerism so often associated with women in the postwar era, the interest that these young men took with their appearance and in consumer goods suggested a narcissistic self-indulgence that made them seem "feminine," at least when compared to the civilian husbands and fathers officially promoted as the ideal masculine figures. On the other hand, the kinds of goods consumed and the behavior they seemed to promote often projected aggression and violence: tight jeans, T-shirts, duck-tail hairdos, and short, often leather jackets were recognizable signs of what many saw as a dangerously aggressive hypermasculinity, one disturbingly redolent of fascist violence and resolutely at odds with more restrained middle-class ideals of manhood. The media resurrected the 1920s term *Halbstarke* (literally, "semi-strong") to describe males whose unconventional behavior seemed to qualify them as only partly masculine.[53]

As in Britain, this sense of male crisis was exacerbated by the growing link between young men and the influx of American popular culture: dancing, jazz and rock music, and films, in particular westerns and thrillers. Here, too, American culture was taken to represent a continuum of "savage" realities, from the African-American elements of popular music to the uncouth cowboys, tough gangsters and private eyes who appeared on celluloid. American films comprised the majority of those released in West Germany during the 1950s, and though only a handful were released in East Germany, officials estimated that in 1956–57 around 26,000 East Germans crossed into West Berlin daily to see these movies. Until the Berlin Wall was erected in 1961,

East Germans seeking dime novels about America could obtain them fairly easily from "exchange" shops along the border areas of West Berlin. Worried East German authorities closely linked juvenile delinquency to the impact of these often violent cultural imports, especially in the wake of the robberies and murders committed by Werner Gladow and his gang in the late 1940s. Authorities made much of Gladow's penchant for American gangster and cowboy tales as an explanation for his criminality.[54] A few years later, teen rebellion films such as *The Wild One* (1955) were thought to provide a "realistic" portrayal of youth culture and gender relations in the US, where no town was safe from leather-clad biker gangs who routinely terrorized residents and corrupted nice local girls. When thirty-six riots between police and mostly male teens erupted across West Germany between April and September 1956, it was generally agreed that *The Wild One* had more or less provoked these disturbances (despite the fact that biker gangs had existed in Germany long before its release).[55]

Following its defeat in 1940 and the subsequent ugly social realities of German occupation, French national self-esteem was at a particularly low point by the end of the war. As Michael Kelly rightly observes, in the postwar era "masculine identity was one of the devastated reaches of French life that had to be reconstructed." Yet the restoration of men to leading roles in politics and the economy did not put to rest misgivings about manhood. Rather, attention began to be directed at the kinds of men who dominated the postwar world. As in Britain and West Germany, in France the economic boom produced "new men" who bore a disturbing similarity to their American counterparts. This new managerial class of highly-educated technocrats, *les jeunes cadres*, allowed older anxieties about the cerebral, non-martial male to resurface, and during the 1950s they posed a stark contrast to the physical virility embodied in peasants and in revolutionary cadres active in Algeria. While the latter groups embodied an ethic of sacrifice that placed a premium on daring and physical strength, the *jeune cadres* spent considerable leisure time engaged in a cult of comfort that negated traditional notions of active and virile manhood. This was, to be sure, a lifestyle that revolved around male dominance in a home that was lovingly maintained by faithful wives, who had at their disposal an army of modern appliances. Yet, as Kristen Ross suggests, "the qualities required of the new middle-class businessman – a certain amorphous adaptability bordering on passivity, serviceability, a pleasant nature, and being on the whole devoid of singularity – amounted to a distinct loss in virility."[56]

Les jeunes cadres seemed especially vulnerable on sexual grounds, where physicians linked their conditions of life to homosexuality and impotence right up to the 1970s. Sexologists concurred that there was something disturbing about bourgeois sexuality, contending that the "more or less morbid intellectualism" of the organization man's lifestyle was a *cause* of the homosexuality they claimed was rife within this professional class.[57] Sexual impotence was also linked to the distinctive lifestyles of the postwar era. "Deprived of its *élan vital* by debilitating conditions of life, comfortable habits, the slackening of bodily functions, and an excess of often adulterated food," observed one study, "the body gives precedence to a cerebrality that is pushed beyond its breaking point ... Among men this ceaseless, overexcited use of intellect leads to the exhaustion of the vital forces."[58] The same point was made in the *Dictionnaire de la virilité*, an A-to-Z of modern impotence which offered what it called a "map of exhausted France." Here, too, male sexual impotence was cast as a primarily urban phenomenon connected to the "breathless rhythm of civilization," the stresses of modern life and the hygienic problems of the bourgeois professions.[59]

The drama of the Algerian war proved a depressing backdrop to these misgivings about modernity and virility; *le jeune cadre* paled in comparison to revolutionary cadres who struggled against political repression and whose sexual virility was a given. As Frantz Fanon observed, fantasies about black manhood often evoked white fears about how the cerebral focus of civilization promoted sexual repression and even impotence among white men. "Every intellectual gain requires a loss in sexual potential," Fanon observed. "The civilized white man retains an irrational longing for unusual eras of sexual licence, or orgiastic scenes, of unpunished rapes, of unrepressed incest ... For the majority of white men the Negro represents the sexual instinct (in its raw state). The Negro is the incarnation of genital potency beyond all moralities and prohibitions."[60] Yet the *jeune cadre*'s less polished "other" did not need to be represented only by a black man, as demonstrated in Christiane Rochefort's *Les Stances à Sophie* (1963). Disillusioned with her marriage to the technocrat Philippe, the working-class protagonist Céline has an affair with an Italian peasant that leads to a familiar conclusion about manhood and modernity: "virility seems to recede as urbanization rises."[61]

Amid the prosperity and technological advances of the postwar era, when the triumph of modernity seemed to validate the efforts of the white middle class, the Gallic organization man suffered from similar concerns as his American cousin. Both observed a widening gap between socio-economic success and masculinity, and each found a semblance of relief in fantasies about civilization's opposite. This is perhaps one reason why, from the 1950s to the present, Club Méditerranée (Club Med) has been able to market itself as an "antidote to civilization" where men and women could escape the wear and tear of modern life. None of this, of course, really represented a rupture with the consumerism that also characterized modern civilization, but a further packaging of the primitive as something capable of existing both within and against modernity.[62]

BARBASOL BARBARIANS

As the above sketch suggests, tensions between polish and primitivity, brains and brawn, and activity and sedentariness, have continued to animate and complicate representations of masculinity in the twentieth century. To be sure, what Tom Pendergast describes in the American context as "modern masculinity" may be characterized by an emphasis on "personality, sexuality, self-realization, and a fascination with appearances, all traits that made men well suited to participate in the social and economic institutions" of the twentieth century.[63] No matter how prevalent such concerns would become, however, the tensions of the postwar era indicate that none of these investments in appearance, leisure or consumption provided unproblematic validations of masculinity. Rather they activated nostalgic longings for simpler realities that have been deemed "lost" as a casualties of the modern world. If the postwar period differs from previous eras, it may be in the systematic celebration and commercialization of "savagery" as a counterpoint to the risks of over-civilization – even as the "nature" on offer is also a product of modernity, often with a price tag, like anything else. Following an older pattern that has grown in intensity since 1900, men have been exhorted to achieve unstable and nearly impossible syntheses of the respectable and the savage. As Christine Castelain-Meunier rightly observes, "This vacillation between the domestic man and the wild man simulates the malaise and ambiguity of modern man."[64]

Thus, postwar mass culture readily reworked the Western tradition of adventure fiction to speak to new generations of males hungry for different realities. On offer were a spectrum of heroic male types whose relationship with civilized refinements were typically complex, from the suave refinement and narcissism of James Bond to the impressive muscular feats of Hercules and Tarzan. Indeed, Edgar Rice Burroughs's fictional jungle man experienced a resurgence in popularity in the early 1960s, with reissued paperback novels selling like hot cakes. As they had earlier in the century, critics drew direct parallels between these fantasies of male strength and the more modest realities that men faced in the real world. According to Gore Vidal, the only function played by these "dreamselves" was the compensatory project of establishing "personal primacy in a world which in reality diminishes the individual."[65] The same could be said of the very popular sword-and-sandal (or "peplum") films produced in Italy just a few earlier, where characters such as Hercules and Maciste (who had been popular during the early fascist years) wowed a new generation of theater-goers both in Europe and North America.[66] With American bodybuilders playing the lead roles, the gratification these films provided could be at once compensatory and nostalgic, for Italy's economic miracle of the 1950s witnessed dramatic migration of muscular labor from the rural south to machine-based jobs in the industrial north. As Richard Dyer usefully suggests, to such viewers the spectacle of muscles was "an affirmation of the value of strength to an audience who was finding that it no longer had such value."[67] A similar nostalgia for the fringes of civilization may be found in the European interest in westerns after 1945, whether in the "spaghetti" variety that predominated in Italy once the peplum cycle had run its course, or in the continuing German fascination with the works of Karl May, whose stories of Winnetou and Old Shatterhand sold a million copies a year from 1945 to 1990 and inspired a number of films.[68]

The devaluation of muscularity in practical terms seems to have occasioned its overvaluation in the world of fantasy, status and symbols. Although images of the mesomorphic superman have circulated widely since the 1890s, it was not until the 1960s that a considerably bulking up of the ideal male body took place (and a greater acceptance of exercise, if not anabolic steroids, as a way to achieve it). If earlier emphases on the well-built body were dogged by suspicions of homoeroticism, during the 1970s champion bodybuilder Arnold Schwarzenegger helped make the practice more respectable as a mainstream ideal for heterosexual men.[69] In recent decades the hyper-muscular male body has become more pronounced as an ideal, notably in commercialized boy culture. American action figures like G.I. Joe and the male heroes from *Star Wars* look like they've been "juicing" since they first appeared in 1960s and 1970s: today one is more likely to find male toy figures with unrealistically slender waists and equally implausible chests and biceps (a tendency that parallels the fantastic proportions of girls' toys, notably Barbie).[70] A recent study of *Playgirl* magazine further illustrates how recent a phenomenon this shift to hypermuscularity really is. Whether the main readers of *Playgirl* are women or gay men, the fact remains that, since 1973, its male centerfolds have gained about 27 lbs worth of muscle.[71] One result of this obsession with muscularity is a growing number of men suffering from body image problems in a way that has hitherto been associated primarily with women.[72] In a society where extreme muscular development has scant functional value in everyday life, the look and feel of strength may be attractive for the aura of control and invulnerability it seems to confer. Muscles have become male fashion accessories in the cult of appearances.

If everyday life provided few opportunities to test one's muscular prowess, grooming and fitness remained important in both professional and romantic terms. In France, for instance, personal appearance and consumer taste became increasingly important for men during *les trentes glorieuses*. In cinema, the attractiveness of the young Alain Delon, whose physical image was often closely associated with the growing consumerism of this period, was enhanced by the contradiction inherent in the icy and tough characters that he often played.[73] Endorsing such narcissism, male beauty guides like *Masculin quotidien* (1969) encouraged men to care for all aspects of their embodied existence. Advice ranged from the proper care of skin, hair, teeth, hands and feet to suggestions on walking, dieting, exercise, weight loss, massage, leisure time, and leading a "life of sexual equilibrium." For *Masculin quotidien* the intimate details of the body demanded attention, inside and out, but the ultimate goal of this daily care was not health or well-being, but "seduction" in all aspects of life. To some extent this outward orientation had always been a rationale for the healthy body, but by the postwar era an emphasis on appearances had clearly reached center stage. "Man should possess all of the 'trump cards' that allow him to maximize his seductive potential," readers were informed. "There is no doubt that a man who feels that he 'looks great' and is 'in shape,' who is relaxed and lively, healthy and attractive, has, at first glance, a power to charm superior to that of a man who is nervous, always tired, [or] fat."[74]

As always, consumer culture was there to complete the male persona, often employing rhetoric that denied that anything so "feminine" as actual consumption was taking place. If one were to believe advertising copy, it would seem that the world of commodities was a rather dangerous place. In ads selling woolen pajamas to men, for instance, references to the product's softness were replaced by language emphasizing its raw, even wild qualities, not to mention its "virile" cut. Fabergé's "Go West" line of toiletries challenged men to "recover your taste for adventure. Even for your skin ... If you're not afraid to be a man." And if selecting the right skin care product proved too much excitement for one day, one could always unwind with the symbolic gesture of the Canadian cigarette, Macdonald's Export "A." Here a man could quietly contemplate his deep connection with the bearded fur trappers who graced the Macdonald's ads, the kind of Frenchmen who had colonized and built Canada centuries before.[75] That the only dangers this Gallic Marlboro Man would probably face included lung cancer and impotence were less important than the fantasies of unfettered manhood such advertisements evoked.

Gender-coded advertising provided another way of putting adventure back into life. The new breed of corporate financiers who made their mark on the banking world from the 1980s onward eagerly embraced bodily maintenance and discipline as keys to their success. This concern was paramount among the London bankers interviewed by Linda McDowell in the 1990s, most of whom offered unsolicited information about their clothes and body weight. More than a third of these men claimed to work out regularly, while nearly half said they engaged in some form of sporting activity. They were also likely to "discipline" their subordinates by exhorting them to care more for their appearance, to lose weight, to get a better haircut, or to select more tasteful clothes. As a result of this obsession with looks, most bankers cut a strikingly

uniform appearance, a point which was often commented upon by inter-
viewees and was a recurring feature in Bret Easton Ellis's Wall Street satire,
American Psycho (1991), where the yuppie serial killer, Patrick Bateman, is constantly being confused with someone else (which is how he escapes detection
for the senseless and brutal murders he regularly commits).[76] Bateman the
refined sociopath could not be accused of losing touch with his savage side.

Reactions to the so-called "metrosexual" exemplify the paradoxes that men
face with regard to competing and contradictory messages about how to be
both masculine and modern at the same time. As defined by the British
columnist Mark Simpson in 1994, whose account was largely ironic, the term
"metrosexual" refers to "the single young man with a high disposable income,
living or working in the city (because that's where all the best shops are)" and
represents "one of the most promising consumer markets" of the 1990s.
Rather than a completely new being, the metrosexual may be more profitably
viewed as a further development of marketing and consumption patterns
already established in the 1950s. "Metrosexuals are the creation of capitalism's
voracious appetite for new markets."[77] By definition situated in urban contexts, the stereotypical metrosexual bore all the signs of the over-civilized
male: a preoccupation with appearances, refined manners and at least the
semblance of culture. Nevertheless, the project of personal refinement is often
represented as an act requiring willpower and pain, and the body being
refined is likened to an industrial object. Skin care through the use of cosmetics, cleansers and shaving products are routinely "masculinized" by being
depicted as boundary-building labor rather than mere beautification. Face and
body scrubs are recommended far more often than moisturizers and softeners,
not least because abrasive exfoliates are likened to an industrial smoothing
that is not unlike sand-blasting. Even something as mundane as personal
grooming can awaken fantasies of metallic hardness, the metrosexual as man
of steel. As a writer for the *Sydney Morning Herald* announced, "Men want
tough skin that isn't a hindrance. They want steel panelling, not silk lining,
and they want to suffer in their efforts to achieve that result. That is why men
like face and body scrubs. They like that gravel rash feeling that only a good
exfoliant can give."[78] The fashion magazine *GQ* even suggested that skin care
was a kind of technical skill, declaring at one point that regular "maintenance
is required" when "tending the well-oiled machine" that is the male body.[79]

Under the rule of the performance principle, bodies have become more and
more like machines, especially when it comes to the installation and replacement of parts. Cosmetic surgery has, in recent decades, come to the rescue of
growing numbers of men seeking to improve their appearance through facial
alterations and implants. Those lacking the time or the inclination to develop
muscles through exercise and/or steroids may, for a hefty price, take advantage of bicep, pectoral and calf implants through muscle contouring surgery.[80]

In addition to helping individuals design their own ideal bodies, such measures "can help build self-confidence in those who were once embarrassed by their appearance."[81] And, of course, bodies that can be so thoroughly remade through surgical means can also be transformed into the opposite sex. If alterations of the male body had once aimed at the restoration of a natural physicality diminished by modern life, technology has increasingly removed "nature" from the equation altogether to render the body almost infinitely malleable.

As has often been the case, male physical performance seemed to receive its harshest reviews in the bedroom. Mid-twentieth-century claims that male sexual impotence was primarily the result of psychological causes, cerebral lifestyles or insatiable women gave way during the late-1980s to the urological concept of "erectile dysfunction," which transformed the problem from a mental state into a thoroughly organic "disease" whose frequency among aging men was said to be on the rise. Studies in the 1990s asserted that around 52 per cent of men over forty could expect to suffer "some degree of erectile dysfunction," leading many to conclude that this constituted an "epidemic" that threatened the emotional well-being of aging men and their partners. With emotional and other psychological factors removed from the scene, erectile dysfunction could now be viewed as a simple mechanical problem treatable through penile implant surgery, which was developed in the early 1960s as a cure for impotence and has increased in popularity ever since.[82]

The language of machine-like power and performance also underlines the attractions of Viagra (sildenafil citrate), which, since its introduction in the late-1990s, quickly transcended its therapeutic purpose to become a party drug in certain circles.[83] The fact that many countries fast-tracked the approval of Viagra reveals the perceived seriousness of the problem, and thus the sorry state of civilized man's sexual reliability. This could be a particular blow to national self-esteem, notably in countries long renowned for the lustiness of their men. The French media not only criticized the intrusion of this American pharmaceutical innovation into their nation, but deeply resented the implication that the fabled French lover would ever need such chemical assistance. Unsurprisingly, many journalists also levelled the blame at women who, in addition to seeking financial independence and equity in the workplace, demanded satisfaction in the bedroom, thus placing even greater strains upon the male machine. Catherine Breillat's controversial film *Romance* (1999), dubbed the "first real film of the Viagra era," generated similar anxieties. Starring the Italian porn star, Rocco Siffredi, widely known as the "Italian Stallion" both for his penis size and claims to have bedded over 4000 women, *Romance* featured an eight-minute scene of explicit penetrative sex where the penis was the real star. Some journalists wondered why a French penis (with an actor attached) could not have been found for this starring role.[84]

Bodies enhanced or altered through chemical means for the sake of appearance or performance have thus become relatively commonplace today, especially in the world of professional sport, where record-breaking performances are applauded by men and women whose own lifestyles demand little physical exertion. Such vicarious experiences may indeed compensate for otherwise sedentary and mundane adult lives. Nevertheless, actual athletic performance and other examples of "tough" behavior remain essential elements of childhood for many boys, among whom the ability and willingness to inflict and endure pain remain essential markers of masculinity, key ingredients in becoming "somebody." Pain thus continues to be a currency that is traded in the formation of acceptable masculine identities.[85] Despite the greater acceptance of female athletic performance since the 1960s and 1970s, it is the male body whose athletic prowess receives the greatest attention and carries the most symbolic capital for growing boys. Even when the female athlete fulfills reigning ideals of maximum performance and efficiency, by challenging prevailing gender stereotypes about how "feminine" bodies should look and act, her success always risks being undermined through the violation of ideals of female beauty and comportment.[86] Complicated hairstyling and long painted "feminine" fingernails sometimes seem to be used by female athletes to offset the apparent maleness of well-developed musculature.

The performance principle thus remains alive and well, even among men in professions hitherto seen as leading to an early grave. By the 1980s a new personality disposition called "hardiness" was developed to identify traits that might protect ambitious men from the negative effects of stress on their mental and physical well-being. The hardy executive was characterized by control, commitment and a tendency to embrace change as a personal challenge. Unlike the pathological Type A man, whose obsessions made him a high risk for coronary heart disease, the hardy executive was described as more controlled, flexible and resilient, and thus able to remain successful and ambitious in the face of the instabilities of modern business. Ruggedly strong and individualistic, this was a

> gentrified version of the populist spirit of the hard and self-made man ... While the construct of Type A man made traditional masculinity into a medical issue, the construct of hardiness redefines and reinvents masculinity for modern middle-class men. Men are now told that they can be committed to the American work ethic without having to pay the health costs for this kind of behavior, if they remain in control and be responsible.[87]

The conduct and health literature to support this body image appears monthly in the men's magazines that have emerged in the 1990s. Aimed at the upwardly-mobile, college-educated, politically-conservative, heterosexual carnivore, mass-circulation magazines like *Men's Health*, which is published in foreign-language editions across the West, confirm the business world's view of the ideal male body as sporting rock-hard abs, bulging biceps and pectorals.[88] That such attributes are presented as evidence of "health" suggests just how far we have come from nineteenth century ideals of balance and harmony.

So central had the allure of primitivity become during the postwar era that even anti-patriarchal revolts against the strictures of modern manhood found inspiration in fantasies of unfettered "nature." As we have seen, in a world of increasing consumption and inactivity, suffering and pain have played important roles in the formation of modern male identities, at least when imagined in terms of their fighting and laboring potential. What differed after the 1950s was the *acceptability* of vocalizing complaints about this suffering. As a recent study of two counter-cultural communities shows, hippie societies often prided themselves on their proximity to the less fettered manhood of Native Americans and African Americans, and thus to its perceived ability to access a more "authentic" way of being a man.[89] In the wake of the women's movement and the civil rights movement, a number of men began asking questions about the wounds they routinely suffered in an effort to meet dominant expectations of masculinity. Male liberationist texts often spoke of how "patriarchy" was damaging for both men and women, emotionally as well as physically, and recommended a relaxation of repressions to allow for the freer expression of feeling. Yet, as Sally Robinson observes, the blocked emotions often cited in these texts usually consisted of anger and resentment, rarely love or fear, and their expression was described in violent terms, all of which allowed these men to masculinize emotion in rather traditional ways. Unlike women who expressed anger at their blocked social opportunities, male liberationists raged against the fact of emotional blockage itself. The direct expression of rage thus becomes a form of therapy for men who have been socialized to repress their feelings.[90]

It is easy to see why these validations of "free" manhood would mutate into more sexist forms over time: regenerative appeals to "nature" always contain anti-modern tendencies that can be pressed toward reactionary as well as progressive ends. Whether informed by sociobiology or mythopoetic therapies, the return to "true" masculinity usually requires a process of getting beneath the sedimented habits of everyday modernity. Robert Bly and his ilk have been rightly associated with the chorus of male victimization observed in American culture since the 1960s; yet the "crisis" to which the members of the men's movement often refer pertains to long-term structural paradoxes of modernity that have only accelerated in recent decades. Bly's influential unpacking of the Wild Man within invokes images of primordial masculinity that have haunted the civilizing process every step of the way. Of course what Bly proposes is getting in touch with a "deep masculine" that is compatible with modernity yet capable of transcending its feminizing tendencies.

Nevertheless, it is difficult to see this kind of man as anything other than fundamentally unstable: "The Wild Man is not opposed to civilization," Bly claims, "but he's not completely contained by it either."[91]

In addition to disaffected white heterosexuals who had grown weary of their own ambiguous manhood, the attractions of "primitive" masculinity appealed to a number of marginalized groups. Spicing up the muscular ethos of early Zionism with the tough-guy posturing of writers like Norman Mailer, many Jewish men continued to refute allegations of effeminacy by emphasizing their virile, fighting qualities.[92] Since the Stonewall riots of 1969, gay men have not only mobilized in defense of their rights, but many resolutely rejected the prevailing stigma of gay effeminacy by donning a proletarian sartorial style (blue jeans, flannel shirts, leather jackets, topped off with short hair and a mustache) and more muscular physiques. While seemingly conforming to the image of the "real man," the so-called "clone" subverted traditional understandings of masculinity while implicitly reinforcing stereotypes about gay men.[93] With the outbreak of HIV/AIDS in the 1980s, moreover, muscularity was understandably taken as a sign of health that distanced many gay men from the emaciated, withered bodies of those who were dying. Gay men are thus not exempt from the prevailing assumptions that "real" men are ideally physically fit and adept at sports.[94]

Few groups know the divided nature of white manhood better than African Americans, whose campaign for civil rights since the 1950s has often foregrounded the interests of the black male breadwinner. Even though Martin Luther King privileged the concerns of African-American males, by the late 1960s the distinction between the peaceful King and more militant civil rights leaders were usually gendered. The overtly martial manhood represented by the Black Power movement constituted a direct refusal of old stereotypes about black docility and cowardice, but also perpetuated stereotypes about black brutality. In a world where the white middle-class was maligned for its complacency and weakness, yet nevertheless retained its dominance in the political, social and economic spheres, conciliation with this kind of manhood seemed as politically futile as it was unmanly. Eldridge Cleaver famously posited a gendered racial distinction between black men ("supermasculine menials") and white men, those "omnipotent administrators" who excel in organizational matters but have relegated physical power to blacks and other subordinates. This is how "THE MAN," as the white establishment was often depicted in Black Power discourses, could represent both power and weakness. The white man compensated for his lack of physical power by seeking to control black bodies, mainly by depriving them of access to education but also by curtailing their access to white women.[95] As Michele Wallace observed, such reductions of racial oppression to the problem of manhood sidelined the concerns of black women, who were expected "to understand that manhood was essential to revolution – unquestioned, unchallenged, unfettered manhood."[96]

In America and elsewhere, many people of color seem to accept and even perpetuate dehumanizing stereotypes of savage black men "as a mark of distinction," as bell hooks notes. In the face of white socio-economic and political dominance, this physical menace is "the edge that they have over white males."[97] Just as the African-American influence on jazz and rock music enhanced the "primitive" liberation that such musical forms and their culture offered, so too does the embrace of "gangsta" culture by white youths provide an imaginative connection with a "savagery" that peddles catharsis while reinforcing blatantly sexist and homophobic sentiments and deeds. But, of course, virile savagery draws upon imagery based on class as well as race. Today the "New Lad" culture of Britain celebrates male irresponsibility and sexism, with rock stars Noel and Liam Gallagher (from the band Oasis) offered as counterpoints to the apparent refinement of the king of metrosexuals, soccer great David Beckham. British men's magazines like *Loaded* (founded in 1994) and imitators like *For Him Magazine* (*FHM*) revel in this renewed focus on working-class styles of masculinity, addressing themselves to single men in their teens and early twenties. New Lads embrace more traditional forms of male consumption, and are thus "dedicated to life, liberty and the pursuit of sex, drink, football and less serious matters." In their negotiation of modernity and masculinity, these recent incarnations of the urban primitive embrace some elements of civilization (material comforts and sedentary lifestyles) while seeking to minimize the impact of others (education and politeness). "We have accepted what we are and have given up trying to improve ourselves."[98]

* * *

The twentieth-first century thus began with more conflicted representations of and prescriptions for male behavior. Alongside movements to rediscover the "wild man" within were a series of novels and films that indulged the widespread complaint that white, middle-class men had become the victims of a politically-correct, pro-woman culture that left them jealous, jobless and powerless. While most situated their narratives in the present, others looked, with Nietzsche, Wells and Huxley, to the distant future to project the possible consequences of contemporary trends. Visions of a feminized future were even humorously floated in the action film *Demolition Man* (1993), which is really just a variation on Huxley's *Brave New World* with all of the gender elements thrown into relief. The eponymous *Demolition Man* is the aptly named "John Spartan," a cryogenically frozen super-cop (played by Sylvester Stallone) who has been thawed to combat a grotesquely maniacal defrosted criminal (Wesley Snipes) who is rampaging through the pacified world of 2032. In a caricature of Huxley's vision, with flashes of *The Time Machine* thrown in for good measure, this is a politically-correct and vaguely New Age utopia/dystopia where all unhealthy and dangerous speech, deeds and substances have been banned. "Things don't happen anymore," proudly declares one police official; "we've taken care of all that." Even love-making has been replaced by the "digitized transference of sexual energies" that delivers thunderous pleasure without demanding anything so coarse as physical contact. One result of this *extensio ad absurdum* of the civilizing process is a laughably inept police force unable to cope with this resurgence of the old ultra violence and thus much in need of the pyrotechnic regeneration that only Stallone can deliver. The proudly unkempt rebels who have chosen a different life for themselves underground are led by the fast-talking, chain-smoking comic Dennis Leary, who appears in the film mainly to launch his trademark tirade about political correctness and healthy lifestyles. The world may have become "a pussy-whipped, Brady-Bunch version of itself," but we know that Stallone and company will fix all that.

Conclusion
The Return of the Repressed

If, like many historical phenomena, representations of gender and the body suggest an interplay between residual and emergent cultural tendencies, then historians need to remain attentive to the dialectic of continuity and change that shapes masculinities throughout the modern era and across national boundaries. Chuck Palahniuk's novel *Fight Club* (1996) is a particularly vivid example of how the gendered discourse of civilization continues to refract popular perceptions of masculinity.[1] In this novel and its acclaimed 1999 film adaptation, a depressed yuppie discovers in bare-knuckle boxing a violent yet rejuvenating alternative to a shallow life devoted to politeness, consumption and appearances. The men who share in his immersion in pain and violence are soon ready for the paramilitary/terrorist organization known as Project Mayhem, which unleashes a more concerted assault upon a modernity that, in their view, has robbed men of virility and the world of values. Project Mayhem's goal, we learn, is none other than "the complete and right-away destruction of civilization," after which a rejuvenated humanity will thrive in post-apocalyptic urban jungles.

> You'll hunt elk through the damp canyon forests around the ruins of Rockefeller Center, and dig clams next to the skeleton of the Space Needle leaning at a forty-five degree angle. We'll paint the skyscrapers with huge totem faces and goblin tikis, and every evening what's left of mankind will retreat to empty zoos and lock itself in cages as protection against bears and big cats and wolves that pace and watch us from outside the cage bars at night.[2]

In *Fight Club* the path back to manhood passes through the body, especially its appetites, activity, endurance and hardness, to emerge rejuvenated from the wreckage of modernity itself. Of course this dream is not borne out at the end of the novel. Rather the struggle against civilization takes on more fascistic and destructive overtones that are even less tolerant of individual expression. Though sometimes accused of glamorizing and even promoting some of the experiences it invokes, it is perhaps fairer to say that *Fight Club* explores the tensions between manhood and modernity without necessarily proposing clear solutions.

Nevertheless *Fight Club*'s relentless obsession with the implications of modernity for men is beyond doubt. In line with the longstanding cultural tendency to elide women with the very experiences that seem to "feminize" men, *Fight Club*'s critique of civilization barely acknowledges that women might also suffer from a world based on consumption and appearances.[3] Instead *Fight Club* foregrounds pain and violence as repressed male experiences that, when released under controlled conditions, are at once cathartic, therapeutic and empowering. Not unlike the Zen Buddhist use of the *kyosaku* stick, each blow that is meted out in bare-knuckle boxing serves to jolt men out of their capitalist-induced existence while forcibly returning them to the "enlightenment" of raw bodily experience and a clear apprehension of "reality." Moreover, by assembling men from a variety of ethnic/racial groups and income levels, the novel implies that the ills of civilization affect all males regardless of race or class. In this way it dramatizes issues similar to those probed in Loïc Wacquant's sociological analysis of lower-class boxers in Chicago. In addition to providing economically disadvantaged men with a semblance of control over their lives (and an illusory sense of someday making it big), professional boxing requires them to "decisively realign the structure and texture of their entire existence – its temporal flow, its cognitive and sentient profile, its psychological and social complexion – in ways that put them in a unique position to assert their agency ... Through the ministry of boxing, fighters' ambition is to remake themselves and the world around them." Significantly, this ambition is most fully realized in the bout itself, which propels boxers into a zone where feelings of mastery are born of the sensation of exuberance:

> Professional pugilism enables its devotees to escape the realm of mundanity and the ontological obscurity to which their undistinguished lives, insecure jobs, and cramped family circumstances relegate them and enter instead into an extra-ordinary, "hyperreal" space in which a purified and magnified masculine self may be achieved. It does this first by thrusting them in the midst of a luxuriant sensory landscape, a broad and varied panorama of affect, pleasure, and dramatic release ... Set against the monochromatic tone of everyday life in the shadow of urban marginality, even the highly reiterative and predictable routine of training is animated and alluring due to the shift it causes in the "balance of the sensorium" and to the continual kinesthetic, visual, tactile, and aural stimulation it procures.[4]

While focused on the economically marginalized, Wacquant's analysis also provides insight into what men from various social groups have historically called real "life" as opposed to the artificiality of modern culture. Even if most middle-class men might shy away from such extreme solutions, the fantasmatic allure of these practices may be located in this perceived gap between the veneer of civilization and the "reality" of intense physical experience. This is why some have perceived in *Fight Club* a kind of developmental tale for males struggling with their identities, while others have even sought to emulate aspects of bare-knuckle culture as a means of gender therapy. In 2001, an organization called "The Real Fight Club" was launched in London, giving white-collar men in their thirties and forties a chance to train as boxers and act out pugilistic fantasies for a price. Within two years more than a thousand men had already joined and the club was set to expand to Germany, South Africa, Australia and New Zealand.[5] Beyond such organized and supervised affairs are the numerous ad hoc teenage and adult fight clubs that have sprung up in Britain, the United States and elsewhere since the film was released. Even techies in Silicon Valley have their own fight club, where they have been discretely beating each other into "reality" since 2000.[6]

As misguided and disturbing as such developments may be (and leaving out of consideration altogether the dubious influence and emulation of media products), they obey a certain logic that this book has endeavored to trace. Many who study the social construction of gender today may subscribe to some version of Elisabeth Badinter's observation that "If masculinity is learned and constructed, there is no question that it can also change ... What has been constructed can therefore be deconstructed in order to be reconstructed anew."[7] The history of masculinities certainly supports this general idea; yet, without some further qualification, statements such as these risk minimizing the entrenched and durable nature of certain dominant images of manhood in Western culture, which – because they are continually counterposed to the gender-blurring tendencies of civilization – necessarily haunt late modern manhood. However diversely masculinities may be lived and represented in everyday life, our culture has yet to divest itself of the entrenched notion that manhood and civilization necessarily exist in a state of tension. Nor does the dismantling of this perception seem imminent. How can one undo deeply ingrained ideals of the rough and hardy masculine when the very conceptual structures of modern society seem geared to invoke such imagery whenever aspects of the "civilizing process" appear to go too far? How can the allure of male violence and risk-taking be dissipated when it continues to be represented as having been unfairly "repressed" along with such vulnerable feelings as love, fear and loneliness? How can we extend the benefits of "civilization" when so many representations of "freedom," "reality," and "life" are so resolutely opposed to it? One might agree with Klaus-Michael Bogdal that

the apparent blurring of genders in contemporary culture "masks a simultaneous tendency toward the reactivation of traditional gender behaviors ... Only
when we are presented with proof that the 'symbolic' construction of masculinity today corresponds to altered gender and power relations and obeys
different discursive rules than those that emerged in the eighteenth century
will we be able to speak of 'New Men.' For the moment, I see few reasons for
doing so."[8]

The international tensions gripping the world today both encourage and
thrive upon a reactivation of what are perceived to be traditional gender
behaviors, even if those behaviors are so often part of the problem. Looking at
foreign affairs through the dubious lens of sociobiology, neoconservative guru
Francis Fukuyama contends that the "feminization of democratic politics" will
never be able to overcome the tendencies of males to "band together for competitive purposes, seek to dominate status hierarchies, and act out aggressive
fantasies toward one another." Such biological drives, Fukuyama informed
readers, might be "rechanneled but never eliminated." Imagining a cauldron
of aggressive drives simmering beneath civilization's veneer is apparently
good news for those worried about the state of contemporary manhood.
However it's less good for Europeans, who, according to Fukuyama, suffer
from such demographic problems that one day their political and foreign pol-
icies might end up being influenced primarily by elderly women.[9]

During the debacle of the Iraq War this view of Europe's diminishing virility
was seconded by another neoconservative, Robert Kagan, who provocatively
declared that "on major strategic questions today, Americans are from Mars
and Europeans are from Venus." Like Fukuyama, Kagan aligns power and
bellicosity with masculinity while locating conciliation and weakness squarely
on the feminine side. Even while claiming to admire the *"mission civilisatrice"*
that Europeans launched in the wake of World War II, Kagan maintains that
Europeans today must toughen themselves up by adopting a more militaristic
spirit. American belligerence might even have a regenerative effect on European virility. "Maybe concerns about America's overweening power really will
create some energy in Europe. Perhaps the atavistic impulses that still swirl in
the hearts of Germans, Britons, and Frenchmen – the memory of power, international influence, and national ambition – can still be played upon ... These
urges are now mostly channeled into the grand European project, but they
could find more traditional expression." While admitting that whether "this is
to be hoped for or feared is another question,"[10] Kagan expends precious little
time exploring this matter, as if the consequences of nationalistic militarism
are somehow unimportant.

Kagan's "analysis" thus amounts to calling Europeans sissies. Yet however
Americans may feel about warfare, their nation's belligerence has little to do
with either the population's physical fitness or its martial capacity.[11] As inhab-

itants of the most materialistic and obese country in the West, they rather seem bent on realizing the "paradise of little fat men" that Orwell predicted. Thus most Americans leave the actual work of fighting, killing and dying to professional warriors while vicariously enjoying carnage through the media, team sports, video games, and any other spectacles where men hurt other men (televised "cage fighting" is just a recent update to the *Rollerball* scenario). Of course male violence is not all vicarious, either in America or elsewhere. In addition to those men who commit violent crimes, there are those who take a more principled stance toward the softness of modern life, and profess a readiness to fight if motivated by the right cause. Some of these causes are disturbing yet familiar. Described as one of the most widely-read books among the American far-right, William Pierce's *The Turner Diaries* (1978), depicts a future race war pitting the extremists of the "Organization" against the US government, which finally ends in the extermination of blacks and Jews across the world. Yet racial minorities are not the only enemies confronted during the so-called Great Revolution. If blacks and Jews have come to dominate white America, Pierce maintains, it is largely because most whites have become so beholden to their soft and comfortable lives. Since the early tactics of the Organization only targeted institutions, life is for most Americans "still moderately comfortable, and comfort is the great corruptor, the great maker of cowards." The persistence of softness becomes the rationale for the use of political terror as tactics that rouse whites from their laziness. "Our attitude is that those whose only concern is to enjoy life in these times of trial for our race do not deserve life. Let them die." This and other murderous wishes are fulfilled at the end of the novel: "As the war of extermination wore on, millions of soft, city-bred, brainwashed Whites gradually began regaining their manhood. The rest died."[12]

These are fringe sentiments, and one hopes they will remain that way; yet they differ from related critiques of civilization only in terms of degree. The religious right's fulminations against modernity since the 1980s have often included a critique of the effeteness and weakness of those educated and latte-sipping "liberals" who, against considerable evidence to the contrary, are said to dominate all aspects of American life. Unlike the upright, hard-working (and well-armed) Christian who defends his country and "his" women, liberals are defined by their "unmanly" intellectuality and refinement as well as their sexually indeterminate bodies. Railing against the "girlie men" he encountered in the White House of Bill Clinton, former FBI agent Gary Aldrich discerned "a unisex quality to the Clinton staff that set it apart from the Bush administration. It was the shape of their bodies. In the Clinton administration, the broad-shouldered, pants-wearing women and the pear-shaped, bowling-pin men blurred distinctions between the sexes. I was used to athletic types, physically fit persons who took pride in body image and good health."[13] This is why conservative critics were able to allege during the 2004 presidential campaign that Democratic candidate John Kerry was not only a "metrosexual," but that he "looked French" and that, if elected, he would make America as "soft" as the nation that refused to support the war in Iraq.[14]

Whatever their views of international affairs, Europeans (the French too) have continued to express concern about the state of manhood in the modern world. The magazine *Esprit* devoted an entire issue to changing gender relations, and featured an article by Claude Fischler that connected the civilizing process to a "féminisation des moeurs" in which ideas and practices "traditionally considered specifically feminine are increasingly adopted by the other sex," a development he saw as especially marked in the areas of consumption, appearance and the body.[15] Similar concerns were raised in 2003 when the women's magazine *Elle* devoted much of an issue to the "malaise" of men by inviting opinions from musicians, novelists, psychologists and philosophers. Popular singer Patrick Bruel observed that contemporary women expect men to be able to do it all, even if it requires contradictory demands: "The man should at once forget the threadbare values of machismo to cast himself in the values of femininity, or at least sometimes seem to cast himself in them. But, once he has integrated those values, the woman will reproach him for his lack of virility."[16] (Not that contradictory demands are the bane of masculine lives only: proverbially women should be cooks in the kitchen, ladies in public and whores in the bedroom.) However, political journalist Éric Zemmour concurs, claiming that today there are "no longer men, there are no longer women, nothing but equal human beings, necessarily equal, even better than equal, identical, undifferentiated, interchangeable ... We indeed live in an age of a totalitarian and castrating mixing of the sexes."[17] Despite this feared erasure of gender distinctions, in France as elsewhere representations of political power still rely on suggestions of male corporeal prowess, as is evinced by the efforts of the magazine *Paris-Match* to manage President Nicolas Sarkozy's body by retouching photos of his "love handles," presumably so he could seem lean as well as mean.[18]

Similar thoughts have been expressed in Britain, whose population once prided itself on being more manly than the French. With women beginning "to take part in every sphere of life that used to be reserved for maleness," complained a writer for *The Times*, "manhood stands, as it were, on the edge of extinction ... Nothing I do anymore, but nothing, marks me out as a man."[19] Others have claimed that "the opinion-formers who talk up this crisis of masculinity want such a crisis to exist because they wish to redefine the male role and masculinity itself out of existence."[20] Dubbed by one critic a "feminized" country in which men have been "neutered," Britain epitomizes the sorry condition of "being a man" in what the writer Robert Twigger colorfully dubbed "the lousy modern world."[21]

This is a truly international refrain, though some sing more loudly and for longer periods than others. At present, the American-style "corporate imaging and representation of men" pervades the European media, where "the ideology of what it means to be a 'real man' is transformed into advertisement images of expensive businessmen's clothing or young stylish men or, in some countries, working clothes."[22] Even Russia and the former Soviet states, which had always looked westward for lessons in modernity, have been experiencing gender trouble as a partial result of their sudden immersion in American-style consumer culture. The decline of the male role as chief breadwinner has been cited as a primary reason for a growing sense of male unease, where incidences of alcoholism, suicide and premature death have increased since the closing decades of the Soviet era.[23] Despite these problems, mass culture continues to provide fantasmatic ways of soothing the hurt caused by economic hardship and social dislocation. Since 1988 tough guy fiction and films from the West have flooded into Eastern Europe, and have in some instances spawned Russian imitations. In the popular political thrillers of Aleksandr Kabakov, such as *The Adventures of a Real Man* (1993) and *The Last Hero* (1995), women are marginalized in favor of active male heroes who are quite comfortable with the new consumerism that has sprung up around them.[24] In August 2007 photographs of the shirtless Russian president Vladimir Putin engaging in rugged outdoor activities elicited numerous comments about his buff physique, and even prompted the popular tabloid *Komsomolskaya Pravda* to publish an exercise guide called "Get a Body Like Putin's."[25]

Despite the enthralling spectacle of male political bodies, some have critiqued the very emphasis on consumption and appearances that has seemingly replaced traditional ideals about austerity in Eastern Europe. Written by the Latvian journalists Alexander Garros and Aleksei Evdokimov, and clearly inspired by the shock tactics of 1990s American and British popular culture, the novel *Headcrusher* (2003) depicts a post-Soviet Riga trapped in the "pseudo-life" promoted by the culture industries of the West.[26] Vadim Apletaev is a journalist-turned-PR man for a major bank, "a petty cog, the lowest link in a long chain of cogs" (p. 24). After murdering his boss, this latter-day Raskolnikov begins killing his way up the corporate ladder, with Tarentinoesque results. As in *Fight Club*, violence is what jolts Vadim out of his commodity-induced reverie, and ends up prompting the usual speculations about how the course of civilization has left men with no outlet for their elemental drives. He comes to realize that modern life satisfies a man's primary needs while creating artificial ones that ultimately have no connection to basic biological life. Commodity culture induces "sensory overload from the visual to the olfactory, battering, flattening, swamping, flooding, cocooning in sensation" (p. 81).

For Vadim the internet and computer games are the logical consequence of this retreat from reality. "Here you have the direct earthing, the virtualisation of the young male's instincts, destructive and otherwise ... so that our young male won't start actualising his destructive potential right here in the social sphere ..." (p. 244). The man who becomes a success in this world ends up being "emasculated, squeezed dry. Used up. All your vital juices had been expended on the attainment of alienated, abstract goals" (p. 79). By killing four people, Vadim comes to see his everyday "reality" as a "grotesque and ludicrous mimetic simulacrum of real life in which there was absolutely nothing worth doing, let alone being afraid of" (p. 182). For this man, one of civilization's many malcontents, the path to authentic rather than "pseudo-life" often seems to lead through violence and pain. That the real and its simulacrum are no longer easily distinguished – that what passes for "life" is also a form of "pseudo-life" – doesn't seem to matter.

  In the face of such widespread concerns about manhood and modernity, it is striking to see that some of the most scathing attacks on the Western world emerge from belief systems that continue to value traditional warrior codes and ultra-conservative gender roles. Indeed, woven into geopolitical and religious critiques about Western interference in the Middle East is the familiar analysis of modern civilization as a feminizing process that leaves men soft, complacent and cowardly. It is for these reasons that fundamentalist Islam explicitly offers itself as a form of "rescue" for the identity problems faced by modern men,[27] and thus dovetails with Christian and other fundamentalist movements whose critiques of modernity often seek a restoration of anti-quated gender roles as part of the "new" world they envision. The fundamentalist challenge to Western achievements in gender and sexual equality is at once vexing and ironic. "The remarkable irony of history," observes Leo Braudy, "is that just at the time that, in the wake of World War II, such attitudes have been open to the most widespread criticism, at a time when women have achieved more structural equality than ever before, when homosexual behavior is no longer so officially stigmatized, the West is faced with an enemy emerging from the ancient lands of the Aryan warriors, whose own canons of sexuality attempt to reestablish a past from which the West has been distancing itself."[28] With what are for women oppressively traditional gender roles high on the list of desirable social transformations, Al-Qaeda, the Taliban and their fellow travelers have launched their own warrior critique of civilization, with striking similarities to the self-critique that has recurred in the West since the seventeenth century. Claiming that "true" manhood has disappeared in Europe and North America, these fundamentalist warriors set themselves up as New Men ushering in a heroic New Age.

  Building upon metaphorical references to the imminent disappearance of manhood, in popular culture today the ultimate challenge that modernity poses to the male body may be literal extinction. This is at the crux of Brian K. Vaughn's acclaimed graphic novel series, *Y: the Last Man*, which began its run in 2002 and is now being planned as a feature film. *Y* explores the matter of "gendercide" where a mysterious plague wipes out all male mammals on earth, save an unemployed former English major and his capuchin monkey.[29] Vaughn's engaging story is an obvious response to recent scientific studies claiming that the disappearance of males is already underway as the result of millennia of evolutionary development. If biologists during the early days of evolutionary theory were of two minds when it came to the relationship between modernization and masculinity, today's geneticists plot the gradual decline and eventual extinction of the Y chromosome as an obsolete vestige of humanity's early history.[30]

Others suggest that we may not need to wait 125,000 years for the extinction of males, and thus of humanity generally. As an increasing number of scientific studies suggest, the industrial chemicals that are now virtually inescapable components of modern life have been linked to growing cancer rates as well as diminishing sperm counts across the Western world. It has also been found that chemicals like DDT alter animal reproduction and development by mimicking the hormone estrogen, and thus block the action of androgens. These stunt the physical development of male animals while leaving females relatively unaffected.[31] The irony that "mother earth" would seem to respond so energetically to male-dominated modernity through the "feminization of nature" has not been lost on contemporary observers. "Gaia's revenge," notes one scientist, "is hitting men where it hurts most."[32]

If such dire predictions reduce Nietzsche's concept of the "last man" to the most corporeal of terms, they are also variations on the recurring cultural theme that this book has endeavored to trace. Although sometimes perceived as being an extension and facilitator of "patriarchal" gender relationships, modernity continues to function as a double-edged sword that, among its many paradoxical effects, extends and supports male dominance while creating the conditions that subvert the "natural" basis for that dominance. The same civilization that bolsters male dominance also contains the seeds of its undoing, which is one reason why this concept has elicited such diverse reactions throughout the modern era. Yet history is not necessity, and the negative patterns of the past might be undone if people are prepared break with modes of thought and behavior that have outlived their usefulness. To return to Raymond Williams's terms, perhaps we can more fully embrace our emergent possibilities by collectively refusing the residual cultural elements that frustrate our attempts to think and behave differently. By probing the durable and entrenched aspects of this tension between masculinity and modernity, this book illustrates both the possibility and the difficulty of moving beyond the constraints of history.

Notes

INTRODUCTION: CIVILIZATION AND ITS MALCONTENTS

1. Isaac Asimov, *The Robots of Dawn* (London: Panther Books, 1985), pp. 9, 18 (Asimov's emphasis)
2. Simone de Beauvoir, *The Second Sex*, trans. H.M. Parshley (1949; New York: Vintage, 1989), p. 267; Max Horkheimer and Theodor W. Adorno, *Dialectic of Enlightenment*, trans. John Cumming (1944; New York: Continuum, 1989), p. 33.
3. See Judith Butler's influential discussion of gender performativity in *Gender Trouble: Feminism and the Subversion of Identity* (New York: Routledge, 1990), pp. 138–9, but also Pierre Bourdieu's insistence on the relative durability of the *habitus* in *La domination masculine* (Paris: Seuil, 1998), pp. 29–30.
4. This idea of "multiple hegemonic masculinities" relative to different contexts is developed in Andrea Cornwall and Nancy Lindisfarne, "Dislocating Masculinity: Gender, Power and Anthropology," in Andrea Cornwall and Nancy Lindisfarne (eds), *Dislocating Masculinity: Comparative Ethnographies* (London: Routledge, 1994), p. 20. On the importance of attending to the temporality of gender, see Gabriela Spector-Mersel, "Never-Aging Stories: Western Hegemonic Masculinity Scripts," *Journal of Gender Studies*, 15 (1) (March 2006): 67–82.
5. On the "patriarchal dividend," see R.W. Connell, *Masculinities* (Sydney: Allen & Unwin, 1995), p. 79.
6. Connell, *Masculinities*, p. 84. This point has been made by many others as well.
7. Sally Robinson, *Marked Men: White Masculinity in Crisis* (New York: Columbia University Press, 2000), pp. 10–11.
8. Melanie Phillips, *The Sex-Change Society: Feminised Britain and the Neutered Male* (London: The Social Market Foundation, 1999), p. xiii.
9. Marshall Berman, *All That is Solid Melts into Air: the Experience of Modernity* (London: Verso, 1995), p. 15. That modernity and the civilizing process generate ambiguous and even contradictory effects is a common theme in sociological treatments of modernization. See, for instance, Zygmunt Bauman, *Modernity and Ambivalence* (Cambridge: Polity, 1993), and Ian Burkitt, "Civilization and Ambivalence," *British Journal of Sociology*, 47 (1) (March 1996): 135–50.
10. Rita Felski, *The Gender of Modernity* (Cambridge, MA: Harvard University Press, 1995), pp. 1–4.
11. Ulrich Beck, *The Reinvention of Politics: Rethinking Modernity in the Global Social Order*, trans. Mark Ritter (Cambridge: Polity, 1997), pp. 63, 67.
12. My understanding of the double logic of civilization owes much to Jacques Derrida's concept of supplementarity. See Derrida, *Of Grammatology*, trans. G.C. Spivak (Baltimore: Johns Hopkins University Press, 1976), pp. 141–64. For a major reconceptualization of modernism, see Roger Griffin, *Modernism and Fascism: the Sense of a Beginning under Mussolini and Hitler* (Basingstoke: Palgrave, 2007). Griffin demonstrates how social, political and aesthetic modernisms often recommended forward-looking reconnections with "lost" sources of spirituality and body culture in order to imagine purified forms of modernity in the future.

13. R.W. Connell, *The Men and the Boys* (Berkeley: University of California Press, 2000), p. 59. As it is employed in social and political discourses, the very concept of "crisis" often features an implicit medical understanding inherited from the ancient Greeks. Crisis thus necessarily points us to the body as a referent, even if only metaphorically. Koselleck, "Crisis," trans. Michaela W. Richter, *Journal of the History of Ideas*, 67 (2) (April 2006): 361.

14. Compare Susan Stanford Friedman, "Definitional Excursions: the Meanings of Modern/Modernity/Modernism," *Modernism/Modernity*, 8 (3) (2001): 493–513.

15. Bruce Mazlish, *Civilization and its Contents* (Stanford: Stanford University Press, 2004). Gail Bederman rightly observes how "different people, with different political agendas, defined and deployed 'civilization' differently," citing how "this very mutability and flexibility" helped make the discourse of civilization such a powerful form of argument during this time. Yet Bederman does not define what "civilization" means or periodize its emergence, but opts instead to examine the "process of articulation" itself. Bederman, *Manliness and Civilization: a Cultural History of Gender and Race in the United States, 1880–1917* (Chicago: University of Chicago Press, 1995), pp. 23, 40–1.

16. Jean Starobinski, *Blessings in Disguise; or, The Morality of Evil*, trans. Arthur Goldhammer (Cambridge, MA: Harvard University Press, 1993), pp. 3, 6 (emphasis in original); see also Raymond Williams, *Keywords: a Vocabulary of Culture and Society* (New York: Oxford University Press, 1983), p. 58.

17. Even in German-speaking (and later in Slavic) countries, the normative principles, values and ideals implicit in the concept of civilization were placed under the rubric of "culture" or *Kultur*, while *Zivilisation* was reserved for the more technical and practical aspects of this idea. Hence "civilization" continued to be an operative principle even in countries that expressed some reservations about the term. Jaroslav Krejcí, *The Paths of Civilization: Understanding the Currents of History* (Basingstoke: Palgrave, 2004), p. 7; Raymond Geuss, "*Kultur, Bildung, Geist*," *History and Theory*, 35 (2) (May 1996): 151–64.

18. Alice Bullard, *Exile to Paradise: Savagery and Civilization in Paris and the South Pacific, 1790–1900* (Stanford: Stanford University Press, 2000), pp. 14–15.

19. As Kathleen Canning notes, in many cases scholars "merely invoke the body or allow 'body' to serve as a more fashionable surrogate for sexuality, reproduction, or gender without referring to anything specifically identifiable as body, bodily or embodied." Canning, "The Body as Method? Reflections on the Place of the Body in Gender History," *Gender & History*, 11 (3) (November 1999): 499.

20. Antony Easthope, *What a Man's Gotta Do: the Masculine Myth in Popular Culture* (Boston: Unwin Hyman, 1990), pp. 35–44.

21. Stefan Dudink, "Masculinity, Effeminacy, Time: Conceptual Change in the Dutch Age of Democratic Revolutions," in Stefan Dudink, Karen Hagemann and John Tosh (eds), *Masculinities in Politics and War: Gendering Modern History* (Manchester: Manchester University Press, 2004), pp. 89–90; see also Harold Mah, *Enlightenment Phantasies: Cultural Identity in France and Germany, 1750–1914* (Ithaca, NY: Cornell University Press, 2003), p. 7.

22. Dominick LaCapra, "Trauma, Absence, Loss," *Critical Inquiry*, 25 (Summer 1999): 696–727.

23. Beck, *Reinvention of Politics*, p. 64.

24. Compare Jeffrey Herf, *Reactionary Modernism: Technology, Culture, and Politics in Weimar and the Third Reich* (Cambridge: Cambridge University Press, 1984).

25. For a classic example of the "crisis" model, see Annelise Maugue, *L'identité masculine en crise au tournant du siècle, 1871–1914* (Paris: Éditions Rivages, 1987); on women

and male sexual impotence, see Angus McLaren, *Impotence: a Cultural History* (Chicago: University of Chicago Press, 2007), pp. 42–4, 61–8, 103, 108–12, 219–21.

26. This was the case in the colonies as well as the metropole, where a female influence was thought capable of smoothing out the "natural" roughness of males. Ann Laura Stoler, "Rethinking Colonial Categories: European Communities and the Boundaries of Rule," *Comparative Studies in Society and History*, 31 (1) (January 1989): 144.

27. Quoted in Paul Birukoff, *Leo Tolstoy: His Life and Work* (New York: Charles Scribner's Sons, 1911), p. 102.

28. Sarah Watts, *Rough Rider in the White House: Theodore Roosevelt and the Politics of Desire* (Chicago: University of Chicago Press, 2003), p. 16.

29. Robert Aldrich, "Homosexuality and the City: an Historical Overview," *Urban Studies*, 41 (9) (August 2004): 1719–37.

30. Harry Oosterhuis, *Stepchildren of Nature: Krafft-Ebing, Psychiatry, and the Making of Sexual Identity* (Chicago: University of Chicago Press, 2000), pp. 33, 53–5.

31. Starobinski, *Blessings*, p. 5.

32. Ann Laura Stoler, *Race and the Education of Desire* (Durham, NC: Duke University Press, 1995), p. 75.

33. Alastair Bonnett, "From White to Western: 'Racial Decline' and the Idea of the West in Britain, 1890–1930," *Journal of Historical Sociology*, 16 (3) (September 2003): 320–48; Mazlish, *Civilization and its Contents*, p. 17.

34. For a discussion of non-Western engagements with the notion of civilization, see Anna Tsing and Gail Hershatter, "Civilization," in Tony Bennett, Lawrence Grossberg and Meaghan Morris (eds), *New Keywords: a Revised Vocabulary of Culture and Society* (Oxford: Blackwell, 2005), pp. 36–9.

35. Richard Slotkin, *Regeneration through Violence: the Mythology of the American Frontier, 1600–1860* (Middletown, CT: Wesleyan University Press, 1973), pp. 29–30.

36. David Cannadine, *Ornamentalism: How the British Saw Their Empire* (London: Allen Lane, 2001), p. 125.

37. Penny Edwards, "On Home Ground: Settling Land and Domesticating Difference in the 'Non-Settler' Colonies of Burma and Cambodia," *Journal of Colonialism and Colonial History*, 4 (3) (2003): paragraphs 12, 25; Eric T. Jennings, "From *Indochine* to *Indochic*: the Lang Bian/Dalat Palace Hotel and French Colonial Leisure, Power and Culture," *Modern Asian Studies*, 37 (1) (February 2003): 159–94; E.M. Collingham, *Imperial Bodies: the Physical Experience of the Raj, c. 1800–1947* (Oxford: Polity Press, 2001), pp. 84–7.

38. Rob Kroes, *If You've Seen One, You've Seen the Mall: Europeans and American Mass Culture* (Urbana, IL: University of Illinois Press, 1996).

39. On Australian misgivings about being "modern," see David Walker, "Modern Nerves, Nervous Moderns: Notes on Male Neurasthenia," *Australian Cultural History*, no. 6 (1987): 49–63; for the classic formulation of the "cultural cringe" see A.A. Phillips, *On the Cultural Cringe* (1950; Melbourne: Melbourne University Press, 2006).

40. George L. Mosse, *The Image of Man: the Creation of Modern Masculinity* (New York: Oxford University Press, 1996), p. 5.

1   FOUR FACES OF CIVILIZATION, *c.* 1500–1750

1. Leo Braudy, *From Chivalry to Terrorism: War and the Changing Nature of Masculinity* (New York: Knopf, 2003).

2. Raymond Williams, "Base and Superstructure in Marxist Cultural Theory," *New Left Review*, no. 82 (November–December 1973): 10–11.

3. Pierre Bourdieu, *Distinction: a Social Critique of the Judgement of Taste*, trans. Richard Nice (Cambridge, MA: Harvard University Press, 1984), p. 207.

4. Norbert Elias, *The Civilizing Process*, trans. Edmund Jephcott (1939; Oxford: Blackwell, 1994), p. 204.

5. Elias, *Civilizing Process*, p. 447.

6. Michael Steppat, "Social Change and Gender Decorum: Renaissance Courtesy," in Jacques Carré (ed.), *The Crisis of Courtesy: Studies in the Conduct-Book in Britain, 1600–1900* (Leiden: E.J. Brill, 1994), p. 29.

7. Martin J. Weiner, "The Victorian Criminalization of Men," in Pieter Spierenburg (ed.), *Men and Violence: Gender, Honor, and Ritual in Modern Europe and America* (Columbus, OH: Ohio State University Press, 1998), p. 200.

8. Robert Bartra, *Wild Men in the Looking Glass: the Mythic Origins of European Otherness*, trans. Carl T. Berrisford (Ann Arbor, MI: University of Michigan Press, 1994), p. 147.

9. Bartra, *Wild Men*, pp. 110–11.

10. Peter Burke, *The Fortunes of the* Courtier: *the European Reception of Castiglione's* Cortegiano (Cambridge: Polity, 1995), pp. 14–15.

11. Anna Bryson, "The Rhetoric of Status: Gesture, Demeanour and the Image of the Gentleman in Sixteenth- and Seventeenth-Century England," in Lucy Gent and Nigel Llewellyn (eds), *Renaissance Bodies: the Human Figure in English Culture, c. 1540–1660* (London: Reaktion, 1990), pp. 140–1; Robert A. Nye, *Masculinity and Male Codes of Honor in Modern France* (Oxford: Oxford University Press, 1993), pp. 16–22.

12. Burke, *Fortunes*, p. 31.

13. Baldassare Castiglione, *The Book of the Courtier* (1527; London: J.M. Dent and Sons, 1944), pp. 33, 35–6, 39.

14. Burke, *Fortunes*, pp. 158–62; Jorge Arditi, *A Genealogy of Manners: Transformations of Social Relations in France and England from the Fourteenth to the Eighteenth Century* (Chicago: University of Chicago Press, 1998), pp. 117, 129.

15. Desiderius Erasmus, *On Good Manners for Boys [De Civilitate morum puerilium]* (1530), in *Collected Works of Erasmus, vol. 25,* J.K. Sowards, ed. (Toronto: University of Toronto Press, 1985), pp. 269–89; Burke, *Fortunes*, p. 16.

16. Giovanni della Casa, *Galateo, or The Book of Manners*, trans. R.S. Pine-Coffin (1558; Harmondsworth: Penguin, 1958), p. 22.

17. Elizabeth A. Foyster, *Manhood in Early Modern England: Honour, Sex and Marriage* (London: Longman, 1999), pp. 35–6.

18. Charles Taylor, *Sources of the Self: the Making of Modern Identity* (Cambridge: Cambridge University Press, 1989), p. 159. See also Dorinda Outram, *The Body and the French Revolution: Sex, Class and Political Culture* (New Haven, CT: Yale University Press, 1989), pp. 69–71.

19. Georges Vigarello, "S'exercer, jouer," in Georges Vigarello (ed.), *Histoire du corps: 1. De la Renaissance aux Lumières* (Paris: Seuil, 2005), p. 236.

20. Elias, *Civilizing Process*, pp. 452–3.

21. Jeroen Duindam, *Myths of Power: Norbert Elias and the Early Modern European Court* (Amsterdam: Amsterdam University Press, 1994), p. 168.

22. Bryson, "Rhetoric of Status," p. 152.

23. This point is clearly illuminated in the history of Russian masculinities. See Rebecca Friedman and Dan Healey, "Conclusions," in Barbara Evans Clements, Rebecca Friedman, and Dan Healey (eds), *Russian Masculinities in History and Culture* (Basingstoke: Palgrave, 2002), p. 229; see also Lyndal Roper, *Oedipus and the Devil* (London: Routledge, 1994), pp. 151–3, 157.

24. Maurice Keen, *Origins of the English Gentleman: Heraldry, Chivalry and Gentility in Medieval England, c.1300–c.1500* (Charleston, SC: Tempus, 2002), pp. 88–9. The same may be said of Dutch nobles, few of whom held military offices in the sixteenth

century. H.F.K. van Nierop, *The Nobility of Holland: From Knights to Regents, 1500–1650*, trans. Maarten Ultee (Cambridge: Cambridge University Press, 1993), p. 22.

25. Maurice Keen, *Chivalry* (New Haven, CT: Yale University Press, 1984), p. 32.

26. Bryson, "Rhetoric of Status," pp. 147–8; James J. Supple, *Arms versus Letters: the Military and Literary Ideals in the 'Essais' of Montaigne* (Oxford: Clarendon Press, 1984), pp. 12–15.

27. Dena Goodman, *The Republic of Letters: a Cultural History of the French Enlightenment* (Ithaca, NY: Cornell University Press, 1994), pp. 92–3.

28. Helen Watanabe-O'Kelly, *Court Culture in Dresden: From Renaissance to Baroque* (New York: Palgrave, 2002), pp. 45–59; Duindam, *Myths of Power*, p. 162.

29. Ronald G. Asch, *Nobilities in Transition, 1550–1700: Courtiers and Rebels in Britain and Europe* (London: Arnold, 2003), pp. 56–60.

30. Supple, *Arms versus Letters*, p. 88.

31. Asch, *Nobilities*, p. 60.

32. Robert Burton, *The Anatomy of Melancholy* (1621; New York: AMS Press, 1973), I: 349, II: 107.

33. Supple, *Arms versus Letters*, pp. 103, 109, 266.

34. On this point, see Ken Plummer, "General Introduction," in Ken Plummer (ed.), *Sexualities: Critical Concepts in Sociology* (New York: Routledge, 2002), I: 1.

35. David Halperin, "How to do the History of Male Homosexuality," *GLQ*, 6 (1) (2000): 93.

36. Joseph Cady, "The 'Masculine Love' of the 'Princes of Sodom' 'Practising the Art of Ganymede' at Henri III's Court: the Homosexuality of Henri III and his *Mignons* in Pierre de L'Estoile's *Mémoires-Journaux*," in Jacqueline Murray and Konrad Eisenbichler (eds), *Desire and Discipline: Sex and Sexuality in the Premodern West* (Toronto: University of Toronto Press, 1996), pp. 132–3.

37. Joachim Bumke, *Courtly Culture: Literature and Society in the High Middle Ages*, trans. Thomas Dunlap (Berkeley: University of California Press, 1991), pp. 199–200.

38. John E. Crowley, *The Invention of Comfort: Sensibilities and Design in Early Modern Britain and Early America* (Baltimore: Johns Hopkins University Press, 2001), pp. 3–7, 69–73; Tomas Maldonado, "The Idea of Comfort," *Design Issues*, 8 (1) (Fall 1991): 35–6.

39. Rahel Hahn, "The Wood, the Word, and the Cure: Ulrich von Hutten's Self-Presentation as a Healed Syphilitic," in Rudolf Käser and Vera Pohland (eds), *Disease and Medicine in Modern German Cultures* (Ithaca, NY: Center for International Studies, 1990), p. 4.

40. Crowley, *Invention*, p. 72.

41. Daniel Roche, *A History of Everyday Things: the Birth of Consumption in France, 1600–1800*, trans. Brian Pearce (Cambridge: Cambridge University Press, 2000), p. 108.

42. Maxine Berg and Elizabeth Eger, "The Rise and Fall of the Luxury Debates," in Maxine Berg and Elizabeth Eger (eds), *Luxury in the Eighteenth Century: Debates, Desires and Delectable Goods* (Basingstoke: Palgrave, 2003), p. 7.

43. Crowley, *Invention*, pp. 141, 149; Cissie Fairchilds, "The Production and Marketing of Populuxe Goods in Eighteenth-Century Paris," in John Brewer and Roy Porter (eds), *Consumption and the World of Goods* (London: Routledge, 1993), pp. 228–48.

44. Edward Hundert, "Mandeville, Rousseau and the Political Economy of Fantasy," in *Luxury in the Eighteenth Century*, 29; E.J. Clery, *The Feminization Debate in Eighteenth-Century England: Literature, Commerce and Luxury* (New York: Palgrave, 2004), p. 63; Crowley, *Invention*, p. 157; Roche, *History of Everyday Things*, pp. 75–6.

45. Laurence Dickey, *Hegel: Religion, Economics, and the Politics of Spirit, 1770–1807* (Cambridge: Cambridge University Press, 1987), pp. 221–2.
46. John P. Mallan, "Roosevelt, Brooks Adams, and Lea: the Warrior Critique of the Business Civilization," *American Quarterly*, 8 (3) (Autumn 1956): 216–30.
47. Mark Seltzer, *Bodies and Machines* (New York: Routledge, 1992), p. 152.
48. Vicesimus Knox, *The Spirit of Despotism* (London, 1795), p. 155.
49. David Kuchta, *The Three-Piece Suit and Modern Masculinity: England, 1550–1850* (Berkeley: University of California Press, 2002), p. 147.
50. Paul A. Silverstein, "The Kabyle Myth: Colonization and the Production of Ethnicity," in Brian Keith Axel (ed.), *From the Margins: Historical Anthropology and its Futures* (Durham, NC: Duke University Press, 2002), p. 136; Ana María Alonso, "The Politics of Space, Time and Substance: State Formation, Nationalism, and Ethnicity," *Annual Review of Anthropology*, 23 (1994): 395; Edwards, "On Home Ground," paragraphs 12–14.
51. Bartra, *Wild Men*, p. 3; see also John K. Noyes, "Nomadic Landscapes and the Colonial Frontier: the Problem of Nomadism in German South West Africa," in Lynette Russell (ed.), *Colonial Frontiers: Indigenous-European Encounters in Settler Societies* (Manchester: Manchester University Press, 2001), pp. 198–215.
52. Jean-Jacques Rousseau, *A Discourse on the Origin of Inequality* [1754], in *The Social Contract and Other Discourses*, trans. G.D.H. Cole (London: Everyman, 1993), p. 91.
53. Keen, *Chivalry*, pp. 111–12.
54. Richard Sennett, *Flesh and Stone: the Body and the City in Western Civilization* (New York: Norton, 1994), pp. 338–42.
55. Richard Mulcaster, *Positions Concerning the Training Up of Children*, William Barker, ed. (1581; Toronto: University of Toronto Press, 1994), pp. 34–5, 62; Marcia Vale, *The Gentleman's Recreations: Accomplishments and Pastimes of the English Gentleman, 1580–1630* (Cambridge: D.S. Brewer, 1977), pp. 112–17.
56. Jacques Gleyse, "La fabrication du corps? Le discours de l'âge classique sur le mouvement et l'exercise," *Stadion*, 23 (1997): 68–70.
57. Burton, *Anatomy*, I: 278, 280.
58. Jean-Jacques Rousseau, *Émile, or On Education*, trans. Allan Bloom (1762; New York: Basic Books, 1979), pp. 199–200.
59. William Buchan, *Domestic Medicine: or, a treatise on the prevention and cure of diseases by regimen and simple medicines* (3rd edition: London: W. Strahan, 1774), p. 90n.
60. Kenneth A. Lockridge, "Colonial Self-Fashioning: Paradoxes and Pathologies in the Construction of Genteel Identity in Eighteenth-Century America," in Ronald Hoffman, Mechal Sobel and Fredrika J. Teute (eds), *Through a Glass Darkly: Reflections on Personal Identity in Early America* (Chapel Hill, NC: University of North Carolina Press, 1997), p. 295.
61. Marianna Torgovnick, *Gone Primitive: Savage Intellects, Modern Lives* (Chicago: University of Chicago Press, 1990), p. 17.
62. Philip A. Mellor and Chris Shilling, *Re-Forming the Body: Religion, Community and Modernity* (London: Sage, 1997), p. 26.
63. Sigmund Freud, *Civilization and its Discontents*, trans. James Strachey (1929; New York: Norton, 1989), pp. 49–50.

2   BALANCING ACTS: THE PARADOX OF THE GENTLEMAN

1. Matthew Head, "'Like Beauty Spots on the Face of a Man': Gender in 18th-Century North-German Discourse on Genre," *Journal of Musicology*, 12 (3) (Summer 1995): 148.

2. John Tosh, *A Man's Place: Masculinity and the Middle-Class Home in Victorian England* (New Haven, CT: Yale University Press, 1999), pp. 111–12.
3. Janet Oppenheim, *"Shattered Nerves": Doctors, Patients, and Depression in Victorian England* (New York: Oxford University Press, 1991), p. 145.
4. Peter Burke, *The Fortunes of the* Courtier: *the European Reception of Castiglione's* Cortegiano (Cambridge: Polity, 1995), pp. 126–7.
5. David Yosifon and Peter N. Stearns, "The Rise and Fall of American Posture," *American Historical Review*, 103 (4) (October 1998): 1057–95.
6. Mark Motley, *Becoming a French Aristocrat: the Education of the Court Nobility, 1580–1715* (Princeton: Princeton University Press, 1990), p. 25; Georges Vigarello, "The Upward Training of the Body from the Age of Chivalry to Courtly Civility," in Michel Feher (ed.), *Fragments for a History of the Human Body, Part Two* (New York: Zone Books, 1989), pp. 157, 168–73, 179.
7. John Locke, *Some Thoughts Concerning Education* (1693; Oxford: Clarendon Press, 1989), section 65, 1.
8. Peter France, *Politeness and its Discontents: Problems in French Classical Culture* (Cambridge: Cambridge University Press, 1992), p. 57.
9. Charles Strachey (ed.), *The Letters of the Earl of Chesterfield to his Son* (London: Methuen, 1901); Ute Frevert, *Men of Honour: a Social and Cultural History of the Duel*, trans. Anthony Williams (Cambridge: Polity Press, 1995), pp. 13–14.
10. Daniel L. Purdy, *The Tyranny of Elegance: Consumer Cosmopolitanism in the Era of Goethe* (Baltimore: Johns Hopkins University Press, 1998), p. 6.
11. Good manners were primarily taught through the short but widely distributed tract, *On the Duties of Man and Citizen* (1783). Catriona Kelly, *Refining Russia: Advice Literature, Polite Culture, and Gender from Catherine to Yeltsin* (Oxford: Oxford University Press, 2001), pp. 8–9, 20, 24, 32–42, 46; Rebecca Friedman, "From Boys to Men: Manhood in the Nicholaeven University," in Barbara Evans Clements, Rebecca Friedman and Dan Healey (eds), *Russian Masculinities in History and Culture* (Basingstoke: Palgrave, 2002) , pp. 33–40. A similar development was under way on the other side of the world, where in eighteenth- and nineteenth-century America advice books were as likely to be imported and/or translated as home-grown. C. Dallett Hemphill, *Bowing to Necessities: a History of Manners in America, 1620–1860* (New York: Oxford University Press, 1999), pp. 115, 118.
12. Harold Mah, *Enlightenment Phantasies: Cultural Identity in France and Germany, 1750–1914* (Ithaca, NY: Cornell University Press, 2003), pp. 52–54; Vigarello, "Upward Training," p. 183.
13. France, *Politeness*, p. 66. See also Anne C. Vila, "Elite Masculinities in Eighteenth-Century France," in Christopher E. Forth and Bertrand Taithe (eds), *French Masculinities: History, Culture and Politics* (Basingstoke: Palgrave, 2007), pp. 15–30.
14. Barbara Alpern Engel, *Women in Russia, 1700–2000* (Cambridge: Cambridge University Press, 2004), p. 22.
15. Philip Carter, *Men and the Emergence of Polite Society, Britain 1660–1800* (London: Pearson, 2001), pp. 68–9.
16. Goodman, *Republic of Letters*, p. 233; Joan B. Landes, *Women and the Public Sphere in the Age of the French Revolution* (Ithaca, NY: Cornell University Press, 1988).
17. G.J. Barker-Benfield, *The Culture of Sensibility: Sex and Society in Eighteenth-Century Britain* (Chicago: University of Chicago Press, 1992), pp. 8–9; Carter, *Men and the Emergence*, p. 105.
18. J.B. Figgis, *Manliness, Womanliness, Godliness* (2nd edition; London: S.W. Partridge and Co., 1886), p. 23.

19. Kelly, *Refining Russia*, p. 46. "The perception of the restlessly laboring and emotion-ally impoverished rational man who draws his identity solely from his profession turns out to be a misleading stereotype and – if valid at all – is a backward projec-tion of the situation as it existed in the late nineteenth century." Charlotte Trepp, "The Emotional Side of Men in Late Eighteenth-Century Germany (Theory and Example)," *Central European History*, 27 (2) (Summer 1994): 135.

20. Dorothée Sturkenboom, "Historicizing the Gender of Emotions: Changing Percep-tions in Dutch Enlightenment Thought," *Journal of Social History*, 34 (1) (2000): 65.

21. Madelyn Gutwirth, *Twilight of the Goddesses: Women and Representation in the French Revolutionary Era* (New Brunswick, NJ: Rutgers University Press, 1992), pp. 3–22; Head, "'Like Beauty Spots,'" pp. 143–67.

22. Immanuel Kant, *Observations on the Feeling of the Sublime and the Beautiful*, trans. John T. Goldthwait (1764; Berkeley: University of California Press, 1960), pp. 59, 101–3; Prince M.M. Shcherbatov, *On the Corruption of Morals in Russia*, trans. A. Lentin (1768; Cambridge: Cambridge University Press, 1969), p. 145.

23. Michèle Cohen, "'Manners' Make the Man: Politeness, Chivalry, and the Construc-tion of Masculinity, 1750–1830," *Journal of British Studies*, 44 (2) (April 2005): 312–29. However chivalry did not merely offer a compromise between warrior and civilized ideals. Rather, as illustrated through Stacey Grimaldi's conduct book, *A Suit of Armour for Youth* (1824), wisdom, virtue, and knowledge corresponded to differ-ent parts of a knight's armor which, though infinitely lighter, offered young men metaphorical boundaries that would protect them from the pitfalls of the modern world. Allen J. Frantzen, *Bloody Good: Chivalry, Sacrifice, and the Great War* (Chicago: University of Chicago Press, 2004), pp. 122–3.

24. Douglas Smith, *Working the Rough Stone: Freemasonry and Society in Eighteenth-Century Russia* (Dekalb, IL: Northern Illinois University Press, 1999), p. 52; Kelly, *Refining Russia*, pp. 138, 140, 144–50.

25. Marjorie Morgan, *Manners, Morals and Class in England, 1774–1858* (New York: St Martin's Press, 1994), pp. 107, 108.

26. Honoré de Balzac, "Physiologie de la toilette," in *Théorie de la démarche et autres textes* (1830; Paris: Pandora, 1978), p. 137.

27. Rousseau, *A Discourse on the Moral Effects of the Arts and Sciences*, in *The Social Contract*, 6. Translation altered.

28. Quoted in Philippe Perrot, *Fashioning the Bourgeoisie: a History of Clothing in the Nineteenth Century*, trans. Richard Bienvenu (Princeton, NJ: Princeton University Press, 1994), p. 32.

29. Purdy, *Tyranny of Elegance*, p. 178.

30. J.C. Flügel, *The Psychology of Clothes* (London: The Hogarth Press, 1930), pp. 74–6.

31. Kaja Silverman, "Fragments of a Fashionable Discourse," in Tania Modleski (ed.), *Studies in Entertainment* (Bloomington, IN: Indiana University Press, 1986), p. 149.

32. Rather what irked the Puritans of this period were *French* fashions, food and goods. In absolutist France the clothes were soft, the food was odd and dainty, the manners over-refined, all of which posed a stark contrast to the supposedly wholesome plain-ness of English culture, liberty and masculinity. Kuchta, *Three-Piece Suit*, pp. 50, 57.

33. Kuchta, *Three-Piece Suit*, pp. 59, 79.

34. Kuchta, *Three-Piece Suit*, pp. 116; Margot Finn, "Men's Things: Masculine Possession in the Consumer Revolution," *Social History*, 25 (2) (May 2000): 133–55.

35. Warren G. Breckman, "Disciplining Consumption: the Debate about Luxury in Wilhelmine Germany, 1890–1914," *Journal of Social History*, 24 (3) (Spring 1991): 490; Russell W. Belk, *Collecting in a Consumer Society* (London: Routledge, 1995), p. 7.

36. Randolph Trumbach, "The Birth of the Queen: Sodomy and the Emergence of Gender Equality in Modern Culture, 1660–1750," in Martin Duberman, Martha Vicinus and George Chauncey (eds), *Hidden from History: Reclaiming the Gay and Lesbian Past* (New York: Penguin 1989), pp. 135–6.

37. Robert McGregor, "The Popular Press and the Creation of Military Masculinities in Georgian Britain," in Paul R. Higate (ed.), *Military Masculinities: Identity and the State* (Westport, CT: Praeger, 2003), p. 144.

38. Theo van der Meer, "Sodomy and the Pursuit of a Third Sex in the Early Modern Period," in Gilbert Herdt (ed.), *Third Sex, Third Gender: Beyond Sexual Dimorphism in Culture and History* (New York: Zone Books, 1993), pp. 182–3.

39. Leo Bersani, "Is the Rectum a Grave?" in Jonathan Goldberg (ed.), *Reclaiming Sodom* (New York: Routledge, 1994), p. 252. As Philip Carter explains, "the ensuing eighteenth-century debate over normative manliness took the form, broadly speaking, of a contest between two rival interpretations – one 'classical', the other 'refined' – both of which defined their subject in terms of a series of social, not sexual, acts." Carter, "An 'Effeminate' or 'Efficient' Nation? Masculinity and Eighteenth-Century Social Documentary," *Textual Practice*, 11 (3) (1997): 440.

40. Michael Zakim, *Ready-Made Democracy: a History of Men's Dress in the American Republic, 1760–1860* (Chicago: University of Chicago Press, 2003), pp. 11–36; Bertram Wyatt-Brown, *The Shaping of Southern Culture: Honor, Grace, and War, 1760s–1880s* (Chapel Hill, NC: University of North Carolina Press, 2001), p. 39; Carroll Smith-Rosenberg, "The Republican Gentleman: the Race to Rhetorical Stability in the New United States," in *Masculinities in Politics and War*, pp. 66–8.

41. Purdy, *Tyranny of Elegance*, pp. 166–7.

42. Lynn Hunt, *Politics, Culture, and Class in the French Revolution* (Berkeley: University of California Press, 1984), pp. 75–86; Purdy, *Tyranny of Elegance*, pp. 180–94; Zakim, *Ready-Made Democracy*, pp. 22–4.

43. Kuchta, *Three-Piece Suit*, p. 147.

44. Jerrold Seigel, *Bohemian Paris: Culture, Politics, and the Boundaries of Bourgeois Life, 1830–1930* (New York: Viking, 1986), p. 11.

45. Christopher Breward, *The Hidden Consumer: Masculinities, Fashion and City Life, 1860–1914* (Manchester: Manchester University Press, 1999), p. 29.

46. Donna C. Stanton, *The Aristocrat as Art: a Study of the Honnête Homme and the Dandy in Seventeenth- and Nineteenth-Century French Literature* (New York: Columbia University Press, 1980), p. 71; on respectability see George L. Mosse, *Nationalism and Sexuality: Middle-Class Morality and Sexual Norms in Modern Europe* (Madison, WI: University of Wisconsin Press, 1985).

47. Kenneth L. Ames, *Death in the Dining Room and Other Tales of Victorian Culture* (Philadelphia: Temple University Press, 1992), pp. 191–5, 202, 212–15; Tomas Maldonado, "The Idea of Comfort," *Design Issues*, 8 (1) (Fall 1991): 41.

48. William M. Reddy, *The Navigation of Feeling: a Framework for the History of Emotions* (Cambridge: Cambridge University Press, 2001), p. 145.

49. John R. Gillis, *Youth and History: Tradition and Change in European Age Relations, 1770–Present* (New York: Academic Press, 1974), p. 77.

50. Margaret C. Jacob, *Living the Enlightenment: Freemasonry and Politics in Eighteenth-Century Europe* (New York: Oxford University Press, 1991), pp. 67–8.

51. Jacob, *Living the Enlightenment*, p. 79.

52. Mary Ann Clawson, *Constructing Brotherhood: Class, Gender, and Fraternalism* (Princeton: Princeton University Press, 1989), p. 55.

53. Smith, *Working*, pp. 34–44, 94.

54. Richard van Dülmen, *The Society of the Enlightenment: the Rise of the Middle Class and Enlightenment Culture in Germany*, trans. Anthony Williams (Cambridge: Polity, 1992), pp. 61–3.
55. Maurice O. Wallace, *Constructing the Black Masculine: Identity and Ideality in African American Men's Literature and Culture, 1775–1995* (Durham, NC: Duke University Press, 2002), pp. 53–81. See also the Free African Society, founded in 1787 in Philadelphia to promote austere moral values and abstention from "gaming and feasting." Christopher B. Booker, *"I Will Wear No Chain!" A Social History of African American Males* (Westport, CT: Praeger, 2000), p. 56.
56. Hemphill, *Bowing to Necessities*, p. 186.
57. Mike J. Huggins, "More Sinful Pleasures? Leisure, Respectability and the Male Middle Classes in Victorian England," *Journal of Social History*, 33 (3) (Spring 2000): 586.
58. Elizabeth A. Foyster, *Manhood in Early Modern England: Honour, Sex and Marriage* (London: Longman, 1999), pp. 40–1; David Tjeder, "The Power of Character: Middle-Class Masculinities, 1800–1900," doctoral dissertation in history, Stockholm University (2003) pp. 66–9, 74; Elaine Frantz Parsons, *Manhood Lost: Fallen Drunkards and Redeeming Women in the Nineteenth-Century United States* (Baltimore: Johns Hopkins University Press, 2003).
59. Friedman, "From Boys to Men," p. 40.
60. Judith Deutsch Kornblatt, *The Cossack Hero in Russian Literature: a Study in Cultural Mythology* (Madison, WI: University of Wisconsin Press, 1992), pp. 16, 18.
61. See also how American colonists embraced Native American garb and paraphernalia around the time of the Boston Tea Party, partly as an attempt to project a distinct, albeit conflicted, "American" identity. Philip J. Deloria, *Playing Indian* (New Haven, CT: Yale University Press, 1998), pp. 10–37.
62. Douglas Peter Mackaman, *Leisure Settings: Bourgeois Culture, Medicine, and the Spa in Modern France* (Chicago: University of Chicago Press, 1998), pp. 76–8.
63. Jane Rendell, "West End Rambling: Gender and Architectural Space in London, 1800–1830," *Leisure Studies*, 17 (1998): 114–16, 119.
64. Joachim Schlör, *Nights in the Big City*, trans. Pierre Gottfried Imhof and Dafydd Rees Roberts (London: Reaktion Books, 1998), p. 170.
65. Kenneth A. Lockridge, "Colonial Self-Fashioning: Paradoxes and Pathologies in the Construction of Genteel Identity in Eighteenth-Century America," in Ronald Hoffman, Mechal Sobel and Fredrika J. Teute (eds), *Through a Glass Darkly: Reflections on Personal Identity in Early America* (Chapel Hill, NC: University of North Carolina Press, 1997), pp. 295–6; Stanton, *Aristocrat as Art*, pp. 75–7.
66. Quoted in Charles Bernheimer, *Figures of Ill Repute: Representing Prostitution in Nineteenth-Century France* (Durham, NC: Duke University Press, 1997), p. 16. Similar arguments were made in Italy. Compare Mary Gibson, *Prostitution and the State in Italy, 1860–1915* (New Brunswick: Rutgers University Press, 1986), pp. 31, 33.
67. Peter N. Stearns, *Be a Man! Males in Modern Society* (2nd edition; New York: Holmes & Meier, 1990), p. 126.
68. *Life in Society, at Home and at Court* (1890), quoted in James von Geldern and Louise McReynolds (eds), *Entertaining Tsarist Russia* (Bloomington, IN: Indiana University Press, 1998), p. 97.
69. Margaret S. Creighton, *Rites and Passages: the Experience of American Whaling, 1830–1870* (Cambridge: Cambridge University Press, 1995), p. 208.

3   THE ARMOR OF HEALTH AND THE DISEASES OF CIVILIZATION

1. Dr F. Foy, *Manuel d'hygiène* (Paris: Baillière, 1845), p. 3.
2. Kaja Silverman, *Male Subjectivity at the Margins* (London: Routledge, 1992), p. 62.
3. Bruce Haley, *The Healthy Body and Victorian Culture* (Cambridge, MA: Harvard University Press, 1978), p. 21.
4. Janet Beizer, *Ventriloquized Bodies: Narratives of Hysteria in Nineteenth-Century France* (Ithaca, NY: Cornell University Press, 1994), pp. 41, 47, 81.
5. Pierre Bourdieu, *The Logic of Practice*, trans. Richard Nice (Stanford: Stanford University Press, 1990), pp. 71–2.
6. Quoted in Haley, *Healthy Body*, pp. 12–13 (Carlyle's emphasis); for a study of how bodily experiences typically recede from awareness, see Drew Leder, *The Absent Body* (Chicago: University of Chicago Press, 1990).
7. Thomas Laqueur, *Making Sex: Body and Gender from the Greeks to Freud* (Cambridge, MA: Harvard University Press, 1990).
8. Karen Harvey, "The Substance of Sexual Difference: Change and Persistence in Representations of the Body in Eighteenth-Century England," *Gender & History*, 14 (2) (August 2002): 204.
9. What was known in the German-speaking world as the "character of the sexes" (*Geschlechtscharakter*) emerged at this time as a way of designating the anatomical and mental qualities that characterized the sexes. Karin Hausen, "Family and Role-Division: the Polarisation of Sexual-Stereotypes in the Nineteenth Century – an Aspect of the Dissociation of Work and Family Life," in Richard J. Evans and W.R. Lee (eds), *The German Family: Essays on the Social History of the Family in Nineteenth- and Twentieth-Century Germany* (London: Croom Helm, 1981), pp. 54–8.
10. Barbara Duden, *The Woman Beneath the Skin: a Doctor's Patients in Eighteenth-Century Germany*, trans. Thomas Dunlap (Cambridge, MA: Harvard University Press, 1991), pp. 11–12.
11. Georges Vigarello, *Concepts of Cleanliness: Changing Attitudes in France since the Middle Ages*, trans. Jean Birrell (Cambridge: Cambridge University Press, 1988); Dorinda Outram, *The Body and the French Revolution: Sex, Class and Political Culture* (New Haven, CT: Yale University Press, 1989), p. 14.
12. Michael Stolberg, "An Unmanly Vice: Self-Pollution, Anxiety, and the Body in the Eighteenth Century," *Social History of Medicine*, 13 (1) (April 2000): 19.
13. "Lâche," *Encyclopédie, ou Dictionnaire raisonné des sciences, des arts et des métiers* (Neufchâtel: chez Samuel Faulche, 1765), IX: 165.
14. Anne C. Vila, *Enlightenment and Pathology: Sensibility in the Literature and Medicine of Eighteenth-Century France* (Baltimore: Johns Hopkins University Press, 1998), p. 248.
15. Christoph Wilhelm Hufeland, *Macrobiotics, or The Art of Prolonging Life* (1796; London: John Churchill, 1859), pp. 83–4.
16. See the discussion of the "cult of invalidism" in Bram Dijkstra, *Idols of Perversity: Fantasies of Feminine Evil in Fin-de-Siècle Culture* (Oxford: Oxford University Press, 1986), pp. 25–63.
17. George L. Mosse, *The Image of Man: the Creation of Modern Masculinity* (New York: Oxford University Press, 1996), pp. 29–35.
18. Ludmilla Jordanova, *Sexual Visions: Images of Gender in Science and Medicine between the Eighteenth and Twentieth Centuries* (Hemel Hempstead, UK: Harvester Wheatsheaf, 1989), p. 58; Philip Carter, *Men and the Emergence of Polite Society, Britain 1660–1800* (London: Pearson, 2001), pp. 105–6.

19. Teresa Sanislo, "Models of Manliness and Femininity: the Physical Culture of the Enlightenment and Early National Movement in Germany, 1770–1819," doctoral dissertation in history, University of Michigan (2001): 106.

20. As Caroline Warman shows, the normative (and implicitly male) body that was the subject of scientific scrutiny in the nineteenth century was also viewed as at once the most sophisticated and vulnerable in the natural world, thus inscribing instability at the heart of the male body. Warman, "From Lamarck to Aberration: Nature, Hierarchies and Gender," *Journal of the History of Sexuality*, 18 (1–2) (January/May 2009), in press.

21. G.J. Barker-Benfield, *The Culture of Sensibility: Sex and Society in Eighteenth-Century Britain* (Chicago: University of Chicago Press, 1992), pp. 8–9; Carter, *Men and the Emergence*.

22. J.-E.-D. Esquirol, *Mental Maladies: a Treatise on Insanity* (1845 English edition: New York: Hafner Publishing Company, 1965), p. 40

23. Hufeland, *Prolonging Life*, p. 135. On concerns about luxury, health and morality, see Mary Lindemann, *Health and Healing in Eighteenth-Century Germany* (Baltimore: Johns Hopkins University Press, 1996), pp. 276–7.

24. Michel Foucault, *The History of Sexuality, Volume 2: the Use of Pleasure*, trans. Robert Hurley (New York: Vintage, 1990), p. 108.

25. William Coleman, "Health and Hygiene in the *Encyclopédie*: a Medical Doctrine for the Bourgeoisie," *Journal of the History of Medicine and Allied Sciences*, 29 (October 1974): 399–421; Outram, *The Body and the French Revolution*, p. 48; Vila, *Enlightenment and Pathology*, p. 188.

26. Jean-Jacques Rousseau, *Émile, or On Education*, trans. Allan Bloom (1762; New York: Basic Books, 1979), p. 55.

27. Although our modern understanding of hygiene was transformed with the advent of microbiology towards the end of the nineteenth century (nowadays the word suggests only external cleanliness), elements of the traditional concept still circulate in alternative medical literature.

28. Hans-Joachim von Kondratowitz, "The Medicalization of Old Age: Continuity and Change in Germany from the Late Eighteenth Century to the Early Twentieth Century," in Margaret Pelling and Richard M. Smith (eds), *Life, Death, and the Elderly: Historical Perspectives* (London: Routledge, 1991), pp. 144–5; see also Hufeland, *Art of Prolonging Life*.

29. Marie Mulvey Roberts, "'A Physic Against Death': Eternal Life and the Enlightenment – Gender and Gerontology," in Marie Mulvey Roberts and Roy Porter (eds), *Literature & Medicine during the Eighteenth Century* (London: Routledge, 1993), pp. 151–67.

30. J.H. Réveillé-Parise, *Physiologie et hygiène des hommes livrés aux travaux de l'esprit* (1834; Paris: Baillière, 1881), pp. 366, 208.

31. Thomas R. Cole, *The Journey of Life: a Cultural History of Aging in America* (Cambridge: Cambridge University Press, 1992), pp. 90–1.

32. M.J. van Lieburg, *The Disease of the Learned: a Chapter from the History of Melancholy and Hypochondria*, trans. D.M. Speer (Oss: Organon International, 1990), p. 11. For more on Caspar Barlaeus's bouts of melancholia, see F.F. Blok, *Caspar Barlaeus: From the Correspondence of a Melancholic* (Amsterdam: Van Gorcum & Co., 1976).

33. Gill Speak, "An Odd Kind of Melancholy: Reflections on the Glass Delusion in Europe (1440–1660)," *History of Psychiatry*, 1 (1990): 191–206.

34. Scipion Pinel, *Physiologie de l'homme aliéné* (Paris: J. Rouvier et E. Le Bouvier, 1833), p. 73.

35. This too became an issue in later attempts to rehabilitate the male body from the debilitating effects of book learning. David Yosifon and Peter N. Stearns, "The Rise and Fall of American Posture," *American Historical Review*, 103 (4) (October 1998): p. 1068.
36. Samuel Auguste Tissot, *De la santé des gens de lettres* (1768; Geneva: Slatkine, 1981), p. 56.
37. Susan Kassouf, "The Shared Pain of the Golden Vein: the Discursive Proximity of Jewish and Scholarly Diseases in the Late Eighteenth Century," *Eighteenth-Century Studies*, 32 (1) (1998): 102; Ute Frevert, *A Nation in Barracks: Modern Germany, Military Conscription and Civil Society*, trans. Andrew Boreham and Daniel Bruckenhaus (Oxford: Berg, 2004), p. 25; Sanislo, "Models of Manliness."
38. Quoted in Lieburg, *Disease of the Learned*, p. 59.
39. Roy Porter and George Rousseau, *Gout: the Patrician Malady* (New Haven, CT: Yale University Press, 1998), pp. 88–92; Roy Porter, *Bodies Politic: Disease, Death and Doctors in Britain, 1650–1900* (Ithaca, NY: Cornell University Press, 2001), p. 95.
40. Uli Linke, *Blood and Nation: the European Aesthetics of Race* (Philadelphia: University of Pennsylvania Press, 1999), pp. 178–80; Kassouf, "Shared Pain," p. 101.
41. Elaine Forman Crane, "'I Have Suffer'd Much Today': the Defining Force of Pain in Early America," in Ronald Hoffman, Mechal Sobel and Fredrika J. Teute (eds), *Through a Glass Darkly: Reflections on Personal Identity in Early America* (Chapel Hill, NC: University of North Carolina Press, 1997), pp. 382–3, 392, 400.
42. Elizabeth Green Musselman, *Nervous Conditions: Science and the Body Politic in Early Industrial Britain* (Albany, NY: SUNY Press, 2006), p. 6.
43. John Pemble, *The Mediterranean Passion: Victorians and Edwardians in the South* (Oxford: Clarendon Press, 1987), pp. 84–96.
44. Douglas Peter Mackaman, *Leisure Settings: Bourgeois Culture, Medicine, and the Spa in Modern France* (Chicago: University of Chicago Press, 1998).
45. Charles Lamb, "The Convalescent," quoted in Maria H. Frawley, *Invalidism and Identity in Nineteenth-Century Britain* (Chicago: University of Chicago Press, 2004), p. 215; Edward Bulwer Lytton, "On Ill Health, and its Consolations" (1832), in *Miscellaneous Prose Works* (London: Richard Bentley, 1868), II: 151.
46. Fyodor Dostoyevsky, *Notes from Underground/The Double*, trans. Jessie Coulson (London: Penguin, 1972), p. 25.
47. Edward Bulwer Lytton, "*The Caxtons.*–Part XII," *Blackwood's Edinburgh Magazine*, 65, no. 402 (April 1849): 430–1.
48. Honoré de Balzac, "Traîté des excitants modernes [1833]," in *Théorie de la démarche et autres textes* (Paris: Pandora, 1978), p. 91.
49. Peter Melville Logan, *Nerves and Narratives: a Cultural History of Hysteria in Nineteenth-Century British Prose* (Berkeley: University of California Press, 1997), pp. 25–7; Thomas Trotter, *A View of the Nervous Temperament* (1807; New York: Arno, 1976).
50. On the longevity of this idea, see Lois Whitney, *Primitivism and the Idea of Progress in English Popular Literature of the Eighteenth Century* (1934; New York: Octagon Books, 1965).
51. Georges Vigarello, "The Upward Training of the Body from the Age of Chivalry to Courtly Civility," in Michel Feher (ed.), *Fragments for a History of the Human Body, Part Two* (New York: Zone Books, 1989), p. 185; Mark Motley, *Becoming a French Aristocrat: the Education of the Court Nobility, 1580–1715* (Princeton: Princeton University Press, 1990), pp. 140–52; Marcia Vale, *The Gentleman's Recreations: Accomplishments and Pastimes of the English Gentleman, 1580–1630* (Cambridge: D.S. Brewer, 1977), p. 118; Elizabeth A. Foyster, *Manhood in Early Modern England: Honour, Sex and Marriage* (London: Longman, 1999), p. 36.

52. Anita Guerrini, *Obesity and Depression in the Enlightenment: the Life and Times of George Cheyne* (Norman, OK: University of Oklahoma Press, 2000), p. 121; Steven Shapin, "Trusting George Cheyne: Scientific Expertise, Common Sense, and Moral Authority in Early Eighteenth-Century Dietetic Medicine," *Bulletin of the History of Medicine*, 77 (2003): 282.
53. Alphonse Quetelet, *Sur l'homme et le développement de ses facultés* (Paris: Bachelier, 1835): I: 49–50.
54. Sanislo, "Models of Manliness": 104–5.
55. G.J. Barker-Benfield, *The Horrors of the Half-Known Life: Male Attitudes toward Women and Sexuality in Nineteenth-Century America* (New York: Routledge, 1999), pp. 32–4.
56. Réveillé-Parise, *Physiologie et hygiène*.
57. Charles Lamb, "The Superannuated Man" (1825), in *Elia and The Late Essays of Elia*, ed. Jonathan Bate (Oxford: Oxford University Press, 1987), p. 221.
58. Louis Chevalier, *Laboring Classes and Dangerous Classes in Paris during the First Half of the Nineteenth Century*, trans. Frank Jellineck (New York: Howard Fertig, 1973), pp. 416–17.
59. Réveillé-Parise, *Physiologie et hygiène*, p. 39.
60. Quoted in Sanislo, "Models of Manliness."
61. William Thomas, *Letters from Scandinavia, on the Past and Present State of the Northern Nations of Europe* (London: G.G and J. Robinson, 1796), I: pp. 375–6, 436.
62. See, for instance, the discussion of civilized organs in L. Dumont, "Civilization as Accumulated Force," *Popular Science Monthly*, 1 (May–October 1873): 610–11; John M. Hoberman, *Mortal Engines: the Science of Performance and the Dehumanization of Sport* (New York: The Free Press, 1992), pp. 37–8.
63. Musselman, *Nervous Conditions*, p. 34.
64. Steven Shapin, "The Philosopher and the Chicken: On the Dietetics of Disembodied Knowledge," in Christopher Lawrence and Steven Shapin (eds), *Science Incarnate: Historical Embodiments of Natural Knowledge* (Chicago: University of Chicago Press, 1998), p. 37.
65. Kathleen Wilson, *The Island Race: Englishness, Empire and Gender in the Eighteenth Century* (London: Routledge, 2003); Hoberman, *Mortal Engines*, pp. 39–40; Suzanne Zantrop, "The Beautiful, the Ugly, and the German: Race, Gender, and Nationality in Eighteenth-Century Anthropological Discourse," in Patricia Herminghouse and Magda Mueller (eds), *Gender and Germanness: Cultural Productions of Nation* (Oxford: Berghahn, 1997), p. 27.
66. George L. Mosse, *Nationalism and Sexuality: Middle-Class Morality and Sexual Norms in Modern Europe* (Madison, WI: University of Wisconsin Press, 1985), p. 79.
67. Ambivalence about muscularity and sexuality may have actually *assisted* white men in their often confused classification of other races, not least because it offered them a variety of yardsticks to employ in different contexts. When facing cultures where male muscular and genital attributes seemed to surpass those of Europeans, colonial observers often emphasized reason and intellect as defining features of white superiority; in places where the men seemed less warlike or "savage," white bodies were described as the enviably robust complements of their superior intellects.
68. Sanislo, "Models of Manliness," pp. 97–8. On the allure of primitivism in early modern Germany, see Erich A.G. Albrecht, *Primitivism and Related Ideas in Eighteenth-Century German Lyric Poetry, 1689–1740* (Baltimore: J.H. Furst Co., 1950).

69. David Leverenz, "The Last Real Man in America: From Natty Bumppo to Batman," *American Literary History*, 3 (4) (Winter 1991): 760.
70. John M. Efron, *Medicine and the German Jews: a History* (New Haven, CT: Yale University Press, 2001), pp. 67–76; Kassouf, "Shared Pain."
71. Quoted in Mrinalini Sinha, *Colonial Masculinity: the 'Manly Englishman' and the 'Effeminate Bengali' in the Late Nineteenth Century* (Manchester: Manchester University Press, 1995), pp. 15–16.
72. Paul Dimeo, "'A Parcel of Dummies'? Sport and the Body in Indian History," in James H. Mills and Satadru Sen (eds), *Confronting the Body: the Politics of Physicality in Colonial and Post-Colonial India* (London: Anthem Press, 2004), pp. 43–4.
73. Gérard de Nerval, *The Women of Cairo: Scenes of Life in the Orient* (1851; New York: Harcourt, Brace and Co., 1930), p. 36. Many thanks to Karen Offen for bringing this quotation to my attention.

4   A DIET OF PLEASURES? THE INCORPORATION OF MANHOOD

1. Nikolai Chernyshevsky, *What is to be Done?* trans. Michael R. Katz (1863; Ithaca, NY: Cornell University Press, 1989), p. 281.
2. Rebecca L. Spang, *The Invention of the Restaurant: Paris and Modern Gastronomic Culture* (Cambridge, MA: Harvard University Press, 2000), p. 38.
3. Roy Porter and Dorothy Porter, *In Sickness and in Health: the British Experience, 1650–1850* (London: Fourth Estate, 1988), p. 55.
4. Anita Guerrini, *Obesity and Depression in the Enlightenment: the Life and Times of George Cheyne* (Norman, OK: University of Oklahoma Press, 2000), p. 6; George Rousseau, "Coleridge's Dreaming Gut: Digestion, Genius, Hypochondria," in Christopher E. Forth and Ana Carden-Coyne (eds), *Cultures of the Abdomen: Diet, Digestion, and Fat in the Modern World* (New York: Palgrave, 2005), p. 108.
5. Fredrik Albritton Jonsson, "The Physiology of Hypochondria in Eighteenth-Century Britain," in *Cultures of the Abdomen*, pp. 16–17.
6. Chevalier de Jaucourt, "Dyspépsie," *Encyclopédie, ou Dictionnaire raisonné des sciences, des arts et des métiers* (Paris: Briasson, 1755), V: 177.
7. Anne C. Vila, *Enlightenment and Pathology: Sensibility in the Literature and Medicine of Eighteenth-Century France* (Baltimore: Johns Hopkins University Press, 1998).
8. Christoph Wilhelm Hufeland, *Macrobiotics, or The Art of Prolonging Life* (1796; London: John Churchill, 1859), p. 107.
9. J.H. Réveillé-Parise, *Physiologie et hygiène des hommes livrés aux travaux de l'esprit* (1834; Paris: Baillière, 1881), pp. 37, 62, 63, 164, 226.
10. P.-J.-G. Cabanis, *Les rapports du physique et du morale de l'homme* (8th edn: Paris: Baillière, 1844), p. 115.
11. Quoted in William M. Reddy, *The Navigation of Feeling: a Framework for the History of Emotions* (Cambridge: Cambridge University Press, 2001), p. 214.
12. Anne C. Vila, "The *Philosophe*'s Stomach: Hedonism, Hypochondria, and the Intellectual in Enlightenment France," in *Cultures of the Abdomen*, p. 95; James C. Whorton, *Crusaders for Fitness: a History of American Health Reformers* (Princeton: Princeton University Press, 1982), pp. 40–2.
13. Petrus Cunaeus to Caspar Barlaeus, 10 June 1632, quoted in F.F. Blok, *Caspar Barlaeus: From the Correspondence of a Melancholic* (Amsterdam: Van Gorcum & Co., 1976), p. 49.
14. John Locke, *Some Thoughts Concerning Education* (1693; Oxford: Clarendon Press, 1989), p. 99.

15. "This physiology demands not the seamless corporeal enclosure that Bakhtin identifies with the classical body but rather the routine excretory processes that he displaces onto lower-class festivity." Michael C. Schoenfeldt, *Bodies and Selves in Early Modern England: Physiology and Inwardness in Spenser, Shakespeare, Herbert, and Milton* (Cambridge: Cambridge University Press, 1999), p. 14.

16. Vila, "The *Philosophe*'s Stomach," p. 98.

17. James C. Whorton, *Inner Hygiene: Constipation and the Pursuit of Health in Modern Society* (New York: Oxford University Press, 2000), p. 22.

18. Jean Anthelme Brillat-Savarin, *The Physiology of Taste, or Meditations on Transcendental Gastronomy*, trans. M.F.K. Fisher (1825; New York: Knopf, 1972), pp. 204–5. See also Steven Shapin, "How to Eat Like a Gentleman: Dietetics and Ethics in Early Modern England," in Charles Rosenberg (ed.), *Right Living: an Anglo-American Tradition of Self-Help Medicine and Hygiene* (Baltimore: Johns Hopkins University Press, 2003), pp. 21–58.

19. Harvey Green, *Fit for America: Health, Fitness, Sport and American Society* (New York: Pantheon, 1986), p. 6; Whorton, *Inner Hygiene*, pp. 22–7.

20. Thomas Laqueur, *Solitary Sex: a Cultural History of Masturbation* (New York: Zone Books, 2003), pp. 232–3, 249.

21. Lutz D.H. Sauerteig, "Sex Education in Germany from the Eighteenth to the Twentieth Century," in Franz X. Eder, Lesley Hall and Gert Hekma (eds), *Sexual Cultures in Europe: Themes in Sexuality* (Manchester: Manchester University Press, 1999), p. 11.

22. Quoted in G.J. Barker-Benfield, *The Horrors of the Half-Known Life: Male Attitudes Toward Women and Sexuality in Nineteenth-Century America* (New York: Routledge, 1999), p. 32; Nick Fiddes, *Meat: a Natural Symbol* (London: Routledge, 1991), p. 147.

23. Dioclesian Lewis, *Chastity, or, Our Secret Sins* (1874; reprint: New York: Arno Press, 1974), p.176.

24. Vernon A. Rosario, *The Erotic Imagination: French Histories of Perversity* (New York: Oxford University Press, 1997), pp. 20–8.

25. Harry Oosterhuis, *Stepchildren of Nature: Krafft-Ebing, Psychiatry, and the Making of Sexual Identity* (Chicago: University of Chicago Press, 2000), p. 40.

26. Porter and Porter, *In Sickness and in Health*, p. 54; Roy Porter, "Consumption: Disease of the Consumer Society?" in John Brewer and Roy Porter (eds), *Consumption and the World of Goods* (London: Routledge, 1993), p. 63.

27. Leslie A. Marchand (ed.), *Byron's Letters and Journals* (London: John Murray, 1974), III: p. 257.

28. Jules Barbey d'Aurevilly, *Du Dandyisme et de G. Brummell*, in *Oeuvres completes* (Geneva: Slatkine, 1979), III: 262–3.

29. Vigarello, "Le corps travaillé," in Alain Corbin (ed.), *Histoire du corps: 2. De la Révolution à la Grande guerre* (Paris: Seuil, 2005), pp. 321–2.

30. Brillat-Savarin, *Physiology of Taste*, pp. 205–6, 208.

31. Fyodor Dostoyevsky, *Notes from Underground/The Double*, trans. Jessie Coulson (London: Penguin, 1972), p. 29.

32. C. Saucerotte, "VIRILITÉ," *Encyclopédie des gens du monde* (Paris: Treuttel et Würtz, 1844), XXII: 638.

33. Quoted in Green, *Fit for America*, p. 31.

34. Réveillé-Parise, *Physiologie et hygiène*, p. 230.

35. Dr Dheur, *Comment on se défend contre l'obésité* (Paris: Société d'éditions scientifiques, n.d.), p. 24. On the association of obesity with impotence since ancient times, see Angus McLaren, *Impotence: a Cultural History* (Chicago: University of Chicago Press, 2007), pp. 10–11, 39, 80, 93.

36. Locke, *Some Thoughts*, pp. 106–7.
37. Ken Albala, *Eating Right in the Renaissance* (Berkeley: University of California Press, 2002), pp. 189–94.
38. Jean-Louis Flandrin, "From Dietetics to Gastronomy: the Liberation of the Gourmet," in Jean-Louis Flandrin and Massimo Montanari (eds), *Food: a Culinary History from Antiquity to the Present*, trans. Clarissa Botsford, Arthur Goldhammer, Charles Lambert, Frances M. López-Morillas and Sylvia Stevens (New York: Columbia University Press, 1999), pp. 429–31.
39. Spang, *Invention of the Restaurant*, pp. 28, 38–9.
40. Margaret C. Jacob, *Living the Enlightenment: Freemasonry and Politics in Eighteenth-Century Europe* (New York: Oxford University Press, 1991), pp. 77, 82.
41. Roy Porter and Lesley Hall, *The Facts of Life: the Creation of Sexual Knowledge in Britain, 1650–1950* (New Haven, CT: Yale University Press, 1995), pp. 113–14.
42. Priscilla Parkhurst Ferguson, *Accounting for Taste: the Triumph of French Cuisine* (Chicago: University of Chicago Press, 2004), p. 93.
43. Jeremy Black, *France and the Grand Tour* (Basingstoke: Palgrave, 2003), p. 67.
44. John Andrews, *An Account of the Character and Manners of the French; with Occasional Observations on the English* (London: C. Dilly, 1770): I: 249–50. Nevertheless a fair number of Britons counted themselves among the devotees of the new cult of good taste, though, whereas Continental cuisine often emphasized refinement, in their search for stimulating tastes they sometimes used spices to excess. Paul Langford, *Englishness Identified: Manners and Character, 1650–1850* (Oxford: Oxford University Press, 2000), p. 49.
45. Priscilla Parkhurst Ferguson, "A Cultural Field in the Making: Gastronomy in Nineteenth-Century France," in Lawrence R. Schehr and Allen S. Weiss (eds), *French Food: on the Table, on the Page, and in French Culture* (London: Routledge, 2001), pp. 13–18.
46. Ferguson, *Accounting for Taste*, p. 93.
47. Ferguson, *Accounting for Taste*, p. 93; Mme J.-J. Lambert, *Manuel de la politesse, des usages du monde, et du savoir-vivre* (Paris: Delarue, n.d. [*c.* 1840s]), p. 116.
48. Philibert-Louis Debucourt, "L'Épicurien: l'embarras des Richesses!!!" (1800–05), in Gerhard Langemeyer, Gerd Unverfeht, Herwig Guratzsch and Christoph Stölzl (eds), *Mittel und Motive der Karikatur un fünf Jahrhunderten* (Munich: Prestel-Verlag, 1985), p. 53.
49. Quoted in Ferguson, *Accounting for Taste*, pp. 102–3.
50. Jean-Paul Aron, *The Art of Eating in France: Manners and Menus in the Nineteenth Century*, trans. Nina Rootes (New York: Harper and Row, 1975), pp. 167, 224–9.
51. James Boswell, *Life of Johnson* (1791; New York: Oxford University Press, 1970), p. 926.
52. A. Debay, *Hygiène et perfectionnement de la beauté humaine* (Paris: E. Dentu, 1864), p. 152.
53. Woodruff D. Smith, *Consumption and the Making of Respectability, 1600–1800* (New York: Routledge, 2002), pp. 147–8.
54. Elizabeth A. Foyster, *Manhood in Early Modern England: Honour, Sex and Marriage* (London: Longman, 1999), p. 40.
55. Smith, *Consumption*, pp. 151–3, 158; Steve Pincus, "'Coffee Politicians Does Create': Coffeehouses and Restoration Political Culture," *Journal of Modern History*, 67 (December 1995): 824–5.
56. Quoted in Bennett Alan Weinberg and Bonnie K. Bealer, *The World of Caffeine: the Science and Culture of the World's Most Popular Drug* (New York: Routledge, 2001), pp. 120–3.

57. Stephen Nissenbaum, *Sex, Diet, and Debility in Jacksonian America: Sylvester Graham and Health Reform* (Westport, CT: Greenwood, 1980), p. 35; Lewis, *Chastity*, pp. 270, 273.

58. Réveillé-Parise, *Physiologie et hygiène*, p. 360.

59. Matthew Hilton, *Smoking in British Popular Culture, 1800–2000* (Manchester: Manchester University Press, 2000), pp. 20–1, 28, 32; Smith, *Consumption*, pp. 167–8.

60. Fiddes, *Meat*, pp. 94–118.

61. Arouna Ouédraogo, "The Social Genesis of Western Vegetarianism to 1859," in Robert Dare (ed.), *Food, Power and Community* (Adelaide, Aus.: Wakefield Press, 1999), p. 158.

62. Nissenbaum, *Sex, Diet, and Debility*, pp. 46–7.

63. Fiddes, *Meat*, pp. 150–3. While this formulation seems to place women on the side of animal nature to be conquered by civilized men, its association of men with hunting and devouring locates the male on the side of the nomadic hunter-gatherer tribes that preceded the earliest human settlements.

64. A Debay, *Hygiène et physiologie du mariage* (1848; 29th edn, Paris: E, Dentu, 1862), pp. 132–3.

65. Arouna Ouédraogo, "Vegetarianism in Fin-de-Siècle France: the Social Determinants of Vegetarians' Misfortune in Pre-World War I France," in Alexander Fenton (ed.), *Order and Disorder: the Health Implications of Eating and Drinking in the Nineteenth and Twentieth Centuries* (Edinburgh: Tuckwell Press, 2000), pp. 212–13.

66. Dr E. Contet, *Le végétarisme: étude critique, indications thérapeutiques* (Paris: Baillière, 1902), p. 11; Darra Goldstein, "Is Hay Only for Horses? Highlights of Russian Vegetarianism at the Turn of the Century," in Musya Glants and Joyce Toomre (eds), *Food in Russian History and Culture* (Bloomington, IN: Indiana University Press, 1997), pp. 103–23; Whorton, *Crusaders for Fitness*, pp. 201–38.

67. Fiddes, *Meat*, pp. 158–9.

68. Quetelet, *Sur l'homme*, II: 21, 79; Ouédraogo, "Vegetarianism," pp. 203–6; Guy Soudjian, "Quelques réflexions sur les statures des jeunes Parisiens sous le second Empire," *Ethnologie française*, 9 (1) (1979): 80.

5   BUILDING BODIES: VIOLENCE, PAIN AND THE NATION

1. G.W.F. Hegel, *Philosophy of Right*, trans. T.M. Knox (1820; Oxford: Oxford University Press, 1967), p. 210.

2. G.W.F. Hegel, *The Phenomenology of Mind*, trans. J.B. Baillie (1807; New York: Harper Torchbooks, 1967), pp. 232–4; Immanuel Kant, "Perpetual Peace: a Philosophical Sketch," in *Political Writings*, ed. Hans Reiss (Cambridge: Cambridge University Press, 1991), pp. 93–130.

3. It should come as no surprise that Hegel also defended dueling as that which prevented the "schism of personality" faced by all middle-class men, who were necessarily engaged in "a perpetual struggle for 'independent unity with the self.'" Ute Frevert, *Men of Honour: a Social and Cultural History of the Duel*, trans. Anthony Williams (Cambridge: Polity Press, 1995), p. 25.

4. Karen Halttunen, "Humanitarianism and the Pornography of Pain in Anglo-American Culture," *American Historical Review*, 100 (2) (April 1995): 318.

5. John Stuart Mill, "Civilization" [1836], in Gertrude Himmelfarb (ed.), *Essays on Politics and Culture* (Gloucester, MA: Peter Smith, 1973), p. 58.

6. Greg Eghigian and Paul Petts, "Introduction: Pain and Prosperity in Twentieth-Century Germany," in Paul Betts and Greg Eghigian (eds), *Pain and Prosperity: Reconsidering Twentieth-Century Germany* (Stanford: Stanford University Press, 2003).

7. A great of deal of scholarship has been devoted to the most spectacular and extreme examples of pain and violence, ranging from murder, torture and executions to warfare and domestic violence, and the key theoretical work on such forms of pain is still Elaine Scarry, *The Body in Pain: the Making and Unmaking of the World* (New York: Oxford University Press, 1985). As defined by the *OED*, however, "pain" refers to a spectrum of physical and emotional experiences, from "a continuous, strongly unpleasant or agonizing sensation in the body" and a "state or condition of consciousness arising from mental or physical suffering" to less excruciating yet still burdensome activities like "labour, toil, exertions; careful and attentive effort." The *OED*'s approach to "violence" has a similar semantic latitude. Of course topping the list is the "exercise of physical force so as to inflict injury on, or cause damage to, persons or property"; yet among the other definitions of violence are "Force or strength of physical action or natural agents; forcible, powerful, or violent action or motion." Not surprisingly, both pain and violence contrast with "comfort," which, among other things, suggests "Pleasure, enjoyment, delight, gladness" as well as "state of physical and material well-being, with freedom from pain and trouble, and satisfaction of bodily needs." In those rare instances where comfort provides "strength" or "refreshment," the point is mainly moral. Most of the physical connotations of a comfort that strengthens are therapeutic, referring to the recuperation from an illness or injury that returns the body to its "normal" state (which may or may not have been particularly strong to begin with). This chapter employs this broader definition of pain as a spectrum of sensations.
8. Robert McGregor, "The Popular Press and the Creation of Military Masculinities in Georgian Britain," in Paul R. Higate (ed.), *Military Masculinities: Identity and the State* (Westport, CT: Praeger, 2003), pp. 145–6.
9. Peter Stanley, *For Fear of Pain: British Surgery, 1790–1850* (Amsterdam: Rodopi, 2003), p. 119. The French, of course, had their own mythologies of heroic endurance of pain: a painting by Bizard shows how a wounded soldier overcomes the pain of amputation by gazing upon the tricolor flag. See Sean M. Quinlan, "Men without Women? Ideal Masculinity and Male Sociability in the French Revolution, 1789–99," in Christopher E. Forth and Bertrand Taithe (eds), *French Masculinities: History, Culture and Politics* (Basingstoke: Palgrave, 2007), p. 38.
10. Ana María Alonso, "The Politics of Space, Time and Substance: State Formation, Nationalism, and Ethnicity," *Annual Review of Anthropology*, 23 (1994): 395.
11. V.G. Kiernan, *The Duel in European History: Honour and the Reign of the Aristocracy* (Oxford: Oxford University Press, 1988), pp. 6–7, 136, 148; Irina Reyfman, *Ritualized Violence, Russian Style: the Duel in Russian Culture and Literature* (Stanford: Stanford University Press, 1999), pp. 97–8.
12. Frevert, *Men of Honour*, p. 27.
13. Kevin McAleer, *Dueling: the Cult of Honor in Fin-de-Siècle Germany* (Princeton: Princeton University Press, 1994), pp. 140–1.
14. Robert A. Nye, *Masculinity and Male Codes of Honor in Modern France* (Oxford: Oxford University Press, 1993), pp. 16–17.
15. Mark Motley, *Becoming a French Aristocrat: the Education of the Court Nobility, 1580–1715* (Princeton: Princeton University Press, 1990), pp. 48–9.
16. Leo Braudy, *From Chivalry to Terrorism: War and the Changing Nature of Masculinity* (New York: Knopf, 2003), pp. 118, 127, 177–9.
17. Kiernan, *The Duel*, p. 57.
18. Reyfman, *Ritualized Violence*, pp. 107–8.
19. Ibid., pp. 86–7, 109.

20. Carl von Clausewitz, *On War*, trans. J.J. Graham (1832; London: Routledge and Kegan Paul, Ltd., 1949), I: 1.
21. Alain Ehrenberg, *Le corps militaire: politique et pédagogie en démocratie* (Paris: Éditions Aubier Montaigne, 1983), p. 45.
22. Anne McClintock, "'No Longer in a Future Heaven': Nationalism, Gender, and Race," in Geoff Eley and Ronald Grigor Suny (eds), *Becoming National: a Reader* (New York: Oxford University Press, 1996), p. 261. See also Nira Yuval-Davis, *Gender & Nation* (London: Sage, 1997).
23. Michel Foucault, *Discipline and Punish: the Birth of the Prison*, trans. Alan Sheridan (New York: Vintage, 1977), p. 169.
24. Ehrenberg, *Le corps militaire*, p. 53. On the role of pain and violence in the formation of society, see Nick Crossley, *Reflexive Embodiment in Contemporary Society* (Maidenhead, UK: Open University Press, 2006), pp. 12–13.
25. Johann Gottlieb Fichte, *Addresses to the German Nation* (1808; Westport, CT: Greenwood Press, 1979), p. 13; on the nation's "internal boundaries," see pp. 223–4.
26. Steven Hughes, "Men of Steel: Dueling, Honor, and Politics in Liberal Italy," in Pieter Spierenburg (ed.), *Men and Violence: Gender, Honor, and Ritual in Modern Europe and America* (Columbus, OH: Ohio State University Press, 1998), p. 70.
27. Quoted in Hal Foster, "Prosthetic Gods," *Modernism/Modernity*, 4, no. 2 (1997): 17.
28. Stephen H. Gregg, "'A Truly Christian Hero': Religion, Effeminacy, and Nation in the Writings of the Societies for Reformation of Manners," *Eighteenth-Century Studies*, 25 (1) (2001): 23.
29. Linda Colley, *Britons: Forging the Nation* (New Haven, CT: Yale University Press, 1992), pp. 1, 9.
30. Joane Nagel, "Masculinity and Nationalism: Gender and Sexuality in the Making of Nations," *Ethnic and Racial Studies*, 21 (2) (March 1998): 242–69.
31. William H. McNeill, *Keeping Together in Time: Dance and Drill in Human History* (Cambridge, MA: Harvard University Press, 1995), pp. 2–3, 127–31.
32. Benedict Anderson, *Imagined Communities: Reflections on the Origin and Spread of Nationalism* (London: Verso, 1991) p. 16.
33. Alonso, "Politics of Space," p. 386.
34. Philip Carter, *Men and the Emergence of Polite Society, Britain 1660–1800* (London: Pearson, 2001), pp. 130–1; Matthew McCormack, "The New Militia: War, Politics and Gender in 1750s Britain," *Gender & History*, 19 (3) (November 2007): 483–500.
35. Jean-Jacques Rousseau, *Discourse on the Arts and Sciences*, in *The Social Contract and Other Discourses*, trans. G.D.H. Cole (London: Everyman, 1993), p. 21.
36. Daniel L. Purdy, *The Tyranny of Elegance: Consumer Cosmopolitanism in the Era of Goethe* (Baltimore: Johns Hopkins University Press, 1998), p. 165.
37. André Rauch, *Le premier sexe: mutations et crise de l'identité masculine* (Paris: Hachette, 2000), p. 48.
38. Dorinda Outram, *The Body and the French Revolution: Sex, Class and Political Culture* (New Haven, CT: Yale University Press, 1989), pp. 86–8; Stefan Dudink, "Cuts and Bruises and Democratic Contestation: Male Bodies, History and Politics," *European Journal of Cultural Studies*, 4 (2) (2001): 158. David's *Oath of the Horatii* (1785) suggests the formation of the nation as a band of brothers that excludes any feminine principle, whether it be softness or women themselves. Moreover, the nation is constituted through a violence that demands that men sacrifice themselves in the name of national duty; Joan B. Landes, *Women and the Public Sphere in the Age of the French Revolution* (Ithaca, NY: Cornell University Press, 1988), p. 156. Yet depictions of heroic adulthood were complemented during the revolutionary era with images

of ephebic male figures in decidedly unheroic and eroticized poses, a fact which partly reveals male attempts to recuperate the "femininity" that had been eradicated from politics through the exclusion of women. Hence, as Abigail Solomon-Godeau shows, patriarchy was capable of being affirmed through both "hard" and "soft" representations of male bodies. Abigail Solomon-Godeau, *Male Trouble: a Crisis in Representation* (London: Thames and Hudson, 1997).

39. Quoted in de Antoine de Baecque, *The Body Politic: Corporeal Metaphor in Revolutionary France, 1770–1800*, trans. Charlotte Mandell (Stanford: Stanford University Press, 1997), pp. 139, 142.
40. After the initial enthusiasm of 1792 many recruits deserted the French army, and subsequent volunteers were less forthcoming, thus prompting the revolutionary government to devise more coercive recruitment techniques. Alan Forrest, *The Soldiers of the French Revolution* (Durham, NC: Duke University Press, 1990), pp. 58–88.
41. Un Citoyen de la Section des Tuileries, *Vues générales sur l'éducation à donner aux garçons dans la République française* (Paris: n.p., c.1800), pp. 3, 6, 9.
42. Sean M. Quinlan, "Physical and Moral Regeneration after the Terror: Medical Culture, Sensibility and Family Politics in France, 1794–1804," *Social History*, 29 (2) (May 2004): 157–9.
43. Norman Bryson, "Géricault and 'Masculinity,'" in Norman Bryson, Michael Ann Holly and Keith Moxley (eds), *Visual Culture: Images and Interpretation* (Hanover, NH: Wesleyan University Press, 1994), p. 147.
44. Suzanne Zantrop, "The Beautiful, the Ugly, and the German: Race, Gender, and Nationality in Eighteenth-Century Anthropological Discourse," in Patricia Herminghouse and Magda Mueller (eds), *Gender and Germanness: Cultural Productions of Nation* (Oxford: Berghahn, 1997), p. 29. Assumptions about the simple, hard and pure lives of ancient Germans, as well as the loss of courage and fighting strength among their modern heirs was expressed long before the Napoleonic invasion. Erich A.G. Albrecht, *Primitivism and Related Ideas in Eighteenth-Century German Lyric Poetry, 1689–1740* (Baltimore: J.H. Furst Co., 1950), pp. 36–7.
45. Ute Frevert, *A Nation in Barracks: Modern Germany, Military Conscription and Civil Society*, trans. Andrew Boreham and Daniel Bruckenhaus (Oxford: Berg, 2004), pp. 25–7. Teresa Sanislo, "Models of Manliness and Femininity: the Physical Culture of the Enlightenment and Early National Movement in Ger-many, 1770–1819," doctoral dissertation in history, University of Michigan (2001): 49.
46. Frevert, *Nation in Barracks*, pp. 18–19.
47. Richard Slotkin, *Regeneration through Violence: the Mythology of the American Frontier, 1600–1860* (Middletown, CT: Wesleyan University Press, 1973), pp. 29–30, 34, 191.
48. Fichte, *Address to the German Nation*. For a further discussion of the tension between "bare life" and political existence, see Giorgio Agamben, *Homo Sacer: Sovereign Power and Bare Life*, trans. Daniel Heller-Roazen (Stanford: Stanford University Press, 1998).
49. Quoted in Frevert, *Nation in Barracks*, p. 28.
50. Clausewitz, *On War*, p. 191.
51. Karen Hagemann, "German Heroes: the Cult of the Death for the Fatherland in Nineteenth-Century Germany," in Stefan Dudink, Karen Hagemann and John Tosh (eds), *Masculinities in Politics and War: Gendering Modern History* (Manchester: Manchester University Press, 2004), p. 120; Karen Hagemann, "Of 'Manly Valor' and 'German Honor': Nation, War, and Masculinity in the Age of the Prussian Uprising against Napoleon," *Central European History*, 30 (2) (1997): 187–220; George L. Mosse, *The Image of Man: the Creation of Modern Masculinity* (New York: Oxford University Press, 1996), p. 44.

52. Abbé Grégoire, *Essai sur la régénération physique, morale et politique des juifs* (1788; Paris, Stock, 1988), pp. 57–64, 163, 168,175.
53. Paula E. Hyman, *The Jews of Modern France* (Berkeley: University of California Press, 1998), p. 47; John M. Efron, "Images of the Jewish Body: Three Medical Views from the Jewish Enlightenment," *Bulletin for the History of Medicine*, 69 (1995): 349–66.
54. Frevert, *Nation in Barracks*, p. 162.
55. Patricia Vertinsky, "Body Matters: Race, Gender, and Perceptions of Physical Ability from Goethe to Weininger," in Norbert Finzsch and Dietmar Schirmer (eds), *Identity and Intolerance: Nationalism, Racism, and Xenophobia in Germany and the United States* (Cambridge: Cambridge University Press, 1998), p. 355.
56. Quoted in Frevert, *Nation in Barracks*, p. 69; Gregory A. Caplan, "Militarism and Masculinity as Keys to the 'Jewish Question' in Germany," in Higate, *Military Masculinities*, p. 180.
57. Robert B. Edgerton, *Hidden Heroism: Black Soldiers in America's Wars* (Boulder, CO: Westview Press, 2001), pp. 7–38.
58. Christopher B. Booker, *"I Will Wear No Chain!": a Social History of African American Males* (Westport, CT: Praeger, 2000), pp. 73–4; Jim Cullen, "'I's a Man Now': Gender and African-American Men," in Catherine Clinton and Nina Silber (eds), *Divided Houses: Gender and the Civil War* (New York: Oxford University Press, 1992), pp. 76–91.
59. McClintock, "'No Longer in a Future Heaven,'" p. 263.
60. William Buchan, *Domestic Medicine: or, a treatise on the prevention and cure of diseases by regimen and simple medicines* (3rd edition: London: W. Strahan, 1774), p. 48n.
61. David Tjeder, "The Power of Character: Middle-Class Masculinities, 1800–1900," doctoral dissertation in history, Stockholm University (2003), p. 135.
62. Jens Ljunggren, "The Masculine Road through Modernity: Ling Gymnastics and Male Socialisation in Nineteenth-Century Sweden," in J.A. Mangan (ed.), *Making European Masculinities: Sport, Europe, Gender* (London: Frank Cass, 2000), pp. 86–111.
63. Mosse, *Image of Man*, pp. 41–2; Sanislo, "Models of Manliness," p. 281.
64. Henning Eichberg, "The Enclosure of the Body – on the Historical Relativity of 'Health', 'Nature' and the Environment of Sport," *Journal of Contemporary History*, 21 (1) (January 1986): 115.
65. Rachel Woodward, "'It's a Man's Life!': Soldiers, Masculinity and the Countryside," *Gender, Place and Culture*, 5 (3) (1998): 281, 292.
66. Hagemann, "German Heroes," pp. 127–8.
67. Johann Jacob Sachs, quoted in Vertinsky, "Body Matters," p. 345.
68. Less demanding exercises like these also allowed older and better-off men to save face: they risked looking ridiculous by attempting anything that required greater strength and effort. To some degree, then, "civilized" gymnastics conferred fitness and dignity on bodies that remained relatively mediocre, at least when compared to the more robust physiques of the "craftsmen" who predominated in other gymnastics societies. This gendered class distinction was one reason more popular groups in turn resisted the free and order practices. Considered adequate only for girls, boys and young men, or as a warm-up for more strenuous exercises, these middle-class practices seemed downright effeminate from a working-class perspective. Berit Elisabeth Dencker, "Class and the Construction of the Nineteenth-Century German Male Body," *Journal of Historical Sociology*, 15 (2) (June 2002): 233, 239, 242.
69. Andrew Warwick, "Exercising the Student Body: Mathematics and Athleticism in Victorian Cambridge," in Christopher Lawrence and Steven Shapin (eds), *Science*

Incarnate: Historical Embodiments of Natural Knowledge (Chicago: University of Chicago Press, 1998), pp. 288–326.

70. John Tosh, *A Man's Place: Masculinity and the Middle-Class Home in Victorian England* (New Haven, CT: Yale University Press, 1999), pp. 118–19.

71. J.A. Mangan, *Athleticism in the Victorian and Edwardian Public School* (3rd edition: London: Frank Cass, 2000).

72. Foucault, *Discipline and Punish*, p. 135.

73. Paul Broca, *Sur la prétendue dégénérescence de la population française* (Paris: E. Martinet, 1867), p. 26.

6   MODERN PRIMITIVES: MANHOOD AND METAMORPHOSIS AROUND 1900

1. Henri-Frédéric Amiel, 19 June 1869, *Journal intime*, Bernard Gagnebin and Philippe M. Monnier (eds) (Lausanne: L'Age d'Homme, 1987), VII: 831; 31 March 1870, *Journal intime*, VII: 1359.

2. When the young Australian Frederic Eggleston had his second nervous breakdown in 1902, his doctor diagnosed him as suffering from nervous exhaustion, or neurasthenia. In addition to prescribing nerve tonic, the doctor informed the studious Eggleston that he was much too civilized and needed to become more of a "barbarian" if he was ever to become well. David Walker, "Modern Nerves, Nervous Moderns: Notes on Male Neurasthenia," *Australian Cultural History*, no. 6 (1987): 60.

3. Mike Hawkins, *Social Darwinism in European and American Thought, 1860–1945* (Cambridge: Cambridge University Press, 1997), pp. 249–71.

4. Lawrence Birkin, *Consuming Desire: Sexual Science and the Emergence of a Culture of Abundance, 1871–1914* (Ithaca, NY: Cornell University Press, 1988), pp. 77–8.

5. Cynthia Eagle Russett, *Sexual Science: the Victorian Construction of Womanhood* (Cambridge, MA: Harvard University Press, 1989), pp. 31–4, 48.

6. Robert Dunn, "Civilisation and Cranial Development: Some Observations on the Influence of Civilisation upon the Development of the Brain in the Different Races of Man," *Transactions of the Ethnological Society of London*, 4 (1866): 33; Paul Broca, *Sur la prétendue dégénérescence de la population française* (Paris: E. Martinet, 1867), p. 49.

7. See, for instance, William C.D. Whetham, *The Family and the Nation: a Study in Natural Inheritance and Social Responsibility* (London: Longmans, Green, and Co., 1909), pp. 73–4.

8. Londa Schiebinger, *Nature's Body: Gender in the Making of Modern Science* (Boston: Beacon Press, 1993), pp. 120–5.

9. Peter Redman and Maírtín Mac an Ghaill, "Educating Peter: the Making of a History Man," in Deborah Lynn Steinberg, Debbie Epstein and Richard Johnson (eds), *Border Patrols: Policing the Boundaries of Heterosexuality* (London: Cassell, 1997), pp. 162–82.

10. For an account of how historians have masculinized their craft, see Bonnie G. Smith, *The Gender of History: Men, Women, and Historical Practice* (Cambridge, MA: Harvard University Press, 1998), pp. 130–56.

11. Hawkins, *Social Darwinism*, pp. 29–30.

12. Birkin, *Consuming Desire*, pp. 79–80.

13. Geneviève Fraisse, *Reason's Muse: Sexual Difference and the Birth of Democracy*, trans. Jane Marie Todd (Chicago: University of Chicago Press, 1994), p. 195.

14. Harry Oosterhuis, *Stepchildren of Nature: Krafft-Ebing, Psychiatry, and the Making of Sexual Identity* (Chicago: University of Chicago Press, 2000), pp. 52–3.

15. Harry Oosterhuis, "Medical Science and the Modernization of Sexuality," in Franz X. Eder, Lesley Hall and Gert Hekma (eds), *Sexual Cultures in Europe: National Histories* (Manchester: Manchester University Press, 1999), p. 228.

16. Georges Vigarello, *Le corps redressé: histoire d'un pouvoir pédagogique* (1978; Paris: Armand Colin, 2001), pp. 90–3.

17. Joanna Bourke, *Dismembering the Male: Men's Bodies, Britain and the Great War* (London: Reaktion, 1996), pp. 173–4.

18. Robin Lenman, John Osborne and Eda Sagarra, "Imperial Germany: Towards the Commercialization of Culture," in Rob Burns (ed.), *German Cultural Studies: an Introduction* (Oxford: Oxford University Press, 1995), p. 13.

19. Henrik Meinander, "Discipline, Character, Health: Ideals and Icons of Nordic Masculinity, 1860–1930," *International Journal of the History of Sport*, 22 (4) (July 2005): 604.

20. Charles Darwin, *Descent of Man*, in *From so Simple a Beginning: the Four Great Books of Charles Darwin*, ed. Edward O. Wilson (1871; New York: W.W. Norton, 2006), p. 874; Paul Crook, *Darwinism, War and History* (Cambridge: Cambridge University Press, 1994), p. 27.

21. Francis Galton, "Hereditary Improvement," *The Eclectic Magazine of Foreign Literature, Science, and Art* (March 1873): 298, 300. Reprinted from *Fraser's Magazine*. See also Elizabeth Green Musselman, *Nervous Conditions: Science and the Body Politic in Early Industrial Britain* (Albany, NY: SUNY Press, 2006), pp. 113–14.

22. Quoted in John M. Hoberman, *Mortal Engines: the Science of Performance and the Dehumanization of Sport* (New York: The Free Press, 1992), p. 87.

23. Janet Brown, "I Could Have Retched All Night: Charles Darwin and his Body," in Christopher Lawrence and Steven Shapin (eds), *Science Incarnate: Historical Embodiments of Natural Knowledge* (Chicago: University of Chicago Press, 1998), pp. 240–87.

24. Alexandre Cullerre, *Les frontières de la folie* (Paris: Baillière et fils, 1888), p. 318.

25. Christopher E. Forth, *The Dreyfus Affair and the Crisis of French Manhood* (Baltimore: Johns Hopkins University Press, 2004), pp. 74–7.

26. Henry Childs Merwin, "On Being Civilized Too Much," *Atlantic Monthly*, 79 (476) (June 1897): 842.

27. M. Potel, "Neurasthénie," *La Grande encyclopédie* (Paris: Société anonyme de la Grande encyclopédie, 1898–99), XXIV: 986.

28. William Mathews, "Civilization and Suicide," *The North American Review*, 152 (413) (April 1891): 483.

29. Fernand Levillain, *La neurasthénie: maladie de Beard* (Paris: A. Maloine, 1891), p. 31.

30. S. Weir Mitchell, "Civilization and Pain," *Annals of Hygiene*, 7 (1892): 26.

31. W.J. Dawson, *The Making of Manhood* (London: Hodder and Stoughton, 1894), p. 77.

32. G.W. Steevens, "The New Humanitarianism," *Blackwood's Edinburgh Magazine*, 163 (January 1898): 103–4.

33. M.G. Mulhall, "Insanity, Suicide, and Civilization," *Contemporary Review*, 43 (June 1883): 905–6.

34. Oosterhuis, *Stepchildren*, pp. 33–4. This was certainly the case with masturbation, whose relationship to the conditions of modern life continued to be observed through the early twentieth century. See Dr Thésée Pouillet, *De l'onanisme chez l'homme* (Paris: Vigor frères, 1897), pp. 41–2.

35. David Walker, "Modern Nerves, Nervous Moderns: Notes on Male Neurasthenia," *Australian Cultural History*, no. 6 (1987): 59.

36. Pouillet, *De l'onanisme*, pp. 41–2.
37. Kevin J. Mumford, "'Lost Manhood' Found: Male Sexual Impotence and Victorian Culture in the United States," *Journal of the History of Sexuality*, 3 (1) (July 1992): 35; McLaren, *Impotence*, pp. 115–17, 132.
38. Vernon A. Rosario, *The Erotic Imagination: French Histories of Perversity* (New York: Oxford University Press, 1997), p. 89.
39. Gert Hekma, "'A Female Soul in a Male Body': Sexual Inversion as Gender Inversion in Nineteenth-Century Sexology," in Gilbert Herdt (ed.), *Third Sex, Third Gender: Beyond Sexual Dimorphism in Culture and History* (New York: Zone Books, 1993), p. 103.
40. Judith Surkis, *Sexing the Citizen: Morality and Masculinity in France, 1870–1920* (Ithaca, NY: Cornell University Press, 2006), p. 84.
41. Oosterhuis, *Stepchildren*, p. 53.
42. Richard von Krafft-Ebing, *Psychopathia Sexualis*, trans. Franklin S. Klaf (New York: Bell Publishing Company, 1965), p. 48; Oosterhuis, *Stepchildren*, p. 54.
43. James C. Whorton, *Crusaders for Fitness: a History of American Health Reformers* (Princeton: Princeton University Press, 1982), p. 157.
44. Angus McLaren, *The Trials of Masculinity: Policing Sexual Boundaries, 1870–1930* (Chicago: University of Chicago Press, 1997), pp. 30–1.
45. Quoted in Michael Kane, *Modern Men: Mapping Masculinity in English and German Literature, 1880–1930* (London: Cassell, 1999), p. 67.
46. Antony Copley, *Sexual Moralities in France, 1780–1980* (London: Routledge, 1989), p. 147; J.-K. Huysmans, *Against the Grain* (1884; New York: Dover, 1969).
47. George L. Mosse, *Nationalism and Sexuality: Middle-Class Morality and Sexual Norms in Modern Europe* (Madison, WI: University of Wisconsin Press, 1985), p. 33; Oosterhuis, *Stepchildren*, p. 69.
48. Louis A. Lurie, "The Endocrine Factor in Homosexuality," *American Journal of the Medical Sciences*, 208 (2) (August 1944): 176.
49. H.G. Wells, *The Time Machine* [1895], in *The Science Fiction, Volume 1* (London: Phoenix, 1995), pp. 24–6, 65. I am grateful to Beth Abraham for drawing this image to my attention.
50. See the discussion of "devirilized" French bureaucrats in Surkis, *Sexing the Citizen*.
51. On the troubled status of bureaucrats in the early nineteenth century, see William M. Reddy, *The Invisible Code: Honor and Sentiment in Postrevolutionary France, 1814–1848* (Berkeley: University of California Press, 1997), pp. 114–16.
52. Clark Davis, *Company Men: White-Collar Life and Corporate Cultures in Los Angeles, 1892–1941* (Baltimore: Johns Hopkins University Press, 2001), pp. 156–7, 166.
53. Tom Pendergast, *Creating the Modern Man: American Magazines and Consumer Culture, 1900–1950* (Columbia, MO: University of Missouri Press, 2000), pp. 51–8, 120.
54. Angel Kwolek-Folland, *Engendering Business: Men and Women in the Corporate Office, 1870–1930* (Baltimore: Johns Hopkins University Press, 1994), p. 55.
55. Kwolek-Folland, *Engendering*, p. 51.
56. Jonathan Wild, *The Rise of the Office Clerk in Literary Culture, 1880–1939* (New York: Palgrave, 2006), pp. 81–100; Davis, *Company Men*, pp. 162–4.
57. In the nineteenth century, consumption was coded differently depending on who was involved in it. Women may have shopped, but men *collected*, a practice that was valorized as a form of investment that could be appreciated with a disinterested eye. Bourgeois men who wrote about collecting fantasized about the act as a form of "hunting" in places where women rarely ventured and which required a range of masculine skills, including intrepidity, discernment, risk-taking, competitiveness

and persistence. Auction houses were arenas where these skills could be tested, while flea markets were imagined as exotic locales populated by unsavory types. Leora Auslander, "The Gendering of Consumer Practices in Nineteenth-Century France," in Victoria de Grazia with Ellen Furlough (eds), *The Sex of Things: Gender and Consumption in Historical Perspective* (Berkeley: University of California Press, 1996), pp. 85–7, 92–3; Russell W. Belk, *Collecting in a Consumer Society* (London: Routledge, 1995), p. 97.

58. Warren G. Breckman, "Disciplining Consumption: the Debate about Luxury in Wilhelmine Germany, 1890–1914," *Journal of Social History*, 24 (3) (Spring 1991): 487–92.

59. Leon W. Fuller, "The War of 1914 as Interpreted by German Intellectuals," *Journal of Modern History*, 14 (2) (June 1942): 150; Geoffrey Cocks, "Modern Pain and Nazi Panic," in Paul Betts and Greg Eghigian (eds), *Pain and Prosperity: Reconsidering Twentieth-Century Germany* (Stanford: Stanford University Press, 2003), p. 92; in the same volume, also see Patricia R. Stokes, "Purchasing Comfort: Patent Remedies and the Alleviation of Labor Pain in Germany Between 1914 and 1933" and Greg Eghigian, "Pain, Entitlement, and Social Citizenship in Modern Germany," pp. 62, 28–9. See also Roslyn W. Bologh, *Love or Greatness: Max Weber and Masculine Thinking – a Feminist Inquiry* (Boston: Unwin Hyman, 1990), p. 43.

60. Farid Chenoune, *A History of Men's Fashion*, trans. Deke Dusinberre (Paris: Flammarion, 1993), p. 95; Herbert Maxwell, "Civilization," *Littell's Living Age*, 74 (2445) (9 May 1891): 331.

61. Gregory L. Kaster, "Labour's True Man: Organised Workingmen and the Language of Manliness in the USA, 1827–1877," *Gender & History*, 13 (1) (April 2001): 55–6.

62. Mark A. Swiencicki, "Consuming Brotherhood: Men's Culture, Style and Recreation as Consumer Culture, 1880–1930," *Journal of Social History*, 31 (4) (Summer 1998): 773–808.

63. Philip Gibbs, *The New Man: a Portrait Study of the Latest Type* (London: Sir Isaac Pitman & Sons, Ltd., 1913), pp. 86, 155.

64. Guy Reel, *The* National Police Gazette *and the Making of the Modern American Man, 1879–1906* (New York: Palgrave, 2006); Erin A. Smith, *Hard-Boiled: Working-Class Readers and Pulp Magazines* (Philadelphia: Temple University Press, 2000); Eugen Weber, "Gymnastics and Sports in Fin-de-Siècle France: Opium of the Classes?" *American Historical Review*, 76 (1) (February 1971): 98.

65. James Gilbert, *Men in the Middle: Searching for Masculinity in the 1950s* (Chicago: University of Chicago Press, 2005), pp. 31–2.

66. Quoted in Jock Phillips, *A Man's Country? The Image of the Pakeha Male – a History* (Auckland: Penguin, 1987), pp. 4–5, 17. To the eugenically-minded, the prospect of a mass exodus of able-bodied men was most worrying: in the decade leading up to World War I, several hundred thousand departed the mother country every year for the colonies, supposedly leaving behind the weak, elderly, and defective who continued to breed. Richard A. Soloway, *Demography and Degeneration: Eugenics and the Declining Birthrate in Twentieth-Century Britain* (Chapel Hill, NC: University of North Carolina Press, 1990), p. 60. This was also evident elsewhere: see Daniel J. Walther, "Gender Construction and Settler Colonialism in German Southwest Africa, 1894–1914," *The Historian*, 66 (1) (March 2004): 1–18.

67. Anne M. Windholz, "An Emigrant and a Gentleman: Imperial Masculinity, British Magazines, and the Colony that Got Away," *Victorian Studies*, 42 (4) (1999): 631.

68. Gail Bederman, *Manliness and Civilization: a Cultural History of Gender and Race in the United States, 1880–1917* (Chicago: University of Chicago Press, 1995), p. 97.

69. Brooks Adams, *The Law of Civilization and Decay* (New York: Macmillan, 1895), p. viii.
70. Edward Carpenter, *Civilisation: Its Cause and Cure* (2nd edn: London: Swan Sonnenschein and Co., 1891), p. 47.
71. Pascal Grosse, "Turning Native? Anthropology, German Colonialism, and the Paradoxes of the 'Acclimatization Question,' 1885–1914," in H. Glenn Penny and Matti Bunzl (eds), *Worldly Provincialism: German Anthropology in the Age of Empire* (Ann Arbor, MI: University of Michigan Press, 2003), pp. 184–6.
72. Carpenter, *Civilisation*, p. 35.
73. Frank Trentmann, "Civilization and its Discontents: English Neo-Romanticism and the Transformation of Anti-Modernism in Twentieth-Century Western Culture," *Journal of Contemporary History*, 29 (4) (October 1994): 589–91.
74. Henning Eichberg, "The Enclosure of the Body – on the Historical Relativity of 'Health', 'Nature' and the Environment of Sport," *Journal of Contemporary History*, 21 (1) (January 1986): 108; Matthew Jefferies, "Lebensreform: a Middle-Class Antidote to Wilhelminism?" in Geoff Eley and James Retallack (eds), *Wilhelminism and its Discontents: German Modernities, Imperialism, and the Meanings of Reform, 1890–1930* (New York: Berghahn, 2003), p. 94
75. Karl Toepfer, *Empire of Ecstasy: Nudity and Movement in German Body Culture, 1910–1935* (Berkeley: University of California Press, 1997), p. 31.
76. Hans Surén, *Man and Sunlight*, trans. David Arthur Jones (1924; Slough, UK: The Sollux Publishing Company, 1927), p. 104.
77. Maren Möhring, "Working out the Body's Boundaries: Physiological, Aesthetic and Psychic Dimensions of the Skin in German Nudism, 1890–1930," in Christopher E. Forth and Ivan Crozier (eds), *Body Parts: Critical Explorations in Corporeality* (Lanham, MD: Lexington Books, 2005), pp. 234–5; Toepfer, *Empire of Ecstasy*, pp. 35–7; Michael Hau, *The Cult of Health and Beauty in Germany: a Social History, 1890–1930* (Chicago: University of Chicago Press, 2003), p. 25.
78. Hau, *Cult of Health*, pp. 15, 33, 46–9.
79. Quoted in Paul Mendes-Flohr and Jehuda Reinharz (eds), *The Jews in the Modern World: a Documentary History* (Oxford: Oxford University Press, 1995), pp. 267–8.
80. Todd Samuel Presner, "'Clear Heads, Solid Stomachs, and Hard Muscles': Max Nordau and the Aesthetics of Jewish Regeneration," *Modernism/Modernity*, 10 (2) (2003): 269–96; David Bathrick, "Max Schmeling on the Canvas: Boxing as an Icon of Weimar Germany," *New German Critique*, 51 (Autumn 1990): 126–7; Matti Bunzl, "Resistive Play: Sports and the Emergence of Jewish Visibility in Contemporary Vienna," *Journal of Sport and Social Issues*, 24 (3) (August 2000): 241.
81. Martin Summers, *Manliness and its Discontents: the Black Middle Class and the Transformation of Masculinity, 1900–1930* (Chapel Hill, NC: University of North Carolina Press, 2004), pp. 25–65.
82. Christopher B. Booker, *"I Will Wear No Chain!": a Social History of African American Males* (Westport, CT: Praeger, 2000), p. 60.
83. Gwendolyn Champion, "Enter Ladies and Gentlemen of Color: Gender, Sport, and the Ideal of African American Manhood and Womanhood during the Late Nineteenth and Early Twentieth Centuries," *Journal of Sport History*, 18 (1) (Spring 1991): 91–3; Bederman, *Manliness and Civilization*, pp. 1–44.
84. Gilbert Andrieu, *L'Homme et la force: Des marchands de la force au culte de la forme (XIXe et XXe siècles)* (Joinville-le-Pont: Éditions Actio, 1988), pp. 222–3.

85. William James, "The Moral Equivalent of War" (1906), quoted in Daniel Pick, *War Machine: the Rationalisation of Slaughter in the Modern Age* (New Haven, CT: Yale University Press, 1993), p. 16.
86. Wild, *Rise of the Office Clerk*, pp. 123–6.
87. Margaret Marsh, "Suburban Men and Masculine Domesticity, 1870–1915," *American Quarterly*, 40 (2) (June 1988): 176; see also Gilbert, *Men in the Middle*, p. 32.
88. Martin Francis, "The Domestication of the Male? Recent Research on Nineteenth- and Twentieth-Century British Masculinity," *The Historical Journal*, 45 (3) (2002): 643.

7 MEN OF STEEL: TECHNOLOGIES OF THE MALE BODY

1. Sandro Bellassai, "The Masculine Mystique: Antimodernism and Virility in Fascist Italy," *Journal of Modern Italian Studies*, 10 (3) (2005): 331–2.
2. Quoted in Karl Toepfer, "Nudity and Modernity in German Dance, 1910–30," *Journal of the History of Sexuality*, 3 (1) (July 1992): 66.
3. Christopher S. Thompson, *The Tour de France: a Cultural History* (Berkeley: University of California Press, 2006), pp. 185–9.
4. Hal Foster, "Prosthetic Gods," *Modernism/Modernity*, 4, no. 2 (1997): 5; Michael Adas, *Machines as the Measure of Men: Science, Technology, and Ideologies of Western Dominance* (Ithaca, NY: Cornell University Press, 1989).
5. George Orwell, *The Road to Wigan Pier* (London: Victor Gollancz, Ltd., 1937), p. 228.
6. Anson Rabinbach, *The Human Motor: Energy, Fatigue, and the Origins of Modernity* (Berkeley: University of California Press, 1990), pp. 64–6; Cecelia Tichi, *Shifting Gears: Technology, Literature, Culture in Modernist America* (Chapel Hill, NC: University of North Carolina Press, 1987), pp. 34–40. On energy as "capital," see Dr Burlureaux, *La lutte pour la santé: Essai de pathologie générale* (Paris: Perrin, 1906), p. 2.
7. Mark Seltzer, *Bodies and Machines* (New York: Routledge, 1992), pp. 152–3.
8. Jeffrey Herf, *Reactionary Modernism: Technology, Culture, and Politics in Weimar and the Third Reich* (Cambridge: Cambridge University Press, 1984), p. 3.
9. Susan Kingsley Kent, *Making Peace: the Reconstruction of Gender in Interwar Britain* (Princeton: Princeton University Press, 1993), p. 49.
10. Henry Ford, *My Life and Work* (1922; New York: Arno Press, 1973), pp. 1, 103.
11. Quoted in Richard Stites, *Revolutionary Dreams: Utopian Vision and Experimental Life in the Russian Revolution* (New York: Oxford University Press, 1989), p. 148.
12. Some have even written of a "natural affinity" of men for the machines they design, operate and maintain, an affective relationship often couched in the language of "love" and "respect." Cynthia Cockburn, *Machinery of Dominance: Women, Men and Technical Know-How* (London: Pluto Press, 1985), p. 172. See also Ruth Oldenziel, *Making Technology Masculine: Men, Women and Modern Machines in America, 1870–1945* (Amsterdam: Amsterdam University Press, 1999), pp. 54–62.
13. Paul Willis, "Shop Floor Culture, Masculinity and the Wage Form," in John Clarke, Chas Critcher and Richard Johnson (eds), *Working-Class Culture: Studies in History and Theory* (London: Hutchinson, 1979), pp. 188–90; Stephen Meyer, "Work, Play, and Power: Masculine Culture on the Automotive Shop Floor, 1930–1960," *Men and Masculinities*, 2 (2) (October 1999): 115–34.
14. Frances L. Bernstein, "Envisioning Health in Revolutionary Russia: the Politics of Gender in Sexual-Enlightenment Posters of the 1920s," *Russian Review*, 57 (April 1998): 199; Catriona Kelly, "The Education of the Will: Advice Literature, *Zakal*, and Manliness in Early Twentieth-Century Russia," in Barbara Evans Clements,

Rebecca Friedman and Dan Healey (eds), *Russian Masculinities in History and Culture* (Basingstoke: Palgrave, 2002), pp. 131, 142

15. Timothy W. Luke, "The Proletarian Ethic and Soviet Industrialization," *American Political Science Review*, 77 (3) (September 1983): 594–5.

16. Toby Clark, "The 'New Man's' Body: a Motif in Early Soviet Culture," in Matthew Cullerne Bown and Brandon Taylor (eds), *Art of the Soviets: Painting, Sculpture and Architecture in a One-Party State, 1917–1992* (Manchester: Manchester University Press, 1993), p. 45; Rolf Hellebust, "Aleksei Gastev and the Metallization of the Revolutionary Body," *Slavic Review*, 56 (3) (Autumn 1997): 501.

17. Katerina Clark, *The Soviet Novel: History as Ritual* (Chicago: University of Chicago Press, 1981), pp. 94–5, 98; Luke, "Proletarian Ethic," pp. 598–9.

18. Quoted in Igal Halfin, "The Rape of the Intelligentsia: a Proletarian Foundation Myth," *Russian Review*, 56 (January 1997): 102.

19. Clark, *Soviet Novel*, pp. 152–3.

20. Clark, *Soviet Novel*, pp. 120, 138–9, 143.

21. Victoria E. Bonnell, *Iconography of Power: Soviet Political Posters under Lenin and Stalin* (Berkeley: University of California Press, 1997), p. 39.

22. Margarita Tupitsyn, "Superman Imagery in Soviet Photography and Photomontage," in Bernice Glatzer Rosenthal (ed.), *Nietzsche and Soviet Culture: Ally and Adversary* (Cambridge: Cambridge University Press, 1994), pp. 287–310.

23. Maurizia Boscagli, *Eye on the Flesh: Fashions of Masculinity in the Early Twentieth Century* (Boulder, CO: Westview, 1996), p. 129.

24. Modris Eksteins, *Rites of Spring: the Great War and the Birth of the Modern Age* (New York: Anchor Books, 1989), pp. 250–1.

25. Robert Wohl, *A Passion for Wings: Aviation and the Western Imagination, 1908–1918* (New Haven, CT: Yale University Press, 1994), p. 29. See also Peter Fritzsche, *A Nation of Fliers: German Aviation and the Popular Imagination* (Cambridge, MA: Harvard University Press, 1992), pp. 133–4.

26. Marinetti, "Multiplied Man and the Reign of the Machine," in *Marinetti: Selected Writings*, ed. R.W. Flint, trans. R.W. Flint and Arthur A. Coppotelli (New York: Farrar, Straus and Giroux, 1971), p. 91.

27. Monica Dall'asta, *Un cinéma musclé: Le surhomme dans le cinéma muet italien (1913–1926)*, trans. Franco Arnò and Charles Tatum, Jr (Paris: Éditions Yellow Now, 1992), p. 97.

28. Marinetti, "Multiplied Man," p. 91.

29. Despite the number of female aviators who also broke records during this time, representations of flight as an exclusively male prerogative abounded in the early twentieth century. The practical obstacles that women faced in their efforts to gain flight training, licensing or employment as pilots helped to preserve aviation's masculine credentials. Siân Reynolds, *France between the Wars: Gender and Politics* (New York: Routledge, 1996), pp. 68–9. In Germany, by contrast, female aviators were often celebrated as exemplars of "the new person" that technology had made possible. Physical differences mattered less when most pilots were relatively small and thin. Fritzsche, *Nation of Fliers*, p. 158.

30. Wohl, *Passion for Wings*, p. 138; Claudio G. Segrè, *Italo Balbo: a Fascist Life* (Berkeley: University of California Press, 1987), pp. 148–9, 192–4; Bellassai, "Masculine Mystique," p. 324. By the 1960s cosmonauts would model themselves on the aviator hero, proudly declaring themselves "Chkalovites." Jay Bergman, "Valerii Chkalov: Soviet Pilot as New Soviet Man," *Journal of Contemporary History*, 33 (1) (January 1998): 131–52.

31. Todd Presner, "Muscle Jews and Airplanes: Modernist Mythologies, the Great War, and the Politics of Regeneration," *Modernism/Modernity*, 13 (4) (2006): 701–28.

32. Farid Chenoune, *A History of Men's Fashion*, trans. Deke Dusinberre (Paris: Flammarion, 1993), p. 144.

33. Clay McShane, *Down the Asphalt Path: the Automobile and the American City* (New York: Columbia University Press, 1994), pp. 153–5.

34. Maria H. Frawley, *Invalidism and Identity in Nineteenth-Century Britain* (Chicago: University of Chicago Press, 2004), p. 114; Motor, "L'Automobilisme et la culture physique," *La Culture physique*, 1 (February 1904): 10.

35. Marinetti, "The Founding and Manifesto of Futurism" (1909), in Umbro Apollonio (ed.), *Futurist Manifestos* (London: Thames and Hudson, 1973), p. 21.

36. Georgine Clarsen, "The 'Dainty Female Toe' and the 'Brawny Male Arm': Conceptions of Bodies and Power in Automobile Technology," *Australian Feminist Studies*, 15 (32) (2000): 155.

37. Christina Cogdell, *Eugenic Design: Streamlining America in the 1930s* (Philadelphia: University of Pennsylvania Press, 2004), pp. 31–2.

38. Quoted in Marshall Berman, *All that is Solid Melts into Air: the Experience of Modernity* (London: Verso, 1995), p. 166.

39. Sinclair Lewis, *Babbitt* (1922; New York: Random House, 2002), p. 55; see also McShane, *Down the Asphalt Path*, p. 156.

40. Quoted in Sean O'Connell, *The Car in British Society: Class, Gender and Motoring, 1896–1939* (Manchester: Manchester University Press, 1998), p. 53.

41. David H. Keller, "The Revolt of the Pedestrians," *Amazing Stories*, 2, no. 11 (February 1928): 1048–59.

42. Walter Camp, *Keeping Fit All the Way: How to Obtain and Maintain Health, Strength and Efficiency* (New York: Harper & Brothers Publishers, 1919), pp. 4–5.

43. Angus McLaren, *Impotence: a Cultural History* (Chicago: University of Chicago Press, 2007), p. 173.

44. Orwell, *Road to Wigan Pier*, p. 227.

45. Roy Helton, "The Inner Threat: Our Own Softness," *Harper's Magazine*, 181 (September 1940): 338, 341.

46. John M. Hoberman, *Mortal Engines: the Science of Performance and the Dehumanization of Sport* (New York: The Free Press, 1992), p.103.

47. Leo Braudy, *From Chivalry to Terrorism: War and the Changing Nature of Masculinity* (New York: Knopf, 2003), pp. 431–2.

48. Cogdell, *Eugenic Design*, pp. 34, 203–7; Gerard Jones, *Men of Tomorrow: Geeks, Gangsters and the Birth of the Comic Book* (New York: Basic Books, 2004), pp. 80–6. Whereas ancient heroes often possessed powers that were the "extreme realization of natural endowments" that ordinary men might possess, Umberto Eco suggests that the conditions of modern industrial society demand a different kind of hero: "Individual strength, if not exerted in sports activities, is left abased when confronted with the strength of machines which determine man's very movements. In such a society the positive hero must embody to an unthinkable degree the power demands that the average citizen nurtures but cannot satisfy." Eco, "The Myth of Superman," in *The Role of the Reader* (Bloomington, IN: Indiana University Press, 1979), p. 107.

49. Ana Carden-Coyne, "Classical Heroism and Modern Life: Bodybuilding and Masculinity in the Early Twentieth Century," *Journal of Australian Studies*, 63 (December 1999): 138–52.

50. Elizabeth Toon and Janet Golden, "'Live Clean, Think Clean, and Don't Go to Burlesque Shows': Charles Atlas as Health Advisor," *Journal of the History of Medicine*, 57 (1) (January 2002): 39–60.
51. Perhaps foreseeing exciting new markets, in one of his many ads Charles Atlas upgraded the disorder to "scourge of the world."
52. J.H. Kellogg, *The Itinerary of a Breakfast* (New York: Funk and Wagnalls Co., 1918), p. 37; Whorton, *Inner Hygiene*, p. 106; Ana Carden-Coyne, "American Guts and Military Manhood," in Christopher E. Forth and Ana Carden-Coyne (eds), *Cultures of the Abdomen: Diet, Digestion, and Fat in the Modern World* (New York: Palgrave, 2005), pp. 79–80.
53. James C. Whorton, *Crusaders for Fitness: a History of American Health Reformers* (Princeton: Princeton University Press, 1982), pp. 175–7, 180.
54. Tom Burns Haber, "The Origin of 'Intestinal Fortitude,'" *American Speech*, 3 (3) (October 1955): 235–7.
55. Ina Zweiniger-Bargielowska, "The Culture of the Abdomen: Obesity and Reducing in Britain, circa 1900–1939," *Journal of British Studies*, 44 (April 2005): 239–73.
56. D.H.S., "Forty – and Fat," *Men Only* (1935): 101–3.
57. Arouna Ouédraogo, "Vegetarianism in Fin-de-Siècle France: the Social Determinants of Vegetarians' Misfortune in Pre-World War I France," in Alexander Fenton (ed.), *Order and Disorder: the Health Implications of Eating and Drinking in the Nineteenth and Twentieth Centuries* (Edinburgh: Tuckwell Press, 2000), p. 211; and idem., "Food and the Purification of Society: Dr Paul Carton and Vegetarianism in Interwar France," *Social History of Medicine*, 14 (2) (2001): 231, 234.
58. "His Clothes," *Man: the Australian Magazine for Men*, 10 (November 1941): 104.
59. Gaylyn Studlar, *This Mad Masquerade: Stardom and Masculinity in the Jazz Age* (New York: Columbia University Press, 1996), pp. 12–13.
60. David Levering Lewis, *When Harlem Was in Vogue* (New York: Oxford University Press, 1981), pp. 114–15; Scott Appelrouth, "Body and Soul: Jazz in the 1920s," *American Behavioral Scientist*, 48 (11) (July 2005): 1496–509.
61. Quoted in Jeffrey H. Jackson, *Making Jazz French: Music and Modern Life in Interwar Paris* (Durham, NC: Duke University Press, 2003), p. 100.
62. Marieke Dubbelboer, "Un univers mécanique: la machine chez Alfred Jarry," *French Studies*, 68 (4) (2004): 471–83.
63. Kevin White, *The First Sexual Revolution: the Emergence of Male Heterosexuality in Modern America* (New York: NYU Press, 1993), pp. 18–19, 31, 156–7.
64. Joanna Bourke, *Working-Class Cultures in Britain, 1890–1960* (London: Routledge, 1994), p. 35.
65. Laure Adler, *Secrets d'alcôve: histoire du couple de 1830 à 1930* (Paris: Hachette, 1983), pp. 93–4.
66. Atina Grossmann, *Reforming Sex: the German Movement for Birth Control and Abortion Reform, 1920–1950* (New York: Oxford University Press, 1995), pp. 26, 34.
67. Here too the metaphor of the body-as-automobile was widely employed. Compare McLaren, *Impotence*, p. 178.
68. Lesley A. Hall, *Hidden Anxieties: Male Sexuality, 1900–1950* (Cambridge: Polity, 1991), pp. 71, 120–4; Rachel P. Maines, *The Technology of Orgasm: "Hysteria," the Vibrator, and Women's Sexual Satisfaction* (Baltimore: Johns Hopkins University Press, 1999), pp. 117–18; Mary Lynn Stewart, *For Health and Beauty: Physical Culture for Frenchwomen, 1880s–1930s* (Baltimore: Johns Hopkins University Press, 2001), pp. 14–115; Ute Frevert, *Women in German History: From Bourgeois Emancipation to Sexual Liberation*, trans. Stuart McKinnon Evans (Oxford: Berg, 1989), pp. 190–2.

69. Wilhelm Stekel, *Impotence in the Male: the Psychic Disorders of Sexual Function in the Male*, trans. Oswald H. Boltz (New York: Liveright Publishing Corp., 1927), I: 2, 5, 53–4; Kevin J. Mumford, "'Lost Manhood' Found: Male Sexual Impotence and Victorian Culture in the United States," *Journal of the History of Sexuality*, 3 (1) (July 1992): 50–1.

70. Stewart, *For Health and Beauty*, p. 140; Jennifer Terry, *An American Obsession: Science, Medicine, and Homosexuality in Modern Society* (Chicago: University of Chicago Press, 1999), p. 162; Chandak Sengoopta, "Glandular Politics: Experimental Biology, Clinical Medicine, and Homosexual Emancipation in Fin-de-Siècle Central Europe," *Isis*, 89 (1998): 445–73.

71. John Hoberman, *Testosterone Dreams: Rejuvenation, Aphrodisia, Doping* (Berkeley: University of California Press, 2005), p. 55; Ad for Vi-Tabs, "Youthful Vigour Restored by New, Simple, Easy Method," *Man: a Magazine for Australian Men*, 6 (1) (June 1939): 113.

72. Walter van Henry, *Glands: a Treatise on their Importance in the Human Machine and their Scientific Hygiene* (Chicago: Walter van Henry, 1924), pp. 4, 18–21; see also Paul de Kruif, *The Male Hormone* (New York: Harcourt, Brace and Co., 1945), p. 92.

73. Herman H. Rubin, *Your Life is in Your Glands* (New York: Stratford House, Inc., 1948), pp. 84–5.

74. Terry, *American Obsession*, pp. 161–2.

75. Nelly Oudshoorn, *Beyond the Natural Body: an Archeology of Sex Hormones* (New York: Routledge, 1994), pp. 59–61; McLaren, *Impotence*, pp. 149–207.

76. Anne-Marie Sohn, "Le corps sexué," in Jean-Jacques Courtine (ed.), *Histoire du corps: 3. Les mutations du regard. Le XXe siècle* (Paris: Seuil, 2005), pp. 108–9.

77. Georges Valois, *L'Homme qui vient: Philosophie de l'autorité* (1905; Paris: La nouvelle librairie nationale, 1923), pp. 47–50, 54.

78. David Forgacs, "Fascism, Violence, and Modernity," in Jana Howlett and Rod Mengham (eds), *The Violent Muse: Violence and the Artistic Imagination in Europe, 1910–1939* (Manchester: Manchester University Press, 1994), p. 5.

79. Emilio Gentile, "'L'homme nouveau' du fascisme: réflexions sur une expérience de révolution anthropologique," in Marie-Anne Matard-Bonucci and Pierre Milza (eds), *L'homme nouveau dans l'Europe fasciste (1922–1945): entre dictature et totalitarisme* (Paris: Fayard, 2004), p. 36.

80. Barbara Spackman, *Fascist Virilities: Rhetoric, Ideology, and Social Fantasy in Italy* (Minneapolis: University of Minnesota Press, 1996), pp. xii, 19–20.

81. John M. Hoberman, *Sport and Political Ideology* (London: Heinemann, 1984), pp. 84, 102.

82. Michael A. Spurr, "'Playing for Fascism': Sportsmanship, Antisemitism and the British Union of Fascists," *Patterns of Prejudice*, 37 (4) (2003): 363–4; Tony Collins, "Return to Manhood: the Cult of Masculinity and the British Union of Fascists," in J.A. Mangan (ed.), *Superman Supreme: Fascist Body as Political Icon – Global Fascism* (London: Frank Cass, 2000), pp. 145–62.

83. Quoted in Philip M. Coupland, "The Blackshirted Utopians," *Journal of Contemporary History*, 33 (2) (April 1998): 264.

84. Leon W. Fuller, "The War of 1914 as Interpreted by German Intellectuals," *Journal of Modern History*, 14 (2) (June 1942): 150.

85. Quoted in David Bathrick, "Max Schmeling on the Canvas: Boxing as an Icon of Weimar Germany," *New German Critique*, no. 51 (Autumn 1990): 117.

86. Eghigian, "Pain, Entitlement, and Social Citizenship in Modern Germany," in Paul Betts and Greg Eghigian (eds), *Pain and Prosperity: Reconsidering Twentieth-Century Germany* (Stanford: Stanford University Press, 2003), pp. 28–30.

87. Arnd Krüger, "Breeding, Rearing and Preparing the Aryan Body: Creating Supermen the Nazi Way," in J.A. Mangan (ed.), *Shaping the Superman: Fascist Body as Political Icon – Aryan Fascism* (London: Frank Cass, 1999), p. 56.
88. Arnaldo Testi, "The Gender of Reform Politics: Theodor Roosevelt and the Culture of Masculinity," *Journal of American History*, 81 (4) (March 1995): 1514, 1519.
89. Bellassai, "Masculine Mystique," pp. 316, 318; Gentile, "L''homme nouveau,'" p. 58; Roger Griffin, *Modernism and Fascism: the Sense of a Beginning under Mussolini and Hitler* (Basingstoke: Palgrave, 2007).
90. George L. Mosse, *The Image of Man: the Creation of Modern Masculinity* (New York: Oxford University Press, 1996), p. 166.
91. Roberta Suzzi Valli, "The Myth of *Squadrismo* in the Fascist Regime," trans. Anne Heaton-Ward, *Journal of Contemporary History*, 35 (2) (April 2000): 139–42.
92. Klaus Theweleit, *Male Fantasies, Volume 1: Women, Floods, Bodies, History*, trans. Stephen Conway (Minneapolis: University of Minnesota Press, 1987).
93. Griffin, *Modernism and Fascism*, p. 140.
94. Rabinbach, *The Human Motor*, pp. 298, 299.
95. Roland Barthes, "L'homme-jet," in *Mythologies* (Paris: Seuil, 1957), pp. 94–6.

8   THE LAST MEN? CONSUMING MANHOOD SINCE 1945

1. Friedrich Nietzsche, *Thus Spoke Zarathustra*, in *The Portable Nietzsche*, trans. Walter Kaufmann (1885; New York: Viking, 1969), pp. 129–30.
2. Aldous Huxley, *Brave New World* (1932; New York: Vintage, 2004), pp. 201, 209.
3. John Osborne, *Look Back in Anger and Other Plays* (1956; London: Faber and Faber, 1993).
4. Marianna Torgovnick, *Gone Primitive: Savage Intellects, Modern Lives* (Chicago: University of Chicago Press, 1990), p. 37.
5. Susan Jeffords, *The Remasculinization of America: Gender and the Vietnam War* (Bloomington, IN: Indiana University Press, 1989), p. 3.
6. Joanna Bourke, *An Intimate History of Killing: Face-to-Face Killing in Twentieth-Century Warfare* (London: Granta, 1999), pp. 77–8, 83–102, 132–6.
7. Christina S. Jarvis, *The Male Body at War: American Masculinity during World War II* (Dekalb, IL: Northern Illinois University Press, 2004), pp. 107–12.
8. Miriam G. Reumann, *American Sexual Character: Sex, Gender, and National Identity in the Kinsey Reports* (Berkeley: University of California Press, 2005), pp. 54–85.
9. Robert D. Dean, *Imperial Brotherhood: Gender and the Making of Cold War Policy* (Amherst, MA: University of Massachusetts Press, 2001), pp. 43–9.
10. Dean, *Imperial Brotherhood*, pp. 180–1.
11. Quoted in Dean, *Imperial Brotherhood*, p. 182.
12. Quoted in Barbara Ehrenreich, *Fear of Falling: the Inner Life of the Middle Class* (New York: Pantheon, 1989), pp. 33–4.
13. C. Wright Mills, *White Collar: the American Middle Classes* (New York: Oxford University Press, 1951), p. xii.
14. This figure increased to eight by 1970, though in America it had dropped to around five by 2004. Barbara Ehrenreich, *The Hearts of Men: American Dreams and the Flight from Responsibility* (New York: Anchor Books, 1983), p. 70; National Center for Health Statistics, National Vital Statistics Reports, 54 (19), 28 June 2006, www.cdc.gov/nchs. Last consulted on 7 January 2007.

15. Ehrenreich, *Hearts of Men*, p. 71; Elianne Riska, *Masculinity and Men's Health: Coronary Heart Disease in Medical and Public Discourse* (Lanham, MD: Rowman & Littlefield, 2004), pp. 32–3; James Gilbert, *Men in the Middle: Searching for Masculinity in the 1950s* (Chicago: University of Chicago Press, 2005), pp. 78–9.

16. Art Buchwald, "Acid Indigestion," *Esquire*, 84 (December 1975): 169.

17. Ehrenreich, *Hearts of Men*, pp. 74–5.

18. Elaine Tyler May, *Homeward Bound: American Families in the Cold War Era* (New York: Basic Books, 1988).

19. Jesse Berrett, "Feeding the Organization Man: Diet and Masculinity in Postwar America," *Journal of Social History*, 30 (Summer 1997): 809, 813, 817.

20. May, *Homeward Bound*, pp. 9–8.

21. Reumann, *American Sexual Character*, p. 185. Arthur Schlesinger's diagnosis of the "crisis of American masculinity" accords well with such claims: "it can be plausibly argued that the conditions of modern life make the quest for identity more difficult than it has ever been before ... [I]f people do not know *who* they are, it is hardly surprising that they are no longer sure what sex they are." Schlesinger, "The Crisis of American Masculinity (1958)," in *The Politics of Hope* (Boston: Houghton Mifflin Co., 1962), pp. 242–3.

22. Mickey Spillane, *One Lonely Night*, in *The Mike Hammer Collection, Volume 2* (1951; New York: New American Library, 2001), p. 6.

23. Mickey Spillane, *I, the Jury*, in *The Mike Hammer Collection, Volume 1* (1947; New York: New American Library, 2001), p. 52.

24. Bill Osgerby, "Muscular Manhood and Salacious Sleaze: the Singular World of the 1950s Macho Pulps," in Nathan Abrams and Julie Hughes (eds), *Containing America: Cultural Production and Consumption in 50s America* (Birmingham: University of Birmingham Press, 2000), pp. 125–50. See also Max Allan Collins, Rich Oberg, George Hagenauer and Steven Heller (eds), *Men's Adventure Magazines in Postwar America* (Köln: Taschen, 2004).

25. Steven Cohan, *Masked Men: Masculinity and the Movies in the Fifties* (Bloomington, IN: Indiana University Press, 1997), pp. 106–21.

26. Robert A. Heinlein, *Starship Troopers* (1959; New York: Ace Books, 1987), p. 171.

27. John P. Mallan, "Roosevelt, Brooks Adams, and Lea: the Warrior Critique of the Business Civilization," *American Quarterly*, 8 (3) (Autumn 1956): pp. 216–17.

28. Richard Matheson, *The Shrinking Man* (1956; London: Gollanz, 2002), p. 67.

29. Joanne Hollows, "The Bachelor Dinner: Masculinity, Class, and Cooking in *Playboy*, 1953–1961," *Continuum: Journal of Media and Cultural Studies*, 16 (2) (2002): 144–5; Bill Osgerby, *Playboys in Paradise: Masculinity, Youth and Leisure-Style in Modern America* (Oxford: Berg, 2001).

30. Cohan, *Masked Men*, p. 266. See also *Esquire* magazine, which initiated many of these ideas in the 1930s: Kenon Breazeale, "In Spite of Women: *Esquire* Magazine and the Construction of the Male Consumer," *Signs*, 20 (111) (1994): 1–22.

31. Candida Taylor, "Zoot Suit: Breaking the Cold War's Dress Code," in *Containing America*, pp. 63–6.

32. David Savran, *Taking It Like A Man: White Masculinity, Masochism, and Contemporary American Culture* (Princeton: Princeton University Press, 1998), pp. 62, 67.

33. Despite their more modest lifestyles, even the Soviets were preoccupied with a tension between instilling in young men the virtues of "culturedness" and growing tendencies toward rowdy behavior like smoking, drinking, sexual adventures and physical aggression. By the 1970s these and other problems constituted what Russian officials dubbed a "Masculinity Crisis." Julie Gilmour and Barbara Evans

Clements, "'If You Want to Be Like Me, Train!': the Contradictions of Soviet Masculinity," in Barbara Evans Clements, Rebecca Friedman and Dan Healey (eds), *Russian Masculinities in History and Culture* (Basingstoke: Palgrave, 2002), pp. 210–22; Jeff Hearn and Keith Pringle (eds), *European Perspectives on Men and Masculinities: National and Transnational Approaches* (Basingstoke: Palgrave, 2006), p. 40.

34. Dan Diner, *America in the Eyes of the Germans: an Essay on Anti-Americanism* (Princeton: Markus Wiener, 1996), p. 56.
35. Richard Kuisel, *Seducing the French: the Dilemma of Americanization* (Berkeley: University of California Press, 1993), pp. 2–3, 13.
36. Alexis de Tocqueville, *Democracy in America*, trans. Henry Reeves (1831; New York: Knopf, 1953), p. 128.
37. John Locke, *Of Civil Government: Second Treatise* (1689; South Bend, IN: Gateway Editions, 1955), p. 39.
38. Charles Sowerwine, *France since 1870: Culture, Politics and Society* (London: Palgrave, 2001), pp. 274–83.
39. Mary Nolan, "Consuming America, Producing Gender," in R. Laurence Moore and Maurizio Vaudagna (eds), *The American Century in Europe* (Ithaca, NY: Cornell University Press, 2003), p. 254.
40. Frank Mort and Peter Thompson, "Retailing, Commercial Culture and Masculinity in 1950s Britain: the Case of Montague Burton, the 'Tailor of Taste,'" *History Workshop Journal*, 38 (Autumn 1994): 114–15.
41. Percy Cerutti, *Be Fit! Or Be Damned* (London: Pelham Books, 1967), p. 19.
42. Sir Adolphe Abrahams, *Fitness for the Average Man* (London: Christopher Johnson, 1952), p. 13; Ina Zweiniger-Bargielowska, "The Culture of the Abdomen: Obesity and Reducing in Britain, circa 1900–1939," *Journal of British Studies*, 44 (April 2005): 272.
43. Patrick Higgins, *Homosexual Dictatorship: Male Homosexuality in Postwar Britain* (London: Fourth Estate, 1996), pp. 20–5, 29–30. In the eyes of some, however, the damage had been done years earlier. The decline of the British Empire had often been attributed to a process of "feminization" by women who just didn't understand the sometimes brutal methods needed to keep indigenous people down. See Helen Callaway, *Gender, Culture and Empire: European Women in Colonial Nigeria* (Urbana: University of Illinois Press, 1987), p. 3.
44. John Hill, *Sex, Class and Realism: British Cinema, 1956–1963* (London: BFI Publishing, 1986), p. 25.
45. D.E. Cooper, "Looking Back on Anger," in Vernon Bogdanor and Robert Skidelsky (eds), *The Age of Affluence, 1951–1964* (London: Macmillan, 1970), pp. 254–67.
46. Ironically, the misogyny expressed by some Angries was appropriated to encourage the consumption they also despised: a critical element of the marketing of menswear by companies like Burton was the ability to affirm a distinctly masculine culture by reinforcing the idea that men could wrest themselves from "female bondage" by selecting clothes for themselves. Mort and Thompson, "Retailing," pp. 120–1.
47. Mark Donelly, *Sixties Britain: Culture, Society and Politics* (London: Longman, 2005), p. 37.
48. Christopher Breward, *Fashioning London: Clothing and the Modern Metropolis* (Oxford: Berg, 2004), pp. 126, 130–5.
49. Erica Carter, *How German is She? Postwar German Reconstruction and the Consuming Woman* (Ann Arbor, MI: University of Michigan Press, 1997), p. 29.
50. Carter, *How German is She?*, pp. 22–6.

51. Michael Wildt, "Continuities and Discontinuities of Consumer Mentality in West Germany in the 1950s," in Richard Bessel and Dirk Schumann (eds), *Life after Death: Approaches to a Cultural and Social History of Europe during the 1940s and 1950s* (Cambridge: Cambridge University Press, 2003), pp. 219–20, 227.

52. Andrew Bickford, "The Militarization of Masculinity in the Former German Democratic Republic," in Paul R. Higate (ed.), *Military Masculinities: Identity and the State* (Westport, CT: Praeger, 2003), pp. 159–62.

53. Uta G. Poiger, *Jazz, Rock, and Rebels: Cold War Politics and American Culture in a Divided Germany* (Berkeley: University of California Press, 2000), p. 80.

54. Uta G. Poiger, "Rebels with a Cause? American Popular Culture, the 1956 Youth Riots, and New Conceptions of Masculinity in East and West Germany," in Reiner Pommerin (ed.), *The American Impact on Postwar Germany* (Oxford: Berghahn, 1995), pp. 94, 100; Poiger, "A New, 'Western' Hero? Reconstructing German Masculinity in the 1950s," *Signs*, 24 (1) (Autumn 1998): 149–50.

55. Poiger, "Rebels with a Cause?" pp. 97–8.

56. Kristin Ross, *Fast Cars, Clean Bodies: Decolonization and the Reordering of French Culture* (Cambridge: MIT Press, 1995), pp. 61, 175; Richard Ivan Jobs, *Riding the New Wave: Youth and the Rejuvenation of France after the Second World War* (Stanford: Stanford University Press, 2007), pp. 83–8. For the origins of this consumer ethos in the inter-war period, see Robert L. Frost, "Machine Liberation: Inventing Housewives and Home Appliances in Interwar France," *French Historical Studies*, 18 (1) (Spring 1993): 122.

57. Antony Copley, *Sexual Moralities in France, 1780–1980* (London: Routledge, 1989), p. 217.

58. Marcel Rouet, *Virilité et puissance sexuelle* (Paris: Productions de Paris, 1971), pp. 9–10.

59. Paul Vincent, *Dictionnaire de la virilité* (Paris: Maloine S.A. Editeur, 1973), pp. 9–10, 84, 289–90.

60. Frantz Fanon, *Black Skin White Masks*, trans. Charles Lam Markmann (1952; St Albans, UK: Paladin, 1970), pp. 117, 125.

61. Ross, *Fast Cars*, pp. 61, 175.

62. Ellen Furlough, "Packaging Pleasures: Club Méditerranée and French Consumer Culture, 1950–1968," *French Historical Studies*, 18 (1) (Spring 1993): 65–81.

63. Tom Pendergast, *Creating the Modern Man: American Magazines and Consumer Culture, 1900–1950* (Columbia, MO: University of Missouri Press, 2000), p. 13.

64. Christine Castelain-Meunier, *Les hommes aujourd'hui: virilité et identité* (Paris: Acropole, 1988), p. 107.

65. Gore Vidal, "Tarzan Revisited," *Esquire*, 60 (6) (December 1963): 264; Torgovnick, *Gone Primitive*, pp. 42–4.

66. Maria Wyke, "Herculean Muscle! The Classicizing Rhetoric of Bodybuilding," *Arion: a Journal of Humanities*, 4 (3) (1997): 51–79.

67. Richard Dyer, *White* (London: Routledge, 1997), p. 169.

68. Christopher Wagstaff, "A Forkful of Westerns: Industry, Audiences and the Italian Western," in Richard Dyer and Ginette Vincendeau (eds), *Popular European Cinema* (London: Routledge, 1992), pp. 253–4; Leo Braudy, *From Chivalry to Terrorism: War and the Changing Nature of Masculinity* (New York: Knopf, 2003), p. 358.

69. Kenneth R. Dutton, *The Perfectible Body: the Western Ideal of Male Physical Development* (New York: Continuum, 1995), pp. 143–7.

70. Dutton, *Perfectible Body*, pp. 143–7.

71. Richard A. Leit, Harrison G. Pope, Jr and James J. Gray, "Cultural Expectations of Muscularity in Men: the Evolution of Playgirl Centerfolds," *International Journal of Eating Disorders*, 29 (2001): 90–3.

72. Harrison G. Pope, Jr, Katharine A. Phillips and Roberto Olivardia, *The Adonis Complex: the Secret Crisis of Male Body Obsession* (New York: The Free Press, 2000), pp. 40–7.
73. Ginette Vincendeau, *Stars and Stardom in French Cinema* (London: Continuum, 2000), p. 175; see also Graeme Hayes, "Framing the Wolf: the Spectacular Masculinity of Alain Delon," in Phil Powrie, Ann Davies and Bruce Babington (eds), *The Trouble with Men: Masculinities in European and Hollywood Cinema* (London: Wallflower Press, 2004), pp. 42–53.
74. Franka Guez, *Masculin quotidien: guide pratique à l'usage des hommes* (Paris: Stock, 1969), p. 7.
75. Georges Fauconnet and Nadine Lefaucheur, *Le fabrication des mâles* (Paris: Éditions du Seuil, 1975), pp. 26–7, 38, 41–3, 52.
76. As Linda McDowell explains, however, none of this emphasis on appearances is terribly new, rather it is a continuation and extension of practices developed decades earlier. "The dominance of a new, slim and fit bodily image has merely displaced the location from old-style male clubs to the sports field and club." McDowell, *Capital Culture: Gender at Work in the City* (Oxford: Blackwell, 1997), pp. 166–71, 186–7, 191; Bret Easton Ellis, *American Psycho* (New York: Vintage, 1991).
77. Mark Simpson, "Here Come the Mirror Men – Metrosexual Men," *Independent* (15 November 1994): 22.
78. Quoted in Jackie Cook, "Men's Magazines at the Millennium: New Spaces, New Selves," *Journal of Media & Cultural Studies*, 14 (2) (2000): 177.
79. However enjoyable such maintenance might be, one must remember that this too is work: "Personal grooming never takes a holiday." Peter Rubin, "Tending the Well-Oiled Machine," *GQ* (May 2002): 153, and "A Whiff of Summer," *GQ* (July 2002): 62. In March 2007, those reading the Qantas in-flight magazine got a "history lesson" about men of the classical world, who "were just as concerned with grooming as today's metrosexuals, bathing in thermal waters of natural springs and spas to soften their skin and to heal wounds gained in battle." Caroline Baum, "Skin Deep," *Qantas: the Australian Way*, no. 165 (March 2007): 130.
80. Body Implants, www.bodyimplants.com. Last consulted on 6 January 2007.
81. iEnhance, http://www.ienhance.com/procedure/description.asp?ProcID=33&BodyID=2&specialtyID=1#2. Last consulted 6 January 2007.
82. Sander Gilman, *Making the Body Beautiful: a Cultural History of Aesthetic Surgery* (Princeton: Princeton University Press, 1999), p. 242.
83. McLaren, *Impotence*, pp. 235–62; Barbara L. Marshall and Stephen Katz, "Forever Functional: Sexual Fitness and the Ageing Male Body," *Body & Society*, 8 (4) (2002): 43–70; Susan Bordo, *The Male Body: a New Look at Men in Public and in Private* (New York: Farrar, Straus and Giroux, 1999), pp. 59–61.
84. Jean-Pierre Boulé, "Viagra, Heroic Masculinity and France," *French Cultural Studies*, 12 (June 2001): 220, and "Virilité in Post-War France: Intellectual Masculinity, Jewishness and Sexual Potency," in Christopher E. Forth and Bertrand Taithe (eds), *French Masculinities: History, Culture and Politics* (Basingstoke: Palgrave, 2007).
85. Jon Swain, "How Schoolboys Become Somebody: the Role of the Body in the Construction of Masculinity," *British Journal of Sociology of Education*, 24 (3) (2003): 299–314; Michael Gard and Robert Meyenn, "Boys, Bodies, Pleasure and Pain: Interrogating Contact Sports in Schools," *Sport, Education and Society*, 5 (1) (2000): 19–34.
86. Susan K. Cahn, *Coming on Strong: Gender and Sexuality in Twentieth-Century Women's Sport* (New York: The Free Press, 1994), pp. 26–7, 173–81, 239, 262–3.

87. Riska, *Masculinity*, pp. 60–7.
88. Fabio Parasecoli, "Feeding Hard Bodies: Food and Masculinities in Men's Fitness Magazines," *Food & Foodways*, 13 (2005): 24–5, 28–30; Arran Stibbe, "Health and the Social Construction of Masculinity in *Men's Health* Magazine," *Men and Masculinities*, 7 (1) (July 2004): 40, 44–7; Cook, "Men's Magazines," p. 177.
89. Tim Hodgdon, *Manhood in the Age of Aquarius: Masculinity in Two Countercultural Communities, 1965–83* (New York: Columbia University Press, Gutenberg-e Project, 2007), available online at http://www.gutenberg-e.org/hodgdon, chap. 2, par. 5–30 (accessed 16 May 2007).
90. Sally Robinson, *Marked Men: White Masculinity in Crisis* (New York: Columbia University Press, 2000), pp. 134–7.
91. Robert Bly, *Iron John: a Book about Men* (1990; Boston: Element, 1999), p. 8.
92. Michael Kimmel, *Manhood in America: a Cultural History* (New York: The Free Press, 1996), pp. 277–8.
93. David Forrest, "'We're Here, We're Queer, and We're Not Going Shopping': Changing Gay Male Identities in Contemporary Britain," in Andrea Cornwall and Nancy Lindisfarne (eds), *Dislocating Masculinity: Comparative Ethnographies* (London: Routledge, 1994), p. 105.
94. Christine Yelland and Marika Tiggemann, "Muscularity and the Gay Ideal: Body Dissatisfaction and Disordered Eating in Homosexual Men," *Eating Behaviors*, 4 (2003): 107–16.
95. Steve Estes, *I Am a Man: Race, Manhood, and the Civil Rights Movement* (Chapel Hill, NC: University of North Carolina Press, 2005), pp. 156, 159.
96. Michele Wallace, *Black Macho and the Myth of the Superwoman* (1978; New York: Verso, 1990), p. 13.
97. bell hooks, *We Real Cool: Black Men and Masculinity* (New York: Routledge, 2004), p. 48.
98. Anna Rogers, "Chaos to Control: Men's Magazines and the Mastering of Intimacy," *Men and Masculinities*, 8 (2) (October 2005): 175–94; Carolyn Jackson, "Motives for 'Laddishness' at School: Fear of Failure and Fear of the 'Feminine,'" *British Educational Research Journal*, 29 (4) (August 2003): 583–98.

CONCLUSION: THE RETURN OF THE REPRESSED

1. Karen Lee Ashcraft and Lisa A. Flores rightly note that *Fight Club* is but one example of the "public performances of white/collar masculinity in crisis [that] are gaining momentum and bear startling resemblance to themes from the turn of the last century." Ashcraft and Flores, "'Slaves with White Collars': Persistent Performances of Masculinity in Crisis," *Text and Performance Quarterly*, 23 (1) (January 2000): 7.
2. Chuck Palahniuk, *Fight Club* (New York: Random House, 1996), p. 124.
3. Of course this is not to suggest that the gendered discourse of civilization has always neglected women. Over the centuries numerous physicians, psychiatrists and social reformers have complained about how modern living conditions can negatively affect the bodies and minds of girls and women. Yet if such voices have proposed a variety of recommendations for how women might live more in accordance with "nature," it was often so that some semblance of "real" femininity could be retained in the face of modernity's liquefying potential.
4. Loïc J.D. Wacquant, "The Pugilistic Point of View: How Boxers Think and Feel about their Trade," *Theory and Society*, 24 (August 1995): 489–535.

5. Courtney Rubin, "The Lords of the Ring," *Time*, no. 37 (22 September 2003): 46–8.
6. "Fight Club Draws Techies for Bloody Underground Beatdowns," *USA Today* (29 May 2006), http://www.usatoday.com/tech/news/2006-05-29-fight-club_x.htm?POE=TECISVA. Nor are men the only ones to find such "therapy" useful and attractive. In Devon, England, four women were arrested on charges of child cruelty after staging and video-taping "toddler fights" where boys were berated as "wimps" if they failed to punch girls. "I didn't see any harm in toughening them up," one explained; "I done the same with my own children." 15 February 2007. BBC News, http://news.bbc.co.uk/1/hi/england/devon/6366255.stm.
7. Elisabeth Badinter, *XY: On Masculine Identity*, trans. Lydia Davis (New York: Columbia University Press, 1995), p. 27.
8. Klaus-Michael Bogdal, "Hard-Cold-Fast: Imagining Masculinity in the German Academy, Literature, and the Media," in Roy Jerome (ed.), *Conceptions of Postwar German Masculinity* (Albany: SUNY Press, 2001), pp. 13, 38.
9. Francis Fukuyama, "Women and the Evolution of World Politics," *Foreign Affairs*, 77 (24) (1994): 36, 38–9.
10. Robert Kagan, "Power and Weakness," *Policy Review*, 113 (June–July 2002): 3, 28. In an apparent parody of Kagan's analysis, Parag Khanna sees in European finesse and style a redefined and more successful version of masculinity. Unlike the coarse United States, Khanna claims, "the world's first metrosexual superpower" is able to balance "hard power with its sensitive side" to great effect. Parag Khanna, "The Metrosexual Superpower," *Foreign Policy*, 143 (July–August 2004): 66.
11. This is what makes the recent film adaptation of Frank Miller's graphic novel *300* so ludicrous. In this stylized dramatization of the Battle of Thermopylae, the massive Persian army exhibits nearly every imaginable form of monstrosity, deformity and perversity as it faces the hard and well-defined bodies of a small band of freedom-loving Spartan warriors. Although Miller published his novel in 1999, in light of the Iraq War the movie *300* seems implicitly to contrast the virtuous hardness of "American" troops against what could only be viewed as the "Oriental" perversity of Iran (present-day Persia). Dana Stevens, "A Movie Only a Spartan Could Love: The Battle Epic *300*," *Slate Magazine* (8 March 2007), http://www.slate.com/id/2161450. Last accessed 21 May 2007.
12. Andrew Macdonald [William L. Pierce], *The Turner Diaries* (Boulder, CO: Paladin Press, 1978), chapters 9 and 11, and Epilogue. http://www.solargeneral.com/library/TurnerDiaries.pdf.
13. Gary Aldrich, *Unlimited Access: an FBI Agent Inside the Clinton White House* (Washington, DC: Regnery Press, 1996), p. 30.
14. Brenton J. Malin, *American Masculinity under Clinton: Popular Media and the Nineties "Crisis of Masculinity"* (New York: Peter Lang, 2005), pp. 1–2; Robert A. Nye, "Afterword," in Christopher E. Forth and Bertrand Taithe (eds), *French Masculinities: History, Culture and Politics* (Basingstoke: Palgrave, 2007), p. 232. This equation of Frenchness with refined effeminacy was spoofed in the film *Talladega Nights: the Ballad of Ricky Bobby* (2006), where a highly skilled, yet effete and openly gay, French stock car racer challenges the good-ole-boy simplicity of ace American driver, Ricky Bobby, and his redneck pals.
15. Claude Fischler, "Une 'féminisation' des moeurs?" *Esprit*, no. 196 (November 1993): 10.
16. "États généraux de l'homme: ce qu'ils ont à nous dire," *Elle* (10 March 2003): 78–112. Nevertheless, as of early 2007 the French were reportedly pressing for a return to manners and politeness like never before. Elaine Sciolino, "France Polishes

its Politesse," *New York Times* (11 January 2007), http://www.nytimes.com/2007/01/11/fashion/11polite.html?_r=3&oref=slogin&oref=slogin&oref=slogin.

17. Éric Zemmour, *Le premier sexe* (Paris: Denoël, 2006), pp. 10, 61.
18. According to Denis Muzet, president of the Institut médiascopie: "The image of Sarkozy's body is extremely important; this body which is in good health, high-performing, dynamic, young, energetic is an element of the political relationship between the French people and our President." Reuters, 27 August 2007. Reuters, http://tvscripts.edt.reuters.com/2007-08-23/20a2db59.html. See also "Hunky Vlad, Slim Sarko – Playing with PR Fire," Reuters, http://www.reuters.com/article/worldNews/idUSL2479635220070824. Last accessed 27 August 2007.
19. Giles Coren, "A Man's Place – The Second Sex? – Day Two," *The Times* (15 October 1996): 19.
20. Melanie Phillips, *The Sex-Change Society: Feminised Britain and the Neutered Male* (London: The Social Market Foundation, 1999), p. xiii. For a more pro-feminist account of British men, see Anthony Clare, *On Men: Masculinity in Crisis* (London: Chatto & Windus, 2000).
21. Robert Twigger, *Being a Man ... in the Lousy Modern World* (London: Weidenfeld & Nicolson, 2002).
22. Jeff Hearn and Keith Pringle (eds), *European Perspectives on Men and Masculinities: National and Transnational Approaches* (Basingstoke: Palgrave, 2006), pp. 104–5. On "transnational business masculinity," see R.W. Connell, "Masculinities and Globalization," *Men and Masculinities*, 1 (1) (July 1998): 3–23.
23. Sarah Ashwin and Tatyana Lytkina, "Men in Crisis in Russia: the Role of Domestic Marginalization," *Gender & Society*, 18 (2) (April 2004): 189–206.
24. Robert Porter, "From *Homo Russicus* to *Homo Sovieticus* – and Back Again?" *Forum for Modern Language Studies*, 34 (3) (1998): 223–4.
25. "Russian Paper Explains How to Copy Putin's Body," Reuters, 22 August 2007, http://www.reuters.com/article/worldNews/idUSL2284998820070822.
26. Alexander Garros and Aleksei Evdokimov, *Headcrusher* (2003; London: Vintage, 2006).
27. Christine Castelain-Meunier, *Les hommes aujourd'hui: virilité et identité* (Paris: Acropole, 1988), p. 73.
28. Leo Braudy, *From Chivalry to Terrorism: War and the Changing Nature of Masculinity* (New York: Knopf, 2003), p. 548. See also Ian Buruma and Avishai Margalit, *Occidentalism: a Short History of Anti-Westernism* (London: Atlantic Books, 2004), pp. 49–73.
29. Brian K. Vaugh, *Y: the Last Man, Volume 1: Unmanned* (New York: Vertigo, 2003).
30. Steve Jones, *Y: the Descent of Men* (London: Little, Brown, 2002); Brian Sykes, *Adam's Curse: a Future without Men* (London: Corgi, 2003).
31. Deborah Cadbury, *Altering Eden: the Feminization of Nature* (London: Hamish Hamilton, 1997).
32. Sykes, *Adam's Curse*, p. 343.

Index